Visit our Web sites:

www.nelson.com
polisci.nelson.com

Your comprehensi
Web reference for
political science

D1314613

1000
$38.00

CONFEDERATION COLLEGE
CHALLIS RESOURCE CENTRE   JUN 2 9 2000

Local Government

in Canada (5th) edition

280101

C. Richard Tindal
and Susan Nobes Tindal

Nelson
Thomson Learning

Australia • Canada • Denmark • Japan • Mexico • New Zealand • Phillipines
Puerto Rico • Singapore • South Africa • Spain • United Kingdom • United States

MAY 2 6 2000

1120 Birchmount Road
Scarborough, Ontario M1K 5G4
www.nelson.com
www.thomson.com

Copyright © 2000 Nelson, a division of Thomson Learning. Thomson Learning is a trademark used herein under license.

All rights reserved. No part of this work covered by the copyright hereon may be reproduced, transcribed, or used in any form or by any means—graphic, electronic, or mechanical, including photocopying, recording, taping, Web distribution or information storage and retrieval systems—without the permission of the publisher.

For permission to use material from this text or product, contact us by
- web: www.thomsonrights.com
- Phone: 1-800-730-2214
- Fax: 1-800-730-2215

Canadian Cataloguing in Publication Data

Tindal, C. R., 1943–
        Local government in Canada

5th ed,
Includes bibliographical references and index.
ISBN 0-17-616791-9

1. Local government – Canada.   2. Municipal government – Canada.
I. Tindal, S. Nobes, 1949– .   II. Title.

JS1708.T55 1999   352.14'0971   C99-931374-6

Editorial Director	Michael Young
Acquisitions Editor	Nicole Gnutzman
Project Editor	Jenny Anttila
Production Editor	Natalia Denesiuk
Production Coordinator	Helen Jager Locsin
Marketing Manager	Kevin Smulan
Art Director	Angela Cluer
Cover Design	Ken Phipps
Proofreader	Ruth Peckover
Cover Image	Comstock/Kingston City Hall
Printer	Webcom

Printed and bound in Canada
1   2   3   4   03   02   01   00

About the Authors

C. Richard Tindal, Ph.D., has been teaching, researching, and writing about local government for more than 30 years. For much of that period, he was a Professor of Government at St. Lawrence College, in Kingston, and was Head of its Centre for Government Education and Training until his early retirement in mid-1998. He has also been an occasional Visiting Professor in the School of Policy Studies at Queen's University. Dick has written a dozen professional training programs in municipal government, as well as three books and numerous articles on government and management. As President of *Tindal Consulting Limited*, a firm established in the early 1970s, he has conducted local government restructuring studies in several areas of Ontario, designed and delivered training seminars across Canada, and continues to undertake consulting and writing projects in his "retirement."

Susan Nobes Tindal, M.Ed., LL.B., is a lawyer and teacher. She has taught courses in law and municipal government for two decades. In addition to her private practice, she acts as legal counsel for a children's aid society in Eastern Ontario. Susan is currently President of the Lennox & Addington County Law Association and is a member of the Family Court Community Liaison Committee. Her community service activities include being a Governor of Kingston General Hospital, past chair of the Kingston Local Architectural Conservation Advisory Committee, past chair of the Kingston, Frontenac and Lennox & Addington District Health Council, and Past-President of the Frontenac Historic Foundation.

Table of Contents

Preface

This edition continues to provide a straightforward, factual overview of municipal government developments across Canada. It examines these developments in relation to their impact on the representative and service delivery roles of municipal government. This is hardly a new approach, but what does distinguish this new edition is its contention that we are in the midst of a new turn of the century reform movement, one which is again trying to make municipalities run more like a business.

While the book retains its institutional focus, public choice theory is used to illuminate discussion of the two key topics of municipal restructuring and "reinventing government." The theory's emphasis on individual choice and competitive market forces is both appealing (in promoting efficiency in service delivery) and worrying (in its lack of support for notions of community and collective responsibility). An underlying theme of the book is how municipalities can blend utilization of business tools and techniques, where appropriate, with a renewed commitment to their political and representative role—a commitment that gives municipalities their best hope for the future.

Chapter 1 introduces the roles of municipal government and traces the developments which have undermined adherence to the representative role. The historical foundations of local government are examined in *Chapter 2*, and *Chapter 3* examines the turn of the century reform movement and its contribution to the machinery and operating philosophy of local government. *Chapter 4* continues the chronological evolution of events through the 20th century, examining the extent, nature, and impact of urbanization. It also describes the shortcomings of the municipal government system and previews the reforms introduced. These reforms were focused on municipal restructuring and amalgamation and are examined in two chapters. *Chapter 5* deals with restructuring in Central Canada and *Chapter 6* explores developments in Eastern and Western Canada. The limits of these structural reforms are discussed in *Chapter 7*, which also examines and illustrates the potential of process reforms. Intergovernmental relations is the theme of *Chapter 8*, which features new material on the potential and abuses of the disentanglement exercises pursued by several provinces, on provincial invasion of the municipal property tax field, and on the potential of new Municipal Acts passed or proposed by several provinces. *Chapter 9* examines the internal governing machinery of municipalities. It begins with traditional machinery, then looks at such coordinating models as the chief administrative officer and executive committee, and concludes with examples of the new business models which are currently coming to the fore. Various aspects of the relationship between the municipality and the public are explored in *Chapter 10*, which looks at the citizen as customer, the citizen as elector, local groups, local political parties, and tools of direct democracy such as the referendum. A number of observations about local political activity are made after a description of such activities in a number of Canadian cities. *Chapter 11* discusses how municipalities can best respond to the new turn of the century reform era in which they find themselves. It puts forth two models of municipal government, reflecting the tension between the representative and administrative roles of municipalities. While citing benefits from the use of many of the business techniques being advocated, it calls upon municipalities to revive their fundamental political role, and to forge closer links with their citizens.

For reviewing all or parts of this manuscript and offering suggestions for its improvement, we are grateful to Sally Bennett of the University of Windsor, James Lightbody of the University of Alberta, Mohawk College's Barb Reavley, and especially Andrew Sancton of the University of Western Ontario. Helpful information was provided by many others, including Alan Artibise of the University of Victoria, George Betts of the University of New Brunswick (retired), Peter Boswell of Memorial University, Martin Corbett of the New Brunswick Department of Municipalities, Chris Leo of the University of Winnipeg, Jack Novack of Dalhousie University, and Patrick Smith of Simon Fraser University.

This is the first edition of this book published by Nelson, and it has been a most pleasant experience working with this company. Special thanks to Nicole Gnutzman, who, as our first contact, set the tone for the friendly dealings which were to follow, and to Jenny Anttila, who was always prompt and helpful in her role as project manager for the book. We also very much appreciate the support and friendly cooperation received from Tracy Bordian, Natalia Denesiuk, Ruth Peckover, and Kevin Smulan.

Richard and Susan Tindal
Inverary, Ontario
May 1999

CHAPTER 1
Whither Local Government?

While it hasn't yet been formally defined as such, municipalities today are in the midst of a new turn of the century reform movement more radical and far-reaching than the one they experienced 100 years ago.

Introduction

As Canada enters the 21st century, local governments are also going through a momentous transition. What is not immediately apparent is whether they are going forward to the future or back to the past. As will be seen, the changes affecting local governments are part of a larger pattern of developments affecting all levels of government which, in turn, are being driven by international economic forces. The most pronounced manifestation of these changes is a diminished role for governments—all governments—and an enhanced role for the market place and for private and individual decision making. At the municipal level, these changes have brought a new wave of amalgamations in the 1990s, promoted in large part by provincial governments which feel that they need larger municipalities to which they can download responsibilities and costs. That downloading, in turn, has increased the fiscal squeeze on municipalities, prompting them to embrace a variety of techniques designed to make them more business-like.

For municipal governments, this emphasis on operating more like a business has a familiar ring, and parallels developments which took place 100 years ago. How they respond this time will go a long way toward determining whether the municipalities of the 21st century will operate more as institutions of local democracy or as business corporations carrying out the dictates of their provincial creators. That they face this difficult choice should not be surprising since, from their earliest years, municipalities have wrestled with the potential conflict and tension between their two fundamental roles of representation and service delivery.

What Is Local Government?

At the outset, we need to clarify the nature of local government. The terms "local government" and "municipal government" or "municipality" are often used interchangeably. But local government is a broader term, which includes municipalities and a variety of boards, commissions, and other local special purpose bodies.

Dealing first with the former, a municipality is a corporation, a legal device that allows residents of a specific geographic area to provide services that are of common interest. It is also a democratic institution, created historically in response to the desire of local communities to exercise self-government. Through its elected council, the municipality provides a vehicle for local citizens to identify and address their local concerns. The chief distinguishing features of a municipality are: (1) its corporate nature, (2) defined geographic boundaries, (3) an elected council, and (4) taxing power.

There are some 4000 incorporated municipalities in Canada, close to half of these found in Ontario and Quebec. The specific classifications include cities, towns, villages, rural municipalities (also categorized as townships, parishes, and rural districts), counties (both single and upper tier), and regional and metropolitan municipalities.

In addition, there are various other local special purpose bodies that defy classification or even precise numbering. In Ontario alone, where the use of such local bodies has been most prevalent, it is estimated that there are at least 2000 of these bodies of 70 different types. Common examples include police commissions, health units, conservation authorities, public utilities commissions, parks boards, and school boards. While many of these boards are long standing, there are also a number of new bodies which have been created to facilitate partnership arrangements amongst local governing bodies or to preside over entrepreneurial operations such as convention centres or arenas.

What Do Local Governments Do?

The most obvious answer to this question (but a dangerously limited one) is that local governments provide a very wide range of services, programs, facilities, and regulations which largely shape our day-to-day lives. Jack Layton, an academic and experienced municipal politician, offers the following categories of local government responsibility:[1] protective services (police and fire), transportation services (roads and public transit), environmental services (sewers, garbage disposal, and water supply), social and health services (welfare administration, day care, homes for the aged, and public health programs), recreation and cultural services, and land use planning. A monograph by Andrew Sancton offers a quite similar list of local government responsibilities, but adds the provision of public education.[2]

What is striking about both lists is that most of the responsibilities can be characterized as services to property. This is true even of such services as education. As Sancton points out, the quality of a local school system can be a major factor in attracting new residential growth and, sometimes, new businesses as well. Many municipalities have also experienced the fact that the location of a new school, or the closing of an existing school, can have a significant effect on the growth and development in the surrounding area. As will be discussed throughout this text, since local governments provide such an extensive range of services to property and also raise much of the money to pay for these services from a tax on property, it is not surprising that their role has long been seen mainly in terms of serving the needs of property owners.

Valuable as all of these services may be, they are not the only reason, or the most important reason, for local governments to exist. More specifically, they are not the main reason why *municipal governments* exist. That reason is to provide a mechanism for inhabitants of defined local areas to express, debate, and resolve local issues and concerns. In other words, municipal governments perform a political role. They provide local citizens with the opportunity to choose representatives who will make decisions which reflect, or at least respond to, the views and concerns of those local citizens. The municipality is an extension of the community, the community governing itself.[3]

---

[1]Jack Layton, "City Politics in Canada," in Michael S. Whittington and Glen Williams (eds.), *Canadian Politics in the 1990s*, 3rd Edition, Scarborough, Nelson Canada, 1990, pp. 405-408.

[2]Andrew Sancton, *Governing Canada's City Regions: Adapting Form to Function*, Montreal, Institute for Research on Public Policy, 1994, p. 11.

[3]For a more complete examination of this concept, see various writings by John Stewart including "A Future for Local Authorities as Community Government," in John Stewart and Gerry Stoker, *The Future of Local Government*, London, Macmillan Education Ltd., 1989, and Michael Clarke and John Stewart, *The Choices for Local Government*, Harlow, Longman, 1991.

It follows then that municipal governments exist to serve two primary purposes:

1. To act as a political mechanism through which a local community can express its collective objectives; and
2. To provide various services and programs to local residents.

These two separate purposes of municipal government are evident when one examines the origins of Canada's municipal government system. From the early years of settlement of the then colony of Canada, local services were provided. As the need for local services increased, more local government responsibilities were assigned to the existing form of local administration—the Courts of Quarter Sessions and their Justices of the Peace. These arrangements resulted in services being provided locally, but local residents had no say in what was done. This situation proved particularly unacceptable to the United Empire Loyalists, many of whom had experienced a form of elected municipal government in the New England colonies from whence they came. The result, as will be described, was constant agitation from the Loyalists which, along with other factors, ultimately led to the provision for elected municipal governments which took over the responsibility for local services from the Courts of Quarter Sessions.

> The key feature of municipal government is the interaction of its representative and administrative roles.

It is the combination and interaction of the representative and administrative roles which can make municipal government so important and desirable. It is not just that there is a level of government close to the people, representing their views and affording the opportunity for public participation. It is not just that municipal government provides a number of important services. The key feature of municipal government is, or ought to be, the fact that the services provided are in accordance with the needs and wishes of the local residents. It is this flexibility, this capacity to respond to varying local preferences, which, if realized, makes municipal government especially attractive. It suggests a level of government which allows the inhabitants of a particular area to decide, through their elected council, which range and level of services is most appropriate for them.

If the representative and administrative roles of municipal government are not interrelated in this manner, neither one appears to be nearly as valuable. Consider a situation in which services are provided without regard to local needs and wants, or in which citizens participate in a government which doesn't have the capacity to deal with the issues that concern them. In either case, much of the potential significance of municipal government is lost.

What, specifically, are the benefits or potential benefits of municipal government?[4] It diffuses the power of government and involves many decision makers in many different localities. This "localness" of municipal government provides greater local knowledge of the situations about which decisions are being made. This arrangement offers the possibility that there will be diverse responses to varying needs of particular localities, thereby allowing the provision of services that better fit local circumstances than would be the case under more distant decision makers. The experimentation which arises may also lead to improved and more efficient approaches than would be possible if only one central standard were to be accepted. This network of municipalities also greatly broadens the opportunities for citizen participation. Municipal governments are more accessible than senior levels of government and more exposed to the possibility of public influence.

Among the potential benefits of municipal government are local knowledge, greater accessibility, and diverse responses to varying needs of particular localities.

Municipal Governments and Democracy

The concept of municipal governments as more sensitive and responsive to local needs is not new. Various writers from de Tocqueville and John Stuart Mill to K. G. Crawford[5] have emphasized the democratic features of municipal government. To some, such as Mill, municipal government constituted a training ground for democracy, wherein elected representatives would "learn the ropes" before going on to service at a more senior level, and local citizens would learn about exercising their democratic rights in the context of issues which were relatively simple and understandable. No better expression of this latter sentiment can be found than the Durham Report. Lord Durham was struck by the lack of municipal institutions in the colony in the 1830s, especially in the rural areas still governed by the Courts of Quarter Sessions. He expressed concern that "the

---

[4]The arguments which follow are partly based on G. Jones and J. Stewart, *The Case for Local Government*, London, Allen & Unwin Inc., 1985.

[5]See Alexis de Tocqueville's *Democracy in America*, J. S. Mill's *Considerations on Representative Government* and *On Liberty*, and *Canadian Municipal Government* by K. G. Crawford.

people receive no training in those habits of self-government which are indispensable to enable them rightly to exercise the power of choosing representatives in parliament."[6]

Others, such as de Tocqueville, with his oft-quoted statement that "municipal institutions constitute the strength of free nations," saw municipal government's democratic role in a much more direct, fundamental light. Indeed, Crawford saw municipal government as far from just a training ground, but as the level at which the democratic ideal was most likely to be fulfilled. The citizen is more likely to understand the issues under consideration locally than the increasingly complex, technical matters which predominate at the senior levels of government. Moreover, because the results of local decisions (or indecision) are readily apparent in the local community, citizens should be able to evaluate the effectiveness of their municipal government and the degree to which elected representatives have fulfilled their campaign promises.

Not everyone shared this positive view of municipalities, however. A contrasting viewpoint is provided by Langrod, who viewed municipal government as "but a technical arrangement within the mechanisms of the administrative system, a structural and functional detail...."[7] Langrod not only rejected the assumption that municipal governments are vital to democracy, he also contended that they could be contrary to the democratic process.

> In some countries local government, with its structured anachronisms, the high degree of its internal functionalisation, the preponderance in practice of the permanent official over the elected and temporary councillor, its methods of work and its obstinate opposition to all modernization, can ... act as a brake on the process of democratisation.[8]

It must be recognized, however, that municipal governments were never intended to be instruments of mass democracy. Kaplan points out that a number of conflicting views influenced the creation of our original municipal institutions. He notes that while reformers pushed for the democratic virtues of local government, the image of local officials as magis-

---

[6]Quoted in Engin Isin, *Cities Without Citizens*, Montreal, Black Rose Books, 1992, p. 132.

[7]Georges Langrod, "Local Government and Democracy," in *Public Administration*, Vol. XXXI, Spring 1953, pp. 25-33. The oft-quoted Langrod and Panter-Brick exchanges on the subject of local government and democracy are reprinted in Lionel D. Feldman (ed.), *Politics and Government of Urban Canada*, Toronto, Methuen, 1981, Section A.

[8]*Ibid.*, pp. 5-6.

trates (arising from the operation of the Courts of Quarter Session) was too firmly established to be completely erased. Landowners liked this latter image, which appeared to provide some reassurance that the new municipal institutions wouldn't embark on costly local improvements. "Rather than seek out local problems and needs and then devise suitable governmental solutions, the municipal officials would wait until individual complaints were brought before them and then would resolve only the case at hand."[9]

In addition to these perspectives, a third view saw local government as a public corporation, drawing its life from a Crown-issued charter, and exercising only those powers assigned to it in the charter. These three premises were obviously inconsistent.

> One cannot model local government on both a judicial tribunal and a business corporation. Local government cannot be both an experiment in mass participatory democracy and a corporation created by and for property owners.[10]

Municipal Governments and Property

The bias in favour of the propertied classes and the lack of participation by the masses is evident from the restricted franchise given to early municipal governments. In the early years only property owners were allowed the right to vote. Consider, for example, the boards of police established in Upper Canada in the early 1830s and heralded as the breakthrough which transferred power from the appointed Courts of Quarter Session to elected councils. As discussed in Chapter 2, membership on the board (council) was limited to freeholders (householders who paid a certain amount of rent per annum for their dwellings). In effect, provision was made for a governing elite. Similarly, Higgins observes that when Halifax was incorporated in 1841, its charter limited the vote to only about 800 people who could meet a property qualification, and restricted candidacy for office to a fraction of that number.[11] To take another example, Baker's study of St. John's, Newfoundland, notes that the incorporation of the city in 1888 was accompanied by strict property qualifications for both voters and candidates. He describes a number of

[9]Harold Kaplan, *Reform, Planning and City Politics: Montreal, Winnipeg, Toronto*, Toronto, University of Toronto Press, 1982, p. 61.

[10]*Ibid.*, p. 63.

[11]Donald J. H. Higgins, *Local and Urban Politics in Canada*, Toronto, Gage, 1986, p. 39.

measures which had the effect of ensuring that it was the merchants, lawyers, and shopkeepers who dominated—within the colonial legislature as well as within the city council.[12] Similarly, Artibise has shown that the municipal governments of the major cities of western Canada were dominated by a business elite, "partly because of a restricted franchise which effectively limited opposition."[13] In addition, businessmen were able to convince many others that their interests and those of the general community coincided.

Magnusson stresses the importance of the fact that the notion of municipal governments reflecting the interests of the propertied classes was well established *before* the franchise was extended to people without real property. This caused a strong resistance to political change even when the franchise was gradually extended.[14]

Authority from the Province, Not the People

The notion of municipalities as extensions of the community was dealt a severe blow by the total lack of any constitutional recognition of municipal governments within the British North America Act which created the country of Canada in 1867. Isin[15] points out that Canada's first incorporated city (Saint John, in 1785) was established by a Royal Charter drafted and confirmed by the Privy Council in Whitehall, but that later incorporations such as those of Montreal and Quebec City in 1832 and Toronto in 1834 were carried out through acts of the colonial legislatures. The result, he argues, is that by the 1830s colonial legislatures were attaining powers to create municipal corporations which were not prescribed in their constitutions. This was to have lasting effects, according to Isin,[16] because during the pre-confederation debates of the 1850s provincial governments

---

[12]M. Baker, "William Gilbert Gosling and the Establishment of Commission Government in St. John's, Newfoundland, 1914," *Urban History Review*, Vol. IX, No. 3, February 1981, pp. 37-39.

[13]Gilbert Stelter and Alan Artibise (eds.), *Shaping the Canadian Landscape: Aspects of the Canadian City-Building Process*, Ottawa, Carleton University Press, 1982, p. 21. See also the Artibise article on pp. 116-147.

[14]Warren Magnusson, "Introduction," in Warren Magnusson and Andrew Sancton (eds.), *City Politics in Canada*, Toronto, University of Toronto Press, 1983, p. 12.

[15]Isin, *op. cit.*, pp. 142-144.

[16]*Ibid.*, p. 144.

were considered to have natural and inalienable rights over municipal governments.

The 1867 British North America Act (now the Constitution Act of 1982) enshrined this concept of municipal governments as "creatures" of the provincial governments which incorporated them. This meant, according to Isin, that the modern municipal corporation would have two essential characteristics:

1. It is created at the pleasure of the legislature, and need not require the consent of the people of the affected locality. The act of incorporation is not a contract between the legislature and the local inhabitants; and
2. The authority conferred on the corporation is not local in nature but derives from the provincial government.[17]

Such an arrangement is obviously not compatible with the concept of municipal government as an extension of the community. Instead, the constitution defined municipalities in terms of the specific classifications they were given which, in turn, determined the powers which they could exercise. As a result, municipal governments have operated since Confederation within a constitutional and legal framework, reinforced by ample case law, which limits their scope to matters specifically delegated to them by the provincial governments which have established them. Broader, more discretionary powers have been delegated in new Municipal Acts passed in a few of the provinces, but as discussed in a later chapter, early indications are that these have not significantly improved the subordinate and restricted status of municipal governments.

Political Role Denied and Decried

A further major setback for municipal governments as instruments of local democracy occurred 100 years ago during the turn of the century reform movement. Advocating more efficient administration and the removal of all corruption, reformers called for the exclusion of politics from municipal government. Decisions should be made on objective, rational grounds. Municipal administrators should be free to provide municipal services without political interference from the elected representatives. In their misguided zeal, the

> According to turn of the century reformers, politics had no place in municipal government.

---

[17]*Ibid.*, p. 2.

reformers substantially undermined the very system of municipal government which the Loyalists and others had fought so hard to obtain only half
a century earlier! From the reform era came a number of structural
changes designed to reduce the influence of the politician and to elevate
the role of the appointed expert, and the lingering notion that politics has
no place in local government.

Yet the efforts of reformers to remove politics from municipal decision making were really designed to remove the political influence which
could now be exercised by growing city populations. In this respect, the
reformers were quite undemocratic or anti-democratic. As Plunkett and
Betts describe the situation:

> ... their intention was not to try to halt the process of making decisions on
> public policy at the local level. Their intention, rather, was to exclude
> various groups from the process.... The reformers were interested in
> restoring the efficiency and effectiveness of municipal service delivery.
> At the same time, they were plainly concerned with restricting the influ-
> ence of the cities' burgeoning population of working people upon the con-
> duct of municipal affairs.[18]

This latter viewpoint reflected the fact that many of the reformers
were middle-class merchants and businessmen who had little sympathy
for the democratic aspects of local government. In their minds, the solution was to run local government more like a business. Of course, this
also meant that citizens should elect more businessmen to councils, an
argument which demonstrated the self-interest in the reform movement.

The reformers tried to reduce the influence of the ward politician,
either by pushing for elections at large or for the establishment of boards
of control, elected at large, which took over many of the important decisions from ward politicians. Yet it was these ward politicians who helped
to ensure representation from all areas of the municipality, including
economically disadvantaged and ethnic neighbourhoods. Election at large
was intended to favour the election of people of class and property. As
with the boards of police of the 1830s, an attempt was being made to secure the position of a governing elite.

The local political process and the opportunities for lively political
debate were also adversely affected by the reform movement and its
fondness for separate boards and commissions. The establishment of
these boards removed from the jurisdiction of elected councils many of
the potentially most important public issues and activities, such as plan-

---

[18]T. J. Plunkett and G. M. Betts, *The Management of Canadian Urban
Government*, Kingston, Queen's University, 1978, p. 27.

ning, policing, public health, children's aid, and public transit. Indeed, this erosion of municipal political vibrancy began much earlier, and Magnusson notes that "some of the heat was taken out of municipal politics in the nineteenth century by the separation of the school boards from the municipal councils and the effective assignment of charitable functions to the churches and other voluntary institutions."[19]

The actions of the reformers in denying any political role for municipal government was misguided and harmful. The fact is that politics inevitably exists in every society because humans have wants and needs that must be satisfied from resources that are scarce and insufficient. As a result, competition and conflict arise, and the central purpose of governments is to resolve these disputes by deciding who gets what resources and how equitably they are distributed. Governments possess legal authority which provides the foundation for their allocation decisions.

It follows that politics is an integral part of local government operations. It is no less true at this level that decisions must be made about allocating scarce resources. Competition and conflict are equally prevalent. Divisions arise on such questions as urban and rural interests, city and suburban, haves and have-nots, for and against development, and ethnic and racial issues. Since municipalities are governments, not just vehicles for service delivery, it is their role to mediate among the diverse interests, to build consensus where possible, to make choices, and to answer for them. "Politics, like sex, cannot be abolished. It can sometimes be repressed by denying people the opportunity to practice it, but it cannot be done away with because it is in the nature of man to disagree and to contend."[20]

> Politics, like sex, cannot be abolished, no matter how much we deny it. It is the process by which decisions are made about the allocation of scarce resources.

Narrowing Scope of Municipal Government

The narrowing of municipal jurisdiction—and, therefore, of the potential scope of the local political process—has continued during the 20th century. The possibility of municipal governments becoming involved in the provision of a wide range of services financed by a variety of sources

[19]Magnusson and Sancton, *op. cit.*, p. 10.

[20]Edward Banfield and James Q. Wilson, *City Politics*, New York, Random House, 1963, pp. 20-21.

appears to have been largely undermined by the impact of the Depression, World War II, and rapid post-war growth. When the Depression began, local governments exercised the main responsibility for the limited social service programs then in existence. Up until World War II, municipalities could finance their expenditures on these and other programs from local sales tax and even income tax as well as from the property tax. With the onset of the Depression, however, municipalities could not afford the financial burden of relief payments. Neither could a number of provincial governments for that matter, and the result was federal government intervention which has since evolved into the modern welfare state. "Canadian municipalities are now almost totally excluded from this crucial area of government policy."[21]

The outbreak of World War II brought the centralization of finances in Canada under federal-provincial tax-rental and tax-sharing agreements. As the federal and provincial levels competed for the largest possible share of the major tax fields, municipal governments were increasingly squeezed out, reverting to their historical dependence upon the property tax. For example, Ontario introduced its first unconditional grant in 1936 when it preempted municipal governments from the income tax field. Access to the corporate tax field was lost just five years later when the various provincial governments entered into a wartime agreement with the federal government which included "renting" this field to the federal level. Instead of tax sources, municipalities were offered more conditional grants, directed to ensuring the provision of services and servicing standards felt to be important to the senior levels of government.

The rapid urbanization of the post-war period further confirmed the narrowing of municipal government's primary role to that of providing the physical services needed to support the continued growth and expansion of our cities. The primary thrust of federal and provincial policies and financial assistance was clearly in this direction, as evidenced by the lending policies of the Central (now Canada) Mortgage and Housing Corporation, and the grants for road construction and for the provision of water supply and sewage disposal systems. Consistent with this viewpoint is Timothy Colton's observation that Metropolitan Toronto was invented to promote what was presumed to be a common and profound interest in rapid urban growth.[22]

---

[21]Andrew Sancton, "Conclusion," in Magnusson and Sancton, *op. cit.*, p. 313.

[22]Timothy J. Colton, *Big Daddy*, Toronto, University of Toronto Press, 1980, p. 175.

Misplaced Emphasis of Municipal Reform

Matters did not improve with the municipal government restructuring initiatives introduced in a number of provinces beginning in the 1960s and continuing, off and on, to the present. For the most part, these have been preoccupied with improving the service delivery role of municipalities. Most of the reforms introduced in the 1960s and 1970s paid very little attention to the more important political role. The end result was new municipal government structures which were often perceived as more bureaucratic and less accountable. The reforms of the 1990s have in many ways been even more one-sided and neglectful of the political role of municipalities. This is especially evident in Ontario, where the province has very aggressively promoted widespread amalgamations. Provincial press releases accompanying each restructuring note approvingly the efficiency gains which are expected and the number of municipal politicians reduced.

(Re)Ascendancy of the Corporate Agenda

The role of municipal government as a business corporation rather than as an instrument of local democracy has come very strongly to the forefront in recent years. In large part, this shift in emphasis has come about because of fundamental changes affecting the world economy and the perceived role of governments therein. We have moved into a post-industrial era, or what is often termed "post-fordism" to reflect the movement beyond the manufacturing assembly line first popularized by Henry Ford.[23] Information technology is the driving force of this new post-industrial era, and new, more flexible forms of production geared not for the masses but for filling specialized needs and market niches.

Another defining characteristic of this new economic era is what amounts to the internationalization of economic activity. Multinational corporations are becoming transnational corporations which have no particular or permanent home base or domestic market. Modern technology allows them to deploy their resources spatially in whatever manner best serves their bottom line. The result is that most mass production, labour-intensive work is shifted to low-wage regions of the world. As these corporations become more mobile, national governments are pressured

---

[23]Stewart and Stoker, *op. cit.*, and Allan Cochrane, *Whatever Happened to Local Government?* Buckingham, Open University Press, 1993.

to accommodate their interests or run the risk of losing them to other jurisdictions.[24]

National governments are also under pressure because of the tremendous volume of foreign exchange activity which has developed over the past couple of decades, creating enormous opportunities for profit for those who buy and sell currencies. From almost nothing, daily trading in foreign exchange markets around the world grew to $150 billion by the mid-1980s, to $880 billion by 1992, and to $1.2 trillion by 1995. Most of this trading is not a reflection of the healthy flow of capital involved in nations trading and investing in each other; it is short-term, speculative buying and selling of currencies to generate profits. Two-thirds of the currency exchanges in 1995, for example, were for fewer than seven days and only one percent lasted as long as a year.[25]

> According to "the market," governments must make major cuts in expenditures and in existing programs.

National governments have been told that unless they conduct their affairs in a manner which "the market" (including particularly the international foreign exchange market) judges prudent, they will face the consequences in the form of a flight of capital. The prudent behaviour called for by the market has centred on policies to eliminate annual government deficits and to reduce the accumulated government debt—and to do so by making major cuts in expenditures and existing government programs. As a result, we are witnessing a profound shift in the role of government.

That role had grown in significance throughout most of the 20th century. There was widespread recognition of the contribution made by governments to the betterment of the human condition. Indeed, in the period from the 1940s to the 1970s, a variety of new programs were introduced (especially at the federal level) which constituted a social safety net for Canadians and which also reinforced the Keynesian fiscal policies of the government. Provincial and municipal governments also expanded their activities throughout this period, largely in response to the servicing needs of a rapidly growing population. These government initiatives re-

---

[24]These developments are discussed in a number of recent books, including Murray Dobbin, *The Myth of the Good Corporate Citizen*, Toronto, Stoddart, 1998, and John Shields and B. Mitchell Evans, *Shrinking the State: Globalization and Public Administration "Reform,"* Halifax, Fernwood Publishing, 1998.

[25]This discussion is based on Linda McQuaig, *The Cult of Impotence: Selling the Myth of Powerlessness in the Global Economy*, Toronto, Penguin Books Canada Ltd., 1998, pp. 153-158.

ceived widespread approval, both for addressing the needs of society and for contributing to economic growth.

Today, however, governments are being portrayed as the cause of most of society's problems, not the solution to them. Social programs are no longer viewed as valuable contributors to economic policy through enhanced consumer spending. Instead, they are criticized as excessively expensive entitlements that breed dependence, create labour market rigidities, and inhibit Canadian competitiveness. The new global economy, we are told, requires the removal of all barriers which might inhibit the effective performance of Canadian companies or cause a flight of investment capital. Many of these "barriers" are found in the government programs and government regulations which were developed in earlier decades in support of a more civilized society.

In response to the dictates of the global economy, Canada (along with a number of other Western nations) has been dismantling the social safety net—either directly through curtailing programs or indirectly by undermining the programs through expenditure cuts. Over the past decade or so, we have witnessed a process in which the federal government cuts transfer payments and shifts responsibilities to the provincial level which, in turn, cuts transfer payments and shifts responsibilities to the local level At the bottom of the pile in this new form of "fend-for-yourself federalism," municipalities, as usual, are adversely affected by the actions of the senior levels of government.[26]

> Fend-for-yourself federalism has meant transfer cuts and downloading of services for municipalities.

Municipalities in some provinces now face the combined impact of reduced provincial transfer payments and increased responsibilities arising from provincial downloading. In Ontario, for example, the one remaining unconditional grant, the Municipal Support Grant, was eliminated in 1998 after being cut by more than 50% over the preceding two years and virtually all conditional grants have also disappeared. Yet municipalities now have increased responsibilities with respect to such functions as social assistance, public health, public housing, ambulances, public transit, water and sewage treatment facilities, and (formerly provincial) highways. While the Ontario government has tried to maintain that the

---

[26]At the end of the 1990s, there are some signs that the federal government may be restoring some spending on social programs, but there is no indication that governments will sustain such action if the market expresses dissatisfaction.

complete swap of functions (which included much of the education cost being taken off the property tax) was revenue neutral, that has clearly not been the case for many individual municipalities.

Much the same situation arose in Nova Scotia. Following the work of a Task Force on Local Government that reported in 1992, that province made municipalities fully responsible for the cost of policing and local roads, while absorbing the costs for the administration of justice and a somewhat larger share of social services costs. This swap was also supposed to be revenue neutral. In fact, the Commission recommending the amalgamation of municipalities in Cape Breton county estimated that the service swap would save those municipalities $7.3 million annually. Instead, the result was an additional cost of $5 million annually.[27]

How are municipalities to cope with this increased revenue squeeze they face? Not by increasing the property tax, and especially not by increasing property taxes on business, that much is clear. Indeed, the Ontario government made a worrisome intrusion into municipal decision making at the end of 1998 when it decided that municipalities had not done all that they could to minimize property tax increases facing businesses in Ontario as a result of the province's assessment and property tax reforms. It passed legislation imposing a ceiling on the permissible level of such tax increases on business properties from 1998 through 2000.

If taxes can't be raised, then expenditures must be cut, leaving municipalities with the same pressure to reduce or abandon public services that the senior levels of government have been experiencing. Municipalities are encouraged to redefine their core business, they are told to develop business plans, to set measurable targets, and to demonstrate to citizens that their tax dollars are well spent. They are encouraged to pursue alternative service delivery strategies, including joint ventures with other local government bodies, public-private partnerships, and even outright privatization. In a move which is consistent with the new public management initiatives which have been occurring at the senior levels of government in a number of countries, municipalities are also being encouraged to separate their service delivery activities from those which involve policy making and to hive off these activities into separate agencies which—freed from the strictures of the traditional bureaucracy—can demonstrate improved customer service and greater entrepreneurship.

---

[27]From Andrew Sancton, Rebecca James, and Rick Ramsay, "Amalgamation vs. Intermunicipal Cooperation: Financing Local and Infrastructure Services," Toronto, ICCUR, forthcoming.

One hundred years after the turn of the century movement which denigrated politics, deplored interference by politicians, and called for municipalities to operate in a more business-like fashion, we find history repeating itself. Political "interference" from councillors is cited as a barrier to expeditious and thoughtful decisions. There are frequent suggestions that ward elections be replaced by elections at large and that the size of council be reduced to produce a body better able to make decisions.

> History repeats, as business principles are again advocated for municipalities.

Just as they moved to limit participation in municipal government by growing city populations at the turn of the century, business interests are now using what they claim are the requirements of the global economy as a means of limiting the opportunity for people to practise politics at all levels. Instead of governments deciding how resources should be allocated, we are told that the market must make these decisions. The requirements of the market place are cited as the reason why governments can't take actions which people might need and want.

Those who persuade us that we must accept a diminished role for government in our lives are essentially trying to deny our democratic rights. Those who deny and decry politics at the local level are also dangerous because they are narrowing the perceived scope of municipal operations. If municipal governments don't have a political role—without which they obviously cannot act as an extension of the community—then they are left only with that other role of service delivery. But what services, and on what basis? Without a political role based on the local community, the answer is whatever services provinces see fit to authorize.

Approach of the Text

This book retains the institutional approach and emphasis of previous editions. It traces the historical origins of municipal governments in Canada, their evolution, adaptation, and restructuring over the years, and the current, reformed municipal governments. It also examines the internal governing machinery of municipalities, including the business models which have recently been introduced. Providing a factual overview of developments across Canada has always been a central feature of this book. A number of important insights are gained from the historical perspective of this approach, and a wealth of fascinating parallels between past and present. These remind us of the enduring nature of certain issues and themes, and also offer opportunities to learn and benefit from what has gone before.

In addition to this institutional emphasis, however, the book also addresses the operating context and environment within which municipal governments function. In so doing, it examines not only intergovernmental relationships and interactions with local groups but also the changing patterns of urbanization and economic development and their impact on municipal operations. In particular, the book explores the economic limits on political action by municipalities, as already noted in this chapter.

Public choice theory is useful in examining major issues facing municipalities today.

It is customary to utilize theories or conceptual frameworks to explore a topic such as municipal politics and policy making. Indeed, the previous edition of this book included a chapter which discussed elite theory and pluralism, public choice, and various theories of economic determinism. This time, however, our examination of theory will focus on public choice only. As explained below, public choice considerations underlie two of the major issues facing municipal government today and featured in this text. They are the renewed emphasis on municipal amalgamation and the revived push to make municipalities operate more like a business.

Public Choice Theory

Public choice or political economy theory incorporates the concepts of classical economics about "economic man," motivated by self-interest, making choices which are reflected through the laws of supply and demand in the operations of the market place. It finds that these basic economic forces don't work as well when applied to public goods and services. Private goods and services are normally available in the market place, and individuals are able to obtain these readily if they are willing to pay the price. Consumer demand (or lack thereof) influences the supply of a private good made available and the price that will apply to it.[28]

Public goods, such as police services, fire protection, or control of contagious diseases, present quite a contrast to private goods. Public goods are enjoyed or consumed by all members of a community. Individ-

---

[28]This discussion is based on Robert L. Bish and Vincent Ostram, *Understanding Urban Government: Metropolitan Reform Reconsidered*, Washington, American Enterprise Institute for Public Policy Research, 1973, Chapter 3.

uals cannot be excluded from enjoying a public good once it is provided for someone else. By their nature, such goods and services cannot be provided on a long-term basis through voluntary efforts and financing. If they were, each citizen would find it in his or her interest to forgo payment, as long as enough others were paying to keep the good or service available. Governments levy taxes as a way of forcing everyone to pay a share of the cost of public goods and services.

Consumers express their preferences for, and their evaluation of, private goods by buying them or not. That choice is not available for public goods, for reasons already indicated. Instead, preferences for public goods and services are expressed through a variety of other means. These include voting, lobbying, public opinion polls, petitions, public hearings, demonstrations, court proceedings, political party organizations, and other indirect means including "taxpayer revolts" and resorts to violence when things are desperate.[29]

Public choice theorists contend that public bureaucracies and representative democracy are both seriously flawed in comparison to the operation of the market place.[30] Private companies, it is argued, must stay lean and efficient because of the existence of competition and alternative sources of goods and services. Not only is government a monopoly (for almost all goods and services), but also the way government operates serves to generate excess growth and spending. This happens, explain public choice theorists, because of the natural instinct of politicians and bureaucrats to pursue their own self-interest. For politicians, this means retaining voter support by promising more and better services to the electorate—although a long-suffering electorate may finally be running out of patience with the idea of being bribed with its own money! Civil servants also pursue expanded programs and services, since the bigger their empires and budgets, the higher their status in the hierarchy. Both politicians and bureaucrats may make common cause with the constituencies which receive goods and services, as a way of developing pressure for their retention and expansion. Interest groups spring up to protect established programs and to advocate their expansion.

Public choice theorists also find deficiencies in the arrangements for expressing consumer preferences concerning public goods and services. The votes cast in an election every few years are not a very good or clear

---

[29]*Ibid.*, pp. 22-23.

[30]The analysis which follows is largely based on Gerry Stoker, *The Politics of Local Government*, London, Macmillan Education Ltd., 1988, Chapter 10.

indication of citizen preferences concerning public goods and services. Voters are responding to a wide range of issues and are not able to signal their response to the provision of a particular good or service. This shortcoming has been referred to as the "all-or-nothing blue-plate menu problem," where à la carte purchasing is not permitted.[31] Citizens also express their preferences in other ways, as listed above, but access to these alternatives varies for different citizens. There are also costs to participating and citizens will only be motivated to express their preferences, therefore, when they feel the benefits of such activity will exceed the costs.

The smaller the political unit and the fewer the services provided, the easier it is for citizen preferences to be indicated precisely. For this reason, public choice theorists reject the creation of large, multi-purpose "regional governments" which have been the objective of most local government reformers. Such structures are held to be too large and bureaucratic and to work against citizen participation. Public choice proponents find the much-maligned fragmentation of local government to be a virtue. They support the retention of separate special purpose bodies. For them, the best structure is to have a large number of small local governments so that the diverse preferences of many different citizens can be satisfactorily accommodated.[32] This approach reflects the contribution of Tiebout, who put forth the view that for each unit of local government there is a natural "optimum community size" based on the mixture of taxes levied and services provided toward which all local governments should strive.[33] This size is achieved as a result of individual consumers "searching around" to find that community which suits their needs best. If taxes increase too much or desired services are not provided, the argument goes, then consumers will respond by expressing their discontent or by "voting with their feet" and moving to another jurisdiction.

As noted, public choice arguments and their merits have been very much in evidence in recent years, especially in relation to two aspects of municipal government. First, the return of widespread municipal amalgamations in the 1990s has pitted those proposing consolidation against public choice advocates who claim that fragmented structures operate more efficiently because of the competition inherent in their make-up.

---

[31]Bish and Ostram, *op. cit.*, p. 23.

[32]Stoker, *op. cit.*, p. 228.

[33]Charles Tiebout, "A Pure Theory of Local Expenditures," *Journal of Political Economy*, Vol. 64, pp. 416-424.

Critics of public choice dispute the notion of well-informed consumers making careful assessments of the package of services and tax levels available to them in their own and neighbouring municipalities.[34] They also point out that most consumers are not that mobile, and can't readily shift locations even if they have information which might suggest more attractive options. This lack of mobility particularly applies to the poor and disadvantaged. As a result, one of the strongest criticisms of public choice theory is that it can serve to justify the establishment or preservation of separate jurisdictions which house the rich and privileged and keep out the poor and undesirable and their expensive servicing needs. This practice has been more evident in the multiple servicing districts and separate jurisdictions found in American urban areas, but cannot be overlooked as a concern in the Canadian context.

Public choice has also come to the fore because of the popularity of books such as *Reinventing Government*[35] with their emphasis on more entrepreneurial municipal governments which focus more closely on their customers, measure the results of their activities, and create a more competitive atmosphere in which greater efficiency is achieved. These enlightened municipalities also appreciate the importance of the distinction between steering and rowing, and they recognize that they can be service arrangers, or enabling authorities, rather than necessarily direct service providers.

> Public choice theory is also reflected in the currently popular proposals for "reinventing government."

Here again, these manifestations of public choice theory generate debate and controversy. As discussed in later chapters, the suggestions in *Reinventing Government* struck a chord because they represented the possibility of significant change and improvement. Process improvements, new initiatives to measure and reward productivity, greater collaboration with other service providers, closer attention to the needs and views of the citizen/customer—all of these changes were warmly welcomed. The introduction of business tools and techniques can be helpful, provided that they remain only tools which assist decision makers, and don't begin to dictate the decisions which are taken. The focus on the

---

[34]For a good discussion of the dubious assumptions underlying the Tiebout hypothesis, see L. J. Sharpe and K. Newton, *Does Politics Matter?* Oxford, Clarendon Press, 1984, pp. 61-68.

[35]David Osborne and Ted Gaebler, *Reinventing Government*, New York, Penguin Books, 1993.

customer or consumer can also be beneficial, but there is a danger that public choice can reduce the relationship between local citizens and their municipality to one based only on considerations of individual economic benefit or loss. Under public choice theory, "democracy is seen less as a system for taking collective decisions than as a mechanism for allowing individuals maximum scope for choice."[36] Any sense of community and collective responsibility is hard to maintain in such an environment. Reducing citizens to the status of customers also represents a diminution of local democracy. According to this perspective, individuals are empowered by action through the market, and the emphasis is on choice, redress, and compensation.[37] A contrary view is that what individuals need is far greater rights to be consulted and wider participation in democratic institutions, "together with a reinvigorated notion of public service as a reflection of shared concerns."[38]

It should be evident from even this brief summary that public choice theory is quite relevant to the discussion of a number of major issues featured in this text. This is why it is the one theory singled out at the outset, even though theories such as pluralism and economic determinism will also be reflected in some later discussions.

Concluding Comments

Municipalities today are in the midst of a turn of the century reform movement far more radical and far-reaching than the one they experienced 100 years ago. The pressures this time come not only from the usual self-interested business classes but from the supposedly unassailable dictates of global economic forces. It is true that municipalities must respond to these pressures. They can't cling to the past in the face of the new realities that confront them. But neither should they embrace without question the new business models currently being advocated. Any such action would also amount to a return to the past, to the narrow view of

---

[36]Michael Keating, "Size, Efficiency and Democracy: Consolidation, Fragmentation and Public Choice," in David Judge, Gerry Stoker, and Harold Wolman (eds.), *Theories of Urban Politics*, London, Sage Publications, 1995, p. 123.

[37]Dilys Hill, *Citizens and Cities*, Hemel Hempstead, Harvester Wheatsheaf, 1994, p. 23.

[38]G. Brown, "Empowerment to the people," *The Guardian*, March 10, 1992, as quoted in *ibid.*, p. 24.

municipal government advocated by the turn of the century movement of 100 years ago. What municipalities must do is steer a middle course. They must find the means to blend the best and most suitable of the business tools and techniques with enhanced democratic principles and practices. How this delicate balancing act might be achieved is one of the issues explored in later chapters of the book.

CHAPTER 2
Foundations of Local Government

It is also noteworthy that where the provincial authorities did encourage or ultimately impose municipal governments on their populace, it was not because of any apparent belief in the values of local democracy. Rather it was motivated by a desire on the part of the provincial administrations to shift at least some of the growing burden of expenditures to the local level.

Introduction

How did our municipal governments evolve, and why in the particular form which we find in Canada? One answer—which is correct as far as it goes—is that they were shaped by decisions made by the provincial governments to which they owe their very existence (and by the federal government in the case of municipalities in the Yukon and Northwest Territories).

This explanation is based on the constitutional, legal arrangements provided by the British North America Act (now the Constitution Act). While both the national and provincial levels of government were given separately defined spheres of operation within which each would act relatively autonomously, municipal governments were accorded no such status. Instead, municipalities were only mentioned in the British North America Act as one of the responsibilities allocated to the provinces.

It follows, therefore, that from a strict legal perspective, municipal governments only exist to the extent that the provincial governments have seen fit to provide for them. The types of municipality and their boundaries, responsibilities, and finances must be authorized through provincial legislation. But since provincial governments are responsible to their legislatures and their electorates, they are unlikely to create municipal institutions which are too out of step with public views and attitudes concerning local government. In any event, the basic features of Canadian local government evolved before Confederation and the new provincial governments established in 1867 inherited existing municipal institutions and/or operating philosophies of how local government ought to operate. It is necessary, therefore, to look beyond the legal explanation, important though it is.

The earliest municipal governments in Canada evolved in response to the settlement of the country. As the population increased, and particularly as it became concentrated in the limited urban centres of the early years, it was necessary to administer a growing variety of programs and regulations. With pockets of population scattered in a vast area, and with very rudimentary forms of transportation and communication, the responsibilities could not be handled directly by a centralized colonial government. While some form of local administration was inevitable for quite practical reasons, therefore, the particular form which did evolve was strongly influenced by the political values and traditions of the settlers of this country and the beliefs which they held or developed about municipal government. In this connection, the extent to which this country was settled through immigration was a significant factor, especially because of the belief in local self-government held by many of the United Empire Loyalists who entered this country in the years during and after the American War of Independence.

These and other influences will be evident throughout this chapter as we trace the historical evolution of municipal government in each of the provinces. No standard time frame is employed; rather, developments in each province are described up to the point where the basic municipal structure was established. But chronological considerations are evident in the sequence of provinces. We begin with central Canada because a comprehensive system of municipal government was first established there (in Ontario)—and this system influenced the municipal institutions subsequently created in a number of other provinces. The chapter then examines developments in the Atlantic provinces, the Western provinces, and, finally, the Northern Territories. It concludes with a number of observations about the nature of the municipal systems established and about the circumstances surrounding their creation.

Central Canada

Local government made its first, although somewhat brief, appearance in Canada under the French regime in the settlements of Montreal, Quebec, and Trois Rivières. As early as 1647 a mayor, councillors, and syndics d'habitations (who made representations on behalf of local residents to the provincial authorities) were elected in Quebec. This practice was strongly discouraged by the very authoritarian and centralized home government in France, which felt that it was a dangerous innovation, and in 1663 the mayor and aldermen of Quebec resigned. The whole issue of local self-government was allowed to lapse until 1760 and the advent of British rule.

After the British conquest all government was vested in the military and subsequently in a Governor and an appointed council. In 1763 a proclamation was issued which promised to introduce English law and the English system of freehold land grants in Quebec, in order to encourage English settlement. In the following year the Governor established the ancient English system of local justices of the peace meeting in the Courts of Quarter Sessions for the three districts around Montreal, Quebec, and Trois Rivières for the trial of unimportant matters.

Despite the rule by British Governors and the promise of the benefits of English law, little occurred to interrupt the traditional running of the affairs of Quebec. There was little interference with the Roman Catholic Church, the Court of Common Pleas continued to administer French civil law, and land was still granted through the feudal French system, "en fief et seigneurie." The Quebec Act of 1774 formally recognized this situation and also extended the Quebec boundaries west to the Great Lakes and Mississippi River and north to Labrador.

The American Revolution broke out soon after and precipitated a flow of United Empire Loyalists to Nova Scotia and the western part of Quebec.[1] The peak years of this immigration were 1782-1783, when 10 000 arrived in the Saint John area of the Bay of Fundy, 25 000 arrived in Nova Scotia (doubling its previous population), and 20 000 arrived in the unsettled areas around Lake Ontario, particularly around Kingston, Toronto, and Niagara.

These immigrants came chiefly from New York and the New England colonies, where they had enjoyed some degree of local self-government. They brought with them the tradition of municipal government through the town meeting. Under this system, selectmen (councillors) were elected at the annual town meeting by the inhabitants residing within one-half mile of the meeting house. These selectmen were to oversee the affairs of the town between meetings. In theory their appointment and actions were to be approved by the Governor but in practice they operated independently of the central authorities.

---

[1]The figures which follow are from K. G. Crawford, *Canadian Municipal Government*, Toronto, University of Toronto Press, 1954, p. 21.

Upper Canada (Ontario)

Needless to say, these Loyalists were unhappy under French civil law, especially the system of land grants under the seigneurial system, and the limited local autonomy. There soon were numerous petitions from the Loyalists around Lake Ontario for some form of local courts and administration, English civil law, and separation from that area of Quebec which was east of Montreal. Because of population growth pressures, but much against their better judgment, the British acquiesced and in 1787 passed an ordinance which divided the western settlements, previously a part of the district of Montreal, into four new districts with various appointed officials including justices of the peace who constituted the Courts of Quarter Sessions. The Quarter Sessions assumed judicial, legislative, and administrative responsibilities including maintaining the peace, regulating domestic animals running at large, the conduct of licensed taverns, the appointment of minor officials, and the superintending of highways.[2] As new problems arose, the Quarter Sessions, which were the only official agency dealing with local matters, were simply given more powers to deal with them.

However, this new system proved to be unworkable under the French feudal laws and institutions which had been established with the Quebec Act and pressure continued for a separate province with English civil law and an English system of land tenure. This continuing pressure finally culminated in the Constitutional Act of 1791 (also known as the Canada Act). Its main provisions were:

1. The creation, from the province of Quebec, of the provinces of Upper and Lower Canada, with the Ottawa River roughly as the dividing line.
2. The provision of a government for each province consisting of a British Lieutenant Governor, an appointed executive council, an appointed legislative council, and an elected legislative assembly.
3. The use of English law and land tenure in Upper Canada.
4. The allotment of land as clergy reserves for the support of the Protestant Clergy.

Both Lord Dorchester and also J. G. Simcoe, the first Lieutenant Governor of Upper Canada, strongly discouraged any form of local government. Their stance reflected the prevailing view of the Colonial Office which was haunted by the prospect of another colonial rebellion. Municipalities were distrusted on the grounds that they were breeding grounds

---

[2]*Ibid.*, p. 23.

for dissent and disloyalty.[3] When the first townships on the upper St. Lawrence were surveyed in 1783, the authorities directed that they be called royal seigniories and not townships, and that they be numbered and not named as was customary, to discourage any strong attachment to a particular place. However, even before the Constitutional Act was passed, the Loyalists had already set up town meetings and designated their settlements townships. In an imaginative act of defiance, they named the townships after King George and members of his family.

In 1792 Simcoe divided Upper Canada into counties for militia purposes and for electing representatives to the newly created assembly. He was very keen to develop an aristocracy in an effort to reproduce the highly classed society found in England. From this privileged class he planned to appoint his executive council to oversee the actions of the assembly. In time an aristocracy known as the Family Compact became organized around the executive branch of the provincial government. This group had both family and economic ties throughout the province.[4] Its members felt it was their duty to "guard the body politic from the corrupting influences of republicanism" and fought all efforts at establishing any kind of responsible government at any level.[5]

On the other hand, the Loyalists, who constituted most of the population of the province, felt that they had proven their loyalty to the Crown by fleeing the rebellious colonies and therefore deserved to have local self-rule. Perhaps it is not surprising then that the first bill introduced in the first session of the legislative assembly of Upper Canada was "to authorize town meetings for the purpose of appointing divers parish officers." Although not passed in that session, it was passed in 1793 as the Parish and Town Officers Act. The Act permitted annual town meetings[6] to appoint a town clerk, assessors, a tax collector, road overseers and fence viewers, a pound-keeper, and town wardens. The town wardens

---

[3]This point is made by Engin Isin, "The Origins of Canadian Municipal Government," in James Lightbody (ed.), *Canadian Metropolitics: Governing Our Cities*, Toronto, Copp Clark Ltd., 1995, pp. 60-61.

[4]In Lower Canada the Family Compact had a counterpart known as the Chateau Clique with whom it also had family and economic ties. An elite group surrounding the Lieutenant Governor, such as the Family Compact and Chateau Clique, was found in most of the provinces.

[5]Adam Shortt, *Municipal Government in Ontario, An Historical Sketch*, University of Toronto Studies, History and Economics, Vol. II, No. 2, undated, p. 8.

[6]In Ontario, town meetings were actually township meetings.

were to represent the inhabitants in the Quarter Sessions of the district in which the town(ship) was located. The only legislative authority the town meeting had was to fix the height of fences and to regulate animals running at large. An assessment act was also passed in 1793 to provide for raising money to pay for the costs of court and jail houses, paying officers' fees, and building roads.

By the turn of the century, urban concerns of sanitation, streets, education, welfare, and local police were sufficiently pressing that the powers of the justices of the peace had to be extended.

A severe fire in Kingston in 1812 persuaded central authorities that some action was needed and in 1816 an act to regulate the police[7] was passed for Kingston. This act gave the magistrates the power to make and publish rules and regulations for the safety and convenience of the inhabitants and to finance local improvements through a special tax. By the end of the year, Kingston had 14 rules which covered such areas as streets, slaughterhouses, weights and measures, and animals running at large.

Another potentially important event in 1816 was the passage of the first public school act. This act enabled local residents to meet together to elect three trustees who were to hire a teacher and authorize school textbooks.

> The first local elections were for school trustees.

This was the first example of true local self-government, whereby local people could elect representatives to administer a local need. Unfortunately, this was not a successful attempt at local government because of the lack of funds and experienced trustees.

The end of the War of 1812 in North America and the Napoleonic Wars in Europe saw the beginning of a new wave of immigration from the British Isles. Between 1815 and 1850 about 800 000 came to British North America, the great bulk of whom settled in Upper Canada. This population growth magnified the existing urban problems and petitioning continued for some form of municipal government. In 1828 Belleville applied to be incorporated as a town. The Legislative Council rejected this application, saying that:

> Since men do not like to be forced, they are pretty certain to elect only such persons as will not make effective rules or adequately enforce them; hence in the interest of efficient administration, such innovations must be discouraged.[8]

---

[7]Use of police in this sense meant regulation, discipline, and control of a community.

[8]Shortt, *op. cit.*, p. 19.

Despite this setback for Belleville, in 1832 the legislature capitulated and created a distinct corporate body in the president and board of police of the town of Brockville. This body was, in essence, the first form of elected municipal council and it assumed responsibility for all of the local government functions previously undertaken by the Quarter Sessions, with the justices of the peace retaining only their judicial functions within Brockville. This movement to representative local government proved to be popular. In 1834 York was created the self-governing city of Toronto and by 1838 there were eight police towns and two cities.

One should not overstate the significance of this development, however.[9] Only the members of the boards of police were incorporated, not the town inhabitants. The qualifications to be a member of the board required that a town inhabitant be a freeholder or a householder paying a certain amount of rent per annum for his dwelling. A governing elite was formed whose obligation was to govern the town. The qualification to be a voter in the election required that the town inhabitant be a male householder, a subject of the King, and possessing a freehold estate. "These qualifications for board membership and voting demonstrate the calculated restrictions that were put upon participation in town politics."[10]

Moreover, the terms of incorporation for these boards suggest that the Upper Canada legislature was very cautious in conferring corporate capacities on towns.

> The boards of police had more duties and obligations than rights and liberties. Or, stated another way, these bodies politic were constituted so as to make them accept the delegated powers of the State; and, by empowering a qualified elite to govern through taxation, these communities also relieved the State of the costs of governance.[11]

While the urban areas of Upper Canada were gaining more local self-government, the rural areas were still functioning under the Parish and Town Officers Act with the magistrates of the Quarter Sessions in almost total control of local affairs. Reform newspapers of the time charged that many magistrates were unfit, intemperate, and ready to stir up the mob against reformers. The magistrates decided which local works were to be carried out, often ignoring areas in which they had no personal interest,

---

[9]See Engin F. Isin, *Cities Without Citizens*, Montreal, Black Rose Books, 1992, pp. 112-114, on which this discussion is based.

[10]*Ibid.*, p. 113.

[11]*Ibid.*, p. 114.

and how much tax revenue was to be raised.[12] The growing unrest culminated in the 1837 Rebellion in Upper and Lower Canada. In response, the Earl of Durham was appointed to investigate the insurrection particularly and the general state of government in all of the provinces. Durham produced a comprehensive report dealing with the conditions in British North America, and of particular importance for our purposes are his recommendations dealing with local government. He wrote that "municipal institutions of local self-government ... are the foundations of Anglo-Saxon freedom and civilization."[13] He also stated: "The latter want of municipal institutions giving the people any control over their local affairs, may indeed be considered as one of the main causes of the failure of representative government and of the bad administration of the country."[14]

Durham recommended that the two Canadas be reunited and that local matters should be looked after by municipal bodies of a much smaller size than the province.

Governor General Sydenham, who replaced Durham in 1840, recognized the importance of the recommendations in Durham's report and he wrote to the Colonial Secretary:[15]

> Since I have been in these Provinces I have become more and more satisfied that the capital cause of the misgovernment of them is to be found in the absence of Local Government, and the consequent exercise by the assembly of powers wholly inappropriate to its functions.

What might have happened if local government clauses had been left in the Union Act?

Sydenham sent the Colonial Secretary a draft bill for union of the Canadas which incorporated Durham's recommendations. Unfortunately at this time Durham had fallen into personal unpopularity and the Colonial Office considered the Family Compact and the Chateau Clique as the loyal heart of the country.[16] The principle of responsible government and the clauses on local government were dropped from the Union Act passed by the English Parliament. One cannot overstate the

---

[12]Fred Landon, *Western Ontario and the American Frontier*, Toronto, McClelland and Stewart Limited, 1967, p. 223.

[13]Gerald M. Craig (ed.), *Lord Durham's Report*, Toronto, McClelland and Stewart Limited, 1963, p. 60.

[14]*Ibid.*, p. 67.

[15]Landon, *op. cit.*, p. 223.

[16]Thomas H. Raddall, *The Path of Destiny*, Toronto, Doubleday and Company, Inc., 1957, p. 31.

importance of this omission. Had the Union Act contained clauses providing for a system of municipal government, then such a separate and distinct provision might well have been reproduced in the British North America Act which brought Canada into existence. Had this happened, municipalities would have gained the constitutional recognition that has always eluded them.

In any event, Lord Sydenham persisted in spite of his initial setback. In 1841 he persuaded the new Canadian legislature to pass an act which established an elected district council to take over the administrative authority formerly exercised by the Courts of Quarter Sessions in rural areas. There were no drastic changes in the general way that local government was carried on; the annual town meeting still elected various officers and passed town laws. But it also elected one or two district councillors from each township. The head of the district council, the warden, was appointed by the Governor General, although subsequently the councils were given the right to choose their own warden. The councils were given responsibility for roads, municipal officers, taxing, justice, education, and welfare. Their expenses could be met by tolls or taxes on real or personal property or both. The Governor General could disallow any by-laws and could dissolve any or all of the district councils.

The District Councils Act is perhaps even more important than any succeeding act because it was the first real break with the system of local government by Courts of Quarter Sessions and preceded by almost 50 years the abandonment of this system in England.[17] While it was too radical for conservative elements in the legislature and not radical enough for the reformers, it did provide for a transition period in the rural areas between no local self-government and full local self-government. The central authorities retained much power because it was genuinely felt that local people would not be able to manage their own affairs.

Despite initial fears, the first district councillors were apparently fairly capable people who were able to stimulate the development of their townships because of their knowledge of local needs. By far the most important functions were the construction and repair of roads and bridges and the laying out and creating of school districts. The councils were hampered, however, by problems with assessment, provincial control, and scarce finances—problems which persist to this day. It has been written of the revenues available to district councils that:

---

[17]Crawford, *op. cit.*, p. 31.

These were paltry sums for the needs of large districts, and it is quite certain that the very light direct taxation on which Canadians long prided themselves was a rather important factor in the backward condition of the country for so many years.[18]

In 1843 the Baldwin or Municipal Act was introduced, but because of a rupture with the Governor General it was not passed until 1849. A primary function of the act was the consolidation of all municipal legislation under one measure. It built upon the District Councils Act while extending certain powers. The Baldwin Act differed *in two major respects*:

1. the county rather than the district became the upper tier of municipal government, and
2. for the first time townships were recognized as a rural unit of municipal government.

As well, the act established villages, towns, and cities as urban municipal units. Cities and separated towns were not a part of the county for municipal government purposes. This municipal system established in 1849 has endured to the present in many areas of Ontario. Moreover, as will be discussed in Chapters 5 and 6, many of the reformed structures introduced in recent decades were essentially modified county systems.

Lower Canada (Quebec)

In Lower Canada, as in Upper Canada, government by the magistrates grew to be very unpopular, and there were frequent demands for improved administration.[19] But it was not until 1832 that Quebec and Montreal were granted charters which enabled the citizens to elect a mayor and two aldermen per ward. According to Isin,[20] the long delay since the 1785 incorporation of Saint John as the first incorporated city in British North America, reflected the caution and hesitancy of colonial and British authorities about the use of this legal device. Indeed, the incorporations were limited to a four year term. When the provisions expired in 1836, they were not renewed until after 1840 because of the political turmoil caused by the 1837 Rebellion.

---

[18]Adam Shortt and Arthur G. Doughty (gen. eds.), *Canada and its Provinces: A History of the Canadian People and Their Institutions*, Toronto, Glasgow, Brook and Company, 1914, Vol. XVIII, p. 437.

[19]*Ibid.*, p. 304.

[20]Isin, *Cities Without Citizens*, p. 142.

Although Lower Canada was subject to almost the same urban pressures as Upper Canada, the first 80 years of British rule saw little progress in the establishment of local government. Lord Durham made the following observation on Lower Canada in 1839:

> In fact, beyond the walls of Quebec all regular administration of the country appeared to cease; and there literally was hardly a single public officer in the civil government except in Montreal and Three Rivers, to whom any order could be directed.[21]

Thus the need for some system of municipal government was apparent and in 1840, under the guidance of Lord Sydenham, an ordinance was passed which provided for a system of local government that in many respects resembled the district councils established soon after in Upper Canada. Lower Canada was divided into districts which were to be governed by an elected council and an appointed warden. Another ordinance passed at the same time provided for the election of a clerk, assessors, tax collector, surveyors, overseers of roads and the poor, fence viewers, drain inspectors, and pound-keepers. Townships and parishes with sufficient population were constituted corporate bodies and elected two councillors each to the district councils. Although the district councils were given the power of taxation, much of the real power remained with the Governor.

Both of the 1840 ordinances were unpopular in Lower Canada. The execution and deportation of rebels of the 1837 Rebellion caused resentment and mistrust and the people were especially wary of Lord Sydenham and his motives. The Union Act itself was unpopular and local government was seen as another means of oppression. But perhaps the most unpalatable measure was the power of taxation which, but for customs duties, had previously been unknown in Lower Canada. Therefore, it is not surprising that in 1845 an act was passed which repealed both ordinances and constituted each township or parish a body corporate with an elected council with most of the duties of the district councils.

In 1847 a county system roughly based on the district councils was established. This system lasted until 1855 when the Lower Canada Municipal and Road Act was passed which became the foundation of Quebec municipal institutions. This act established parishes, townships, towns, and villages, while retaining the county level as an upper tier unit. The heads of the local councils sat on the county council and chose their own warden. Each level could appoint the officers it felt were necessary and

---

[21]Shortt and Doughty, *op. cit.*, p. 290.

could levy taxes. Cities continued to be provided for by special charters rather than being incorporated under the provisions of the general act. This system remained in effect with minor changes until the beginning of the 20th century.

TABLE 1

Historical Highlights: Central Canada

ONTARIO

1763	British rule of the colony begins
1774	Quebec Act
1782-83	United Empire Loyalists immigrate
1791	Constitutional Act, creating Upper & Lower Canada
1793	Parish & Town Officers Act
1816	Public School Act
1832	Board of Police (Council) in Brockville
1837	Rebellion, followed by Durham's Report
1840-41	District Councils Act
1849	Baldwin (Municipal) Act

QUEBEC

1777	Ordinance regulating police of Quebec & Montreal
1832-36	Quebec City & Montreal granted charters
1840	System similar to District Councils
1845	Townships and parishes incorporated
1847	Townships and parishes abolished, in favour of county government
1855	Lower Canada Municipal and Road Act

Atlantic Provinces

The development of municipal institutions in the Atlantic provinces initially paralleled that in Ontario. In the early 1700s the area known as Acadia was ceded by France to Britain. The area soon became known as Nova Scotia and gradually people from New England spread north and settled in the new province. They brought with them a tradition of local government through town meetings, although officially local government was to be carried on by the Courts of Quarter Sessions and a grand jury.

After the American Revolution, a wave of Loyalists migrated to the area, this time less from New England than from New York, New Jersey, Pennsylvania, and the South. The Southern Loyalists brought with them a different tradition of local government based on the classed society of the American South in which the Courts of Quarter Sessions discharged local government functions and the Governor appointed local officials. Because of anti-American feelings caused by the Revolution, the New England Loyalists were unsuccessful in promoting local self-rule. Despite dissatisfaction with corrupt practices of certain magistrates, the system of the Courts of Quarter Sessions was to prevail for over 100 years.

At this point, developments in the Atlantic provinces proceeded on a different course from those in Ontario. Far from fighting for local municipal institutions, many Loyalists actively discouraged their development. Many reasons have been suggested for this attitude. They include the feeling that the town meeting had contributed to the revolutionary tendencies of the Americans, a fear of increased taxation, a concern that local officials would lose patronage, and public apathy. In addition, the compactness of the area and the availability of cheap water transportation rendered road construction, one of the major municipal functions, less important. Developments in each province will now be briefly examined.

Nova Scotia

Early local government in Nova Scotia was provided by Courts of Quarter Sessions established by the British authorities around 1750. A wave of immigration from New England at the beginning of the 1760s brought settlers accustomed to the town meeting form of local government. The colonial authorities were unwilling to consider such a democratic approach, especially after the American War of Independence. It wasn't until 1841 that the first municipal incorporation took place, with the granting of a charter to Halifax.

After the introduction of responsible government in 1848 the authorities showed more willingness to allow local government. Legislation permitting the incorporation of counties was enacted in 1855, and the following year the incorporation of townships was authorized. Ironically, now that the right to local government was finally granted, Nova Scotians did not exercise it. According to Higgins, the early enthusiasm waned with the realization that incorporation would bring with it higher taxation.[22]

---

[22]Donald J. H. Higgins, *Local and Urban Politics in Canada*, Toronto, Gage, 1986, pp. 39-40.

However, the provincial government was determined to shift some of the financial burden for local services on to local residents. The result was the 1879 County Incorporation Act.

> That Act was conceived in secrecy at the provincial level and it was the direct offspring of the financial difficulties of the provincial government. The then Attorney General, J.S.D. Thompson, who later became Prime Minister of Canada, frankly stated that the main object of the Act was "to compel Counties to tax themselves directly to keep up their roads and bridges."[23]

Under the Act, the rural areas of the province were incorporated as counties or districts, single tier municipalities governed by a warden and an elected council. Urban areas were dealt with in the Towns Incorporation Act of 1888. It stipulated geographic and population requirements which would enable a town to apply for a charter of incorporation. (Eight such towns had already been incorporated by charter prior to the passage of the statute.) These provisions for separate rural and urban municipalities have remained the basis for the Nova Scotia system to this day.

Prince Edward Island

In 1769 Prince Edward Island separated from Nova Scotia. Two years earlier the island had been divided into counties, parishes, and townships for judicial purposes and for the election of representatives to the provincial legislature, but these areas were never used as municipal units. Indeed, there wasn't any obvious need for municipal government, or even for a decentralization of the colonial administration, given the small size and tiny population of Prince Edward Island.

The first municipal government appeared in 1855 with the incorporation of Charlottetown as a city. In 1870 an act was passed which enabled the resident householders of a town or village to petition the provincial authorities to allow the election of three or more wardens who could appoint local officers and pass by-laws with regard to finance and police matters. Summerside was incorporated as a town in 1875 but, presumably because of the very small population of most settlements, only six more towns had been incorporated by the time the procedure fell into disuse, in 1919. It was abolished in 1950. That same year, the Village Services Act was passed, but the villages established under this statute were not mu-

---

[23]A. William Cox, Q.C., in a 1989 paper, "Development of Municipal-Provincial Relations," quoted in *Task Force on Local Government*, Report to the Government of Nova Scotia, April 1992, Briefing Book, p. 13.

nicipalities. Instead of elected councillors, they were governed by commissioners appointed by the provincial government. These villages are now known as communities, of which there are presently about 80. The main difference between towns and communities is that the town councils adopt their own budgets whereas communities must get their budgets approved at an annual meeting of residents.[24] Half of the province's area and 40% of its population is still not municipally organized, with the province continuing to provide many usual local government services.

New Brunswick

Fifteen years after Prince Edward Island separated from Nova Scotia, New Brunswick followed suit, with the break being precipitated by an influx of United Empire Loyalists. The following year, 1785, Saint John was incorporated as a city, preceding by almost 50 years the creation of cities in the rest of Canada. Elsewhere in the colony, however, local government was carried on by the Courts of Quarter Sessions and a grand jury. The local citizenry, according to Higgins, seems to have been largely indifferent to the idea of local self-government.[25] This attitude has been partly attributed to the smaller population of Loyalists who came from New England and had thus experienced local government. Whalen, however, rejects this viewpoint, contending that only about 7% of the Loyalists came from the Southern Colonies with their system of Quarter Sessions and that, in any event, even the Loyalists from New England made little demand for more democracy at the local level.[26] Nor did the province's substantial French population, with its tradition of centralism, make such demands.

Interestingly, much of the impetus for the incorporation of municipalities came from the central authorities who were concerned about "reducing the time consumed on endless debates and squabbles over parish and county issues in the legislature" and anxious to shift a growing expenditure burden.[27] Finally, in 1851 an act was passed for the incorporation of counties, but its provisions were permissive and only six counties

---

[24]Allan O'Brien, *Municipal Consolidation in Canada and its Alternatives*, Toronto, Intergovernmental Committee on Urban and Regional Research, May 1993, p. 27.

[25]Higgins, *op. cit.*, p. 40.

[26]H. J. Whalen, *The Development of Local Government in New Brunswick*, Fredericton, 1963, Chapter Two.

[27]*Ibid.*, p. 20.

were established over the next three decades. However, the Municipalities Act of 1877 made county incorporation mandatory, thus bringing the entire population and area of the province under municipal government. The county system was two-tiered like that in Ontario, but differed in that councillors from the rural areas were directly elected to county council while all urban areas, except Fredericton, were represented at the county level, usually by ex-officio members.

During this period a number of urban communities sought corporate status. Fredericton had received its charter in 1848, over 60 years after the first urban incorporation in Saint John. By 1896 nine towns had been established by separate charter. In that year the Town Incorporation Act was passed providing for a uniform system for the creation of towns with an elected council consisting of a mayor and aldermen.

The basic municipal system of New Brunswick was established in this 1896 statute and the 1877 Counties Act. Cities each have their own charter of incorporation and a 1920 act provided for the incorporation of villages. As discussed in Chapter 6, however, a major reorganization of local government in New Brunswick begun in 1967 resulted in the abolition of county governments and a number of other major changes.

Newfoundland

The development of municipal institutions in Newfoundland has been a slow and arduous process, attributed to several factors.[28] The settlements which developed in the early years were numerous but geographically isolated from each other, generally quite limited in population, and financially unable to support any form of local government. Moreover, since Newfoundlanders only gained the right to own property in 1824, they jealously guarded this right against the taxation which would inevitably come with local government.

Newfoundland, because of its geographic isolation, was not influenced by the development of municipal government elsewhere; nor did its early settlers have prior experience with such a system. There was little apparent need for municipal government in much of the province, since transportation needs were partly served by water and the central government provided local services such as roads.

After some unsuccessful attempts, St. John's was created a town in 1888, but once again the impetus was not the demand for local democracy but the desire of the colonial authorities to shift some of their ex-

---

[28]Higgins, *op. cit.*, pp. 33-34.

penditure burden. As Higgins explains, municipal status for St. John's was imposed partly to facilitate costly improvements to the sewerage and street systems and partly to be a mechanism whereby the privately owned and heavily in debt St. John's Water Company would become the financial responsibility of the City—a Water Company in which the Premier of Newfoundland and other prominent government supporters and business people were shareholders![29]

TABLE 2
Historical Highlights: Atlantic Provinces

PRINCE EDWARD ISLAND

1769	P.E.I. separated from Nova Scotia
1855	1st municipal government, city of Charlottetown
1875	Summerside incorporated as a town

NEW BRUNSWICK

1784	New Brunswick separated from Nova Scotia
1785	Saint John incorporated as a city
1851	Legislation allowing incorporation of counties
1877	Municipalities Act
1896	Town Incorporation Act

NOVA SCOTIA

1841	Halifax received charter
1879	General Municipal Act
1888	Town Incorporation Act

NEWFOUNDLAND

1888	St. John's created a town
1949	Province joined Confederation
	General local government act passed

No other municipalities were formed for fifty years. Acts were passed in 1933 and again in 1937 providing for the incorporation of municipalities. However, no community requested incorporation and the central authorities did not use their authority to impose such incorporations. Instead, a new approach was attempted which offered subsidies and provided a special act giving a municipality any taxation form it desired if it would

---

[29]*Ibid.*, pp. 34-35.

incorporate. By 1948 20 municipalities had been incorporated by special charter and only five of these imposed the real property tax.[30]

After Newfoundland joined Confederation in 1949, the provincial legislature passed a general local government act which bestowed municipal status by proclamation for areas with a population of at least 1000, and also provided for rural districts. Since that time the number of municipalities has grown steadily as have local improvement districts and local government communities. Chapter 6 describes Newfoundland's prolonged efforts to bring about restructuring in the St. John's area and its ambitious municipal consolidation program.

Western Provinces

The provinces of Manitoba, Saskatchewan, and Alberta were part of the original Hudson's Bay Company land grant and later of the Northwest Territories. For most of their early history these provinces were governed by the Company, which had complete judicial, legislative, and administrative authority. In 1869 the Company's rights in Rupert's Land and the Northwest Territories were acquired by the newly created Dominion of Canada. It was not until late in the nineteenth century that a substantial amount of settlement occurred in the Prairie provinces. When population growth pressures finally necessitated the provision of local services and subsequently a local government system, it was only logical for these provinces to look to their nearest eastern neighbour, Ontario, for a model upon which to base their systems. Because of the different physical characteristics of the West, the Ontario model was somewhat modified to suit local needs.

Manitoba

In 1870 Manitoba was created a province separate from the Northwest Territories. The first provincial legislature provided for a system of local government by a grand jury and Courts of Sessions which were to administer a County Assessment Act and a Parish Assessment Act. As well, the judges of the Sessions chose local officers such as treasurers, assessors, highway surveyors, pound-keepers, and constables from lists presented by the grand jury.

---

[30]Crawford, *op. cit.*, p. 41.

The first municipality was established in 1873 with the incorporation of Winnipeg as a city—although not without a struggle. Apparently the Hudson's Bay Company and four other property owners, who together owned over half of the assessable property in Winnipeg, had opposed the incorporation and the resultant taxation of that property.[31] In that same year, general municipal legislation was also passed which provided for the establishment of local municipalities upon petition of the freeholders within a district. Only six areas became incorporated during the decade that this act was in force.

This permissive approach was dropped in 1883 when the Manitoba government decided to introduce a municipal system for the whole province modelled on the two tier county system of Ontario. The new act established 26 counties with councils composed of the heads of both rural and urban local (lower tier) municipal councils. The county council elected a warden from among its own members. This Ontario county system proved to be ineffective, however, because of the large areas covered, the often sparse and scattered population, and the local objections to a two tier system. It was abandoned after only three years and the province was divided into smaller rural municipalities.

In 1902 a general act established cities, towns, villages, and rural municipalities as the basic units of local government, although Winnipeg was given its own special charter. This system has continued to the present, except for major changes in the structure of government for the Winnipeg area as discussed in Chapter 6.

Saskatchewan

Like Manitoba, Saskatchewan had been part of the lands granted to the Hudson's Bay Company. It was taken over by the Canadian government in 1870 and administered essentially as a colony until it gained provincial status in 1905. The territorial council first provided for municipal government in 1883 by enacting a municipal ordinance which was patterned on the previously cited Manitoba legislation of that year which, in turn, had been modelled on the 1849 Municipal Act of Ontario. The ordinance provided for either rural municipalities or towns depending on area and population and on whether local citizens petitioned for municipal status. Regina received town status that very year and four rural municipalities were organized in 1884, but little initiative was evident thereafter. By 1897 only one additional town had been created and two rural municipalities

---

[31]Higgins, *op. cit.*, pp. 50-51.

had dropped their municipal status. One major problem was the vast area and small, scattered population which made it difficult to generate the financial base needed to support municipal government.

However, since some form of local organization was necessary to provide roads and protection against prairie and forest fires, an ordinance was passed allowing the creation of "statute labour and fire districts" in areas not organized as rural municipalities. By 1896 these local improvement districts, as they were now called, were made mandatory and the following year legislation was passed which allowed for elected committees to administer the districts. In 1903 the districts were reorganized into larger units made up of four of the former districts, each with one elected councillor on a municipal district council. Meanwhile, a revision and consolidation of municipal ordinances in 1894 provided for the incorporation of cities, towns, and rural municipalities.

> An influx of settlers, some with municipal experience, gave an impetus to municipal incorporations.

Throughout this period the federal government strongly encouraged Western settlement and large numbers of settlers arrived from Europe and from Eastern Canada, the latter bringing previous experience with municipal government. The impetus which these developments gave to the creation of municipal institutions is evident from the fact that when Saskatchewan became a province in 1905 there were already 4 cities, 43 towns, 97 villages, 2 rural municipalities, and 359 local improvement districts.[32]

The new province appointed a Commission to carry on with a study previously started by the assembly of the Northwest Territories, which was to consider all aspects of municipal government. In 1908 Saskatchewan adopted the Commission's recommendation that a system of municipal units be established with a separate act covering each type of unit. Accordingly, the City Act, Town Act, and Village Act were passed in 1908 and the Rural Municipalities Act in the following year. One result was a very rapid increase in rural municipalities—to 200 by 1912. However, many rural residents opposed municipal organization, mainly because of a fear of increased taxes,[33] and the province had to force remaining local improvement districts to become rural municipalities. The municipal structure has remained basically unchanged through to the present.

---

[32]Horace L. Brittain, *Local Government in Canada*, Toronto, Ryerson Press, 1951, p. 179.

[33]Higgins, *op. cit.*, p. 53.

Alberta

Since Alberta was also part of the federally administered Northwest Territories from 1870 until 1905, its municipal background resembles that of Saskatchewan. The first municipal government was introduced in Calgary, which was incorporated as a town in 1884 under the previously described municipal ordinance of 1883. In what has by now become a familiar pattern, incorporation efforts were initially thwarted by large landowners, among them the CPR, opposed to the prospect of property taxes.[34] Two more urban municipalities were created over the next decade (Lethbridge and Edmonton in 1891 and 1892, respectively), but because of the sparse, scattered rural population, there were no petitions for the creation of rural municipalities under the ordinance. As in the area which later became Saskatchewan, the main form of local government was the statute labour and fire district or local improvement district.

Toward the end of the century, however, the large influx of settlers began to stimulate the creation of local governments. When Alberta became a province in 1905 its population was about 170 000 (compared to 18 000 in 1881) and it had 2 cities, 15 towns, and 30 villages. By 1912 a new municipal system was established with cities, towns, villages, and local improvement districts. The latter could be erected into rural municipalities upon reaching a specified population, but here again few incorporations were requested because of local fears about tax increases.

British Columbia

The area of what is now British Columbia was also under the jurisdiction of the Hudson's Bay Company during its early years of settlement. In 1849 the British assumed responsibility for Vancouver Island. By this time there was a general movement of population to the west side of the continent because of the discovery of gold in California (in 1848). A significant influx of population to the mainland of British Columbia occurred with the discovery of gold on the Fraser River in 1858, and that year the British also assumed control of the mainland from the Hudson's Bay Company. The mainland and Vancouver Island were administered as two separate colonies until 1866.

The physical characteristics of British Columbia played a significant role in the development of municipal institutions in the province. Because of the mountainous terrain, early settlements were scattered and isolated.

---

[34]*Ibid.*, p. 54.

New Westminster, the capital of the mainland colony, became a municipality in 1860, and two years later Victoria, the capital of the Vancouver Island colony, was incorporated as a town. Shortly after gaining provincial status in 1871, British Columbia enacted the Consolidated Municipal Act providing for local petitions for municipal incorporation, but by the end of 1874 there were still only five municipalities in the province.

In 1892 the Municipal Clauses Act was passed, governing all new municipalities formed and providing for a system similar to that in Ontario, but without a county level. Municipalities were either cities with a mayor and council or rural districts with a reeve and council. By 1900 there were some 52 of these municipalities. In 1920 a Village Municipalities Act was passed, allowing smaller urban areas to incorporate with limited powers.

TABLE 3
Historical Highlights: Western Provinces

MANITOBA

1870	Created a province
1873	City of Winnipeg incorporated as first municipality
1873	General Municipal Act
1883	Municipal Act based on Ontario, 26 counties established
1902	General legislation for cities, towns, villages, and rural units

SASKATCHEWAN & ALBERTA

1872	Surveyed into townships
1883	Ordinance for creating municipal units
1897	Won right of responsible government
1905	Separate provinces created
1908	Saskatchewan passed City, Town, and Village Acts Established first Municipal Affairs Department
1909	Saskatchewan passed Rural Municipalities Act
1912	Alberta appointed Municipal Affairs Minister Established general local government system

BRITISH COLUMBIA

1871	Became a province
1872	Permissive municipal legislation
1886	Vancouver incorporated
1892	Municipal Clauses Act

Northern Territories

The area of the Yukon and Northwest Territories was controlled by the Hudson's Bay Company until acquired by the federal government in 1870.[35] Its territory was reduced that year by the establishment of Manitoba as a separate province, and further reductions occurred in 1905 when Alberta and Saskatchewan became provinces and in 1912 when the northern boundaries of Ontario, Quebec, and Manitoba were extended north to their present positions. The discovery of gold in the Klondike in 1896 sparked a rapid increase in the population of the Yukon and in 1898 it was established as a separate territory.

Dawson City was incorporated as the first municipality in 1901, but its charter was revoked in 1904 and the provision of local services reverted to the territorial administration for a number of years. Also in 1901, a provision was made for the establishment of unincorporated towns upon petition. These units were not full municipal governments, however, since residents could only elect one official and only a very limited range of services could be provided. In any event, the one unincorporated town created was disbanded when its population subsequently declined.

This often temporary nature of northern settlements has added to the problems caused by the extremely small, scattered population. Therefore, while both the Yukon and Northwest Territories have municipal ordinances authorizing the establishment of municipal governments, very few units were created until the past couple of decades. As late as 1964 there were only three incorporated municipalities—the towns of Yellowknife and Hay Bay and the village of Fort Smith.

Prior to 1960, virtually all real government within the Northern Territories came from Ottawa. With the relocation of the Territorial Council from Ottawa to Yellowknife in 1967, however, new municipal structures were introduced which allowed for more decision making at the local level. The category of city was introduced in 1969, with Yellowknife becoming the first city.

> The decentralization of government from Ottawa to Yellowknife brought new municipal structures.

There has been increasing emphasis on the passing of authority down from the territorial government to local governments, along with an attempt to strengthen the political role of the municipalities. One government study claimed that "[In] the NWT the importance of the local level

---

[35]The description in this section is partly based on Higgins, *op. cit.*, pp. 59-60.

of government is of particular magnitude because of the cultural diversity and the vast distances between communities."[36]

While only a very small portion of the vast area of the Northern Territories is organized municipally, the organized portion contains three-quarters of the population.[37] The few villages, towns, and cities, which contain most of the population, are basically modelled upon the structure of municipal government found in Southern Ontario. In addition to these tax-based municipalities, there are some 40 non-tax-based municipalities (mostly hamlets) with more limited powers. Of particular interest is a relatively new form of municipal unit called the charter community, whose specific features depend on what is spelled out in the charter establishing it. This flexibility is especially useful in areas where band councils have provided the traditional leadership in the community. Natives have tended to view municipalities as "foreign" structures. The charter community approach allows the creation of a new governing arrangement which can combine elements of the band council structure and of municipalities.

In addition to these municipal structures, a very large number of local boards and special purpose committees are found in the Northern Territories.[38] Many of these bodies were established to obtain feedback from the local communities, to compensate for the fact that there were few elected members of the territorial council (now the legislative assembly) and few elected municipal councils. Even though municipal councils are now more widespread, these special purpose bodies have proven difficult to eradicate—a problem also experienced in Southern Canada.

Further changes and boundary adjustments are occurring as a result of reviews carried out in response to the several aboriginal land claim settlements which are changing jurisdictions in the north. Particularly dramatic is the Nunavut land claim of the Eastern Arctic which led to the Nunavut Political Accord signed in October 1992 and the establishment of a new territorial government in the Eastern Arctic effective April 1999, with jurisdiction over an area that covers approximately 20% of Canada.

---

[36]*Constitutional Development in the Northwest Territories, Report of the Special Representative* (Drury Report), Ottawa, 1980.

[37]This discussion is based on Government of the Northwest Territories in conjunction with the Association of Municipal Clerks and Treasurers of Ontario, *Municipal Administration Program*, 1984, Unit 1, Lesson Two.

[38]See Report of the Project to Review the Operations and Structure of Northern Government, *Strength at Two Levels*, November 1991.

Summary

By the beginning of the 20th century, most provinces had in place, or were about to establish, a system of municipalities. The one major exception is the Northern Territories where the development of municipal institutions was much slower because of the very small, scattered, and largely migratory population and the concentration of government in Ottawa until the mid-20th century. All of the systems were fairly similar, in large part because of the influence of the Ontario model established in 1849. The systems generally consisted of cities, towns, and villages as urban units, a rural unit variously known as a township, municipal district, or rural municipality, and some times an upper tier county unit. Councils were for the most part directly elected, with the notable exception of the county level in Ontario, Quebec, and, to some degree, New Brunswick. An Assessment Act was usually passed, providing municipalities with their main source of revenue.

These municipal systems were quite appropriate for the conditions of the time. They were generally based on a differentiation between urban and rural municipal classifications, on an expectation that municipalities would provide a quite limited range of services, primarily services to property, and on an

> The original municipal systems were appropriate for the agricultural and rural conditions of that time.

assumption that the property tax would be both appropriate and adequate to finance the cost of these limited services. However, the primarily agricultural and rural nature of the economy and society in which these municipal systems were established was to undergo a fundamental change over the next 50 to 100 years. As Chapter 4 describes, this change made the traditional municipal systems increasingly inadequate.

Concluding Comments

Over the years, a romantic notion has developed concerning the long, bitter struggle waged by our ancestors to wrest local self-government from an unsympathetic and paternalistic regime both in the colonies and in Britain. This vision is used to defend the status quo whenever change threatens "historic" boundaries.

Yet the true record is considerably less stirring. While something approaching this chain of events did take place in Ontario, municipal government was less warmly received in Quebec where it was viewed as simply another means of oppression because of the power of taxation. In the Atlantic provinces, this fear of the property tax prompted strong opposition to the introduction of municipal government. An editorial in the *New Brunswick Courier* in 1843 about a proposed municipal bill stated that had the bill been passed, "it would have cut loose that many-headed monster, Direct Taxation and its Myrmidon, the Tax-Gatherer, into the happy home of every poor man throughout the land."[39] Indeed, the history of municipal government in Newfoundland, far from being a tale of local agitation and central government resistance, was instead a case of central government overtures complete with financial incentives, all of which were largely ignored by the local people.

It is also noteworthy that where the provincial authorities did encourage or ultimately impose municipal governments on their populace, it was not because of any apparent belief in the values of local democracy. Rather, it was motivated by a desire on the part of the provincial administrations to shift at least some of the growing burden of expenditures to the local level. This pattern is evident in the historical developments in the Atlantic and Western provinces—and there are some fascinating parallels with developments today.

From the historical developments in the various provinces it is clear that municipal governments were mainly established in response to population growth and consequent service demands. Even in Ontario where pressure for local self-government was most pronounced, an important factor in the creation of municipal institutions was the inability of the Courts of Quarter Sessions to deal with growing urban problems. The preoccupation with local government as a provider of services has remained a central feature of the system to the present day.

However they came into being, Isin disagrees with the view that a democratic, autonomous system of municipalities had emerged by the 1840s.[40] He points out that the municipal system which was established reflected a compromise solution on the part of the British authorities. They responded to the demands for more local decision making while still retaining a good deal of central control over the municipal institutions which were authorized. As will be seen, that central control has expanded greatly over the intervening years.

---

[39]Quoted in Whelan, *op. cit.*, pp. 20-21.

[40]Isin in Lightbody, *op. cit.*, pp. 80-82.

CHAPTER 3
Turn of the Century Reform Era

The net result of the reforms was a more complex, less accountable municipal government, more responsible to economy and efficiency than to the voters.

Introduction

By the onset of the 20th century Canada was at the end of 25 years of industrialization and in the midst of large-scale immigration. During this period of unprecedented economic and population growth, Canadians developed a "boom" mentality and municipal councils were no exception. They began to compete with each other for the location of industry, population growth, and new residential and commercial construction. An indication of the extent of this growth is the fact that the number of real estate agents in Halifax, Saint John, Montreal, Vancouver, Ottawa, Toronto, London, Winnipeg, Regina, Calgary, Edmonton, and Victoria increased from 506 in 1901 to 4250 in 1913.[1] This surge of development brought with it not only prosperity but also new servicing demands and problems. As discussed in Chapter 4, the physical nature of this development changed the urban environment and the human interaction taking place there. In this chapter we will examine the impact that this growth had on Canadian municipal institutions and on the operating philosophy of municipal government.

Urban Problems Develop

Between 1901 and 1911 Canada led the Western world in population growth. Much of this growth was due to immigration, with the foreign-born population of Canada increasing by over 2 000 000. While many of

---

[1]John C. Weaver, *Shaping the Canadian City: Essays on Urban Politics and Policy 1890-1920*, Toronto, Institute of Public Administration of Canada, Monographs on Canadian Urban Government, No. 1, 1977, p. 12. This monograph provides an excellent insight into the reform era and is a partial basis for this chapter.

these immigrants were in Canada as temporary labour, a significant number were permanent arrivals seeking employment in urban centres. For example, Calgary and Edmonton multiplied their populations 40 times and changed almost overnight from villages to cluttered cities. Winnipeg, which had already shown an impressive increase in population from 1800 to 40 000 between 1874 and 1899, surged to 150 000 by 1913. The bulk of this increase came from immigration, and by 1911 no other city in Canada had as high a proportion of European-born residents. The problems of assimilation which resulted led to what Artibise called a "Divided City."[2]

Even without these ethnic and cultural strains, however, the sheer numbers involved generated greatly increased service demands. The years 1900-1913 saw a tremendous jump in urban land values which was accompanied by extensive land speculation. In 1913 an English traveller wrote of the Victoria land boom that in two and one-half years values increased 900%.[3] The increase in land values precipitated a change in downtown land use from that of a mix of small businesses and residential housing to high-rise office towers. This change in land use and higher real estate prices also served to push the working class out to the suburbs. These new settlement patterns continued to unfold throughout the 20th century, with disturbing results which are discussed in the next chapter. Despite a building boom accompanied by large-scale land assembly and suburban development, all major Canadian cities were soon faced with a serious housing shortage and the subsequent development of ghettos and slums.

> Canadian cities faced scarce housing, strained water and sewer systems, and health and transportation problems.

Besides a scarcity of housing, Canadian cities were confronted with other new servicing problems. To accommodate immigrant workers, inferior housing units were hastily built, often without sanitary conveniences. Families frequently shared accommodation and overcrowding became a strain on already overworked municipal water and sewer systems. In 1910 in Canada, 57 systems of inland water were receiving raw sewage from 159 municipalities, and 111 water supply systems were obtaining their water from bodies of water into which raw sewage had been discharged. The combination of these factors produced a serious

[2] Alan F. Artibise, "Divided City: The Immigrant in Winnipeg Society, 1874-1921," in Gilbert A. Stelter and Alan F. Artibise (eds.), *The Canadian City: Essays in Urban History*, Toronto, McClelland and Stewart, 1977.

[3] J. B. Thornhill, *British Columbia in the Making*, London, Constable and Company, 1913, pp. 126-127, as quoted in Weaver, *op. cit.*, p. 13.

health hazard which became only too apparent in the early 1900s with an alarming increase in the number of epidemics. During this period, one of every three deaths was caused by tuberculosis, and typhoid and flu epidemics produced more casualties than World War I.[4]

Other major problem areas were transportation and the provision of utilities. The overcrowding of the downtown district plus the increased numbers commuting from the suburbs created the need for new modes of transportation or, at the very least, the construction of more roads and sidewalks. By 1913 most cities had electrified streetcar systems, which were often privately owned monopolies, and at the same time municipalities were being pressured into providing municipal electric power plants. The mayor of Medicine Hat proclaimed, "The municipal ownership town is in a better position to deal with industrial institutions.... Municipal ownership (of utilities) and industrial progress go hand in hand."[5] These new and expanded services in turn meant increased costs and therefore higher municipal taxes. Wickett pointed out in 1907 that:

> The annual expenditure of Winnipeg clearly exceeds that of Manitoba; Montreal's that of the province of Quebec; and until the present year Toronto's that of the province of Ontario.[6]

These growth pressures resulted in the development of various reform movements throughout Canadian society which were also part of a larger international movement common to most industrialized nations. At this time groups such as the Women's Christian Temperance Union, YMCA, YWCA, Salvation Army, and White Cross Army were founded to help stamp out crime, vice, and poverty, evils associated with the emergence of the wicked city. In response to the servicing and financial pressures facing municipal governments, groups were formed such as the Civic Art Guild of Toronto, City Improvement League of Montreal, Union of Canadian Municipalities, Good Roads Association, and the Civic Improvement League of Canada. The goals of these various groups included

---

[4]The above figures on the pollution and health problems are from Alan H. Armstrong, "Thomas Adams and the Commission on Conservation," in L. A. Gertler (ed.), *Planning the Canadian Environment*, Montreal, Harvest House, 1968, pp. 20-22.

[5]Mayor Foster, "Development of Natural Resources Under Municipal Ownership," *Canadian Municipal Journal*, II, April 1906, p. 133, as quoted in Weaver, *op. cit.*, p. 38. See Weaver's monograph, pp. 37-39, for a detailed discussion of public ownership of utilities.

[6]As quoted in Paul Rutherford, "Tomorrow's Metropolis: The Urban Reform Movement in Canada, 1880-1920," in Stelter and Artibise, *op. cit.*, p. 376.

social justice, a healthy and beautiful city, regulation of utilities, and the restructuring of municipal government. Two movements which had a significant impact on local government were those that encouraged municipal planning and the reform of municipal government.

Development of Municipal Planning

There were three main forces which affected the development of municipal planning. The first to emerge was the civic enhancement or "city beautiful" movement which was often embraced by civic boosters. While city beautiful had supporters who wanted to improve the city for its own sake, councillors and businessmen frequently regarded it as simply another means of attracting industry and growth. The central belief of the boosters was the desirability of growth and the importance of material success.[7] Their views were very influential, partly because not to be a booster was portrayed as lacking both community spirit and business sense. "Good citizenship and boosterism were synonymous."[8]

> The city beautiful, city healthy, and city efficient movements all affected municipal planning.

The city beautiful movement was embraced by Canadian architects, engineers, and surveyors unhappy with the squalor and the ugly environment developing in Canadian communities with the rapid urbanization of the time. Their objective was the achievement of civic grandeur through the development of civic centres featuring monumental public buildings grouped around a public square and a broad tree-lined avenue leading to it.[9] The grand designs provoked criticism of the city beautiful movement as "mere adornment" and extravagance, which failed to address the "real problems" of city housing and sanitation.[10]

---

[7]Alan J. Artibise, "In Pursuit of Growth: Municipal Boosterism and Urban Development in the Canadian Prairie West, 1871-1913," in Gilbert Stelter and Alan Artibise (eds.), *Shaping the Urban Landscape: Aspects of the Canadian City-Building Process*, Ottawa, Carleton University Press, 1982, p. 124.

[8]*Ibid.*, p. 125.

[9]Gerald Hodge, *Planning Canadian Communities*, 2nd Edition, Scarborough, Nelson Canada, 1991, p. 53.

[10]*Ibid.*, p. 56.

A second force which influenced planning resulted from the deteriorating health conditions in urban areas. For example, Fort William tripled its population between 1896 and 1905 as the result of railroad expansion. In the winter of 1905-1906 a sewer which emptied into the city's water supply caused approximately 800 cases of typhoid.[11] This and other similar situations gave rise to the "healthy city" movement, with public health advocates pressing for better public water supplies and sewer systems and for the eradication of slums.[12]

People became convinced that housing conditions were related to public health. Toronto's Medical Officer of Health described slums as "cancerous sores on the body politic, sources of bacteria spreading disease, crime, and discontent throughout the city."[13] The middle and upper classes were continually warned that disease did not respect social standing and they pressed for measures which expanded the powers of health and building inspectors and legislated housing standards. J.J. Kelso, an Ontario lobbyist for children's aid, advocated a form of urban renewal:

> Rear houses and those built in the notorious alleys and lanes of the city should be pulled down. There should be a by-law that every dwelling must front on a forty or sixty foot street and that only one dwelling should be created to each 20 by 100 foot lot.[14]

Unfortunately, because many dwellings were subsequently condemned, these measures only served to make the existing housing shortage worse.

The early public health movement was to have a very significant effect on the development of municipal government. The prevention of illness called for municipal action on a wide range of matters. Municipal public works departments grew out of the public health movement, and so did urban planning, parks, housing, and social service functions.[15] As the 20th century advanced, however, advances in medicine shifted the emphasis of health from prevention to the treatment of sickness and from municipal government preventive programs to massive expenditures on hospitals and doctors. It is only recently, through the revival of a "healthy communities" movement, that we are rediscovering the links between

---

[11]Weaver, *op. cit.*, p. 28.

[12]Hodge, *op. cit.*, p. 83.

[13]Rutherford, *op. cit.*, p. 375.

[14]*Labour Gazette*, July 1910, p. 128, as quoted in Weaver, *op. cit.*, p. 33.

[15]Trevor Hancock, Bernard Pouliot, and Pierre Duplessis, "Public Health," in Richard Loreto and Trevor Price (eds.), *Urban Policy Issues: Canadian Perspectives*, Toronto, McClelland and Stewart, 1990, p. 192.

the services provided by municipalities and the maintenance of a healthy population.

The two reform themes we have been discussing, those of city beautiful and city healthy, were brought together with the creation in 1909 of a federal Commission for the Conservation of Natural Resources. The impetus for its establishment was a recognition that "industrial processes were consuming natural resources at an alarming rate, often leaving in their wake waste and pollution."[16]

Thomas Adams was appointed Advisor on Town Planning to the Commission in 1914. Adams, a native of Scotland, had studied law and then been attracted to the Garden City Movement, which aimed to disperse the population and industry of a large city into smaller concentrations and to create more amenable living conditions in what we would now call "new towns" or "satellite towns."[17] He had served on the board which administered the British Town Planning and Housing Act and when he arrived in Canada he already had a reputation as "an eloquent author and speaker on the Garden City Movement, on agricultural land use and on town planning and housing as aspects of local government."

Adams proceeded to draft local plans and model provincial town planning acts based on the British Act, and by 1916 only British Columbia and Prince Edward Island did not have a planning statute of Adams' making in force. His model created a separate honorary planning board, influenced by American prototypes, with the mayor as the only elected representative. Adams also assisted many Canadian municipalities in the preliminary stages of local planning and promoted the creation of provincial departments of municipal affairs in Ontario and Quebec.

A third force, and one which also influenced municipal structural reforms, was the "city efficient" movement. In this movement the goals of city beautiful and city healthy—that is beauty, order, convenience, and health—were interpreted as economy and efficiency. Planning became a rational scientific process in which experts would provide technical solutions. As one speaker explained, "if all the facts can be collected ... then a solution of any town planning problem becomes comparatively simple."[18] This point of view was consistent with, and reinforced by, the new ideas of "scientific management" which were becoming popular at

---

[16]Hodge, *op. cit.*, p. 86.

[17]*Ibid.*, p. 50.

[18]Gilbert Stelter and Alan Artibise, "Urban History Comes of Age: A Review of Current Research," *City Magazine*, vol. 3 no. 1, September-October 1977, p. 31.

this time. Its disciples claimed that there was only "one best way" to run any organization, to be discovered by rational inquiry.

Although most reformers claimed that they were working to improve the plight of the slum dwellers, a certain amount of self-interest can be detected in reforms actually implemented. Zoning by-laws were often passed to protect middle- and upper-class property values and neighbourhoods since, according to one of the supporters of the Manitoba Tenement Act of 1909, tenement houses "may ... to a large extent spoil the appearance of a neighbourhood."[19]

Development of Municipal Reform Movement

By 1900 urban reformers were advocating changes in the structure of local government as a means of eliminating corruption and improving efficiency. Structural reforms had first been popularized by newspapers covering the corruption of the Tammany Society in New York City (and other American political machines) and subsequent American efforts at municipal reform. In fact, much as American immigrants had influenced the original development of Canadian municipal government, Americans also exerted a strong influence on Canadian reforms at the turn of the century. But while the corruption of municipal government had reached crisis proportions in the United States, the situation in Canada was somewhat less severe.

This is not to say that Canadian municipal politicians were immune to the opportunities presented by the sudden urban growth and get-rich mentality of the times.[20] In Toronto, corporations bidding on contracts and franchises complained that aldermen were "shaking them down" and precipitated an inquiry in which only a few were found guilty but the whole council was tarnished by association. It was also soon after discovered that the Montreal Police Commission was running a protection racket, the Toronto zoo keeper was stocking his own kitchen with food meant for the

> Municipal corruption was not limited to areas "south of the border."

---

[19]John C. Weaver, "Tomorrow's Metropolis Revisited: A Critical Assessment of Urban Reform in Canada, 1890-1920," in Stelter and Artibise, *The Canadian City*, p. 407.

[20]The examples which follow are from Weaver, *Shaping the Canadian City*, pp. 56-59.

animals, and Regina city councillors were being given unusually low assessments and utility bills. These revelations and others left the public disillusioned and prompted calls for action.

In the forefront of the municipal reform movement were middle-class merchants and businessmen. Many of these people had little sympathy for the democratic aspects of local government. They were mainly concerned with expanding local services in order to attract more growth (often on land they owned) which in turn would expand the local tax base to help pay for new services. To these business people, most of whom were part of the boosterism discussed above, local government was just a tool to serve personal and community prosperity. "It was merely a device to be used for the benefit of the people who managed to gain political power or influence."[21] It was business people, of course, who gained control very early and used it for their ends.

As the labour movement developed, working people tried to exert influence as a counterbalance to the strength of business interests. The Industrial Workers of the World (I.W.W.), later known as the One Big Union (O.B.U.), was a force to be taken in earnest in the second decade of the 20th century—pledged to the overthrow of the capitalist system.[22] By the end of World War I, it had begun to attract allies in several countries, including Canada. With the end of the war, returning soldiers swelled the labour force, jobs were scarce, and many workers were dissatisfied with their wages and their hours. On May 13th, 1919, the growing labour unrest in Canada exploded in a general strike in Winnipeg, leaving Canada's third largest city half paralyzed. Sympathy strikes broke out in a dozen other cities, including Toronto, Vancouver, Edmonton, and Calgary, but not with the same intensity. Gradually, the civilian authorities reasserted their authority and, more than a month after it began, the strike was ended with the arrest of its alleged leaders. This polarization of business and labour contributed to ongoing clashes between these two interests for control of council in Canada's major cities, as described in Chapter 10.

Businessmen were not prepared to accept any responsibility for the problems caused by urban expansion since this growth was perceived as only allowing nature to follow its own course. Instead, they blamed corrupt local politicians and inefficient municipal governments for the situation. While the initial purpose of municipal reforms was to eliminate

---

[21]Stelter and Artibise, *Shaping the Urban Landscape,* p. 128.

[22]The description which follows is based on Ralph Allen, *Ordeal By Fire,* Toronto, Doubleday, 1961, p. 175.

corruption, a second important purpose was to improve efficiency. The obvious solution, to business at any rate, was to take the politics out of municipal government and to run it on business principles. In Hamilton, reform mayor Captain McLaren ran on the slogan that "civic business is not politics."[23]

The business community was not alone in its perception of municipal government as a business venture which should be run on business principles. Many contemporary newspapers felt this way and often carried editorials promoting municipal reform. Typical of this view is this comparison of a municipality and a joint stock company:

> Municipalities should be run like a business, and political influence reduced.

> If we could only manage our business as private corporations manage theirs we certainly would not have such a queer lot of directors— aldermen we call them—or make presidents—mayors as we call them— out of men who have never proven themselves as good businessmen....[24]

Business people were also concerned about the power and narrow focus of ward-based politicians who failed to understand the importance of municipal reforms and hindered their implementation. In many cities these ward politicians were elected from areas where foreigners constituted most of the electorate and as Winnipeg's Mayor Sharpe stated: "The city's many foreigners could not comprehend civic issues and hence the role of the wards which gave them a degree of influence should be reduced in any new system."[25]

Much of the reform fervour was also due to a certain amount of enlightened self-interest since many businessmen stood to gain financially through municipal actions. Winnipeg's Mayor Sharpe was a wealthy contractor who specialized in sidewalks. In Regina the reform candidate was known as "the Merchant Prince." He claimed that he paid $3 out of every $100 of local taxes. In Montreal the leaders of the business community, including the president of the Street Railway Company, privately financed a plebiscite on structural reforms.[26]

The reforms advocated by the business community really only served to give it a greater hand in municipal affairs. Businessmen had ambitions to have certain public works undertaken, but they found that in municipal

---

[23]Weaver, "Tomorrow's Metropolis Revisited," p. 42.

[24]*Saturday Night*, 1899, quoted in Weaver, *Shaping the Canadian City*, p. 41.

[25]*Ibid.*, p. 62.

[26]*Ibid.*, pp. 62-63.

politics they were only one of many competing interests, including newly enfranchised lower classes. Since they were "unwilling to fully accept the realities of political pluralism they worked to scupper the rules of the game,"[27] as outlined below.

The Reforms

The American schemes of municipal reform which were to influence Canadian reformers had two main thrusts: first, to give more power to the mayor and, second, generally to separate legislative and executive powers. The reforms actually implemented in Canada seemed to have been tempered by British traditions and the main concession made toward obtaining a strong mayor was the move to "at large" elections for the head of council—a change prompted by the spread of Jacksonian democracy to Canada earlier in the 19th century. But there was a greater acceptance of the need to remove certain responsibilities from the control of council and in effect create separate executive and administrative bodies.

Changes to the Electoral Process

One of the structures most under attack was the council-committee system which seemed to allow ward aldermen a great deal of power in specific areas and thus "opened the door to corruption." In a move to reduce this power, reformers called for the complete abolition of the ward system in favour of "at large" elections for all of council. One of the more convincing arguments for abolishing wards was that they fostered a parochial view of municipal issues instead of a broader view of city-wide concerns. This situation frequently resulted in "back scratching" and "log rolling," or "I'll give you what you want in your ward if you'll give me what I want in mine." An editorial in the *Financial Post* in 1912 stated that the ward system was one of the dominant evils of municipal life and that "all aldermen should hold their seats by the vote of all the electors and should represent all the city at all times."[28]

Of course, at large elections, plus a concurrent move to raise the property qualification for voters, would reduce the influence of foreign-born and slum residents. As early as 1857 Montreal changed from alder-

---

[27]*Ibid.*, p. 64.

[28]*Financial Post*, February 10, 1912, as quoted in Weaver, *Shaping the Canadian City*, p. 67.

men choosing their mayor to the mayor being elected at large and in 1873 Toronto followed suit. In 1891 Toronto reduced the number of wards and in 1894 both Saint John and Fredericton abolished wards completely. In Toronto and Montreal an unsuccessful attempt was made to extend the franchise to companies.

Board of Control

Another reform involved the board of control, which was directed at strengthening the executive at the expense of council. The board of control made its first appearance in Toronto in 1896 in response to a water and sewer crisis. It was influenced by local business models and by the commission system popular in the United States. Only one Canadian city, Saint John, New Brunswick, specifically adopted the commission system. In 1912 its council was abolished and provision made for the election at large of a five member commission. Democratic control features of the commission system included public recall, initiative, and referendum. Each commissioner would be responsible for a particular field or department, thereby gaining expertise in that area.

> The board of control was influenced by business models of the time.

The Canadian board of control differed significantly from the American commission system in that it retained a council. Initially the members of the board of control were chosen by the councillors from among themselves but subsequently they were elected at large. The purpose of the board of control was to take important executive functions out of the control of council by allowing the board to prepare the budget, appoint and dismiss department heads, and award all contracts. Board decisions could only be overturned by a two-thirds vote of council which was difficult to accomplish since council included the board of control members. This form of executive committee proved to be popular in Ontario where it became mandatory for municipalities of a certain size. It also spread to other provinces and in 1906 was adopted by Winnipeg, in 1908 by Calgary where it was called a commission, and in 1910 by Montreal. The Montreal board of control, which was actually part of a more comprehensive reform which also cut the size of council in half, was seen as a managing commission whose powers were subject to the majority approval of council.

Proponents of the board of control often drew an analogy between the board and the provincial or federal cabinets. Yet the most important element of a cabinet was missing because there was no party loyalty and the controllers were not responsible to the rest of council, but instead to their own electorate. Unfortunately the board of control did not live up to reformers' expectations because the same people were still in the executive and administrative positions and the standing committee structure was usually retained. Friction often arose between the board of control and the committees because of overlapping jurisdiction. It was also far too easy to pass the buck and postpone decisions when contentious issues arose. One observer described the results as follows:

> Our councillors have long ago discovered the truth of the maxim that there is safety in numbers. When any ticklish matter comes up, the board of control passes it on to the council; council refers it back to the board.[29]

According to this observer, after all have had their say it is customary to ask some senior staff member for a detailed report and "when that long-suffering individual, after much waste of valuable time, has prepared his report no one any longer has interest enough to read it."

In Western Canada most politicians were reluctant to adopt the extreme measures of the American commission system or even the somewhat more democratic board of control. Western cities adopted a system of appointed commissioners. Instead of electing commissioners who would specialize in specific fields, these cities retained their councils and appointed experts to be administrators without any formal role in policy making. Edmonton was the first city to implement this system in 1904; Regina, Saskatoon, and Prince Albert followed in 1911-1912.

Chief Administrative Officer

Another American reform adopted by many Canadian municipalities was the city manager system. This was especially popular in Quebec after 1920. The system entailed the appointment of a chief administrator who was to coordinate and supervise all of the departments and affairs of the municipality. The system was premised on the assumption that policy making, which was to be the exclusive concern of a small elected council, could be completely separated from policy implementation. It was an extremely popular reform in the United States where it was expected to solve the problem of coordinating the various people who had been given bits and pieces of power, by centralizing authority in one person. Despite

---

[29]Frank H. Underhill, "Commission Government in Cities (1911)," in Paul Rutherford (ed.), *Saving the Canadian City: The First Phase 1880-1920*, Toronto, University of Toronto Press, 1974, p. 327.

the somewhat different conditions in Canada, the city manager system was appealing to reformers because it appeared to be one step closer to the corporate model. In 1919, Guelph adopted the system and the city clerk described the organization as similar to a joint stock company with the aldermen as directors and the mayor as president. According to him:

> The city manager through his different departments, plans the work, submits same to council for their approval. When approved, it is up to the city manager to carry it out in a businesslike manner, without interference from the aldermen.[30]

In some cities it was even suggested that the elected council should be abolished and local affairs should be managed by an appointed executive. In London, Ontario, it was proposed that this appointed executive should be composed of representatives of special-interest groups such as Rotary clubs, ratepayers associations, and the Board of Trade. In Montreal it was intended to retain the council with the mayor, two members elected by council, one by the Board of Trade, and one by the Chambre de Commerce as the executive committee. While most of these proposals were not adopted for councils, in the 1940s Montreal did have a council consisting of a mayor and 99 councillors, of whom 66 were elected and 33 were appointed by public associations.[31] The idea of special-interest group representation also became a popular plan when establishing special purpose bodies.

Boards and Commissions

In a further effort to reduce council's control, reformers advocated the creation of various boards and commissions which would oversee activity in a specific area and thus remove it from the political arena. Although these special purpose bodies were not a new phenomenon, Ontario having had police commissions and boards of health as early as the 1850s, they flourished between 1890 and 1920. To some extent this is understandable. The pressures of urban growth and new technological developments made municipal government more complex. Municipalities now faced decisions in areas relating to sewers, pumping stations, streetcars, power systems, street and sidewalk paving, building codes, assessments, department budgets, tenders, debentures, and sinking funds.

---

[30]*Ibid.*, p. 68.

[31]Paul Hickey, *Decision Making Processes in Ontario's Local Governments*, Toronto, Ministry of Treasury, Economics and Intergovernmental Affairs, 1973, p. 203.

Goldwin Smith, a member of a Toronto municipal reform group, summed up the general attitude in 1890 when he said that in the past city government was a proper setting for debates on principles, but now "a city is simply a densely peopled district in need of a specially skilled administration."[32] The age of the experts or the professionals had arrived and their coming was seen as the panacea for urban problems. The creation of a committee of experts was that much better.

Boards were valued for attracting expertise and for isolating functions from control by politicians.

Another argument in favour of creating special purpose bodies was that a commission could attract "the services of bright, able men who have not the time to serve in the council."[33] What this also meant was that business people were more likely to serve in an appointed position than they were to engage in an election contest and, if successful, to endure the tedious task of attending to constituents' requests. In any event, lobbying for appointed commissions increased; in Toronto for a parks commission, fire commission, hydro-electric commission, and transportation commission; in Montreal for a parks commission; and in Vancouver for a water works commission. As previously discussed, the impetus for town planning also included the creation of a separate planning board or commission. As well, when municipalities took over the operations of street railway systems in the name of efficiency, they usually established a separate body to oversee the administration of this very important function.

By 1917 the proliferation of special purpose bodies was causing concern over the amount of decentralization and fragmentation which had resulted. The October issue of *Municipal World* that year carried an article with the following statement:

> Decentralization has been carried too far. Town Planning Commissions, Suburban Road Commissions, Railway Commissions, Police Commissions, Boards of Education, Hospital Trusts, Utilities Commissions have usurped Council powers. The Council today is little more than a tax-levying body with little or no control.[34]

---

[32]Weaver, *Shaping the Canadian City*, p. 72.

[33]Mayor Bethune, Vancouver (1907), as quoted in *ibid.*, p. 70.

[34]S. M. Baker, "Municipal Government Reform," *Municipal World*, Vol. 27, October 1917, p. 154, as quoted in Weaver, "Tomorrow's Metropolis Revisited," p. 411.

As will be seen in Chapters 5 and 6, these criticisms of excessive boards and resulting fragmentation were still being heard when local government reform initiatives were launched in many of the provinces in the 1950s and 1960s. In response, most of the reforms called for the abolition of boards and municipal consolidations to create a more coordinated structure for efficient delivery of services. However, as will also be seen, boards have been making something of a comeback in recent years.[35] They have been established in, or proposed for, a number of urban areas, in part because of the near-impossibility of gaining agreement on municipal boundary changes, or because boundary changes fail to keep pace with ongoing urban sprawl.

Summary: The Legacy of the Reform Era

Each of the reform movements had its own vision of what tomorrow's city should be like: a city beautiful, filled with parks, trees, boulevards, and stately buildings; a nation full of Garden Cities in which development was controlled to ensure all the basic amenities of life; the Canadian city converted into a Christian community where poverty, crime, and vice were eliminated; or an orderly community with a municipal government run on principles of economy and efficiency.[36]

While many of the reformers undoubtedly were sincere in their efforts, others had less noble motives behind their reform proposals. C. S. Clarke, an opinionated Torontonian, denounced those crusaders who wanted to purify city life as "a small group of pious fanatics who bothered the respectable and terrorized the weak."[37] In only slightly more generous terms, Kaplan states that "the reform doctrine was self-congratulatory, contemptuous of outsiders, and thus highly vulnerable to charges of hypocrisy,"[38] especially since, as indicated above, its main advocates were prominent businessmen seeking to expand their influence. Keating describes the concern of the business community and also much of the

---

[35] A number of examples are found in Dale Richmond and David Siegel (eds.), *Agencies, Boards and Commissions in Canadian Local Government*, Toronto, Institute of Public Administration, 1994.

[36] Rutherford, *Saving the Canadian City*, p. xvii.

[37] Rutherford, "Tomorrow's Metropolis," p. 371.

[38] Harold Kaplan, *Reform, Planning and City Politics: Montreal, Winnipeg, Toronto*, Toronto, University of Toronto Press, 1982, p. 173.

professional middle class about the demands of an increasingly assertive working class, armed with the franchise.[39] These demands had produced "machine politics" in the United States and a socialist movement centred mainly in Western Canada. Both of these troubling developments (in the minds of the business community) could be curtailed by limiting the role of the poor and working class in local politics through institutional reform and by reasserting the ideology of non-partisanship and good government. As Keating points out, "attacks on politics or partisanship often mask objections to the use of political power to counteract inequalities in the social or economic spheres. Non-partisanship thus tends to be a conservative rallying cry."[40] This bias will become evident with the examination of activities of local political parties in a later chapter.

> Politics and partisanship were attacked because political action might be used to counteract inequities.

The reforms pertaining to municipal government were partly meant to eliminate corruption and to improve efficiency. The primary method of achieving this was to remove powers from council control by decreasing the number and importance of ward politicians, by increasing the power of a small executive through the board of control, by increasing the powers of the administration through the commissioner and city manager systems, and, finally, by creating separate special purpose bodies to take over completely certain important functions which could not be entrusted to politicians. Municipal government was regarded less as a level of government and more as a business. The right to vote was viewed as less important than ensuring a well-run municipal organization which would provide services efficiently. In discussing the municipal franchise, Goldwin Smith asked:

> What is the power which we now exercise, and which is largely illusory so far as the mass of us are concerned, compared with our health, our convenience, and the rescue of our property from the tax-gatherer?[41]

The net result of the reforms was a more complex, less accountable municipal government, more responsible to economy and efficiency than to the voters. Yet even in these former respects the success of the new municipal organizations was questionable. As early as 1899 there was

---

[39]Michael Keating, *Comparative Urban Politics*, Aldershot, Edward Elgar, 1991, pp. 43-46.

[40]*Ibid.*, p. 43.

[41]Weaver, *Shaping the Canadian City,* pp. 45-46.

some recognition in Toronto that structural reforms had not eliminated waste and corruption. A *Toronto Star* editorial claimed that council and the board of control were playing "a game of shuttlecock and battledore."[42] In 1909 the Fort William-Port Arthur Utilities Commission had to admit that service was poor. In 1913 Calgary's commissioners purchased a $5000 car with special paint and a special siren horn for their use,[43] perhaps not the most efficient use of public funds. The problem, of course, was that even businessmen and experts were as prone to self-interest and corruption as those municipal officials they had previously chastised. In 1895 the *Telegram* observed that "the fault is not with the system but with the people,"[44] an insight that might be borne in mind by those who remain preoccupied with structural change.

It is ironic that while many of these turn of the century reforms were prompted by the excesses of party politics and the "spoils" system in American local government, they were adopted by Canadian municipalities which, for the most part, were not organized on party lines. A number of indigenous factors have been suggested to explain this different pattern of development in Canada.[45] Because urbanization came later to Canada, Canadian cities were smaller and more homogeneous and lacked the patronage potential found in American cities with a heavily immigrant population. In addition, since provincial governments controlled their local governments more than state governments did, "the sandbox politics of City Hall offered little incentive for organized partisan activity or division."[46]

These indigenous factors changed with the passage of time, of course, and reference has previously been made, for example, to the extensive immigrant population in Winnipeg by the first decade of the 20th century and the "Divided City" which resulted. But as Anderson noted:

> By the time Canadian cities reached the size and complexity sufficient to make them attractive to political parties, the reform ideology and the accompanying structural innovations imported from the U.S. had become

---

[42]*Ibid.*, p. 72.

[43]*Ibid.*, pp. 72-73.

[44]*Ibid.*, p. 48.

[45]See J. D. Anderson, "Nonpartisan Urban Politics in Canadian Cities" in Jack K. Masson and J. D. Anderson (eds.), *Emerging Party Politics in Urban Canada*, Toronto, McClelland and Stewart, 1972.

[46]James Lightbody, "The Rise of Party Politics in Canadian Local Elections," in Masson and Anderson, p. 196.

firmly established, and provided an effective barrier to the entry of parties.[47]

Instead, what we got in a number of Western Canadian cities was business groups backing slates of candidates for municipal office, ostensibly to keep out political parties, but really to keep the socialist party (first the CCF, then the NDP) from gaining control of city hall.

Concluding Comments

There is a striking similarity between the challenges and problems of 100 years ago and those of today. Common to both periods are concerns over the adequacy of the municipal infrastructure, housing shortages and resistance to low-income housing, concerns about rapid consumption of resources and environmental degradation, the promotion of preventive health programs, conflict of interest and corruption charges surrounding municipal councillors, and a feeling that structural changes make little difference if people and their practices remain unchanged.

The legacy of the reform era is evident in the continued existence of many of the structural reforms from the early 1900s and in the continued denial of the relevance of politics at the local level. Indeed, there has been a resurgence in the criticism of politics and politicians as we proceed through another turn of the century era. Once again, municipalities are told to embrace business principles and practices as the key to their survival. Cities pursue with great vigour the coveted title of being "the best city for business," often at the expense of more balanced policies and practices. Business interests continue to expect (and demand) special treatment.

We are told that those who don't learn from history are condemned to repeat it. Fortunately, the turn of the century reform era provides many lessons that can help to guide municipalities as they face developments today.

---

[47]Anderson, *op. cit.*, p. 12.

CHAPTER 4
Pressures of Growth and Change

By the middle of the 20th century, approximately 100 years after the establishment of local government in Canada—if the Baldwin Act of Ontario is used as a major starting point—the local government system had become increasingly inadequate, largely because of the pressures of industrialization and urbanization.

Introduction

The foundations of Canada's municipal system were laid as long as 200 years ago. They were developed for a small and scattered population comprising a primarily agricultural and rural society. The 20th century has seen the population of Canada increase from 5 million to 30 million, and that much larger population has been concentrated first in rapidly growing cities and then has shifted outward to suburbs surrounding those cities. We have gone from an industrial economy to an information economy and to a new world economic order in which the demands of investment capital and the dictates of the foreign currency traders seem to exert more influence than the decisions of national governments.

These developments significantly altered the nature of Canadian society and our interactions with government. They influenced and constrained the roles and responses of government, even as they were in turn influenced by the policies pursued by governments, at all levels. This chapter explores the nature and impact of Canada's urbanization and suburbanization and the way that these developments have affected, and been affected by, the actions of our governments. Particular attention, of course, is given to municipalities and how they been affected by the pressures of growth and change. In addition, this chapter outlines a number of the ways in which municipalities have adapted to these pressures. Many of these adaptations have involved structural reform, and the discussion in this section previews the more detailed examination which follows in the next two chapters.

The Pattern of Urbanization

Sir John A. Macdonald has been credited with (or accused of) many things, but it may seem surprising to cite him as a key player in determining the pattern of urban development in Canada. Yet, his "national policy" of 1879, and especially its emphasis on high tariffs to protect the new domestic manufacturing industries of central Canada, was to lead to the early (and continuing) concentration of manufacturing in a central corridor extending from Quebec City to Windsor. This development, in turn, contributed to the growth of a number of cities throughout this area, and to the dominance of the Montreal and Toronto urban areas.

The transformation was described by the Economic Council of Canada in its fourth Annual Review, a document which helped to focus attention on the problems of urbanization.

... economic change in Canada has thus been marked by a relative shift in the focus of employment and output from the on-site exploitation of the natural resource base to the processing of materials, to manufacturing and advanced fabrication, and to the provision of a rapidly widening range of modern private and public services. Inevitably this change has implied a shift in the location of economic activity away from the rural area and its small service centres towards the larger urban centre.[1]

Figures on both overall population growth and the growth in urban populations mirror the developments in the Canadian economy. The early years of the 20th century saw rapid population growth. Almost half of this growth was caused by the extensive immigration of this period. The rate of increase in population then slowed during each successive decade reaching a low of only 10.9% during the intercensal decade of 1931 to 1941. During this period of the "Great Depression" there was not only a decline in immigration but also a marked reduction in the movement of rural populations to urban centres. With jobs hard to find in the cities, many able-bodied adults who had migrated to urban areas moved "back to the land," where they might hope for regular meals.[2] After 1941 population growth again accelerated to a near-record expansion rate of 30.2% between 1951 and 1961. In subsequent periods the rate of increase has steadily declined, largely because of the reduction in birth rates.

---

[1]Economic Council of Canada, *Fourth Annual Review*, 1967, p. 181.

[2]John Marshall, "Population Growth in Canadian Metropolises, 1901-1986," in F. Frisken (ed.), *The Changing Canadian Metropolis: A Public Policy Perspective*, Toronto, Canadian Urban Institute, 1994, Vol. 1, p. 49.

Of particular interest is the classification of the population as between urban and rural. The Census of Canada defines as urban all persons living in an area having a population concentration of 1000 or more and a population density of at least 386 per square kilometre. On this basis, Canada's population was classified as 75.5% urban in the 1976 Census. Indeed, at this point Canada's urban growth since the end of World War II had exceeded that of any Western industrial nation and three-quarters of the nation's population was concentrated on less than one per cent of its land area.[3]

More significant than this general shift from rural to urban has been the concentration of that urban population. In 1871 only 9 municipalities had populations of over 10 000, but by 1971 there were 246 such municipalities. Although representing only 5.7% of all municipalities, they contained 62% of the Canadian population.[4]

Even greater concentration is evident from the fact that in 1971 more than 50% of the population was centred in 19 census metropolitan areas (census areas comprised of at least two adjacent municipal entities, each at least partly urban, with an urbanized core of 100 000 or more). By 1991 there were 25 of these areas, containing just over 61% of the Canadian population.[5] In that census year, Ontario had over 70% of its population concentrated in census metropolitan areas, and Alberta, Quebec, and British Columbia had over 55% of their populations in these areas.[6] In that same year, the 10 largest metropolitan areas accounted for half of the country's population.[7] Even greater concentration of population is evident in the Toronto, Montreal, and Vancouver areas which alone

> In 1991, the 10 largest census metropolitan areas contained 50% of the population of Canada.

---

[3]Len Gertler and R. W. Crowley, *Changing Canadian Cities: The Next 25 Years*, Toronto, McClelland and Stewart, 1977, p. 41.

[4]Institute of Local Government, *Urban Population Growth and Municipal Organization*, Kingston, Queen's University, 1973, p. i.

[5]From *Statistics Canada, Census, 1991*, as quoted in Richard M. Bird and Enid Slack, *Urban Public Finance in Canada*, Toronto, John Wiley & Sons, 1993, p. 1.

[6]Christopher R. Bryant and Daniel Lemire, *Population Distribution and the Management of Urban Growth in Six Selected Urban Regions in Canada*, Toronto, ICURR, December 1993, p. 10.

[7]F. Frisken, "Jurisdictional and Political Constraints on Progressive Local Initiative," in Timothy L. Thomas (ed.), *The Politics of the City*, Toronto, ITP Nelson, 1997, p. 155.

accounted for 32% of the Canadian population in 1991[8] and 33% by the time of the 1996 intercensal figures.

Compounding this growth and its attendant pressures was what Gertler and Crowley called the "mushrooming growth in a few metropolitan agglomerations." Chief among these were what they identified as the "Lower Mainland" in British Columbia; the Calgary-Edmonton "Transportation Corridor" in Alberta; the "Golden Horseshoe" in Southwestern Ontario; the "Golden Triangle" in Southern Quebec, and the "Central Corridor" in the Maritimes.[9]

In recent years, the Canadian economy has been going through a pronounced economic restructuring—not only in response to the free trade agreements signed with the United States and Mexico but, more fundamentally, in response to the development of an increasingly integrated world economy. The result has been a shift of industrial capital to countries offering lower labour costs and less restrictive regulatory environments and the downsizing of firms that have stayed behind and are trying to remain competitive in the world market.[10] The proportion of manufacturing jobs in the economy has declined. While the primary sector (agricultural) now accounts for only 10% of employment and the secondary sector (manufacturing) only 20%, the tertiary sector (service industries and government) now accounts for 70%.[11]

One of the results of this economic restructuring is that cities in the Windsor-to-Quebec industrial heartland are now "at a structural disadvantage when compared with cities in the peripheral regions such as Atlantic Canada and the Western provinces."[12] A shift in growth momentum is evident from the fact that the census metropolitan areas of Western Canada, as a group, have grown more rapidly during the 20th century than those of any other region—including southern Ontario.[13] In part, this growth reflects the fact that western centres such as the Vancouver and Calgary regions are in the forefront of the rapidly expanding information technology. One estimate states that "half of the labour force of Canada works in occupations involving the collection, processing and

---

[8]Bird and Slack, *op. cit.*, p. 1.

[9]Gertler and Crowley, *op. cit.*, p. 5.

[10]F. Frisken, *Canadian Metropolis*, Vol. 1, p. 5.

[11]Marshall, in *ibid.*, p. 45.

[12]*Ibid.*

[13]*Ibid.*, p. 58.

dissemination of information and almost three-quarters of Canadians work in the service sector."[14]

The city of Moncton, New Brunswick, has revitalized its urban area by providing telemarketing and other communications services for large parts of Eastern Canada and beyond, and was the only city named both in 1992 and 1993 by the *Globe and Mail Report on Business Magazine* as one of Canada's top five cities in which to do business.[15] Even in Central Canada, information technology has been the basis for much economic growth. Ottawa, the ultimate government town, has survived massive cutbacks in public service employment in the 1990s largely because of its growing attraction as "Silicon Valley North."

By the very nature of the technology, information-based industries do not need to locate close to raw materials or large populations of consumers, factors which restricted the locations of traditional manufacturing industries. This new economic reality is contributing to the shift of economic activity and population from urban centres to outlying suburbs or even beyond census metropolitan areas. One study found that during the 1980s, "almost 60 per cent of the net growth in Canada's CMAs and almost 50 per cent of Canada's net growth was located in the CMAs' fringe areas beyond the urbanized core, and CMA fringe areas account for an increasingly large share of CMA population."[16] Emerging economic centres or "edge cities" beyond the urban core are becoming important sources of growth and prosperity. One U.S. study identified over 200 edge cities dotting the urban landscape of America.[17] This pattern is also evident in Canada,[18] with Toronto facing a challenge

> There has been a shift of economic activity and population to the suburbs and beyond, to edge cities.

---

[14]According to Jerome Durlak, "The Effects of Information Technologies on Large Urban Regions," in Frisken, *Canadian Metropolis*, p. 75.

[15]Andrew Sancton, *Governing Canada's City Regions: Adapting Form to Function*, Montreal, Institute for Research on Public Policy, 1994, pp. 47 and 54.

[16]Christopher Bryant and Daniel Lemire, *Population Distribution and the Management of Urban Growth in Six Selected Urban Regions in Canada*, Toronto, Intergovernmental Committee on Urban and Regional Research, 1993, p. 14.

[17]Joel Garreau, *Edge City: Life on the New Frontier*, New York, Doubleday, 1991, p. 61.

[18]Katherine A. Graham, Susan D. Phillips, and Allan M. Maslove, *Urban Governance in Canada*, Toronto, Harcourt Brace & Company, Canada, 1998, pp. 75 and 79.

from cities like Mississauga and Oshawa, and Montreal confronted by Laval, the second largest city in Quebec. In addition to this competition from neighbouring municipalities, Canada's major urban centres have also been facing the challenge of competing in the global economy. In the view of many, this challenge has been made more difficult by the number of separate municipalities within urban centres.

A Fragmented Municipal Structure

Most municipal institutions had originated a century or more ago, and had been designed only "to carry out the public functions and to operate within the restricted area boundaries considered appropriate for the time." Yet the pace of change since had brought about "a complex trans-formation in functions of municipal government and the complete obliter-ation of many previously significant territorial boundaries."[19] For example, within the 18 metropolitan areas identified in the 1961 census, "there were some 260 separate municipal government jurisdictions, together with an additional unknown number of semi-independent single purpose special authorities such as school boards, water boards, transit and utility commissions, and sewerage districts."[20]

To most observers, such a fragmented structure made concerted action to deal with urban problems both difficult and unlikely. In response to this situation, the 1960s and early 1970s saw a wave of municipal re-structuring in most provinces. The number of separate municipalities was significantly reduced through amalgamation, and regional and metro-politan governments were established in many of the urban areas. As will be discussed in the next two chapters, these reforms had a number of shortcomings, not least of which was the fact that they were soon under-mined by the relentless pace of urbanization and suburbanization.

By the 1990s areas that had already been restructured were once again being cited as too fragmented and too small to meet the planning and servicing needs of their areas. Greater Montreal, an area comprising well over 100 municipalities, has been the subject of two reports in the 1990s, both recommending the equivalent of a third level of government. Legislation was passed in mid-1997 to establish a commission de dével-oppement pour la métropole, but no action has been taken at the time of

---

[19]Economic Council of Canada, *op. cit.*, pp. 209-210.

[20]*Ibid.*, p. 210.

writing. An embryonic third level of local government has recently been established in the Toronto area, in the form of the Greater Toronto Services Board. It is striking that this action has been deemed necessary even though the six municipalities which had made up the municipality of Metropolitan Toronto were recently amalgamated into the "megacity" of Toronto, a single municipality of 2.4 million people.

While there is no denying the fragmentation of municipal boundaries found in Canada's urban areas, it is not clear that the municipal restructuring pursued in response has resolved the problem. Instead, as will be discussed, we seem to end up with enlarged municipal structures which are (or soon become) too small to deal with the servicing challenges of their areas and yet have become too large to constitute "local" government as we have known it.

The Nature of Urbanization

Urbanization involves much more than the concentration of population. It arises from, and gives rise to, fundamental changes in the nature of our economy and society. As noted above, it was industrialization, and especially the development of mass production, which encouraged the concentration of population in cities. With this shift in population, other changes occurred. The movement from farm to factory created growing numbers of workers who were dependent upon industrial employment and its attendant uncertainties instead of being relatively self-sufficient by living off the land. They increasingly turned to government to provide them with some protection and security, and gradually the "positive state" evolved with its elaborate range of services and programs designed to ensure all citizens a minimum standard of living conditions. All levels of government were affected by this development, and the resultant increase in services demanded of local government represented a heavy burden for most municipalities.

> Urbanization led to greatly increased service demands for municipalities.

The shortage, expense, and inadequacy of urban housing led to greater government involvement by all levels. The concentration of low income families in inner-city neighbourhoods strained the social service system. The loss of spacious country living, for those who had moved to the city, led to growing demands for parks and recreational facilities. The higher living standards and leisure time of a technological society accentuated this demand. Transportation and traffic movement required increasing government attention, as did the provision of an adequate supply of water and the disposal of domestic and industrial waste. Governments had to deal with air pollution concerns, in large part because of the exhaust from the concentration of motor vehicles. New problems of subdivision control and urban renewal and redevelopment also claimed the attention of the urban municipality. Population sprawl caused the conversion of land from agricultural production to urban uses and government action was needed to protect against developments which had an undesirable impact on the natural environment.

It should be noted that rural municipalities also experienced new servicing pressures, largely because of the influx of the non-farm rural population. Improved road maintenance and fire protection were demanded and such urban amenities as sidewalks and streetlights were expected in many hamlets. New recreational facilities were requested. Extensive cottage development on scenic lakes and rivers and excessive residential development on unsuitable soil often caused pollution problems requiring government action. Where these problems arose in a concentrated area, the municipality often faced the very heavy financial burden of a water supply and sewage treatment system. Residential development and farming activities proved an uneasy mix and the resulting friction provided one more example of the need for land use planning policies and controls in rural areas.

Functional and Financial Constraints

The ability of municipal governments to respond to urban problems was complicated by the fact that a number of traditionally local responsibilities "outgrew" the local level in terms of their significance, importance, and impact. The result, in fields such as health, education, and welfare, has been a gradual shift of responsibility to the senior levels of government and an increasing sharing of responsibilities between two or more levels of government.

At the same time, a parallel but reverse trend was under way in which senior governments launched new initiatives but delegated responsibility to the local level for at least some aspects of program delivery. This pattern was evident in such areas as housing, urban renewal, and environmental protection. The combined result was that municipal operations became increasingly intertwined with those of the senior governments.

In many traditional areas of local competence, provincial supervision, regulation or outright control have been deemed the acceptable solutions.... Their overall effect has incorporated municipal affairs more completely in the broader contexts of provincial and federal public administration. Indeed, local autonomy in all but a few ... areas is extinct.[21]

Thus, not only were municipal governments facing the pressures of an urbanizing trend largely shaped (as will be discussed) by the policies of the senior levels of government but they were also constrained in responding to these pressures by the extent to which their responsibilities were entangled with those senior governments. A number of provinces had established departments of municipal affairs around the turn of the century, but these departments—and often municipal boards as well—really came to the fore during the depression of the 1930s. In the years that followed, their supervision and control of local governments steadily increased. More recently, disentanglement initiatives were launched in several provinces, but with mixed results. These and other intergovernmental developments are examined in Chapter 8.

In addition to its structural and functional shortcomings, the traditional municipal government system also faced increasing financial problems. When municipalities were first established, it was expected that they would meet their revenue needs through the real property tax. This tax could be administered effectively on a local basis and it appeared adequate to finance the limited servicing requirements of the day, mainly related to education, local roads, and the care of the poor. The property tax seemed appropriate since property was the main form of wealth in the early days, and it wasn't considered particularly burdensome since the local taxpayer was not subject to the income tax and other forms of direct and indirect taxation which subsequently made their appearance.[22]

However, as the 20th century advanced, a number of the traditional responsibilities of local government became much more significant and costly, including the above-mentioned examples of education, roads, and welfare. A growing number of new service demands also arose, largely because of urbanization, as has been amply illustrated in the preceding discussions. Yet the real property tax remained the primary source of municipal revenues.

---

[21]H. J. Whalen, *The Development of Local Government in New Brunswick*, Fredericton, 1963, p. 90.

[22]T. J. Plunkett, *The Financial Structure and the Decision Making Process of Canadian Municipal Government*, Ottawa, Central Mortgage and Housing Corporation, 1972, p. 21.

The inadequacy of this financial base became all too evident during the 1930s, when the entire burden for unemployment relief assistance was initially considered to be within the scope of municipal responsibility for poor relief. Even when the federal and provincial levels had assumed 80% of the costs, municipalities still had difficulty financing their share for the substantial unemployed population of the urban industrial centres. They cut back on services and postponed expenditures for maintenance and new construction. Further postponements occurred with the diversion of resources and the massive centralization of government which occurred during the Second World War.

Thus, an enormous backlog of expenditures had already built up even before the municipalities faced the greatly increased demands of post-war urbanization. Goldenberg describes the challenge which this posed:

> They (the municipalities) faced the problem of financing not only the expenditures which had been deferred during fifteen years of depression and war, but also vast new expenditures on works and services required to meet an unprecedented growth in population and economic activity.[23]

The resultant upsurge in municipal spending in the post-war years is vividly illustrated by the fact that total urban municipal expenditures increased by 131% over the 8 year period from 1945 to 1953 compared to an increase of only 13% during the 15 year period 1930 to 1945.[24]

The property tax fell from 80% of municipal revenues in 1930 to 31% by the mid-1980s, before increasing again in the 1990s.

Not surprisingly, the property tax couldn't generate sufficient revenues to meet this explosion of municipal expenditures. While this tax was still providing over 80% of municipal revenues in 1930, the proportion had fallen to 53% by 1953 and to 47% by 1963.[25] By 1974-75, it had dropped below 40% according to the Report of the Tri-Level Task Force on Public Finance in 1976. By the mid-1980s, the proportion was just over 31%,[26] but it has been climbing back up recently, for reasons discussed below.

The growing shortfall in municipal revenue needs in the post-war period has, until the past decade or so, been remedied almost entirely by

---

[23]H. Carl Goldenberg, "Municipal Finance and Taxation," in *Forecast of Urban Growth Problems and Requirements 1956-1980*, Montreal, Canadian Federation of Mayors and Municipalities, 1955.

[24]Plunkett, *op. cit.*, p. 33.

[25]Economic Council of Canada, *op. cit.*, p. 219.

[26]Bird and Slack, *op. cit.*, p. 64.

grants from the senior levels of government. This assistance accounted for over 40% of gross general revenues of Canadian municipal governments at the beginning of the 1970s. While these transfer payments allowed municipalities to meet their expenditure obligations, they were a mixed blessing. The municipal submission to the first national tri-level conference in 1972 noted that approximately 90% of this financial assistance was in the form of conditional grants which reflected the priorities of the senior levels of government. It warned that this situation threatened to turn local governments into "hollow receptacles into which the values of the federal and provincial governments are poured."[27]

In fairness, one could find considerable justification for a number of the provincial conditional grant programs which then existed. Many traditional local government responsibilities were recognized as having much wider than local significance and it had become necessary to find some means of ensuring that these responsibilities were exercised to at least a minimum standard across the province. Given a multiplicity of municipal jurisdictions with widely varying financial capacities, the most effective means of ensuring these standards was through the grant structure. Whatever the rationale, it seems clear that this process had been carried too far. A basic difficulty is that "there is a rapidly diminishing relationship between the taxes paid to any one level of government and the services rendered by it."[28] The main problem with such arrangements, which also apply to federal-provincial relations, is described below:

> Through the development of a complex transfer system, each level of government can influence the nature and scope of the services provided, take a share in the political rewards, maintain the fiction of autonomy, and have a convenient excuse for avoiding any criticism for inadequate services. The only drawback is that the public never knows who is responsible for what or how much the services provided really cost.[29]

As the 1980s unfolded, however, both senior levels of government became increasingly preoccupied with their annual deficits and accumulated debts. As a result, the federal level has tightened up on the amount of money transferred to the provinces and they, in turn, have decreased their transfer payments to the municipal level. According to Bird and

---

[27]Municipal Submission to the first National Tri-Level Conference, *Policies, Programs, and Finance*, Ottawa, 1972, p. 20.

[28]Ontario Economic Council, *Government Reform in Ontario*, Toronto, 1969, p. viii.

[29]*Ibid.*, p. 19.

Slack, transfers as a proportion of municipal revenues declined from 46.4% in 1971 to 37.2% in 1991.[30] This decline in transfer payments is even more marked in Statistics Canada figures, which indicate that these payments represented only 25% of total local government revenues in 1993 and just 20% by 1997.[31]

> There has been a sharp decline in transfer payments over the past three decades.

The transfers that remain, however, are still overwhelmingly conditional in nature. That is, they provide funds, but only if they are spent on the purpose specified and, usually, only if the municipality provides some matching share. Four-fifths of the transfers provided to local governments in 1997 were conditional in nature.[32] In recent years, Alberta and Ontario made their grants more unconditional. But they did so as part of a process in which these grants were then drastically cut or abolished entirely.

The Impact of Urbanization

A number of analysts stress that urban problems are not just found in urban areas but are *inherent in the process of urbanization* itself. For Lithwick, the distinctive feature to be observed is that the growth of cities produces "competing demands for the one common feature of all cities, scarce urban space, driving core prices upward and households outward." He suggests that transportation, pollution, and poverty problems flow from this. Moreover, he argues that because of these interdependencies, efforts to deal with each problem in isolation have inevitably failed.

> Housing policy has added to the stock of urban accommodations, but has led to urban sprawl and fiscal squeeze for the municipalities. Transport policies have moved people faster initially, but have led to further sprawl, downtown congestion, pollution, and rapid core deterioration.[33]

---

[30]Bird and Slack, *op. cit.*, p. 64.

[31]Statistics Canada, CANSIM, Matrix 7093, *Local General Government Revenue and Expenditure, Canada*, as found at its web site, www.statcan.ca, on March 30, 1999.

[32]*Ibid.*

[33]N. H. Lithwick, *Urban Canada: Problems and Prospects*, Ottawa, Central Mortgage and Housing Corporation, 1970, p. 15.

Fowler is also very critical of the process of urbanization pursued in North America, the urban sprawl and suburban development, and the extensive transportation network criss-crossing the landscape. He describes how we ended up with cities "where we sleep en masse in huge residential complexes and work en masse in huge retail or industrial developments—and spend our lives travelling between them, from living room to kitchen, so to speak."[34] He is even more critical of the built environment of our cities and its lack of physical diversity. He cites the proliferation of large-scale projects, the deconcentration and decentralization of development (not just with respect to low-density residential development, but also affecting office and factory space), and the homogeneity of architecture and of land use. Fowler contends that we are squandering billions of dollars in North America because of the built environment in our urban areas which involves us in "an extravagant transportation system, life-threatening levels of pollution, a needlessly large infrastructure of utilities such as water mains and trunk sewers, and significantly more expensive housing and consumer goods."[35]

A 1995 report on *Economics of the Urban Form* concluded that huge savings are possible if a more compact form of development is adopted in the future. In the Toronto area, for example, it estimated that taxpayers could save up to $4 billion in operating and maintenance costs over the next 25 years if more compact neighbourhoods were built, along with as much as $16 billion in reduced capital costs for roads, transit, and utilities. Similarly, the Greater Vancouver Regional District concluded that $2.2 billion could be saved on transportation costs if new growth were more concentrated.[36]

Extensive urban sprawl and suburban development, and attendant financial problems for central cities, have long been characteristic of urban areas in the United States.[37] As business, industry, and middle-class homeowners moved to the suburbs, the tax base of the cities shrank. Yet they faced increased expenditures for fire, police, welfare, education, and other services for the primarily lower-class population which remained.

---

[34]Edmund P. Fowler, *Building Cities That Work*, Kingston, McGill-Queen's University Press, 1992, p. 31.

[35]*Ibid.*, p. 69.

[36]These examples are cited in David K. Foot, *Boom, Bust & Echo*, Toronto, Macfarlane Walter & Ross, 1996, p. 133.

[37]The description which follows is based on Edward C. Banfield and James Q. Wilson, *City Politics*, New York, Random House, 1963, p. 14.

The flight to the suburbs intensified as the cities experienced an influx of Blacks, racial tensions increased, and yet the revenue base of the cities continued to erode—setting up a downward spiral from which it was difficult to escape.

Writing in 1986, Goldberg and Mercer contended that Canada's urban experience had been both different and more positive.[38] In comparison to the United States, they found that Canada's cities were more compact, had not been losing population or jobs to the same extent, were still attractive as places of residence for middle-class homeowners, had a much lower incidence of violent crime, and did not have an "urban under-class" made up of members of one or more racial minorities. As a result, city and suburb differences in income and population characteristics were not as evident in Canada. This meant that Canadian cities were in better financial shape than cities in the United States and less dependent upon grants.[39]

> Are Canada's problems of sprawl more limited or just slower to develop?

Less than a decade later, Frisken found that Canadian metropolitan areas may just be slower to develop many of the features found in their American counterparts, notably:

> ... a decline in the economic strength of central cities within their metropolitan areas, as jobs and middle-class residents relocate to the suburbs; the differentiation of peripheral from central city populations by income and race, with central cities coming to house a disproportionately large share of their regions' most disadvantaged residents; and the outward dispersal of population and jobs at densities likely to result in a high level of automobile dependency.[40]

Effect of Government Policies

Another similarity between the American and Canadian experiences is the fact that, to varying degrees, the urban problems which developed were caused or aggravated by senior government policies. Describing the American situation, Banfield writes that from the New Deal onward, the

---

[38]Michael Goldberg and John Mercer, *The Myth of the North American City: Continentalism Challenged,* Vancouver, University of British Columbia Press, 1986, quoted in Frisken, *Canadian Metropolis,* p. 2.

[39]*Ibid.*

[40]*Ibid.,* p. 4.

flight to the suburbs was encouraged, albeit inadvertently, by the federal government through its transportation and housing policies and programs. Indeed, he contends that these two programs account for 90% of the federal government expenditure for the improvement of the cities, that neither is directed toward the really serious problems of the cities, and that both make the problems worse![41] The improvement of transportation serves to encourage further movement of industry, commerce, and relatively well-off residents (mostly white) from the inner city. Federal housing programs have subsidized home building on a vast scale by ensuring mortgages on easy terms, mostly for the purchase of new homes which were being built in the suburbs. Urban renewal initiatives have also been harmful, forcing hundreds of thousands of low-income people out of low-cost housing to make room for luxury apartments, office buildings, hotels, civic centres, industrial parks, and the like.[42] Far from being productive, Banfield demonstrates that these federal programs actually work at cross-purposes. The expressway program and the housing mortgages in effect pay the middle-class whites to leave the central city for the suburbs; at the same time, the urban renewal and mass transit programs pay them to stay in the central city or to return.

A rather similar pattern is evident in Canada, particularly with respect to federal housing and urban renewal initiatives. Since the 1935 Dominion Housing Act, and especially since the establishment of the Central (now Canada) Mortgage and Housing Corporation (CMHC) in 1946, federal financial assistance for single-family dwellings has reinforced low-density sprawl.[43] The actions of the CMHC also contributed to neighbourhood dislocations and attendant problems because of what has been described as a bulldozer approach to urban renewal. It is evident that in Canada, as well as in the United States, urban growth became a prime instrument of public policy to stimulate and maintain high levels of economic activity.[44] After studying federal housing policy, Fallis concludes that it is mainly influenced by federal macroeconomic policy and he observes that "the

---

[41]Edward C. Banfield, *The Unheavenly City*, Boston, Little, Brown and Company, 1968, p. 14.

[42]*Ibid.*, p. 16.

[43]For a description of the role of the CMHC, see Donald J. H. Higgins, *Urban Canada: Its Government and Politics*, Toronto, Macmillan, 1977, pp. 76-81.

[44]Michael Goldrick, "The Anatomy of Urban Reform in Toronto," in Dimitrios Roussopoulos (ed.), *The City and Radical Social Change*, Montreal, Black Rose Books, 1982, p. 264.

federal government has always used housing programs as instruments of fiscal policy."[45]

Leo describes how all three levels of government became involved in a massive program of government support for suburban development, pursuing policies which not only reinforced the rapidly growing popular preference for the private automobile over public transportation, but gave it free reign and entrenched it.[46] He notes that this state action was quite consistent with the demands of the public at the time. These demands, to a large extent, were a function of changing demographics. The baby boom following World War II meant families of young children in search of the back yard and the quiet street which were to be found by commuting to the suburb.[47] But Leo points out the state was also responding by its actions to "the demands of E. P. Taylor and other development magnates, to the professional biases of bureaucrats in the Department of Finance and the CMHC, to the sensitivities of Liberal Party contributors, and to the interests and concerns of a variety of other parties."[48] It was these influences which led to the specific government response found in Canada, as opposed to, for example, the situation in Europe where suburban development has been less automobile-dominated. According to Leo, the costs of Canada's form of suburban development are evident in deteriorating transit systems, inner city decay, and crumbling infrastructure.[49]

Lorimer contends that "most of the development of Canadian cities in the three boom decades from the Forties to the Seventies was a direct consequence of the economic development strategy chosen by Ottawa for Canada."[50] In his view, this strategy had two principal components—the exploitation of natural resources for use mainly by the major metropolitan economies, and the expansion of a branch-plant secondary manu-

---

[45]George Fallis, "The Federal Government and the Metropolitan Housing Problem," in Frisken, *Canadian Metropolis*, p. 376.

[46]Christopher Leo, "The State in the City: A Political-Economy Perspective on Growth and Decay," in James Lightbody (ed.), *Canadian Metropolitics: Governing Our Cities*, Toronto, Copp Clark Ltd., 1995, p. 31.

[47]This point is well developed in Foot, *op. cit.*, Chapter 7, who also explains how the aging population has brought about a decline in public transit ridership and a growth in the suburbs and the reliance on cars.

[48]Leo, *op. cit.*, p. 32.

[49]*Ibid.*, p. 33.

[50]James Lorimer, "The post-developer era for Canada's cities begins," in *City Magazine Annual 1981*, Toronto, James Lorimer and Company, 1981, p. 7.

facturing industry in Southern Ontario. Local government's primary role was to provide the physical services needed to support growth and development. As a result, according to Lorimer, local governments became the servants of the development industry that they were supposed to regulate.[51]

Magnusson describes the federal government's efforts to support the housing market to ensure an expansion of the economy.[52] But, he also notes that the provinces were just as concerned as the federal level about removing any possible checks on growth, which was one of their reasons for increasing conditional grants for improving public facilities in the cities. He also suggests that provincial legislation on planning and zoning was based on the assumption that urban development would be undertaken through private initiative, with municipalities playing a regulatory role, but one which facilitated private enterprise.[53]

In contrast to those who fault the actions taken by government, another view is that the problems in our cities are caused by a lack of sufficient government intervention and the excesses of private decision making.[54] Those who hold to this viewpoint have numerous examples to support their contention. Perhaps the most blatant example is the land speculation in and around our cities. The extension of services, at public expense, often brings windfall profits to the private speculator who purchased and held land against such an eventuality. Escalating land costs then push the cost of housing beyond the reach of more and more Canadians.

> Some cite the excesses of private decision making for the problems in the cities.

Another example has been the widespread disruption (some would say destruction) of the city to meet the needs of the private use of automobiles without anything like this degree of support for public transit.

---

[51]See, for example, *The Real World of City Politics*, Toronto, James Lewis and Samuel, 1970; *A Citizen's Guide to City Politics*, Toronto, James Lewis and Samuel, 1972; *The Developers*, Toronto, James Lorimer, 1978; and *After the Developers* (with Carolyn MacGregor), Toronto, James Lorimer, 1981.

[52]Warren Magnusson, "Introduction," in Warren Magnusson and Andrew Sancton (eds.), *City Politics in Canada*, Toronto, University of Toronto Press, 1983, p. 27.

[53]*Ibid.*

[54]See, for example, Boyce Richardson, *The Future of Canadian Cities*, Toronto, New Press, 1972, on which this section is based.

Indeed, public transit services have been struggling to maintain ridership, hesitating to increase fares which would likely lose more riders, yet faced with growing deficits and, traditionally, very little financial support from the senior levels of government. According to the Science Council of Canada's report, *Cities for Tomorrow*, "it appears that barely one-half of the cost incurred by the automobile is returned to different levels of government in gasoline taxes and license fees."[55]

Not only do public transit services face unfair competition because of this subsidy, but too little consideration is given to the broad social benefits which they bring—and the social costs of our devotion to the automobile. It is true that provincial governments played a key role in the development of urban mass transit systems in the Toronto, Montreal, and Vancouver areas in the 1970s and 1980s,[56] but the level of government support remains far below that which has already been provided for the automobile. For example, one study found that private cars in the Vancouver area enjoy public subsidies of $2700 a year each, seven times the subsidy for public transit.[57] Yet the Ontario government, as part of service swap in 1997, removed all public transit grants and left the responsibility for financing this critical service to the municipal level.

Private enterprise has also been deficient in providing adequate and appropriate housing for the varied needs of the Canadian population. Here again, the forces of urbanization have played a part by making land very scarce and therefore very valuable. As land prices increase, it becomes necessary to have buildings which will generate a large income for the landowner.

> ... poor houses inhabited by poor people must be swept away, their occupants with them; new places go up, let at high rents; young men and women, married couples, or the rich, move in where poor people lived before; the poor people just "disappear"—most of the time we don't even take the trouble to find out where they go.[58]

While Richardson's analysis of the shortcomings of private decision making may seem quite critical, to some it is far too tame. A more radical viewpoint is that such "problems" as too many cars in the streets, insufficient affordable housing, lack of green space, and environmental pollu-

---

[55]Quoted in *ibid.*, p. 130.

[56]F. Frisken, "Provincial Transit Policy-Making in the Toronto, Montreal, and Vancouver Regions," in Frisken, *Canadian Metropolis*, p. 528.

[57]Foot, *op. cit.*, p. 133.

[58]*Ibid.*, pp. 155-156.

tion are but symptoms of more fundamental causes.[59] According to this view, "it is impossible to understand both the urban sprawl which passes for development and the urban conflict it has produced unless one recognizes the determining power of the capitalist mode of production which governs these processes."[60]

Rather than being haphazard and random, city growth is seen as intimately linked with the changing needs of the economic system. "The city is developed, redeveloped and moulded over time according to long term cycles in how profits are made and investment decisions taken."[61] As Western nations emerged from the depression of the 1930s, they faced the need to stimulate consumption to sustain the capitalist system. The response was to introduce a series of policies to facilitate urban growth. By shifting the focus of capital from production to consumption and by emphasizing urban development as a key vehicle to achieve it, these actions effectively changed the function of cities from that of workshops to "artifacts of consumption."[62] The impact of the resulting urban development has already been noted. The chief beneficiaries have been the property development industry, including developers, financiers, real estate companies, construction companies, property managers, and others.

Unfulfilled Political Role

One of the most important inadequacies of local government to be highlighted by the pressures of post-war urbanization was its ineffectiveness in fulfilling its political role—that is, in representing the views of the local inhabitants, choosing between alternative courses of action, setting priorities for the allocation of scarce resources, and then answering for these decisions to the local electorate.

As we have seen, the turn of the century reformers vigorously denied the relevance of a political role for local government. They viewed this role much too narrowly, equating politics with excessive divisiveness and abuse of power through patronage and the pork barrel. In addition, many of the reformers who purported to want politics removed from local

---

[59]Dimitrios Roussopoulos, "Understanding the City and Radical Social Change," in Roussopoulos, *op. cit.*, p. 61.

[60]M. Castells, as quoted in *ibid.*, p. 111.

[61]Goldrick, *op. cit.*, p. 263.

[62]*Ibid.*, pp. 264-265.

government actually wanted to impose their own notion of what the local priorities should be. As Leftwich has pointed out, "there is nothing *more political* than the constant attempts to exclude certain types of issues from politics."[63] (emphasis in the original)

Whatever their motivations, however, the reformers left us with a deeply ingrained notion of municipal government as administrative and not political in nature, with the council performing a caretaker or custodial role and preoccupied with considerations of efficiency. According to this viewpoint, councillors were not politicians, but "local worthies who kept an eye on one or two amenities."[64] Also from this reform period came the belief that servicing questions were best resolved by the application of technical expertise, with "politics" being kept entirely out of the picture if possible.

Given the growth pressures and challenges of the post-war period, this concept of municipal government became increasingly unworkable. The issues which now demanded the attention of municipalities involved widespread controversy about the best course of action. Concern about the quality of life and the preservation of established neighbourhoods increased as rapid development threatened the fabric of the city. The traditional reliance on technical expertise was found unacceptable and the public demanded that decision makers show a greater awareness of social and environmental considerations. For example, whether to meet transportation needs through expressways or public transit has been an ongoing dispute, with the battle over the Spadina expressway in Toronto providing a good illustration, along with similar disputes in Vancouver and Edmonton.[65] The fondness for single-family dwellings on sizeable lots, supported by the lending policies of the Central (now Canada) Mortgage and Housing Corporation, has had to be reconciled with the cost and space demands of such housing compared with the economics of higher-density construction. Urban renewal projects have aroused strong opposition from neighbourhoods where residents wanted rehabilitation of existing stock rather than the traditional response of tearing down and

---

[63]A. Leftwich (ed.), *What Is Politics?* London, Blackwell, 1984, p. 144.

[64]B. Walden, "Apply the brakes to our local politicians," *Sunday Times,* July 26, 1987, quoted in John Gyford, Steve Leach and Chris Game, *The Changing Politics of Local Government,* London, Unwin Hyman Ltd., 1989, p. 1.

[65]See Christopher Leo, *The Politics of Urban Development: Canadian Urban Expressway Disputes,* Monographs on Canadian Urban Development, No. 3, Toronto, Institute of Public Administration of Canada, 1977.

building anew. Even more, they wanted full consultation before any decisions were made.[66]

Nor were the tensions confined to urban areas. Rural residents also debated the desirability of growth and the validity of new service demands. There has been a growing concern about the loss of farmland and, paradoxically, about controls intended to protect the farmland but which were felt to be too restrictive. Conflicting views about both the style and substance of municipal government were presented by the non-farm rural dweller and the farmer, the new resident and the long-time settler, the seasonal population and the permanent inhabitants.

Given these developments, the caretaker or custodial role of local government became less and less appropriate, as did the notion of periodic voting as the primary method of citizen involvement. Instead, citizens and citizen groups increasingly questioned the actions of their councils and demanded a more open,

> Citizens became increasingly active and less content with municipalities playing a caretaker role.

consultative decision-making process which considered their views at least as much as the technical advice provided by staff. An even more direct response was evident in some cities where reform candidates and local parties ran for municipal office. These developments, which are examined in a later chapter, were not new. Kaplan provides examples of both citizen group and party activity in the early years of local government in our major cities and notes that "a culture that ascribed a high mission to local government and forbade all forms of 'politics' co-existed alongside an intensive, undignified scramble for specific facilities."[67]

However, the upsurge in this activity in the post-war period reflected a growing public conviction that municipalities must demonstrate responsiveness and accountability in discharging their responsibilities. But here again the traditional system was inadequate in several respects. The fragmentation of the structure made it very difficult to assign responsibility for action. Not only was power divided among the council and various local boards, but in addition responsibilities were shared between the local and senior levels of government, and an extensive network of conditional grant payments further blurred the focus of responsibility.

---

[66]For an excellent account of one such battle, see Graham Fraser, *Fighting Back*, Toronto, Hakkert, 1972.

[67]Harold Kaplan, *Reform, Planning and City Politics: Montreal, Winnipeg, and Toronto*, Toronto, University of Toronto Press, 1982, p. 146.

Nor was accountability any clearer within the council of most municipalities. All councillors were collectively responsible for everything, and
yet none were specifically responsible for anything! Except in the few
instances where organized political parties operated, councils were made
up of a group of individuals with potentially different interests and concerns and no sense of cohesion or collective purpose. There wasn't any
particular governing group responsible for taking the initiative in dealing
with the problems facing the municipality. Nor was there any group responsible for scrutinizing and criticizing the initiatives taken to ensure that
they were in the best interests of the public. It was almost impossible for
citizens to know where to direct criticism or praise. Any particular councillor could claim that he was for (or against) the matter at issue but was
outvoted by the other councillors. The chances for buck-passing in this
system were endless.

Even if councils wanted to be accountable and responsive, previously
mentioned legal and financial limitations acted as severe constraints.
Often councils couldn't do what their local citizens wanted them to because they lacked the authority or had failed to receive provincial approval, or felt unable to finance the expenditures involved. These limitations
are well summarized by Plunkett and Graham:

> When many of the apparent characteristics of contemporary urban local
> government in Canada are taken into account (the tendency to adhere to
> a purely service role, increased dependence on conditional provincial
> grants, fragmentation of responsibilities, intergovernmental linkages
> based on professional and functional ties rather than on broad policy
> issues, lack of policy direction and the failure to furnish an identifiable
> government), we have to conclude that local governments are adhering to
> their role as agents of provincial interest to the detriment of their role as
> interpreters of the local scene.[68]

The various explanations for the unfulfilled political role offered above
reflect the conventional view that the problems lie in inadequacies in the
traditional municipal structure. It would be misleading to leave the im-
pression that a different municipal structure would provide the openness
and responsiveness desired by all citizens' groups. First of all, Sancton
notes[69] that these groups shared no common view about the role which

---

[68]T. J. Plunkett and Katherine A. Graham, "Whither Municipal Government,"
in *Canadian Public Administration*, Winter 1982, p. 614.

[69]See Andrew Sancton, "The Municipal Role in the Governance of Cities," in
Trudi Bunting and Pierre Filion (eds.), *Canadian Cities in Transition*, Toronto,
Oxford University Press, 1991, p. 473.

municipal governments should play in creating the ideal urban environment. While some were genuinely committed to various forms of neighbourhood self-government, most were concerned only with the particular issue at hand and were interested in their municipal government only to the extent that it had any decision-making power with respect to that issue. Nobody in the new urban reform movement argued for truly multifunctional municipal governments subject to reduced provincial supervision. "In fact, many new urban reformers seemed profoundly suspicious of any political institutions, including municipal governments and local political parties, that would have the potential to overrule the expressed preferences of local neighbourhoods and their leaders."[70]

Sewell goes so far as to suggest that neighbourhood groups, which were the building block for the reform efforts in the 1960s and 1970s, will be the stumbling block for any new reform movement.[71] He describes the earlier reform period as one in which neighbourhood groups fought to preserve the city built before the Second World War—a city whose neighbourhoods contained a range of incomes and family sizes, a mix of uses and building forms. Residents wanted to preserve that diversity against the destructive impact of urban renewal, expressways, and private redevelopment. Then came Don Mills, Canada's first corporate suburb, and a new definition of neighbourhood based on exclusivity. This was the message presented in the carefully designed homes, the enforced colour coordination, the looping, curvy street design, and the modern house form.[72] According to Sewell, the land mass of most Canadian cities is now predominantly filled with the progeny of Don Mills. "Exclusivity has become the dominant characteristic of the urban area and the Not in My Backyard (NIMBY) lullaby is frequently sung to consistent applause."[73] Sewell contends that NIMBY has hijacked the neighbourhood concept embraced by the reformers and has used the idea that local decision making is best to create an exclusive closed community and a limiting approach to city possibilities.

As discussed earlier in this chapter, Fowler is also critical of the lack of diversity in modern cities. He finds that the physical characteristics of

---

[70]*Ibid.*

[71]John Sewell, *Prospects for Reform*, Research Paper 180, Toronto, Centre for Urban and Community Studies, University of Toronto, January 1991.

[72]*Ibid.*, p. 13. Sewell has since elaborated his views about urban design in *The Shape of the City*, Toronto, University of Toronto Press, 1993.

[73]*Ibid.*

the post-war urban environment do have an adverse impact on our social behaviour, including our political activities. He quotes Theodore Lowi, who contends that suburbs represent a failure of citizenship.

> We have removed ourselves not only from the responsibilities of civic participation but also from the challenges of social relations by zoning poor families out of our neighbourhoods. The social and political skills of adults have declined; we have lost the ability, at a personal level, to say how we feel, to negotiate, to solve problems creatively—in short, to be publicly responsible individuals.[74]

Another failure of citizenship may be occurring with the new, highly mobile knowledge workers who have emerged in the information society of today. According to Lasch, this new élite relocates frequently, has little attachment to place, and prefers to seclude itself in "homogeneous enclaves of walled suburbs and private schools."[75] Members of this élite aren't particularly dependent on public services, and aren't keen to support such services for others who may be less fortunate. Lasch contends that the new élites are at home only in transit and that "theirs is essentially a tourist's view of the world."[76] If his rather negative and pessimistic view is borne out, municipal governments are unlikely to benefit from active participation by this segment of society.

According to Jane Jacobs, the physical diversity which has been disappearing from our cities made neighbour contact more likely and encouraged people to care about what went on in their neighbourhood.[77] The mixture of workplaces and residences ensured the presence of users throughout the day. Short blocks maximized the number of corners and therefore meeting places. The result was streets filled with activity and under constant observation.

The physical features of urban areas adversely affect social behaviour.

> The web of mutual recognition among habitual users of the street, who need be only a minority, is the natural outgrowth of an urge to be responsible for the territory surrounding one's place of work, one's front door,

---

[74]Theodore Lowi, *The End of Liberalism*, 2nd Edition, New York, W. W. Norton, 1979, p. 267, quoted in Fowler, *op. cit.*, p. 73.

[75]Christopher Lasch, *The Revolt of the Elites*, New York, W. W. Norton, 1995, as quoted in K. A. Graham and S. D. Phillips, *Citizen Engagement*, Toronto, Institute of Public Administration of Canada, 1998, p. 16.

[76]Lasch, *op. cit.*, p. 6.

[77]Jane Jacobs, *The Death and Life of Great American Cities*, New York, Random House, 1961.

and even the parks and shopping areas one frequents. This is *civic govern-ment at its most local*, but perhaps most crucial, level.[78] (emphasis added)

What Fowler terms "authentic politics" is, he contends, only possible in small-scale, diverse spaces where a variety of casual face-to-face inter-actions occur naturally, a development pattern disappearing as our cities have been rebuilt in the post-war period. Moreover, he argues that the lack of physical diversity in our cities "encourages the perception that politics does not take place at the local level, but only at the regional and national levels. Alternatively, local politics is considered petty, and pro-vision of local services is considered an administrative job, not a political issue."[79]

To the extent that there is local politics in our cities, Fowler observes, it is mainly concerned with the planning, approval, and servicing of large new developments. This, of course, is a very widely held view. Indeed, Sancton contends that "Canadian municipal politicians have little choice but to build their political careers on policies designed to make their city more prosperous, more appealing, and more pleasant than other com-peting cities."[80] For the most part, politically salient cleavages based on class, ethnicity, or even neighbourhood, are absent, so municipal politi-cians are rarely in a position to profit politically by mobilizing one sector of the community against another. A candidate's election prospects de-pend on convincing voters that his or her policies and abilities are best suited to promoting the general well-being of the whole city. "This means that Canadian city politics is, above all, about boosterism."[81]

Lightbody makes the same point in noting that Canadian cities regard it as a coveted form of recognition to be singled out in a survey by a na-tional publication as one of "Canada's best cities for business." The busi-ness community believes:

> that the expansion of economic enterprise should be the primary focus for local government; all of its energies and concerns ought to be directed towards sustained commercial growth even if such an approach were to mean the neglect of other objectives.[82]

---

[78]Fowler, *op. cit.*, p. 87.

[79]*Ibid.*, p. 132.

[80]Sancton, "Conclusion," in Magnusson and Sancton, p. 293.

[81]*Ibid.*

[82]Lightbody, *op. cit.*, p. 9.

Peterson goes even farther by arguing that cities are obliged to pursue economic development strategies, that they are limited to an urban growth agenda.[83] In his view, local politics is limited to matters of production while redistribution is, and must be, a matter for the central governments. Redistributive policies, he contends, will prejudice a city's chances of attracting growth by driving away high-income residents and business and attracting welfare claimants. While critics claim that Peterson overstates and oversimplifies,[84] his explanation fits the behaviour observed in many cities.

Summary

By the middle of the 20th century, approximately 100 years after the establishment of local government in Canada—if Ontario's Baldwin Act is used as a major starting point—the system had become increasingly inadequate, largely because of the pressures of industrialization and urbanization. To many observers, the problems went much deeper than the local government system itself. They were inherent in the process of urbanization and in the nature of the built environment of our cities with its lack of physical diversity. They were the result of misguided policies of the senior governments, notably using housing and urban development as tools of economic growth. They were the inevitable result of the capitalist mode of production and of the demands of investment capital.

The more conventional assessment, however, and the one which was reflected in the reforms introduced over the past 50 years, was that the main problems were within the existing local government system, were "cracks in the foundation" that had been established in the previous century. These included:

1. Inappropriate municipal boundaries arising from an excessive number of small municipalities and from the fragmented municipal structure found in most urban centres.
2. An erosion of the powers of the municipality to separate boards and commissions and to the senior levels of government.
3. Insufficient municipal revenue sources and an increasing dependence upon provincial grants, heavily conditional in nature.

---

[83]Paul Peterson, *City Limits*, Chicago, University of Chicago Press, 1981.

[84]See, for example, Clarence N. Stone and Heywood T. Sanders (eds.), *The Politics of Urban Development*, Lawrence, University Press of Kansas, 1987.

4. An incompatibility between the non-political tradition inherited from the turn of the century reform era and the controversial issues and value judgments facing municipalities today.
5. Municipal governing bodies that were ineffective in providing leadership, coordination, and a clear focus of accountability.

Concluding Comments

It is clear from these five issues that even within the existing municipal government system there were many significant problems to address. Individual municipalities often adapted to these problems in various ways that showed considerable flexibility and ingenuity. Gradually, however, most provincial governments decided to introduce reform initiatives. These reforms have been mainly concerned with the structure of municipal government, and have involved enlarging municipalities through amalgamation and the creation or enlargement of metropolitan and regional governing bodies. For the most part, the reforms have not addressed the functional, financial, and political issues which are at least equally important. To the contrary, the representative and political role of municipalities is arguably more difficult to fulfil as a result of a number of the reforms. The nature and limits of these reforms are examined in the next two chapters.

CHAPTER 5
Local Government Reform I
Central Canada

The initiatives in both Ontario and Quebec share a major limitation. They are preoccupied with improving the service delivery capability of municipal government, largely to facilitate provincial downloading, and have paid little attention to the representative role of municipalities.

Introduction

This is the first of two chapters summarizing the extensive reform initiatives which have altered municipal structures in most provinces over the past half-century. Chapter 7 then analyzes the effectiveness of these reforms and the extent to which they strengthen municipalities in fulfilling their fundamental roles and also explores the potential of reforms which focus on process rather than structure.

Selecting a starting point for the modern era of local government reform is inevitably arbitrary, because local governments have undergone considerable adaptation since their establishment. Examples include the shift of functions upward to more senior levels of government, the establishment of intermunicipal special purpose bodies and servicing agreements, boundary extensions through annexations and amalgamations, and increased financial assistance from the senior levels of government.

The first local government reform initiative of the post-war period occurred in Alberta, which embarked on a program of consolidating rural units of both municipal and educational administration which culminated in the County Act of 1950. It was the much-publicized establishment of the Municipality of Metropolitan Toronto in 1953, however, that is usually taken as the starting point of the modern period of local government reform in Canada. In the ensuing decade, we witnessed a period of what might be termed *ad hoc metropolitan reform*, extending to Montreal and Winnipeg by the beginning of the 1960s. These reforms were *ad hoc* in the sense that they represented unique responses to very serious servicing problems in the three urban areas involved, rather than arising from any comprehensive study of local government in that particular province.

In contrast, the decade of the 1960s was distinguished by not only a great increase in reform activities but also much more comprehensive approaches in several of the provinces. For example, fundamental examinations of the provincial-local relationship were carried out in New Brunswick in 1963 and Manitoba in 1964, although only New Brunswick's recommendations were acted upon. Reform initiatives were introduced in British Columbia and Quebec in 1965, with particular emphasis on the creation of upper tier governments for the urban areas and, in the case of Quebec, voluntary amalgamations of small municipalities. The establishment of regional governments was the central feature of Ontario's local government reform efforts during this period.

Reform initiatives were much more limited during the 1970s and 1980s. Apart from the completion of Ontario's regional government reforms, the only major structural changes were the creation of Winnipeg Unicity in 1972 and the introduction of regional county municipalities (RCMs) in Quebec in 1979. Major local government studies in both Nova Scotia and Newfoundland were completed in 1974, but were not acted upon except for some gradual changes in recent years.

In the 1990s, however, local government reform and restructuring returned to prominence. Initiatives were launched in all four Atlantic provinces, some very dramatic school board restructuring took place in Alberta and Ontario, and in the latter province the number of municipalities has been reduced by close to 300, as a result of a very aggressive campaign of amalgamations.

TABLE 1
Municipal Reform Highlights

1950s to early 1960s	Ad hoc metropolitan reform Toronto, Montreal, and Vancouver
1960s	Comprehensive reform in New Brunswick Upper tier units for British Columbia, Quebec, and Ontario (regional governments)
1970s and 1980s	Limited reform activity, featuring Unicity, regional county municipalities in Quebec, and remainder of regional governments in Ontario
1990s	Reform initiatives in all Atlantic provinces and extensive amalgamations in Ontario

In an attempt to make more manageable the coverage of this wide range of reform activities, it was decided to use two chapters. Employing the same distinctions found in the review of historical developments in Chapter 2, we begin by discussing reforms in Central Canada (Ontario and Quebec) and then examine the experiences of Atlantic and Western Canada in the next chapter.

Ontario

The Toronto area has been in the forefront of local government reform in Ontario. It was the site of the first major structural reform, the creation of Metropolitan Toronto in 1953, a reform which became the unofficial model for the regional governments established over two-thirds of the population of Ontario in the ensuing decade. Forty-five years later, reforms in Toronto again exerted influence of municipal reforms elsewhere in the province. This time, the Ontario government's determination to impose an amalgamation of all six lower tier municipalities and Metropolitan Toronto in spite of widespread local opposition, led many smaller municipalities trying to resist amalgamation pressure to conclude that their wishes were even less likely to be respected.

Metropolitan Toronto

The pressures of change rendering the traditional local government system increasingly inadequate have been previously described as arising because of urbanization. With the post-war "population explosion," the rapid growth of a number of the municipalities surrounding the city of Toronto produced serious servicing difficulties. Most pressing were the problems of water supply and sewage treatment facilities, arising from the fact that only 6 of the 13 municipalities involved had direct physical access to Lake Ontario. Arterial road development could not keep pace with the rapidly increasing volume of traffic. Public transportation and the existing highway network were poorly integrated. There was a desperate need for new schools. Many of the outlying municipalities were particularly ill equipped to finance these service demands since, as dormitory suburbs, they lacked industrial assessment to help relieve the tax burden on the residential taxpayer.

The city of Toronto also faced serious economic and social problems, with a large backlog of public works because of the disruption of the depression and war years, and a greatly increased demand for welfare services. There was growing traffic congestion because of the extent of commuter population, and urban renewal and redevelopment needs were increasingly obvious. With each municipality seeking capital funds on its own credit, borrowing by the burgeoning suburbs became more and more difficult as interest rates rose.

In response to these problems, a federated form of government embracing the city of Toronto and the 12 surrounding municipalities was introduced, effective January 1, 1953. As the lower tier in a two tier structure, these 13 municipalities retained their existing boundaries and continued to exercise a wide range of responsibilities. In addition, an upper tier unit, the municipality of Metropolitan Toronto, was established with the responsibility for such major functions as assessment, debenture borrowing, water supply and trunk mains, sewage treatment works and trunk sewers, and designated metropolitan roads. A number of responsibilities were also to be shared between the two levels of government. The fact that the metropolitan council was indirectly elected, that is, composed of individuals elected initially to designated positions on the lower tier councils, made the new structure similar to the century-old county system. The major differences were the inclusion of the city in the metropolitan system and the much stronger powers given to the upper tier council.

> Metro was similar to the old county system but with the city included and with more powers for the upper tier.

In its early years, Metropolitan Toronto was substantially successful in combating the servicing problems facing the member municipalities, particularly as regards sewers, water supply, education, and general financial stability. To a considerable extent, these early successes have been attributed to the forceful, skilled leadership of the first chair of the Metro council, Fred Gardiner, who held this position from 1953 to 1961. Gardiner's personal philosophy was clearly consistent with the founding objectives of the new metropolitan system, to develop the servicing infrastructure needed to accommodate the growth pressures.

But Colton notes that there were concerns even before Gardiner retired.[1] Yes, there was a massive expansion of housing, but primarily in the form of high-rise apartment construction which was accompanied by an increasing concentration of power in the development industry. Toronto enjoyed a boom in downtown development but fears mounted about an

---

[1]Timothy J. Colton, *Big Daddy*, Toronto, University of Toronto Press, 1980, pp. 177-178.

excessive growth mentality and the disruption of established neighbour-hoods—as reflected in the activism of citizens and citizen groups in the 1960s. This activism was also reflected in a growing anti-expressway sentiment culminating in the "Stop-Spadina" movement.

Quite apart from these changing public attitudes, Kaplan offers some interesting explanations for the decline in Metro Toronto's momentum after the first few years.[2] He emphasizes the significance of the indirect election of Metro councillors, noting that they stood, succeeded, or failed largely on the basis of their records in their lower tier council, only referring to Metro when it was politically expedient to blame it for not delivering enough for the local municipality in question. Ironically, according to Kaplan it was this parochialism of councillors which helped to explain Metro Toronto's initiatives and successes in the early years. Gardiner astutely avoided issues which would threaten local municipalities, and councillors were largely indifferent to everything else and prepared to accept Gardiner's persuasive leadership. However, when Metro turned to the more complex issues of the 1960s, especially under the less forceful chairs who succeeded Gardiner, the limitations of this passive support became increasingly apparent. Noting that Metro Toronto's main achievements were between 1953 and 1957, Kaplan contends that "in retrospect, the early burst of activity was the aberration and the subsequent prolonged retreat a more accurate expression of the system's character."[3]

Some problems and limitations were documented by the Royal Commission on Metropolitan Toronto established in 1963 to examine the first decade of operation. However, the Commission's 1965 report endorsed continuation of the two tier system.[4] The main change, introduced effective January 1st, 1967, was a consolidation of the original 13 municipalities at the lower tier into 6. In addition, the Metro council was increased to 32 members, with the city retaining its 12 representatives but the 5 suburban municipalities now sending 20 in recognition of their much greater population growth since the establishment of Metropolitan Toronto. A few responsibilities, notably waste disposal and social assistance, were transferred from the lower tier municipalities to Metro Toronto, continuing a trend which had become evident throughout the 1950s.

---

[2]Harold Kaplan, *Reform, Planning, and City Politics: Montreal, Winnipeg, Toronto,* Toronto, University of Toronto Press, 1982, pp. 685-690.

[3]*Ibid.*, p. 694.

[4]*Report of the Royal Commission on Metropolitan Toronto* (H. Carl Goldenberg, Commissioner), Toronto, Queen's Printer, 1965.

As Kaplan observes, there was little in these reforms to revive Metro.[5] While the suburban municipalities now enjoyed a majority position, they had no regional aspirations on which to use their power. They had received the necessary expansion of their basic services during the first decade. Now it was the city of Toronto which needed Metro more—to help finance the renewal of aging facilities. But Kaplan concludes that with a complacent suburban majority, Metro Toronto was even less inclined to blaze new trails.

Major changes in the election of the Metro Toronto council were introduced at the time of the 1988 municipal elections. While the mayors of the 6 lower tier municipalities continued to serve as members, the remaining 28 were directly elected, and did not hold seats on the lower tier councils. Provision was also made for the chair of Metro to be chosen by the Metro council from among the directly elected members. These changes appeared to reflect a belated concern by the Ontario government for the representative role of local government and its accountability and responsiveness.

From Metro to the GTA

The area of urban development that Metropolitan Toronto was established to embrace and to stimulate has long since expanded beyond its boundaries. Just as the population growth of the city of Toronto failed to keep pace with that of the suburban lower tier municipalities within Metro, so too did Metro itself fall behind the rapid pace of growth of areas adjacent to it. It found itself "hemmed in" on all sides by four regional governments (discussed below) and by Lake Ontario. Until 1971 Metropolitan Toronto absorbed the bulk of the new population growth in this area—now known as the Greater Toronto Area (GTA)—but since then its growth has dropped off sharply. In fact, Metro's share of the population of the GTA fell from 77% in 1961 to 54% in 1991.[6]

The growth pressures in the GTA and the lack of coordination in managing this growth led in 1988 to the creation of the Office of the Greater Toronto Area (OGTA), reporting directly to a provincial cabinet minister. The OGTA did not have any legislative mandate, but defined its role

---

[5]Kaplan, *op. cit.*, p. 697.

[6]Frances Frisken, "Planning and Servicing the Greater Toronto Area," in Donald N. Rothblatt and Andrew Sancton (eds.), *Metropolitan Governance: American/Canadian Intergovernmental Perspectives*, Berkeley, Institute of Governmental Studies Press, 1993, p. 157.

as one of fostering communication among government bodies, seeking solutions to immediate problems that no single government could solve on its own and helping governments in the area to develop a consensus on what the GTA should look like in the future.[7] The OGTA also acted as a secretariat for the Greater Toronto Coordinating Committee, which included senior staff representatives from the 5 upper tier municipalities in the GTA (Metro, Halton, Peel, York, and Durham) and the 30 lower tier municipalities in this area.[8]

Gradually, however, the view developed that a new governing body was needed for the GTA. A major impetus for this approach came from the "Golden Report," which proposed replacing the five existing regional governments with a single, streamlined Greater Toronto Council and giving lower tier municipalities added powers and responsibilities to deliver a wider range of services.[9] This proposal was subsequently endorsed by the *Who Does What* panel headed by David Crombie.[10] The stage seemed set for the abolition of the regional governments in the GTA, including Metro, especially since even the Trimmer Task Force on the GTA, set up by the Conservatives before their election victory, recommended abolishing the Metro government as part of a series of changes designed to strengthen the lower tier municipalities.

The Creation of the "Megacity"

Given this background, most were caught off guard when the province announced in late 1996 that all six lower tier municipalities and the metropolitan government would be combined to form a new city of Toronto embracing some 2.4 million people, thereby creating a municipality more populous than five of Canada's provinces. The main rationale for this about-face seemed to be the savings which the amalgamation was supposed to generate. Opposition to the so-called megacity was very strong, highlighted by the large majority voting against it in referenda held in all six of the lower tier municipalities. But the government pushed ahead,

---

[7]*Ibid.*, p. 161.

[8]Andrew Sancton, "Canada as a Highly Urbanized Nation," in *Canadian Public Administration*, Fall 1992, p. 290.

[9]Report of the GTA Task Force, *Greater Toronto*, Queen's Printer, January 1996.

[10]The panel was established "to ensure the very best service delivery by reducing waste, duplication and the overall cost of government...." It produced a series of reports between May and December 1996.

endured an opposition filibuster, and passed the legislation in April 1997. Effective January 1, 1998, the area previously under two tier metropolitan government is now one municipality, governed by a council of 57, elected by ward, plus the mayor, elected at large.

The most striking thing about this reform, apart from the fact that there was no previous rationale for it, either in restructuring studies or in the Conservative Party's past positions, is that it created a municipality with boundaries both too large and too small. Its massive size, at least in the Canadian context, presents major challenges for representation and local democracy. Yet its creation did nothing to address the need for an overall governing body for the GTA. If one overall governing body is needed for an urban area, as was commonly argued, the creation of the megacity did nothing to advance this cause.

> There was no rationale for the megacity, which is both too large and too small.

The Greater Toronto Services Board

To respond to this latter need, the government appointed (in December 1996) Milt Farrow, a former senior public servant in the Ministry of Municipal Affairs, to make recommendations for a Greater Toronto Services Board (GTSB). He proposed a board that would develop a long-term infrastructure coordination strategy; resolve interregional servicing issues, implement decisions, and apportion associated costs; develop a long-term, post-collection waste management strategy; and operate GO Transit (a commuter train service running from Oshawa to Hamilton). Farrow's model called for the GTSB to be operated by a 28 member executive committee, comprising 14 councillors from the city of Toronto and 14 in total from the 5 other lower tier municipalities, plus 3 members from Hamilton-Wentworth Region when GO Transit items were on the agenda.

The GTSB as proposed by Farrow was attacked by some for being too weak, especially with a governing body made up of politicians who would depend on their local councils for legitimacy and direction. Critics argued that the Board was a far cry from the Greater Toronto Council recommended in the Golden Report. Others, however, were opposed to the creation of a GTSB of any significant powers. In the forefront were the regional governments of the area, who feared that such a Board would gradually supersede them. Toronto politicians were also concerned, especially that the Board might fall under the control of suburban politicians.

In the end, the particular model established by the government, effective January 1, 1999, has only one specific power, the control of GO

Transit. In addition, the Board is to provide a forum for promoting better coordination and integration of interregional services in the GTA. It can provide advice to GTA municipalities on key infrastructure investments and provide a mechanism to coordinate economic development across the area. In a departure from the recommendations of Milt Farrow, the Board is composed of 40 members plus a chair, plus 1 member from Hamilton-Wentworth appointed only with respect to transit matters. Every GTA municipality is represented on the Board, with weighted voting to achieve representation by population. There are also special quorum and voting provisions designed to ensure that Board actions have widespread support. However, the complicated weighted voting system could result in political deadlock, since the 11 members coming from Toronto city council have exactly as many votes (55) as all the other politicians from the outer cities.[11]

Proponents of a strong GTSB clearly hope and expect that the obvious need for improved planning and coordination across the GTA will inevitably reinforce the Board's mandate. That prospect is far from clear at the moment. Any significant increase in the role of the GTSB, however, will also bring us closer to three levels of local government within the GTA. Whether that situation will be resolved through abolition of the regional governments—as was originally assumed—or whether the Toronto example will be followed and the lower tier municipalities abolished, is also unclear at the moment.

The Other Regional Governments

The ongoing developments in the Toronto area are by no means the only local government reform activities which have occurred in Ontario. As already noted, the original Metropolitan Toronto was really the first of the regional governments and within a decade it had been transplanted to a dozen other areas. While Metro has been characterized as an ad hoc response to specific servicing problems, the broader regional government program developed, at least officially, from an overall government policy.

That policy, as set out in *Design for Development, Phase Two* at the end of 1968, was potentially quite broad and imaginative, largely because of guidelines and a philosophical base taken from the *Report of the Ontario Committee on Taxation* the previous year. The policy recognized the need to provide not only efficient delivery of services but also adequate

---

[11]David Lewis Stein, "It's okay to take time choosing chair," *Toronto Star*, January 22, 1999.

access and effective representation of local views and concerns. It called for regional governments based on such criteria as community of interest, an adequate financial base, and sufficient size to generate economies of scale.[12] The policy also proposed varied structural approaches including both two tier and one tier governments and the direct election of upper tier councillors in the former instance.

> The regional governments were modified versions of the traditional county system.

In practice, the reforms introduced were all regional governments closely resembling Metro Toronto. As such, they can best be described as a modification of the traditional county system in Ontario. The reformed structures all contained two tiers, with the upper tier closely paralleling the boundaries of one or more counties in most cases. All or major municipal responsibility for such functions as welfare, roads, water supply, sewage disposal, planning, and capital borrowing were vested in this upper tier. The lower tier units in the structure were formed by a consolidation of constituent municipalities and included cities and separated towns, previously not part of the county system. With minor exceptions, election to the upper tier closely resembled the indirect election of county councils, although direct election has been introduced in a number of instances in more recent years. The costs of regional services were apportioned to lower tier municipalities according to their assessment in essentially the same manner as under the county system.

In the decade from the commissioning of the first local government reform study (of Ottawa-Carleton) in May 1964 to the coming into operation of the Regional Municipality of Haldimand-Norfolk in April 1974, 11 regional governments were established,[13] covering over one-third of the population of Ontario. If we add the prototype, Metro Toronto, and the Restructured County of Oxford (described below), we had 13 regional governments in Ontario, containing two-thirds of its population. As the unpopularity and political cost of the reforms became increasingly apparent, however, the government announced that it was winding up the program which, it claimed, had served its purpose.

---

[12]See the Honourable John Robarts and Darcy McKeough, *Design for Development: Phase Two*, Statements to the Legislature of Ontario, November 28th and December 2nd, 1968, and *The Ontario Committee on Taxation, Volume Two*, Toronto, Queen's Printer, 1967, Chapter 23.

[13]These were Ottawa-Carleton, Niagara, York, Waterloo, Sudbury, Peel, Halton, Hamilton-Wentworth, Durham, Haldimand-Norfolk, and Muskoka, with the latter being known as a District Municipality.

In its place, a County Restructuring Program was announced in early 1974. From the conditions required to qualify as a restructured county, it seemed apparent that the new program was little more than an effort to continue promoting regional governments under a new and less threatening name. In any event, very little action was taken on the studies carried out under this program, and the prolonged period of minority government in Ontario in the latter part of the 1970s forestalled any new initiatives. Ironically, the one restructured county, Oxford, was created prior to the County Restructuring Program being announced.

County government reform—or what might be termed the "third coming of regional government" as it has been practised in Ontario—resurfaced at the end of the 1980s. As with the earlier regional government program, a primary impetus for these new county reform proposals was the need to meet certain servicing challenges, including planning and waste management. Once again, much of the emphasis was on strengthening the upper tier by bringing in any cities or separated towns, and strengthening the lower tier through municipal consolidations. But, as with the previous county restructuring program of the mid-1970s, virtually no action was taken on the county studies carried out, and the whole initiative was allowed to lapse.

In place of a comprehensive county government reform program, Ontario reverted for a while to ad hoc boundary adjustments. Many of these were made under a Municipal Boundary Negotiations Act passed in 1981, but they mainly related to towns, villages, and townships, not major urban areas.[14] The beginning of the 1990s also saw municipal amalgamations in Lambton and Simcoe counties and in the London area. However, the attention of the provincial government was increasingly focused on matters of function (disentanglement) and finance (deficit reduction). No new regional governments had been established for more than 20 years, and it began to look as if major municipal restructuring activities were a thing of the past. But then June 1995 brought the election of the Conservatives, led by Mike Harris.

Municipal Restructuring Returns

Within a few months of taking office, the Conservatives introduced a number of legislative provisions in a Savings and Restructuring Act (the very controversial Bill 26) which they claimed were intended to make it

---

[14]Andrew Sancton, *Local Government Reorganization in Canada Since 1975*, Toronto, ICURR Press, April 1991, p. 13.

easier for municipalities to implement annexations and amalgamations. These provisions essentially laid out a two-pronged approach to municipal reform, clearly constructed in such a way as to put enormous pressure on municipalities to act. Reform could be achieved by reaching local agreement, provided that the change had the support of a majority of the affected municipalities containing a majority of the population and, where applicable, a majority of the members of the upper tier council as well. If no local agreement could be reached, however, and if even only one municipality so requested, the minister could appoint a commission with total authority to determine the new structure for the municipal area defined by the minister. This two-stage process, coupled with various statements made by the province about reducing the number of municipalities in Ontario, created an atmosphere in which municipalities felt great pressure to pursue amalgamation.

Two dramatic events added significantly to this pressure. When the province forced through the amalgamations in Toronto, most smaller municipalities understandably wondered what chance they had to resist if the wishes of such a large population area were ignored. Events in Kent County were even more threatening. A commission was appointed and recommended the amalgamation of all municipalities within the county, the county government, and the separate city of Chatham—against the wishes of 22 of the 23 municipalities affected! It may be that the new municipality of Chatham-Kent will be successful, but the way in which it was created sent a powerful message to the rest of the municipalities in Ontario. There was no telling what might happen to them if a commission was appointed. Better to make changes yourself, however unpalatable, than to have even more drastic changes imposed upon you.

> Better to do it to yourself, than to have it done to you!

The high-pressure campaign pursued by the province was quite effective in achieving the substantial pace of restructuring it desired. The term of municipal office following the November 1997 municipal elections began with 200 fewer municipalities than the 815 which existed prior to the elections. All but seven were dissolved by ministerial or commission orders issued under Bill 26. Those seven were the Toronto municipalities merged by legislation to form the megacity. Nor has the reform process stopped with the municipal elections. Since then a number of additional restructurings have been announced and more are under active discussion. It will not be long before the number of municipalities in Ontario will be fewer than the 539 which existed at Confederation.

TABLE 2
Reform Highlights: Ontario

January 1, 1953	Municipality of Metropolitan Toronto
January 1, 1967	Metropolitan Toronto consolidation
December 1968	Reform Policy, Design for Development: Phase II
1969-1974	Regional Governments
January 1996	Municipal Savings and Restructuring Act
January 1, 1998	Megacity and 200 municipal amalgamations
January 1, 1999	Greater Toronto Services Board

Quebec

By the 1960s, the local government system in Quebec had become, after more than a century of existence, very fragmented and was characterized by an excessive number of very small municipalities. Over 90% of the more than 1600 municipalities had less than 5000 population and nearly 50% had less than 1000 population. At the same time, problems of urban concentration and sprawl were evident, with the cities of Montreal, Quebec, and Hull (Outaouais) containing 30% of the population.[15] Efforts at municipal reform have focused on the amalgamation of small municipalities, the creation of regional governments in the three largest urban areas, and the establishment of upper tier governments to replace counties in the remainder of the province.

Municipal Consolidations

The Voluntary Amalgamation Act of 1965 allowed two or more municipalities to amalgamate following a council's resolution to that effect. Not surprisingly, this voluntary approach was ineffective, with fewer than 100 municipalities abolished between 1965 and 1971, hardly enough to reduce the badly fragmented municipal structure in Quebec. While new legislation in 1971 gave the Minister of Municipal Affairs more power to force amalgamations where he felt that it was desirable, this power was little used because of opposition and because (as will be seen) the government was by then preoccupied with metropolitan reforms. According to

---

[15]These figures are from Jean Godin, "Local Government Reform in the Province of Quebec," in Advisory Commission on Intergovernmental Relations, *A Look to the North: Canadian Regional Experience*, Washington, 1974, p. 50.

O'Brien,[16] the peak period for municipal consolidations was between 1971 and 1975, when the number of municipal units was reduced by 84. A limited number of voluntary consolidations (and a few forced ones) continued over the next couple of decades—although provincial government financial policies which gave larger subsidies to smaller municipalities than to larger ones certainly did not encourage the consolidations. Two examples from this period were Lévis and Lauzon (located across the river from Quebec City), which after amalgamation were joined by adjacent St. David, and—in 1992—the city of Sorel and the parish of St. Pierre de Sorel.[17]

In the 1990s, the Quebec government has taken an increasing tough stand with respect to amalgamations. As has been noted in other jurisdictions as well, a major motivating factor was the apparent desire of the province to create larger municipal institutions to which responsibilities could be downloaded. The Liberal budget of April 1990 outlined the downloading of about $400 million in responsibilities to municipalities, mostly in the areas of public transit and police services and local roads in rural areas. The Minister, Claude Ryan, did not deny accusations that these measures were designed to pressure municipalities into combining, and acknowledged that such a consequence would not be unwelcome.[18]

The Parti Québécois took power in 1994 and the following year announced new measures to promote municipal amalgamation. The first and primary phase of the new policy was directed at villages, parishes, and small communities of less than 10 000 population. In May

> Progress was slow in spite of new measures and incentives to promote amalgamation.

1996, the government released a map showing the municipalities being singled out during this first phase. New financial incentives were provided to encourage a municipal response, along with a financial penalty in the form of decreased grants for those who had not responded by January 1, 1999.[19] Progress has been slow, however, and an analysis presented in

---

[16]Allan O'Brien, *Municipal Consolidation in Canada and its Alternatives*, Toronto, ICURR Press, May 1993, p. 39.

[17]Details on these consolidations are provided in *ibid.*, pp. 41 and 46.

[18]Robert Cournoyer, *Municipal Amalgamation in the Nineties in Quebec*, paper presented at the conference on *The State of Unicity—25 Years Later*, Winnipeg, Institute of Urban Studies, 1998, p. 58.

[19]Igor Vojnovic, *Municipal Consolidation in the 1990s: An Analysis of Five Canadian Municipalities*, Toronto, ICURR Press, 1997, pp. 53 and 60.

October 1997 revealed that only 11 amalgamations had taken place during the first year of the new policy (1996), and only 7 more to that date. Moreover, the Ministry has indicated that rather than an automatic penalty for lack of municipal action, each case would be evaluated on its own merits.[20]

Metropolitan Government for Montreal

Annexations were also used early and often in response to problems of urban sprawl in the Montreal area. Indeed, beginning as early as 1883, Montreal proceeded to annex 33 municipalities in roughly as many years. By 1920 this policy had halted, but the provincial government wanted the city to annex four island municipalities recently declared bankrupt. Instead, a regional agency was established—the Montreal Metropolitan Commission—which was to have the authority to approve or veto all local decisions on borrowing and capital expenditures of Montreal and 14 island municipalities. Under pressure from Montreal, however, the province amended the legislation to remove the Commission's authority over the city's financial decisions. The Commission was governed by a 16 member board, 8 named by Montreal, 7 by the suburbs, and 1 by the province.

With its limited jurisdiction, the Montreal Metropolitan Commission was never a very significant body and by the 1950s two studies had confirmed that it was not settling basic intermunicipal problems and that its existence was no more than a makeshift solution to a financial dilemma.

In 1959 the Commission was replaced by the Montreal Metropolitan Corporation. At the outset the new body appeared to represent much more than a change in name. It was authorized to exercise a number of important functions including sewers, water distribution, arterial roads, planning, mass transit, major parks, and all other services considered as intermunicipal by agreement among the municipalities or by decision of the Corporation. Moreover, its jurisdiction extended to the city of Montreal as well as to the 14 island municipalities under its predecessor.

The governing body comprised 14 representatives from the city, 14 from the suburbs, and a chair appointed by the province. This balancing of city and suburbs ensured the vigorous opposition of Montreal's Mayor Drapeau, who, as Sancton notes, was like most central city mayors in resisting any form of metropolitan government which he could not control. As Sancton points out, another and unique reason for Montreal's opposition was the concern that any metropolitan government, by extending

---

[20]Cournoyer, *op. cit.*, p. 60.

to the suburbs and their higher proportions of English-speaking citizens, would decrease the influence of the French.[21] In any event, Montreal's refusal to cooperate effectively sabotaged the new Metropolitan Corporation, which was never a major innovation in spite of its greatly expanded terms of reference.

As an alternative approach, Drapeau and his chief lieutenant, Lucien Saulnier, pursued annexation with a view to establishing one city covering the entire island. The provincial government, not surprisingly, had no desire to see Montreal grow so large as to rival the importance of the province itself, and the city only managed the annexation of three virtually bankrupt suburbs in 1963, 1964, and 1968, respectively.

The Liberals were replaced by the Union Nationale in 1966, and the new government seemed to have little interest in urban reform. But civil servants in Municipal Affairs were impressed with structural reforms introduced in France in the form of "communautés urbaines"—upper tier, indirectly elected governments. In June of 1969 the Minister of Municipal Affairs tabled plans for the creation of communautés urbaines in Montreal and Quebec City and a communauté regionale around Hull. Strong negative reactions, especially from Montreal, prompted an announcement that the plans would be postponed for a year.

> The MUC was created to access suburban funds to help finance the settlement of a police strike.

Ironically, the Montreal Urban Community (MUC) came into existence just three months later, on January 1, 1970 (as did two others around Hull and Quebec City, discussed below). The governing council of the MUC consisted of the mayor and councillors of the city of Montreal and one delegate from each of the other 29 municipalities under its jurisdiction, with the city having 7 of the 12 members on the powerful executive committee and providing the first chair in the person of Lucien Saulnier.

The new structure owed little to the prior recommendations of the Quebec civil service; instead it was a hastily implemented response to the devastating effect of a police strike which hit Montreal on October 7th, 1969. A prompt end to the strike was engineered by none other than Saulnier, whose strategy was "in essence, to promise to pay the police what they wanted and then to force the suburbs and the provincial government

[21]Andrew Sancton, "The Impact of Language Differences on Metropolitan Reform in Montreal," in Lionel D. Feldman (ed.), *Politics and Government of Urban Canada*, Toronto, Methuen, 1981, p. 372.

to finance the increases."[22] The vehicle for this redistribution of funding was the new MUC, "organized such that in many ways it was a mere extension of the city of Montreal."[23]

Contrast the background to the establishment of Metro Toronto, with Frederick Gardiner having several months to acquire staff and organize his approach even before the new structure came into effect. As Sancton observes, the way in which the MUC came into existence without planning or any administrative structure "is a vivid illustration of the fact that its original purpose was to act as a conduit of funds rather than as an important force in the management of Montreal's urban development."[24]

By January 1, 1972, all of the police forces on the island had been unified into the MUC police department but controversy over this decision and related policing issues dragged on for a number of years. It is important to realize, however, that while public security still accounts for almost half of the annual budget of the MUC, the new upper tier government has also become involved in several other areas of activity. In financial terms, the major initiatives have been with respect to subways and sewers, although these projects have come under considerable provincial influence because of the extent of provincial funding. The provincial government has also been extending its influence with respect to regional planning issues. In part, this may reflect the more interventionist philosophy of the Parti Québécois, which came to power in 1976. But to a large extent it results from the failure of the MUC to take initiatives in this area, largely because of a city-suburb split and the effectiveness of the suburban veto. While the city of Montreal has a majority of the votes on the MUC, reflecting its population dominance, a motion cannot pass unless supported by at least half of the suburban delegates present.

An analysis by Sancton concludes that the original hopes that the MUC would evolve into a genuine metropolitan government have never been realized. He notes that suspicion between the city of Montreal and the suburbs has paralyzed the structure from the beginning.[25] While the original legislation contemplated that internal boundary adjustments would be made, any such changes would involve some merging of French-speaking and English-speaking populations—a task no politician wanted

---

[22]*Ibid.*, p. 376.

[23]*Ibid.*

[24]*Ibid.*

[25]Andrew Sancton, "Montreal's Metropolitan Government," Hanover, *Quebec Studies*, No. 6, 1988, p. 23.

to tackle. Without significant boundary changes, Sancton observes, it was only possible "to tinker with the Community's clumsy institutions."[26] The principle that a double majority (city and suburb) was needed before action could be taken meant that often no decision was made. As a result, the provincial government, which held most of the financial power anyway, seized most of the initiative. Instead of being a counterweight to provincial influence, the MUC "passively accepts provincial funds and implements provincial decisions."[27]

The population of the suburbs has been increasing at a faster rate than that of the city of Montreal. As a result, the suburbs have been gaining more voting strength on the MUC governing council, where votes are weighted according to population. Amendments to the MUC Act in 1982 also provided parity between the suburbs and Montreal on the executive committee. At the same time, changes were made in the selection of the chair of the MUC, the ostensible political leader of the metro government. Under the new arrangements, the chair must still be a member of council to be chosen, but must resign his or her local municipal position on taking office for a four year term.

Most growth is beyond the MUC, which is hemmed in by the adjacent RCMs.

A major problem facing the MUC is the declining relevance of its boundaries. In 1971 it contained 71% of the population of the Montreal census metropolitan area, but by 1991 the proportion was down to 57%. The MUC does not have any jurisdiction where most development is now taking place—in the outer suburbs.[28] Expansion of the MUC boundaries seems unlikely, since the adjacent areas have now been established as regional county municipalities (discussed below), rather like the situation in which Toronto finds itself, hemmed in by adjacent regional governments.

In April 1992, the Minister of Municipal Affairs established a Task Force on Greater Montreal, an area encompassed by the MUC and the 12 regional county municipalities surrounding it. The mandate of the Task Force[29] was essentially concerned with issues of "governance," that is, how responsibility for planning and management within the metropolitan

---

[26] *Ibid.*

[27] *Ibid.*, p. 24.

[28] Sancton, *Canada's City Regions*, p. 84.

[29] Canadian Urban Institute, *The Future of Greater Montreal: Lessons for the Greater Toronto Area?* Toronto, 1994, p. 13.

area should be shared among the various municipalities and levels of government. The main recommendation of its December 1993 report was that a Montreal Metropolitan Region be established, "the territory of which would correspond exactly to that of the CMA and which would automatically be adjusted to match future CMA boundary changes."[30] The governing body of the new region would be comprised of 21 mayors and city councillors from the municipalities in the region, with representation weighted according to population.

Even though there are well over 100 municipalities within this area (as contrasted with the 30 lower tier municipalities in the Greater Toronto Area), the Task Force did not recommend any amalgamations. It called instead for the abolition of the 12 regional county municipalities (whose establishment, only 10 years earlier, is discussed below) and the creation of four Intermunicipal Service Agencies or ISAs, each covering a group of existing municipalities.[31] The ISAs would be legal entities with authority to borrow money, but they would only take on responsibilities if enabling motions were approved by a two-thirds vote (weighted by population) of their member municipalities.[32] Concerns were expressed that these proposals would, in effect, establish three levels of municipal government in the Montreal area.

One assessment suggests that the Task Force proposal was designed to "allay municipal fears of centralization and domination."

> By recommending only indirectly elected councillors on the Metropolitan Council, by decentralizing many services to the ISAs, and by proposing that tax inequities be addressed by diversifying taxation sources rather than pooling property on a regional level, the Task Force tried to engineer a compromise between the central city and the suburban municipalities.[33]

These efforts failed, and suburban mayors emerged as the most vocal opponents of the Task Force report. Their main fear appeared to be that a new overall metropolitan government would prevent them from competing with the municipalities of the MUC and would, therefore, undermine their plans for growth.

---

[30] Sancton, *Canada's City Regions*, p. 88.

[31] Canadian Urban Institute, *op. cit.*, p. 26.

[32] Sancton, *Canada's City Regions*, p. 89.

[33] Ray Tomalty, *The Compact Metropolis: Growth Management and Intensification in Vancouver, Toronto and Montreal*, Toronto, ICURR Press, 1997, pp. 163-164.

Upon assuming office in 1996, Lucien Bouchard designated Serge Menard as Minister for the Montreal Region. Menard proposed the creation of a single metropolitan region for the whole Montreal area, but this was rejected by the government.[34] Since the PQ had strong support from the South and North Shores, and little support from within the MUC, its lack of action on the report is not surprising.[35] In addition, there is a view that any true regional government for Montreal would be seen by many (especially sovereignists) as a first step toward a new territorial entity which might seek to secede from Quebec in the event of a "yes" victory. According to this view, "the idea of regional government is a non-starter and will remain so until the constitutional question is resolved."[36]

Legislation was passed in mid-1997 to establish a 40 member commission de développement pour la métropole (CDM). It is to be presided over by the Minister for the Montreal region, with the remaining 39 members to be elected municipal councillors (two-thirds) and appointed representatives of socio-economic groups (one-third).[37] The CDM is to have advisory functions only, mainly related to issues concerning economic development, planning, transportation, and the environment. All existing municipal structures, including the Montreal Urban Community, continue in existence, although the CDM is supposed to make recommendations for streamlining. As of early 1999, however, no members had yet been appointed to the CDM, raising questions about the province's commitment to proceed.

April 1999 saw the release of yet another study, from a commission headed by public administration professor and former provincial civil servant Denis Bedard. Its more than 100 recommendations include very contentious proposals to amalgamate the 29 municipalities on the island of Montreal to a maximum of 5, and to create regional superstructures overseeing urban centres such as Montreal and Quebec City. These new

---

[34]Katherine A. Graham, Susan D. Phillips, and Allan M. Maslove, *Urban Governance in Canada*, Toronto, Harcourt Brace & Company, 1998, p. 80.

[35]*Ibid.*, p. 164. This situation parallels that found in Ontario, where the Conservative Party enjoys strong support from the suburban areas (the so-called 905 area, known for its telephone area code) and much less support within Toronto.

[36]Mario Polèse, "Montreal: A City in Search of a Country," *Policy Options*, September 1996, p. 33.

[37]This description is from Andrew Sancton, "The Municipal Role in the Governance of Cities," in Trudi Bunting and Pierre Filion (eds.), *Canadian Cities in Transition*, 2nd edition, Toronto, Oxford University Press, forthcoming.

regional bodies would take over management and long-term planning for garbage collection and the environment, regional roads, public transit, and social housing.[38] Since the report also recommends that provincial grants relating to public transit, roads, and social housing be cut, it seems to promote the downloading of provincial responsibilities and costs to enlarged municipalities, in much the same way as has happened in Ontario. Concerns have been expressed about the impact of a number of the reforms on the rights of Quebec Anglophones.[39] The proposed amalgamations would absorb predominantly English-speaking areas into new municipalities with a majority of French-speaking residents. In addition, while the new system of linguistic school boards in Quebec is less than a year old, the Bedard report recommends that they be scrapped and that schools eventually be placed under the new regional superstructures, a change which would rob Anglophones of any control over educational matters. Whether the province will act on this report, when it has ignored the recommendations of two other studies earlier in the 1990s, is far from clear at this point.

Other Urban Communities

The December 1969 legislation which created the Montreal Urban Community also provided for an urban community for Quebec City and for a similarly constituted regional government for Hull and environs known as the Regional Community of Outaouais.

The latter municipality faced municipal opposition based on a feeling that the reform was introduced without sufficient prior consultation. A primary motivation for its establishment was apparently the perceived need to provide a counterweight to the adjoining Regional Municipality of Ottawa-Carleton in Ontario, and to represent the area's interests to the National Capital Commission. A somewhat more positive attitude was evident in the Quebec Urban Community where more consultation with local leaders occurred.

In neither instance, however, has the regional level attracted much feeling of loyalty. Instead, there has been some movement for municipalities to consider amalgamation to better defend their interests against the new regional units. Indeed, the number of lower tier municipalities within

---

[38]The discussion in this section is based on a number of articles in the *Montreal Gazette*, April 21, 1999.

[39]This discussion is based on "Treading on Anglo Turf," Editorial, *Montreal Gazette*, April 22, 1999.

Quebec and Outaouais has been reduced from 26 to 13 and from 32 to 8, respectively—a consolidation which is even more striking when compared with the total absence of any such change in the MUC.

The extent of the change within the Outaouais Urban Community may partly reflect the fact that, unlike Montreal and Quebec City, it contained major portions of rural as well as urban territory. This resulted in an uneasy partnership which placed strains on the organization. In 1989, for example, only 23% of the budget went for services used in common, with the rest going to services which were largely urban.[40] Following a ministerial statement and a study (the Giles Report) in 1990, two new structures were put into place effective January 1, 1991—a new regional county municipality covering the rural areas, and a modified Outaouais Urban Community confined to the urban areas of Gatineau, Hull, Aylmer, Buckingham, and Masson. A proposal to amalgamate the first three of these municipalities was put to a referendum and failed to win majority support in all three municipalities as required.

Regional County Municipalities

As a result of legislation passed in 1979 (the Land Use Planning and Development Act), the three upper tier urban communities were joined by a network of 95 new upper tier units called regional county municipalities, or RCMs. These new units replaced all the 72 former county municipalities, which had consisted entirely of rural units and had exercised very limited responsibilities.

Municipalities were grouped together to form these RCMs on the basis of "affinity"—a criterion which was very similar to the community of interest concept specified (but almost never applied) in Ontario's regional government program. The specific boundaries for the RCMs and the exact composition of their governing councils were worked out locally, often with great difficulty and under threat of withdrawal of provincial funds, through tripartite committees comprising representatives of the old counties, the lower tier municipalities, and the Minister of Municipal Affairs.[41] Under the provisions of the legislation, cities (which had been politically separate from their surrounding counties) had to become part of the new RCM system—just as Ontario's cities became part of the new regional municipalities established in that province. In addition, each RCM had to adopt a regional land use plan, and was also to take over the

---

[40]O'Brien, *op. cit.*, p. 48.

[41]Sancton, *Local Government Reorganization*, p. 15.

functions of the old counties, at least for the mainly rural areas in which counties had been operating.[42]

Each RCM is governed by a council composed only of the head of council (or representative) of each member municipality. In Sancton's view, the message was clear: "a new source of elected political authority was *not* being established." The RCMs were to represent existing municipalities acting together—nothing more.[43] Tomalty's assessment supports this interpretation.[44] He finds that the RCMs failed to become a political forum of action independent from the local municipalities. Their ineffectiveness as regional planning agencies he attributes in part to the fact that they do not have responsibility for providing infrastructure, such as roads and sewage treatment, and thus have little leverage with local municipalities. He also cites the indirectly elected governing councils and elaborate voting arrangements as further constraints.

In about half of the RCMs, voting rules give each representative a number of votes proportional to the population of his or her municipality, and 38% of them have some form of veto as part of the delicate balancing of city and rural interests.[45] A further complication is that when the RCMs are performing the functions of the old county councils, representatives from the cities are excluded altogether and the remaining mayors have one vote each, as had been the case under the former county system.[46]

Concerns about the adequacy of the representation arrangements have increased as the expenditures of the RCMs have grown. Costs are shared by municipalities in proportion to their share of the area's taxable assessment. Cities with a healthy assessment base are, not surprisingly, critical of the fact that their voting strength on council is not nearly as large as their expenditure burden.

In response, the Quebec government passed legislative amendments in 1987 which set out three options relating to the voting arrangements within the RCMs, including an opportunity for member municipalities to determine their own rules if agreement could be reached by municipalities representing at least 90% of the population of the area. Conditions

---

[42]Louise Quesnel, "Political Control over Planning in Quebec," *International Journal of Urban and Regional Research* 14, 1990, pp. 25-48, quoted in Sancton, *Local Government Reorganization*, pp. 15-16.

[43]*Ibid.*, p. 16.

[44]The discussion which follows is based on Tomalty, *op. cit.*, p. 159.

[45]These figures are from Quesnel, *op. cit.*, p. 33.

[46]Sancton, *Local Government Reorganization*, p. 17.

were also set forth in the amendments under which RCMs could acquire new responsibilities, where supported by a majority vote of two-thirds of the members of an RCM council.[47]

The RCMs differ from Ontario's county governments in several key respects. First, negotiations leading up to the establishment of the RCMs led to boundaries quite different from the old counties, something Ontario has been unable to achieve even with its restructured counties and regional governments. Second, cities are included within the RCMs, but cities remain separate from the unreformed county systems still found in Ontario. Third, for better or worse, RCMs are designed as flexible mechanisms through which the province and the existing municipalities can better perform their assigned responsibilities, not as genuine political institutions. In that regard, they are probably closer to the regional districts of British Columbia than to Ontario's county and regional governments.[48]

Some expansion in the role of RCMs may occur as a result of the amalgamation policy (referred to above) introduced in the mid-1990s. The third phase of this policy is focused on the 700 some municipalities which are referred to as base communities, three-quarters of them with populations of less than 1500 people. To support these small municipalities, the government has proposed that the power of the RCMs will be reinforced to enable them to provide the municipalities with adequate technical and administrative services.[49] This initiative supports the notion of the RCMs as flexible mechanisms akin to British Columbia's regional districts.

Intermunicipal Agreements

Since 1979, the Cities and Towns Act has authorized three types of intermunicipal agreement: for a municipality to purchase a service from another, for one municipality to delegate its authority to another in order to pursue a defined objective, and for the establishment of intermunicipal corporations to deliver particular services agreed to by the participating municipalities.[50] These arrangements have been used mainly for leisure programs and fire protection. They have been particularly useful when residents of a rural municipality (parish) use services of a nearby village.[51]

---

[47]O'Brien, *op. cit.*, pp. 36-38.

[48]Sancton, *Local Government Reorganization*, p. 23.

[49]Vojnovic, *op. cit.*, p. 54.

[50]Sancton, *Local Government Reorganization*, p. 39.

[51]O'Brien, *op. cit.*, p. 38.

TABLE 3
Reform Highlights: Quebec

1965   Voluntary Amalgamation Act, with limited results
1970   Urban communities for Montreal, Hull, and Quebec City
1979   RCMs replace county governments
1995   PQ measures to promote extensive amalgamation
1997   Legislation to establish CDM for Montreal region

Concluding Comments

Given that Ontario and Quebec had similar municipal structures featuring two tier county systems and a substantial number of small municipalities, it is not surprising that their approaches to reform have also been rather similar. In both provinces, the needs of major urban areas were addressed through the establishment of regional governments or urban communities. Quebec's urban communities appear to have been weaker and less effective, a contrast most evident in comparing the performance of the MUC and Metro Toronto. On the other hand, Quebec moved much earlier to reform the century-old county system, replacing all of their counties with regional county municipalities in 1979. While a dozen of Ontario's counties were converted into regional governments, most of the rest of the county governments remain, albeit with consolidated lower tier municipalities in a number of areas.

So far, however, Quebec's RCMs have been a very limited form of upper tier unit, acting more as the representative of their constituent lower tier municipalities than as a separate government. In contrast, Ontario's regional governments have steadily expanded their responsibilities and have increasingly moved to direct election of their members to give them greater legitimacy as upper tier governments with their own mandate, not agents of the lower tier. The Quebec government has indicated that the RCMs will play an increased role in support of small municipalities as part of the reform policies introduced in the mid-1990s, but where this will lead remains to be seen.

Those mid-1990s reforms in Quebec parallel initiatives also taken by Ontario, and both have centred on ambitious amalgamation programs, designed to create larger municipalities which are supposed to be better able to handle the increased responsibilities and costs being downloaded by the fiscally constrained provincial governments. In this respect, the initiatives in both provinces share a major limitation. They are pre-occupied with improving the service delivery capability of municipal government, largely to facilitate provincial downloading, and have paid little attention to the representative role of municipalities.

CHAPTER 6
Local Government Reform II
Atlantic and Western Canada

Rather than building new foundations for a modern system of municipal government based equally on considerations of effective representation and efficient service delivery, most of the reforms did little more than patch up the cracks in the traditional foundation, leaving the system overbalanced in favour of the service delivery function.

Introduction

This is the second of two chapters summarizing the extensive reform initiatives which have altered municipal structures in most provinces over the past half-century. It begins with experiences in the four Atlantic provinces and then examines developments in Western Canada. Chapter 7 then analyzes the effectiveness of these reforms and the extent to which they strengthen municipalities in fulfilling their fundamental roles, and also explores the potential of reforms which focus on process rather than structure.

New Brunswick

The first province to undertake comprehensive local government reform initiatives in the 1960s was New Brunswick, and it did so by appointing a *Royal Commission on Finance and Municipal Taxation*. The emphasis on fiscal matters implicit in the title reflected the difficulties facing local government in New Brunswick at the time. The level of municipal services compared unfavourably with other provinces and there were wide variations in the standard of service within New Brunswick, notably in education. A multitude of assessment and tax acts resulted in a variety of taxes, again differing from one municipality to the next. There were marked inequities in municipal taxation and high tax arrears. Moreover, municipalities faced increasing difficulties in financing their servicing demands and by the 1960s three of the single tier rural counties were virtually bankrupt.

To its credit, the Byrne Commission, as it came to be known, did contend that the problems facing local government in New Brunswick were not just a matter of allocation of tax fields but also involved government organization and structure. In its 1963 report it made an attempt to distinguish between services appropriate for the provincial level and for the local level. On this basis it recommended the transfer of a number of functions to the provincial level and called for the New Brunswick government to provide services directly for rural areas, hitherto governed by the counties. Recommendations such as these caused some observers to conclude that the Commission's preoccupation with finances had led it to overemphasize efficiency and administrative rather than representative considerations.[1]

Equal Opportunity Program

Following extensive public discussions, the New Brunswick government launched a Program for Equal Opportunity in 1967 under which the main recommendations of the Byrne Commission were implemented. The provincial government took over responsibility for the administration of justice, welfare, and public health, and also financial responsibility for the provision of education, with the number of school districts reduced from 422 to 33. All types of municipal taxation except the real property tax were abolished, and assessment—now to be at market value—and collection of taxes became provincial responsibilities. The 15 single tier rural counties were abolished and, in partial compensation, some 90 new villages were created.

Nonincorporated local service districts were also created, as administrative units for the province to use in providing services which had been delivered by the now-abolished county councils. Under the Municipalities Act, the Minister acts as the mayor and council for all local service districts.[2] Provision was made for the establishment of advisory local service

---

[1]Indeed, T.J. Plunkett in his "Criticism of Byrne Report," in Donald C. Rowat, *The Canadian Municipal System*, Toronto, McClelland and Stewart Limited, 1969, p. 180, charged that the Commission's proposed solutions "make the continuance of municipal government in New Brunswick of doubtful value."

[2]Igor Vojnovic, *Municipal Consolidation in the 1990s: An Analysis of Five Canadian Municipalities*, Toronto, ICURR Press, 1997, p.71.

district committees, if a sufficient number of local inhabitants actively participated in forming them.[3] To discharge the expanded responsibilities, the province set up a number of field offices in rural areas.

The reforms were beneficial in bringing about a substantial improvement in the quality of such services as education, justice, health, and welfare—although this gain was essentially at the expense of the municipal level, which lost all or partial responsibility for these functions to the province. As the years passed, two areas of concern came increasingly to the fore: the lack of municipal government in rural New Brunswick and the failure to deal with boundary changes needed in urban areas. The response to these issues is examined next.

> Key concerns were a lack of government in rural areas and outdated urban boundaries.

Governing Rural New Brunswick

One major problem not resolved, arguably even worsened by the Program for Equal Opportunity, concerned the approximately 250 000 people (one-third of the population of New Brunswick) left without any form of municipal government.[4] These people looked to nearby villages and towns for some local services. They demanded some form of municipal government and, at the same time, the incorporated municipalities complained that these residents of nonincorporated areas were not paying fully for some local services they received.

In response to this situation, a *Task Force on Nonincorporated Areas* was established in June 1975. The resultant report[5] found not only the predictable concern about the lack of elected councils to represent the people but also inequities in the financing of services. It noted that many services underwritten by property taxation in the incorporated municipalities were, in the case of the unincorporated areas, provided by the New Brunswick government without the imposition of any property taxation. Moreover, the report stated that some of the services provided by the provincial government, notably community planning, could not be implemented effectively by that level of government and that more opportunity

---

[3]Edwin G. Allen, *Municipal Organization in New Brunswick*, Ministry of Municipal Affairs, Fredericton, 1968, p. 12.

[4]See Harley d'Entremont and Patrick Robardet, "More Reform in New Brunswick: Rural Municipalities," in *Canadian Public Administration*, Fall 1977.

[5]*Report of the Task Force on Nonincorporated Areas in New Brunswick*, Fredericton, Queen's Printer, 1976.

for local citizen input was necessary. The report recommended that all existing legislation pertaining to local service districts be repealed and that 11 new municipalities with the status of "Rural Municipalities" be incorporated. No action was taken on this recommendation, and one analysis concluded that the report was a piecemeal response to the problems facing the New Brunswick municipal system, handicapped by narrow, and narrowly interpreted, terms of reference.[6]

Another possible response to the problems of rural areas was provided in the April 1993 summary report of the *Commission on Land Use and the Rural Environment*. It expressed great concern about the general lack of support and priority for planning, and the amount of sprawl and ribbon development which had been occurring in the unincorporated areas. The Commission called for the rationalization of existing local service districts into "Rural Communities."[7] These communities would have elected councils which would appoint members to sit on district planning or management commissions, along with members representing municipalities within the districts. The change would, according to the Commission, provide better representation for rural residents, more accountable decision making, and more integrated planning for urban and rural areas. In response, one pilot community, Beaubassin East Rural Community, was established in 1995 and apparently a number of other unincorporated areas have expressed interest in this model.[8]

For the most part, services in rural areas are provided by local service districts administered by the department responsible for municipal affairs. In addition, over 80 villages have been incorporated where population densities call for a higher level of services under the direction of elected councils.[9]

Another response has been the creation of single purpose boards to deliver services which transcend political boundaries. Some 300 of these bodies have been established in New Brunswick, to handle such regional services as economic development, sewage, transit, hospitals, ambulance service, emergency planning, pest control, libraries, and solid waste man-

---

[6]d'Entremont and Robardet, *op. cit.*, p. 480.

[7]Government of New Brunswick, *The Commission on Land Use and the Rural Environment: Summary Report*, April 1993, pp. 6-7.

[8]Communication from the New Brunswick Department of Municipalities and Housing, March 12, 1999.

[9]Kell Antoft and Jack Novack, *Grassroots Democracy: Local Government in the Maritimes*, Halifax, Dalhousie University, 1998, p. 32.

agement.[10] Many of these boards have representation from both local service districts and municipalities. For example, O'Brien found that Moncton, Riverview, and Dieppe were involved in some 10 separate regional single purpose agencies which also served the unincorporated areas in the adjacent geographic counties of Albert and Westmorland.[11] Interestingly, the spirit of municipal cooperation reflected in these extensive joint arrangements, and the economic revival of Greater Moncton, were factors which influenced the decision not to impose amalgamation on the area in the 1990s, as discussed below.

Strengthening Urban Centres

While the Byrne Commission and Equal Opportunity Program failed to address the issue of restructuring in New Brunswick's urban areas, some boundary changes were introduced in the Fredericton and Saint John areas, and in the Moncton area with the consolidations which created Riverview and Dieppe, respectively, out of the English-speaking and Acadian suburbs.

A December 1992 government report[12] acknowledged that the Equal Opportunity reforms had not addressed the problems of urban areas. Seven of these have populations of 20 000 or more, and the report noted that they have been developing a variety of ad hoc regional bodies to deal with the provision of local services to their region, a trend cited above. The proliferation of these boards, according to the report, weakened the accountability and added to the fragmentation within urban centres.

After considering options for restructuring, the report cited amalgamations to produce larger single tier municipal units or a formalized regional structure which would preserve existing municipalities but with an intermunicipal body to coordinate and administer regional services. To recognize the unique features of each of the seven urban areas, and to minimize disruption, the report called for a phased approach, with a limited number of areas considered at any one time.[13]

---

[10]Miramichi Local Government Review Panel, *Miramichi City: Our Future—Strength through Unity*, Fredericton, 1994, p. 4.

[11]Allan O'Brien, *Municipal Consolidation in Canada and its Alternatives*, Toronto, ICURR Press, May 1993, p. 14.

[12]Ministry of Municipalities, Culture and Housing, *Strengthening Municipal Government in New Brunswick's Urban Centres*, December 1992.

[13]*Ibid.*, p. v.

The first two areas selected for study were the Moncton and Miramichi areas, with reports appearing in April 1994.[14] The latter report proposed the amalgamation of all 11 communities in the study area (only five of which were incorporated municipalities) into one municipality—a restructuring which made Miramichi the fourth largest municipal unit in New Brunswick. The Moncton report acknowledged the distinctive English and French communities of Riverview and Dieppe in ruling out amalgamation as the response. Instead, it called for a joint services board comprised of appointed and elected officials from the three municipalities.[15] The board would exist at the pleasure of the municipal governments to perform a municipal-like function. The report emphasized that it should not be allowed to become a new level of government, but rather a mechanism to permit the three municipalities to work in greater harmony. Funding for the board would be through the three councils, with their shares based on their proportions of the total tax base of the three communities. To what extent the existing single purpose agencies would be replaced by the new joint services board would be the decision of the three councils. In the interim, the new board was expected to provide coordination, liaison, and financial control over those special purpose bodies providing services to two or more municipalities in the Greater Moncton area. Greater service integration is occurring with respect to such areas as fire services, 911, and regional policing via the RCMP.[16]

Instead of amalgamation, the Moncton area is using a joint services board and pursuing service integration.

In its Throne Speech in the spring of 1996, the government renewed its commitment to strengthening New Brunswick's urban municipalities. Shortly after, it announced studies of Greater Saint John, Greater Campbellton, Madawaska, and Greater Dalhousie. Commissioners were named for each area, along with an appointed community advisory committee.

In the Saint John area there was fierce opposition from the outlying areas to the possibility of a merger of all nine municipalities to form a single city of Saint John. Instead, the government came up with a com-

[14]See Local Government Review Panel, *Greater Moncton Urban Community: Strength Through Cooperation*, and the previously cited Miramichi report, Government of New Brunswick, April 1994.

[15]For details on this interesting concept, see Moncton report, *op. cit.*, pp. 37-38, on which the following description is based.

[16]Communication from the Department of Municipalities, *op. cit.*

promise solution which, effective January 1, 1998, consolidated the eight suburban municipalities into three and left the boundaries of Saint John unchanged.[17] Another key reform saw the establishment of a Regional Facilities Commission to integrate the financing of major facilities (such as Harbour Station, the Aquatics Centre, and other facilities in the city of Saint John) that are of regional benefit. Work is also continuing on the potential establishment of a Regional District Planning Commission.[18]

In the case of the Dalhousie area, the Commission concluded that full amalgamation was not appropriate, given the cultural and linguistic differences, strong public opposition, and difficult economic circumstances. Recommended instead was the creation of a Joint Services Commission for managing and coordinating services on a regional basis. The government supported the call for unified regional service delivery, but rejected the proposed Joint Services Commission in favour of an inter-community forum, the preferred vehicle of the affected municipalities. It is understood that the next step is up to the municipalities.

Intermunicipal cooperation instead of amalgamation was also the outcome of the Campbellton study, which recognized that a number of services were already integrated on a regional basis and which called for closer collaboration with respect to the Campbellton Civic Centre and the provision of water and sewer services. On the other hand, three municipalities and a portion of one local service district were amalgamated with the city of Edmundston.

Nova Scotia

Local government reform initiatives in Nova Scotia have come in two main waves, almost 20 years apart. A comprehensive report and recommendations appeared in the early 1970s, with some changes gradually introduced over the ensuing decade. The 1990s brought a number of new studies and a major restructuring in the Halifax area.

Graham Commission: Too Much at Once?

June 1974 saw the release of the massive report of the *Royal Commission on Education, Public Services, and Provincial-Municipal Relations in the*

---

[17]The Saint John information is based on G. M. Betts, *Municipal Restructuring New Brunswick Style: The Saint John Experience*, unpublished paper, 1997.

[18]Communication from the Department of Municipalities, *op. cit.*

Province of Nova Scotia. Chaired by Professor John F. Graham, this study began in March 1971 and dealt with not only local government organization but also with the reorganization of provincial departments and agencies, although the latter proposals are of less relevance for our purposes.[19]

As with the Byrne Commission in New Brunswick a decade earlier, the Graham Report examined the most appropriate distribution of provincial and local responsibilities and concluded that municipal government should be relieved of such "general services" as education, health, social services, housing, and administration of justice. It also called for the Nova Scotia government to provide such "support services" to municipal governments as capital borrowing, assessment, tax collection, water and sewer user billing and collection, and the administration of municipal pension funds.

In relation to the municipal structure, the Graham Report recommended that 11 one tier counties be established throughout Nova Scotia replacing the existing rural municipalities, towns, and cities. To facilitate citizen participation in this new structure, the report called for the establishment of community associations supported by county council staff in areas of common interests. Considerable attention was devoted to the internal organization of the new county system, with specific recommendations concerning the make-up of councils, and the use of executive committees and chief administrative officers.

The lack of action on the Graham Report has been attributed, in at least one analysis, to "the degree of detail, the vast and comprehensive nature of the recommendations, the lack of detailed argumentation of alternatives...."[20] Instead, informal discussions involving representatives from the Union of Nova Scotia Municipalities and the Department of Municipal Affairs evolved into what became known as the Task Force on Municipal Reform. Its deliberations culminated in a February 1978 White Paper entitled *New Directions in Municipal Government in Nova Scotia.*

The main emphasis of the White Paper was on the reform of some aspects of the provincial-municipal financial relationship, although not in relation to the most expensive local services such as education, health and social services, housing and justice. Proposals included an uncondi-

---

[19]For a useful summary of the main recommendations of the Graham Commission, see the Appendix prepared by W. Hooson in C. Richard Tindal, *Structural Changes in Local Government*, Toronto, Institute of Public Administration of Canada, 1977, on which this section is partially based.

[20]Lionel D. Feldman and Katherine Graham, *Bargaining for Cities*, Toronto, Butterworths, 1979, p. 164.

tional general grant, provincial grants in lieu of taxes, road user charges, and a revenue guarantee. Strong emphasis was given to the expansion of user-related charges, such as in relation to water and sanitary sewerage. While the proposals were relatively modest, their positive reception is a tribute to the consultative process which was followed.

In the ensuing years, most of the major proposals of the 1978 White Paper have been implemented.[21] These include the development of an unconditional municipal operating and capital grant program and a restructuring of educational administration which saw the municipal school districts consolidated into 21 district school boards comprised of one-third municipally appointed, one-third provincially appointed, and one-third elected representatives. The number of boards had been further reduced to 18 when they were all eliminated in September 1996. Education matters are now handled by the province and by 18 district councils.

Annexations and Amalgamations

While the major boundary changes inherent in the restructuring recommendations of the Graham Commission were not pursued, a number of boundary changes have been occurring over the past three decades using the time-honoured process of annexations and amalgamations. The cities of Halifax and Dartmouth both secured large annexations in the 1960s. In 1961 Dartmouth annexed portions of adjacent Halifax County, increasing its population by 90% and increasing its area by nine times. A 1969 annexation by the City of Halifax nearly quadrupled its area and increased its population by a third.[22] In 1980 Bedford was carved out of Halifax County to provide a focal point for urban development at the head of the Bedford Basin, which separates Halifax from Dartmouth.[23]

The increasingly intertwined relationships between the municipalities in this Greater Halifax area was reflected in the establishment of the Metropolitan Authority of Halifax.[24] It was originally set up to operate a regional jail and over the years it took on the operation of a regional

[21]Correspondence from Shingai Nyajeka, Nova Scotia Department of Municipal Affairs, April 17, 1989, on which this section is based.

[22]These figures are from David M. Cameron and Peter Aucoin, "Halifax," in Warren Magnusson and Andrew Sancton (eds.), *City Politics in Canada*, Toronto, University of Toronto Press, 1983, p. 183.

[23]*Ibid.*, p. 184.

[24]Sancton, *Local Government Reorganization*, p. 35.

transit system and a sanitary landfill operation. Bedford became the fourth member of this authority in 1986, joining Halifax, Dartmouth, and Halifax county. The authority was governed by a 12 member Board comprised of elected representatives appointed from the councils of each of the member municipalities.

The Metropolitan Authority's ineffectiveness led to its replacement by an enlarged Halifax regional municipality.

The ineffectiveness of the Metropolitan Authority prompted growing pressure for municipal restructuring in the Halifax area. According to one analysis,[25] "it was constantly beset by internal political wrangles over financing its work and different visions about priorities." It failed to pursue regional planning, was ineffective in dealing with challenges such as the environmental cleanup of Halifax harbour, and was really only successful in establishing a metropolitan public transit system. As will be seen, new provincial initiatives in the 1990s led to the abolition of the Metropolitan Authority and its replacement by a greatly enlarged city of Halifax.

Task Force on Local Government

The prelude to the Halifax reform was the establishment by the Minister of Municipal Affairs in late 1991 of a *Task Force on Local Government*. Its April 1992 report recommended a significant realignment of functions between the province and municipalities. Rural municipalities would have to start providing their own policing and their own roads (as the urban municipalities had been doing) and the province would take over the administration and financing of the non-federal share of the costs of general welfare assistance. As discussed in Chapter 8, these proposals were very similar to those arising from the "disentanglement" process launched by Ontario during this period.

In addition, the Task Force recommended a major restructuring of municipal governments in the five most urbanized counties in the province—including Halifax County—which together contained 67% of the total population of Nova Scotia. After considering a number of options, the Task Force stated that one tier municipal governments would be the preferred model for the restructuring in these areas,[26] with existing county

[25]Katherine A. Graham, Susan D. Phillips, and Allan M. Maslove, *Urban Governance in Canada*, Toronto, Harcourt Brace & Company, 1998, p. 83.

[26]Report to the Government of Nova Scotia, *Task Force on Local Government*, April 1992, p. 33.

boundaries representing the likely maximum sizes for any such new units. The possible amalgamation of many of the smaller rural municipalities in the province was also raised.

1993 saw the release of reports from the Municipal Reform Commissioners of both Cape Breton County and Halifax County. These studies were follow-ups to the recommendations from the Task Force. Both reports recommended the amalgamation of all municipal units in their study areas into a single municipality.

The Cape Breton Regional Municipality

Both a 1968 Finnis Report and the 1974 Graham Commission had recommended amalgamation of the municipalities in the county of Cape Breton. There was growing criticism of the complex network of special purpose bodies set up in the area, including the Cape Breton Joint Expenditure Board which operated the regional correction centre, a home for special care, regional tourism efforts, and harbour ports.[27] The report of the Cape Breton Reform Commissioner, Charles Campbell, calling for amalgamation of all eight municipalities including the county, was not immediately accepted by the new Liberal government which replaced the Conservatives in 1993. However, when the Cape Breton Development Corporation (Devco) announced that it was reducing its payment-in-lieu by 50% and when the city of Sydney began annexation proceedings, the province decided it was time to act.[28] The new municipality commenced operations on August 1, 1995.

The limited resistance to this significant change (with the notable exception of Louisbourg) probably reflected a recognition of the serious financial difficulties facing a number of the municipalities in this area, and also some public willingness to consider fewer governments and less bureaucracy in the hope that savings would result. Initially, at least, these hopes were not realized. The Commissioner had estimated annual savings of $13.8 million, $7.3 million of which were to come from the realignment of provincial and municipal services which had been introduced across Nova Scotia. In fact, the service swap resulted in an additional cost of $5 million a year, contributing to the $15 million shortfall which the new municipality faced in its 1995/96 operating budget. The

---

[27]The discussion which follows is based on Andrew Sancton, Rebecca James, and Rick Ramsay, "Amalgamation vs. Intermunicipal Cooperation: Financing Local and Infrastructure Services," Toronto, ICURR, forthcoming.

[28]*Ibid.*

province responded with a series of special measures, including the provision of a $2 million interest-free loan (forgivable after three years if certain terms were met).[29] Overall, the fact that tax bills have not gone down since amalgamation is largely the result of developments beyond the control of the new municipality, which is generally regarded as well governed and administered.[30]

The Halifax Regional Municipality

In contrast with Cape Breton, there was considerable opposition to the Halifax amalgamation proposal. The province proceeded nonetheless, and the Halifax Regional Municipality came into existence on April 1, 1996. It was formed from an amalgamation of the cities of Halifax and Dartmouth, the town of Bedford, and Halifax county. The result is a very large municipality approximately the size of Prince Edward Island and containing 40% of the population of Nova Scotia. While 70% of its population is located in an urban/suburban core, 70% of its land area is distinctly rural.[31] The regional council is made up of 23 members representing 23 districts (wards) and is headed by a mayor elected at large. One of the difficulties facing the new council, not surprisingly, has been a "clash of cultures" between the rural and urban councillors, notably over service and tax levels.[32]

As usual, there were suggestions that substantial savings (in this case, $10 million annually) would result from amalgamation and, as usual, costs have increased initially. Indeed, the transition costs of amalgamation reached $26 million. There have also been problems relating to collective bargaining, pressures to increase the cost structure by selecting the highest denominator for service levels and standards and compensation packages, and a perceived loss of community identity. However, according to the CAO of the new municipality,[33] its benefits include clearer lines of authority and accountability, increased equity in sharing resources and costs, an enhanced opportunity to plan and implement regional initiatives,

---

[29]*Ibid.*

[30]Communication from Jack Novack, March 18, 1999.

[31]Figures from K. R. Meech, "Impacts of Amalgamation: The Halifax Regional Municipality Experience," paper presented at the Insight Conference on *Municipal Amalgamation and Restructuring*, April 10-11, 1997, p. 8.

[32]Novack, *op. cit.*

[33]Speaking Notes of K. R. Meech, November 18, 1996.

and the potential for long-term economies of scale. That potential has presumably not yet been realized, since Halifax's projected operating deficit for 1998-99, while "a moving target," is still some $12 million.[34]

Prince Edward Island

The need for municipal reform in Canada's smallest province was raised in a 1990 *Royal Commission on the Land* Report. It commented on the failure in the past to adjust municipal boundaries to reflect population overspill, and took the position that "where the outlying ribbon development begins, so should the municipal borders."[35] The report gave particular attention to the Charlottetown area, where nine suburbs and the city had struggled with what the Commission termed the "herculean" task of achieving a coordinated approach on a volunteer basis. It noted that there had been some instances of successful collaboration, but felt that these had not been as cost-effective efficient or rational as the coordination that could be achieved under one unified jurisdiction.[36] The Commission contended that the municipal consolidation needed for the area would only come about through strong provincial leadership.

June 1993 saw a *White Paper on Municipal Reform*, whose objectives included strengthening the urban centres of the province, improving the decision-making process, achieving greater equity, effecting economies of scale, and improving land use planning. In particular, the White Paper singled out restructuring for the Summerside and Charlottetown areas, which it found overgoverned. It considered several reform options and expressed a preference for amalgamation, while not ruling out annexation or regionalization. A Commissioner was appointed to examine further the implications of municipal reform in these two areas.

The *Report of the Commission on Municipal Reform (Charlottetown and Summerside Areas)* was completed in December 1993. It called for three sets of amalgamations in the Charlottetown area, one of them creating an enlarged city of Charlottetown. It also recommended the complete merger of the five municipalities in the Summerside area, along with some unincorporated territory. Legislation implementing these changes was passed in 1994 and the new cities began operations in 1995.

---

[34]Novack, *op. cit.*

[35]The summary which follows is based on O'Brien, *op. cit.*, pp. 27-30.

[36]*Ibid.*, p. 28.

Newfoundland

Major changes in the municipal structure in Newfoundland were recommended by a Royal Commission study completed in 1974 (the Whalen Commission). It called for the gradual creation of as many as 20 regional governments envisaged as two tier structures with the upper tier units similar to, but much stronger than, British Columbia's previously described regional districts.[37] It also recommended tightening up incorporation procedures and some modifications in municipal classifications, as well as the introduction of the real property tax because of the poor financial conditions in most municipalities. The latter recommendations were gradually incorporated into revisions to the Municipalities Act, but no action was taken with respect to a system of regional governments.

Studying St. John's

Considerable attention was directed, however, to the government structure in the St. John's area. This area had been excluded from the Royal Commission study, but it has been the subject of at least four other studies of its own. Until amalgamations in 1992 (discussed below), the St. John's metropolitan area was comprised of the central city of St. John's and about 20 smaller surrounding municipalities largely dependent on the central city for employment and retail services.[38] The initial study of this metropolitan area in 1957 led to one change—the creation in 1963 of the St. John's Metropolitan Area Board. A second study in 1971 offered three alternative reforms for the area, and this prompted the government to appoint a commission to conduct hearings and make recommendations concerning an appropriate governmental structure for the area. The Henley Commission, as it came to be known, recommended in January 1977 that a two tiered structure of regional government be established along with an expanded city of St. John's. Draft legislation was introduced twice, with the Henley recommendations substantially incorporated except for the lack of a provision for the enlargement of St. John's. Following the defeat of the second bill, the regional government concept appeared to be dropped. The Municipalities Act of 1979-1980 included enabling legislation

[37]Donald J. H. Higgins, *Urban Government: Its Government and Politics*, Toronto, Macmillan, 1977, pp. 127-128.

[38]See Peter G. Boswell, "Regional Government for St. John's?" in *Urban Focus*, Institute of Local Government, Queen's University, January-February 1979, on which this section is based.

for the establishment of regional governments anywhere in the province, but no action has been taken in this regard.

In the meantime, the St. John's Metropolitan Area Board continued to grow and evolve.[39] It spent its first six years developing a municipal plan. It then began to supply urban services in a number of subdivisions outside the towns and city. In 1978, the Board took over responsibility for administration of the regional water supply system on behalf of the province. During the 1980s, the Board had nine members appointed by the province, two of whom represented the city of St. John's and one the town of Mount Pearl, a major suburb of the city. It employed a staff of 37 and generated revenues by levying property taxes and user fees.[40]

Municipal Consolidations

Shortly after the election of the Liberal government headed by Clyde Wells in 1989, Newfoundland launched an ambitious program of municipal consolidations. When the program commenced, the province had 310 municipalities and 165 local service districts, ranging in population from 15 to 95 000 (in the city of St. John's).[41] Not surprisingly, many of these municipalities operated on very high provincial subsidies to provide even a basic level of services.

The community consolidation program (as it was called) identified communities on the basis of physical proximity and a combined population of 1250. Some 110 municipalities were selected using these criteria, and the declared objective was to reduce these to 43.[42] Municipal objections to this reform process centred particularly on what was perceived to be insufficient consultation—both in advance of the reform initiative and during each of the consolidation studies—and on the perceived bias of Commissioners carrying out the consolidation studies, since they were also senior staff of the Ministry of Municipal Affairs.

By the time the consolidation program was put on hold in 1992, to allow for a review of the process and its accomplishments, 31 former communities had been reduced to 13. The main changes occurred in the

---

[39]The summary which follows is based on O'Brien, *op. cit.*, p. 24.

[40]*Ibid.*

[41]Donald Peckham, "Amalgamation Program Undertaken in the Province of Newfoundland and Labrador," in *The Boardroom Files*, Halifax, Maritime Municipal Training and Development Board, Spring/Summer 1993, p. 15.

[42]*Ibid.*, p. 16.

Northeast Avalon area, which included the cities of St. John's and Mount Pearl, 17 towns, and the St. John's Metropolitan Area Board. Effective January 1, 1992, the number of municipalities was reduced to 13, with the city of St. John's absorbing two municipalities and most of the area previously under the Metropolitan Board which was abolished at the same time. The new arrangements also gave St. John's new regional responsibilities for public transit, solid waste management, water supply, fire protection, and secondary processing of sewage.[43] In effect, it has become a regional service provider with respect to these responsibilities, a role which it has not welcomed. St. John's claims that it is paying a disproportionate share of regional costs and is carrying neighbouring municipalities. It would prefer to see its boundaries extended "to incorporate the majority of the surrounding urban and suburban development."[44]

> St. John's has replaced the Metropolitan Board as a regional service provider.

New Regional Initiatives

Since the mid-1990s, the Newfoundland government has given increasing attention to a regional focus for service delivery. Following a report on Community Economic Development, the province was divided into 20 economic zones to facilitate economic development. In the fall of 1996 the government released a consultation document, *Reforming Municipal Government in Newfoundland and Labrador*, which stated that municipalities could be expected to play a greater role in economic development in their respective regions, and which suggested that the boundaries of the new economic zones might logically be used to delineate new regional groupings of municipalities.

In the spring of 1997 the government appointed a three person Task Force to follow up on the matters proposed in the consultation document. After a series of meetings, including one in each of the 20 economic zones, the Task Force reported in September 1997. It called for the establishment of a regional county services board in each of the 20 economic zones, to be governed by a board of directors comprised of both elected and appointed members representing unincorporated areas and municipalities, respectively. The Task Force recommended few initial powers for these boards, but proposed that they take on additional functions as required and approved by the board of directors and that municipalities

---

[43]This discussion is based on Sancton et al., *op. cit.*

[44]March 1997 submission by St. John's, quoted in *ibid.*

and unincorporated communities be allowed to opt in and opt out of the services offered.[45] On the surface, the proposed boards seem quite similar to British Columbia's regional districts (discussed in the next section) and they represent a worthwhile option. However, no action had been taken on the Task Force recommendations at the time of writing.

TABLE 1
Reform Highlights: Atlantic Canada

NEW BRUNSWICK

1963   Byrne Commission on Finance and Municipal Taxation
1967   Program for Equal Opportunity, abolition of rural counties
1995   New city of Miramichi
1996   Studies of several urban areas, leading to joint boards

NOVA SCOTIA

1974   Graham Commission
1992   Task Force on Local Government,
        calling for service swap and restructuring in urban areas
1995   Regional municipalities of Halifax and Cape Breton

PRINCE EDWARD ISLAND

1993   White Paper on Municipal Reform
1995   New cities of Charlottetown and Summerside

NEWFOUNDLAND

1963   St. John's Metropolitan Board
1989   Municipal consolidation program
1992   New city of St. John's replaces Board as service provider
1997   Task Force proposes regional county services boards

To recap, the 1990s have seen extensive amalgamations in areas such as Cape Breton, Charlottetown, Halifax, the Miramichi, and Summerside, but perhaps the most striking feature of the reform efforts in the Atlantic provinces is the widespread and continuing reliance on joint boards and other means of intermunicipal service coordination. Bodies such as the Halifax Metropolitan Authority and the St. John's Metropolitan Board no longer exist, but the use of joint agencies instead of amalgamation has

---

[45]Final Report, *Task Force on Municipal Regionalization*, September 10, 1997, p. 9.

recently been agreed upon for areas such as Campbellton, Dalhousie, and Moncton. In addition, St. John's acts as a regional service provider for a number of municipalities within its area and joint services boards have been suggested for all 20 economic zones in Newfoundland.

British Columbia

British Columbia's approach to local government reform has been very pragmatic and directed to specific problems as perceived by the provincial government. To a large extent these problems were related to the absence of a municipal structure over much of the province. In 1966 only 2870 square miles out of the 266 000 square miles in British Columbia were within organized municipalities.[46] The remainder of the province, containing one-sixth of its population, received services directly from the provincial government—although much of the affected populace resented paying taxes without some form of municipal government. The provincial administration was felt to be too small to deal with the vast territory involved, particularly when people moved into this unorganized area to avoid municipal taxes and then expected municipal services.

There are no municipalities over much of the province, many small municipalities, and a history of joint boards.

The organized municipalities also faced problems, with small, financially weak areas finding it difficult to provide necessary services. Some municipalities suffered from sprawl and poor land use, and the need for a joint approach to the provision of services in the Greater Vancouver area had already prompted the establishment of a number of regional special purpose agencies—the Greater Vancouver Sewerage and Drainage District (1914), the Greater Vancouver Water District (1926), four area health boards (set up between 1936 and 1948), the Lower Mainland Regional Planning Board (1948), the Greater Vancouver Parks District (1966), and the Greater Vancouver Hospital District (1967). A form of metropolitan government for the Greater Vancouver area had been recommended in 1960, but the province did not act on this proposal.

---

[46]The figures are from D.W. Barnes, "The System of Regional Districts in British Columbia," in Advisory Commission on Intergovernmental Relations, *A Look to the North: Canadian Regional Experience*, Washington, 1974, p. 110.

Creation of Regional Districts

Instead, the British Columbia government provided for the creation of regional districts to administer certain functions over wide areas. The specific objectives of this reform were not made clear by the government. However, this may well have been deliberate since one analysis contends that the provincial government was especially interested in the potential of these regional districts in the two major urban centres of Vancouver and Victoria. It argues that the government used a strategy of "gentle imposition" to implement potentially significant regional governments, particularly for Greater Vancouver.[47]

Whatever the government's motives, since the enabling legislation was passed in 1965, 29 regional districts have been established, covering all of British Columbia except the northwest corner. That number has been reduced to 27, as a result of the amalgamation of the 3 regional districts in the Fraser Valley in December 1995. Each district is governed by a regional board of directors comprising representatives from incorporated municipalities within the regional district and from the population of the unorganized territory. The regional districts vary greatly in size.[48] The Greater Vancouver Regional District (GVRD) is a major metropolitan area encompassing seven cities, eight districts (urban municipalities, not to be confused with regional districts), three villages, and three unincorporated areas, known as electoral areas. In contrast, the Central Coast Regional District, with a population of 3000, does not have any municipalities within it, but encompasses five electoral areas.

Because of the previously referred to strategy of gentle imposition, the regional districts originally did not have any assigned responsibilities. Instead it was left to the board of directors of each district to decide on the responsibilities they wished to assume. Individual municipalities or unorganized electoral areas were free to opt in or opt out of any of the servicing arrangements at their own discretion. Gradually, however, this discretion was reduced with certain responsibilities becoming mandatory and the opting-out provision being removed. Thus, all regional districts became responsible for the adoption of an official plan, for the development of community planning services in their constituent electoral areas, for building inspection, and for certain "local works and services." In

---

[47]Paul Tennant and David Zirnhelt, "Metropolitan Government in Vancouver: the strategy of gentle imposition," in *Canadian Public Administration*, Spring 1973, pp. 124-138.

[48]The two examples which follow are from O'Brien, *op. cit.*, p. 53.

addition, individual districts voluntarily adopted a variety of other responsibilities including ambulance service, pest control, recreation facilities, refuse disposal, sewers, and water.[49] The end result is that regional districts are hybrids, delivering a mixture of upper and lower tier services.[50]

The regional districts do not levy taxes. They send a separate requisition for each service, which includes the appropriate share of the administrative costs, to each municipality—and the municipality must pay.[51] In the case of services provided to unincorporated areas, the requisition goes to the province, which, in turn, collects property taxes from inhabitants of these areas.

The overall impact of the British Columbia reforms is difficult to assess. There was some feeling that the regional districts would be a transitional stage toward a strong regional government system in which the existing municipalities would be amalgamated. There is no indication, however, that this was the provincial government's intention and, except for the Greater Vancouver and Victoria (Capital) areas, the regional districts have not developed into an important level of government. But if, as previously mentioned, the government's main purpose was to strengthen local government in these two metropolitan areas, it may feel that this objective has been largely met. The GVRD, for example, provides some 12 distinct functions, employs a staff of 1000, and has an annual budget of over $350 million.[52]

The regional districts have proven to be a flexible structure for dealing with a variety of considerations. They have assumed direct responsibility for the provision of municipal services to the population in unorganized areas. They have also acted as the administrative agency for certain functions or projects which some of their member municipalities wished to pursue jointly. In addition, they have assumed responsibility for various functions delegated to them by their constituent municipalities and they can acquire other functions through the affirmative vote of two-thirds of the directors of the regional district having among them at least two-thirds of the votes on the board of directors.

---

[49]Barnes, *op. cit.*, p. 116.

[50]Brian Walisser, *Understanding Regional District Planning: A Primer*, Victoria, Ministry of Municipal Affairs, June 1987, unpaginated.

[51]O'Brien, *op. cit.*, p. 53.

[52]Alan F. J. Artibise, *Regional Governance Without Regional Government*, Background report prepared for the Regional Municipality of Ottawa-Carleton, April 1998, p. 13.

One analysis of the regional district scheme cites several positive features.[53] Existing municipal units are allowed to continue under this structure, thereby contributing to the preservation of an existing sense of community, allowing for diversity within the regional area, and helping to ensure accessibility and responsiveness in the municipal system. At the same time, the services provided by the regional districts have promoted the common interests of area municipalities, and the fact that these regional services have been assigned by the area municipalities means that they are determining their common interests themselves rather than having this definition imposed from above. But this analysis also noted that because of the structure of the regional districts, notably the indirect election of board members, there appears to be little public discussion of board activities and decision making appears very insulated.

> The flexible structure of the regional districts allows diversity and preserves a sense of community, but accessibility concerns exist.

A Regional District Review Committee was set up by the government in 1977. Its report, the following year, identified several problems.[54] The relationship between the public and the regional district was found to be negative, with the public feeling that the district was inaccessible, dictatorial, and a secretive organization. The Committee felt that the regional districts needed to do more to explain their responsibilities and to encourage public involvement. The Review Committee report also described problems in the provincial-local relationship, stemming from the heavy-handed way in which the provincial level, and particularly the Ministry of Municipal Affairs, dealt with the regional districts.

That observation was borne out by provincial initiatives in the 1980s. Patrick Smith describes the resulting situation as one of "regional structures under attack."[55] He cites the 1983 legislation declaring null and void all regional plans and removing the right of regional districts to plan for their regions as a whole, and the 1985 legislation centralizing the transit function at the provincial level. Oberlander and Smith explain the loss of

---

[53]Lionel G. Feldman Consulting Ltd. and the Institute of Local Government, Queen's University, *Evaluation of Alternative Structures and a Proposal for Local Governance in the Edmonton Region*, January 1980, especially pp. 37-42.

[54]Regional District Review Committee, *Report of the Committee*, Victoria, Ministry of Municipal Affairs and Housing, 1978.

[55]Patrick J. Smith, "Regional Governance in British Columbia," in *Planning and Administration*, 13, 1986, pp. 7-20.

the regional district planning function as the result of a continuing conflict between the GVRD and the provincial government.[56] Agricultural land reserves had been created under the provisions of the 1973 Land Commission Act, passed by the NDP government of that time. But appeals to the cabinet to release such lands for other (development) purposes became increasingly frequent with the return to power of the Social Credit. Matters came to a head over a land reserve in the Vancouver suburb of Delta. The GVRD opposed provincial plans to release this land from the agricultural designation. The government responded, in October 1983, by stripping regional districts of their planning and zoning authority.

Some changes were introduced at the end of the 1980s as a result of another Review Committee which was appointed in 1983 and reported in November 1986.[57] This Committee reiterated the concern about lack of public understanding about the roles of regional districts. It observed that the provincial level had reduced its support for the regional districts over the years and was sending out very mixed signals about the future of these organizations (as noted above). The Committee called for, among other matters, closer liaison between the regional districts and the Ministry of Municipal Affairs and clear and consistent statements of public policy with respect to the regional districts.

In 1989 the legislation governing the regional districts was revised. There were no drastic changes, but for the first time the local services that potentially fall within regional district jurisdiction are listed in the statute. It is still left to each regional district to determine the functions it will provide. However, they can now make service decisions by by-law, rather than by having to get the province to revise letters patent, as was formerly required.[58] To provide a degree of self-government in isolated rural areas, the 1989 amendments encourage regional districts to create community commissions to cover part of an unincorporated area.[59] These commissions would consist of four specially elected commissioners and the director who would be elected to the board from the surrounding unin-

---

[56]See H. Peter Oberlander and Patrick J. Smith, "Governing Metropolitan Vancouver," in Donald Rothblatt and Andrew Sancton (eds.), *Metropolitan Governance: American/Canadian Intergovernmental Perspectives*, Berkeley, Institute of Governmental Studies Press, 1993, pp. 361-363.

[57]Regional District Survey Committee, *Summary Report of the Regional District Survey Committee*, Victoria, Queen's Printer, 1986.

[58]O'Brien, *op. cit.*, p. 52.

[59]The description of these bodies is based on *ibid.*, p. 53.

corporated area. The by-law setting up the commission sets out the administrative powers being delegated to it.

There was also a significant new planning initiative by the GVRD in 1989, in spite of the fact that it had been stripped of its planning authority a few years before. Changes in the region and a significant increase in development pressures led the regional district to begin preparation of a new regional plan, to update its "Livable Region Plan" from 1975. It embarked upon a very successful consultative process self-described as "preparing plans by consensus and implementing them through partnership."[60] By the time it finished this process, in 1995, the province had passed a Growth Strategies Act requiring municipalities to plan regionally, and the GVRD Livable Region Strategic Plan was approved in October 1995. Smith points to this experience as evidence that effective regional initiatives can be undertaken without municipal restructuring. He also suggests that the GVRD experience serves as a rebuttal to the contention in the Golden Report on the Greater Toronto Area that the consensual model inherent in the regional districts was "inherently weak," and suffered from a "lack of mandate."[61]

However, Smith has recently expressed concerns about the extra responsibilities being given to the regional districts, such as the shift of public transit from the province to the Greater Vancouver area, effective April 1, 1999. He and Stewart conclude[62] that a municipal accountability crisis is looming, in part because of the way the regional boards are chosen, and they call for direct election of a Greater Vancouver Authority to replace the GVRD.

Artibise also believes that reform of the GVRD is necessary. He argues that its mandate is too limited, since it is delegated to the district by member municipalities and "changes with the fortunes of the regional interest at the local ballot box."[63] Because all the board members are part-

---

[60]For a good outline and analysis of this process, see Patrick Smith, "More Than One Way Towards Economic Development: Public Participation and Policy-Making in the Vancouver Region," in K. A. Graham and S. D. Phillips, *Citizen Engagement: Lessons in Participation from Local Government*, Toronto, Institute of Public Administration of Canada, 1998, pp. 49-77.

[61]*Ibid.*, p. 54.

[62]Patrick J. Smith and Kennedy Stewart, *Making Accountability Work in British Columbia*, Report for the Ministry of Municipal Affairs and Housing, June 1998.

[63]Artibise, *op. cit.*, p. 23.

time regional politicians, no one speaks out forcefully and consistently for the region, and as a result, the staff of the GVRD have too much influence. Artibise also points to the complex and confusing system of weighted voting and argues that the principles of representative democracy are violated when, for example, the 647 citizens of Lions Bay village have one GVRD vote and so do 104 210 citizens of the city of Vancouver.[64]

Alberta

Alberta had one very early initiative, when it embarked on a program of consolidating rural units of both municipal and educational administration which culminated in the County Act of 1950. Under this Act, the educational and municipal units were combined, initially on a voluntary basis, to form one tier county governments which covered the majority of the populated rural area of Alberta. However, legislative reforms in 1995 effectively removed school jurisdiction from the counties and established school districts in their place, leaving the counties as little more than municipal districts.

The Calgary and Edmonton Areas

No comprehensive restructuring was introduced in urban areas, although the population increase which accompanied the development of the petroleum industry strained the existing municipal organization, especially in the Calgary and Edmonton areas. The result was the frequent annexation of adjacent territory (notably some 19 separate annexations involving Edmonton between 1947 and 1980), usually at the initiative of land owners and developers wishing an extension of services. However, this piecemeal approach frustrated both Calgary and Edmonton. Further concern arose when the Alberta government, between 1974 and 1976, unilaterally imposed restricted development areas around both cities. While intended as utilities and transportation corridors, these RDAs were also seen as potential barriers to future expansion.

Edmonton's response took the form of a March 1979 application to the Local Authorities Board for a massive annexation, including the City of St. Albert and the entire county of Strathcona (an application which would add some 467 000 acres to the city's existing 80 000). The subsequent Board hearings lasted almost a year, comprising 106 days of

---

[64]*Ibid.*, p. 24.

testimony, the hearing of about 200 witnesses, the examination of 299 official exhibits, and the generation of 12 235 pages of transcript—at a cost of over $6 million! After all of that, the outcome was a compromise solution. While the Local Authorities Board approved a very large expansion of Edmonton's boundaries in December 1980, the Cabinet issued a revised order in June 1981, awarding the city 86 000 acres of land but not its dormitory suburbs. According to Feldman, there weren't really any winners or losers and none of the protagonists was severely harmed. "Edmonton got land on which to expand, but possibly not the lands and assessment it really wanted. St. Albert ... lost no territory. Strathcona saw 54 000 acres ... go to Edmonton."[65]

Quite apart from the great cost involved, this approach to developing reformed structures for Alberta's major urban areas has other drawbacks. It is at best a piecemeal, fragmented approach which does not consider the overall needs of the entire urban area, but instead focuses on particular territories affected by proposed annexation, and in an inevitably confrontational atmosphere. Moreover, the relentless pace of urban sprawl makes frequent annexations necessary in an attempt to keep up. Lightbody contrasts the aggressive annexation efforts of Calgary with Edmonton's more cautious approach, one which supported limited population dispersal to its established satellite communities. While Calgary still has over 90% of its regional population within its boundaries, Edmonton finds itself ringed by four cities and four urbanizing rural municipalities.[66] As discussed in the next chapter, Lightbody contends that the more fragmented structure in the Edmonton urban area is both more costly than Calgary's and less effective in promoting economic growth.

> Calgary more than Edmonton pursued the annexation efforts needed to contain sprawl.

Since the abolition of regional planning commissions in 1994 (described below), there have been two initiatives designed to provide some form of broader, regional jurisdiction which could deal with intermunicipal issues affecting the Edmonton area. The Alberta Capital Region Forum was created in March 1995, comprising 14 of the 19 former planning commission municipal members and relying on voluntary funding, especially from Edmonton. One analysis concludes that during its short

---

[65]Lionel Feldman, "Tribunals, Politics and the Public Interest: The Edmonton Annexation Case—A Response," *Canadian Public Policy*, Summer 1982, p. 371.

[66]James Lightbody, *The Comparative Costs of Governing Alberta's Metropolitan Areas*, Edmonton, Western Centre for Economic Research, Information Bulletin Number 48, January 1998, p. 4.

life the Forum was unsuccessful either in land use planning or in developing any coherent regional economic strategy.[67]

At the beginning of 1999 the Forum was replaced by the Alberta Capital Regional Alliance, comprising the city of Edmonton and 19 surrounding communities. The Ministry of Municipal Affairs has pushed for this new body as a way of gaining more cooperation in governing a region that is viewed as being inefficient because it has so many local governments and not enough regional direction.[68] In addition, the Minister announced (in December 1998) a formal review of municipal operations in the Edmonton CMA, but its terms of reference and accompanying statements by the Minister don't suggest that major restructuring is likely to result.[69] If not, matters requiring intermunicipal attention are likely to be addressed by means of joint service agreements and agencies which, as discussed below, have been prominent in Alberta local government.

Intermunicipal Agencies

Regional Planning Commissions were originally authorized in 1929, although the first (in the Edmonton area) wasn't established until 1950. Eventually 10 of these were established, covering about 70% of the area of the province.[70] Their most important function was to prepare a regional plan with which the plans of all member municipalities were expected to conform. The members of the regional planning commissions were elected representatives from the councils of the member municipalities. According to Masson,[71] while the larger municipalities were given multiple votes, they were still underrepresented on these commissions— which provided an ongoing source of friction. The commissions were abolished by the province in 1994, supposedly as an economy measure.

Alberta also has another intermunicipal agency known as the regional services commission. According to the 1981 enabling legislation, the objective of these commissions is to provide water, sanitary and storm sew-

---

[67]*Ibid.*, p. 14.

[68]Allan Chambers, "Council unprepared for regional talks," *Edmonton Journal*, November 25, 1998.

[69]James Lightbody, "Tracking Edmonton's Quest for Regional Government," *Municipal World*, forthcoming.

[70]O'Brien, *op. cit.*, p. 60.

[71]Jack Masson, with Edward Lesage, Jr., *Alberta's Local Governments: Politics and Democracy*, Edmonton, University of Alberta Press, 1994, p. 422.

erage, and waste management services, or any of them, with respect to more than one municipality. Of the 15 in existence, 6 are suppliers of water, 3 are organized for the collection of sewage, 4 are concerned with waste management, while the remaining 2 have dual responsibilities.[72] Members of the commission are representatives from the councils of member municipalities—the same indirect election arrangement found with the regional planning commissions described above. Masson claims that it is not a coincidence that the functions and political structures of regional service commissions resemble those of the regional service districts of British Columbia.[73]

Yet another example of the intermunicipal activity in Alberta is found in the more than 500 intermunicipal agreements through which municipalities purchase and sell municipal services to each other. The services most commonly subject to these arrangements are fire protection, ambulance service, recreation facilities, garbage disposal, libraries, family and community support services, airports, roads, and disaster services.[74]

Saskatchewan

The large-scale amalgamations found in a number of other provinces have not been in evidence in Saskatchewan. According to O'Brien, as urban places have grown in Saskatchewan, they have usually been able to annex land required for urban development, partly because rural municipalities don't appear to have approved of suburban fringe development within their boundaries.[75] He notes that since 1979 there have been 315 annexation and incorporation initiatives in Saskatchewan, of which 280 were approved, and that 12 of these were annexations to Regina and Saskatoon.[76] On the other hand, O'Brien finds only one example of an amalgamation in recent years, and it involved two rural municipalities.

Intermunicipal agreements have been common in Saskatchewan, especially for fire protection and road maintenance, and single purpose intermunicipal agencies are used for economic development, planning, and water.

---

[72]Masson, *op. cit.*, p. 128.

[73]*Ibid.*, p. 500, n. 62.

[74]O'Brien, *op. cit.*, p. 60.

[75]*Ibid.*, p. 58.

[76]*Ibid.*

Manitoba

The opportunity for a comprehensive reform of the overall system of local government in Manitoba was presented by a Royal Commission report in 1964.[77] It attempted a new delineation of provincial and municipal responsibilities, fairly similar to the services to people versus services to property distinction used in New Brunswick and discussed earlier in this chapter. The report also called for the division of Manitoba into 11 administrative regions, each to have a regional council composed of elected representatives from municipalities within the region. These regional councils were not to constitute another level of government, as do county councils in Ontario for example, but were to serve as a forum for developing and carrying out joint works of the municipalities. Executive authority and the responsibility for formulating policy and imposing taxes would remain with the individual municipal councils. The municipalities themselves would be considerably changed, however, with the report recommending that the existing 106 municipalities in Manitoba be amalgamated to form 40 or 50 units.

Whatever its merits, this major study was largely ignored. With strong opposition to the creation of larger municipal units, the province moved instead to formalize a system of single purpose districts for joint municipal services.[78] The system involves a combination of both intermunicipal and provincial-municipal services for rural residents on a more affordable basis than a single municipality could deliver. Examples include planning districts, conservation districts, regional development corporations, community round tables, weed control districts, veterinary services districts, and a recreational opportunities program.

Local government reform activities in Manitoba have focused instead on Winnipeg which, as the provincial capital and the centre for over half the population of the province, understandably dominates the local government scene.

Metropolitan Winnipeg

The factors leading to restructuring in Winnipeg were quite similar to those leading to the creation of Metro Toronto. The population growth af-

---

[77]*Report of the Manitoba Royal Commission on Local Government Organization and Finance* (popularly known as the Michener Report, after its chair, Roland Michener), Winnipeg, Queen's Printer, 1964.

[78]The description which follows is based on O'Brien, *op. cit.*, p. 31.

ter World War II brought the by now familiar urban problems. Expenditures soared, notably in education, while the revenues were distributed unevenly and there were wide variations in property assessment. There was inadequate sewage disposal for the area and water rationing became common. A considerable number of intermunicipal special purpose bodies operated in the Greater Winnipeg area and, while they enjoyed some success, their very existence was seen as pointing to the need for some form of area-wide government. In fact, it has been suggested that the Metro Planning Commission established in 1943 helped to shape thinking about wider planning issues and thus to create the more unified outlook which was needed for subsequent reforms.[79]

A Greater Winnipeg Investigating Commission was established in 1955 and reported in 1959 with recommendations for the establishment of a two tier system of metropolitan government in the area. Apparently the Commission was strongly influenced by the newly created system of Metropolitan Toronto and frequent consultations were held with its chair, Fred Gardiner.[80]

The reform introduced by the Manitoba government in 1960 was more modest than the Commission's recommendations and it also differed from Metropolitan Toronto in certain significant respects. A two tier system of municipal government was established, with 10 municipalities completely within the jurisdiction of the new Metropolitan Winnipeg upper tier government and 9 more partly within and partly in the outlying "additional zone" over which Metro Winnipeg had planning authority. The metro government was given full authority over all planning, zoning, and issuing of permits as well as such operating functions as assessment, civil defence, flood protection, sewage disposal (but not collection), and water (excluding local distribution). Many responsibilities which had previously been exercised by separate special purpose bodies were vested directly in the metro council and no new boards were established—in marked contrast to the Toronto system in which the numerous separate boards were retained.

In a notable departure from the Toronto approach, the 10 members of the metropolitan council were directly elected from special pie-shaped districts including both central and suburban areas. Moreover, metro

---

[79]Harold Kaplan, *Reform, Planning and City Politics: Montreal, Winnipeg, Toronto*, Toronto, University of Toronto Press, 1982, pp. 501-504.

[80]T. Axworthy, "Winnipeg Unicity," in Advisory Committee on Intergovernmental Relations, *op. cit.*, p. 90.

councillors could not also hold local office. It was hoped that this type of district and method of representation would encourage an area-wide perspective. This it did do, but almost too successfully! The metropolitan council contained a strong core of metro supporters and with more specific, parochial demands being directed at lower tier councils, they were able to take the broader view. However, in their enthusiasm they were rather aggressive in their initiatives and insufficiently sensitive to the concerns of the local councils. Municipalities which questioned whether they were getting a share of metropolitan expenditures commensurate with their financial contribution were informed that decisions were made objectively, in the public interest, not on the basis of the pork barrel.

> The direct election of Metro brought area-wide thinking, but strong local opposition.

This approach certainly contrasts with Gardiner's skilful balancing of city and suburban benefits in the Metro Toronto system. As Kaplan points out, if Metropolitan Toronto had insufficiently strong boundaries between it and its lower tier and could not avoid being exploited and manipulated by the municipal governments (especially after Gardiner), "Metro Winnipeg's problem was that it forged impermeable boundaries between it and the municipalities and thus remained singularly obtuse about the wishes of those municipalities."[81] Adding to the problems was the extent of the opposition to the new metropolitan system. Some negative reaction had been expected since the suburbs had wanted the status quo and the city of Winnipeg had wanted complete amalgamation.

> What occurred instead was a virtual municipal insurrection, an assault on metro far exceeding anyone's expectations. During its ten year history, but especially in 1961-65, metro lived under a state of siege.[82]

In the face of these attacks, "metro became even more insular and self-righteous."[83]

The attack on the metropolitan system was led by Stephen Juba, the long-time mayor of Winnipeg, and was "conducted without restraint or let-up in the mayor's characteristically strident, affectively charged, assaultive style."[84] The criticisms were kept up partly because of the provincial government's lukewarm support for its creation. Premier Roblin

---

[81]Kaplan, *op. cit.*, p. 684.

[82]*Ibid.*, p. 554.

[83]*Ibid.*, p. 556.

[84]*Ibid.*, p. 562.

had stated that there wouldn't be any review of the new system until 1965, but in the face of mounting criticism of the system he appointed a review commission in 1962. The Commission's report in 1964 reaffirmed the basic system, although some changes were made in the status of municipalities partly in and partly outside Metro Winnipeg's jurisdiction.

Attacks on the system subsided somewhat after 1965, with Premier Roblin's assertion of stronger support. Instead, attention increasingly shifted to the possibility of amalgamation of the municipalities within the system. The 1969 election of an NDP government suddenly made such a change quite probable because of the NDP's long-time support for an amalgamated approach. Indeed, even though a Local Boundaries Commission appointed by the previous government was still continuing its studies, the new provincial government began preparation of a White Paper, *Proposals for Urban Reorganization*, released December 22, 1970. From this initiative came an exciting and imaginative new structure for urban government with the establishment of Winnipeg Unicity, effective January 1st, 1972.

Winnipeg Unicity

As its name implies, Unicity replaced the two tier metropolitan system with one enlarged city government. But much more than amalgamation of municipalities was involved, and the administrative centralization for efficiency in service delivery was to be offset by various provisions for political decentralization. To understand the new structure, one needs to appreciate the philosophy and objectives of local government on which the reform was based.

Of particular note was the emphasis on the representative role of local government and the importance of citizen access and participation. In part, this was reflected in the provision for an unusually large council of 50 members, each elected from a separate ward. In addition, the Unicity legislation established 13 community committees, each covering a number of wards and consisting of the councillors from these wards. The committees were originally seen as providing a forum for public involvement and for the political decentralization of certain functions. They were to maintain close two-way communication between Unicity and its residents concerning present and potential policies, programs, and budgets. Each committee was also to be responsible for preparing its own budget for services with a local orientation which were assigned to it, a provision which suggested the possibility of some variation in local services. To advise and assist each committee, the legislation also provided for the election of a resident advisory group (RAG). In sharp contrast to most of the reform initiatives of recent years, Unicity was not created with the objective of reducing governments or cutting costs; it was intended to increase the capacity of municipal government to control and shape urban development and to promote greater social and economic equality.[85] As the preceding features of the new system suggest, Unicity was also designed "to weaken the alliance between public officials and land-based business by promoting the formation of alternative governing coalitions."[86]

A second significant feature of the new system was the attempt to build in the elements of the parliamentary model of government, particularly in terms of a separate executive responsible for providing leadership and answering to the elected council. A key provision of this model, proposed in the White Paper but deleted from the legislation, was the stipulation that the mayor be chosen by and from the members of council. Through this process, mayors could provide leadership on council because of majority support. At the same time, they would only remain in this position so long as they retained the confidence of the councillors. It was envisaged that the members of the executive committee would be chosen in the same way and, with the mayor as chair, this body would be akin to the cabinet in the parliamentary system. An important element of this system, of course, was the existence of organized political parties. Some form of political party activity had been evident in Winnipeg since 1919, but it was hoped that a more formalized party system would evolve to complement the new structure.

> Unicity's features included an emphasis on citizen participation, an attempt to create a parliamentary model, and an elaborate internal governing structure.

A third distinctive feature of Unicity was the emphasis given to the internal organization of the municipality. An attempt was made to concentrate council's role on representation and policymaking, while delegating much of the executive power of council to committees and staff, and attempting to ensure coordination of the administrative activities of the municipality. To this end, a fairly elaborate internal structure was established, some aspects of which are discussed in Chapter 9.

---

[85]Andrew Sancton, "Why Unicity Matters: An Outsider's View," in Nancy Klos (ed.), *The State of Unicity—25 Years Later*, Winnipeg, Institute of Urban Studies, 1998, p. 4.

[86]Paul G. Thomas, "Diagnosing the Health of Civic Democracy: 25 Years of Citizen Involvement With City Hall," in Klos, *op. cit.*, p. 47.

Unfortunately, the actual performance of Unicity has been increasingly disappointing. To some extent, this was inevitable, given the innovative, ambitious objectives which had been initially set for the system. Other difficulties and shortcomings were inherent in the Unicity structure or were created by changes introduced over the intervening years. These changes, and their failures, are seen by some as "related to the unwillingness, or inability, of the Manitoba government to take the necessary steps and give the new structure the resources and responsibilities it needed."[87]

A Committee of Review appointed in 1975 found that the principle of unification under a one tier government had apparently been well accepted.[88] The Committee also noted that greater equity in distributing the burden of taxation had resulted from the establishment of a single tax rate throughout the urban area, and that disparities in the level of services provided in the former separate municipal jurisdictions had been considerably reduced. On the other hand, Axworthy claims that capital works expenditures between suburbs and inner city ran as high as 7-1 in favour of the suburban areas.[89]

The Committee of Review also found that a number of the primary objectives of the new structure had not been realized. It laid much of the blame for Unicity's shortcomings on the fact that the mayor was directly elected rather than chosen from council, thereby removing the focus of leadership and accountability central to the parliamentary model. This lack of strong political leadership was especially significant given the large size of the council and the potentially fragmented outlook inherent in election by ward. Indeed, there is considerable evidence to suggest that traditional attitudes, outlooks, and practices continued to prevail within the council in spite of the changes in approach envisaged in the legislation.[90] Parochialism remained, and considerable attention was directed to the securing of public services for particular wards—often taking the

---

[87]This is the view, for example, of Paul Diamant, "Unicity: Bureaucratic Success, Political Nightmare," in Klos, *op. cit.*, pp. 17-18.

[88]*Report and Recommendations, Committee of Review, City of Winnipeg Act*, Winnipeg, Queen's Printer, October 1976.

[89]Lloyd Axworthy, "The Best Laid Plans Oft Go Astray: The Case of Winnipeg," in M.O. Dickerson, S. Drabek, and J.T. Woods (eds.), *Problems of Change in Urban Government*, Waterloo, Wilfrid Laurier Press, 1980, p. 114.

[90]According to P.H. Wichern, Jr., *Winnipeg's Unicity After Two Years: Evaluation of an Experiment in Urban Government*, a paper for the 46th annual meeting of the Canadian Political Science Association, Toronto, June 3-6, 1975.

form of a city/suburbs division, rather than the establishment of overall policies for the Unicity area. After reviewing the new system, Plunkett and Brownstone concluded that "city policy making has not been altered drastically, and that it has only been improved slightly from what it seems likely to have been if the former structure had remained unchanged."[91]

Gerecke and Reid are much more critical, labelling Unicity "a disaster." In their view, because only 16 of Unicity's original 50 seats on council were allocated to the inner city, suburban interests have dominated ever since.[92] While the amount of economic development in the Toronto area allowed both the city of Toronto and the suburbs to enjoy considerable growth (especially with the skilful balancing act of Fred Gardiner, the first Metro chair), Winnipeg's slower growth resulted in suburban development taking place at the expense of the city. Unicity Council, as discussed below, had been reduced to 15 seats in 1992, with only three members from the inner city, leaving the old city of Winnipeg as "nothing more than three wards on the rump of a suburban council."[93]

So much has the power of the inner city declined, argue Gerecke and Reid, that the fringes of Unicity are being allowed to crumble away. This comment stems from legislation in 1992 which allowed a part of Winnipeg known as Headingley to secede from Unicity and to become the 106th rural municipality in Manitoba. When presenting the legislation, the Minister characterized Headingley as a semi-rural community with no municipal water or sewer service and more in common with neighbouring rural municipalities than with Winnipeg.[94] He stressed that the secession of Headingley was not setting a precedent, and that the government remained fully committed to the concept of Unicity. Gerecke and Reid note, however, that this development has caused other fringe communities on the edge of the city, such as St. Norbert and St. Germain, to consider leaving as well. They express concern that Winnipeg may be "unravelling as a coherent unit of government."[95]

---

[91]Meyer Brownstone and T. J. Plunkett, *Metropolitan Winnipeg: Politics and Reform of Local Government*, Berkeley, University of California Press, 1983, p. 173.

[92]Kent Gerecke and Barton Reid, "The Failure of Urban Government: The Case of Winnipeg," in Henri Lustiger-Thaler (ed.), *Political Arrangements: Power and the City*, Montreal, Black Rose Books, 1992, pp. 123-142.

[93]*Ibid.*, p. 127.

[94]O'Brien, *op. cit.*, p. 32.

[95]Gerecke and Reid, *op. cit.*, p. 127.

Another major issue of concern with respect to Unicity's performance has been the effectiveness of the new structure in facilitating citizen involvement, especially through the community committees and the resident advisory groups. The roles of these bodies were insufficiently clear from the outset, although the Unicity legislation certainly gave them less power than had been envisaged by the White Paper. As discussed in the next chapter, these bodies failed to live up to their potential, and the resident advisory groups have disappeared entirely.

In June 1977 the Manitoba government adopted a number of amendments to the Unicity structure but, ironically, these changes did little to resolve the weaknesses identified and, in some cases, have intensified them. In several respects, the amendments undermined the recommendations of the Committee of Review just as the original Unicity legislation had weakened the approach of the White Paper. The Committee of Review had recommended that the mayor be elected from within the council and that the mayor appoint the chairs of the standing committees. These chairs and certain other specified members would constitute the executive and would be given the powers necessary to function as a cabinet. The Committee further recommended that the mayor and executive committee should be confirmed or replaced in their positions annually by a vote of council and that a chief critic should also be elected annually by those councillors not voting for the mayor. While it could not legislate a party system, the Committee expressed the hope and conviction that such a system would evolve "under the influence of the parliamentary characteristics of our model."

Instead, however, the revised legislation removed the mayor from the board of commissioners, and he was also replaced on the executive policy committee by a council-elected chair. These changes, together with the continuation of direct election of the mayor, seemed intended to reduce the position to the largely ceremonial role found in most Canadian municipalities. A further change saw the reduction in the size of council from 50 to 29. The number of community committees (12 since 1974) was reduced to 6 and their vague and limited powers were further reduced. They now exercised discretion only with respect to libraries, parks and recreation, and some planning functions,[96] a reflection of the growing trend toward centralization in program design and service delivery. Moreover, with greatly increased areas and populations of about 100 000, the community councils and RAGs lost the close contact and familiarity with

---

[96]Feldman Consulting Ltd., *op. cit.,* p. 67.

local issues which had been their main (and just about only) strength. Overall, the changes made in 1977 "essentially kept a weak-mayor political system, but strengthened the professional administration through centralizing power in their hands at the expense of the Community Committees and the Standing Committees."[97]

In June 1984, the Manitoba government appointed a Committee to review the Unicity legislation and governing system. The committee's 1986 report found a lack of identifiable and consistent leadership within the Unicity Council, as well as confused roles and relationships among the various elements of the city governing machinery.[98] The Committee recommended that significant powers of the city be delegated to an executive committee composed of six councillors and chaired by the mayor. The Review Committee also recommended that the community committees be given greater powers concerning the initiation, preparation, and approval of local plans and zoning.

The government's response, in a 1987 White Paper,[99] was mixed. It rejected any change which would eliminate the standing committee system. While it agreed with the mayor chairing the executive committee, the government proposed that this committee consist of 12 members not 6, with the additional members being councillors from each of the community committees as elected by those committees. Once again, therefore, the government's approach seemed designed to prevent the mayor from exercising the kind of strong leadership intended. There is no reason why these additional six members of the executive committee would necessarily follow the mayor's direction. The government agreed with increasing the planning powers of the community committees, but without any increase in financial resources to these committees—here again limiting the potential of the change.

With the defeat of the NDP government and the election of a minority Conservative government at the end of the 1980s, a Winnipeg Wards Review Committee was appointed (in February 1991) and charged with recommending a new Unicity council of between 12 and 15 members.

---

[97]Greg Selinger, "Urban Governance for the Twenty-First Century: What the Unicity Experience Tells Us," in Nancy Klos (ed.), *The State of Unicity—25 Years Later*, Winnipeg, Institute of Urban Studies, 1998, p. 90.

[98]Ministry of Urban Affairs, *Discussion Paper*, "Strengthening Local Government in Winnipeg: Proposals for Changes to the City of Winnipeg Act," Winnipeg, February 27, 1987, p. 10. The summary of recommendations which follows is based on this Discussion Paper.

[99]*Ibid.*

The resulting legislation (Bill 68) reduced the Unicity council from 29 to 15 members. This change was supposed to reduce parochialism and encourage the council to take a broader, city-wide approach to planning. It was also expected to streamline and speed up the decision-making process. The result was to be a smaller and more cohesive group to manage city hall.[100] Other changes in Bill 68 saw the community committees further reduced in number from six to five, and the RAGs abolished outright. The bold experiment in citizen participation launched in 1972 was all but gone 20 years later!

Even viewed from the narrower perspective of service delivery, the Unicity structure has not stood the test of time all that well. It is true that Unicity still contains most of the population of Winnipeg's census metropolitan area (94.5% in 1991), but much urban-related development has been taking place beyond the Unicity boundaries in recent years.[101] Over the period from 1971 to 1991, Unicity's population increased a modest 15.2%, while the population in the surrounding municipalities increased by 69.4%.[102] As a result, Unicity is becoming the home of the poor, the disadvantaged, and the unemployed. Social inequities are developing between the city and the surrounding region. If these trends continue, the city "will be called upon to address growing social problems with declining revenues from an eroding tax base...."[103]

The 1986 report of the Review Committee anticipated these problems, recommending the establishment of a new advisory and coordinating organization which would link all municipalities within the Winnipeg commuting area. While stressing that it was not recommending a new layer of regional government, the Committee acknowledged that the boundaries of Unicity were too limited for such municipal purposes as regional planning, environmental assessments, and refuse disposal.[104]

> Both population growth and service demands are undermining Unicity's boundaries.

In 1989 the Manitoba government established what became known as the Capital Region Committee, comprising three provincial ministers

---

[100]O'Brien, *op. cit.,* pp. 31-32.

[101]Andrew Sancton, *Governing Canada's City Regions: Adapting Form to Function*, Montreal, Institute for Research on Public Policy, 1994, p. 27.

[102]Institute of Urban Studies, University of Winnipeg, *Prairie Urban Report*, Issue No. 1, Volume 1, May 1996.

[103]*Ibid.*

[104]Sancton, *Canada's City Regions*, p. 27.

and the heads of council for Winnipeg and 14 surrounding municipalities. In the early years, the committee's limited meetings focused mainly on developing a strategy for sustainable development.[105] There was no indication that this committee would develop into a full-fledged upper tier government, but its very existence demonstrated that even with Unicity there were still servicing problems which overlap municipal boundaries.

In June 1998, the Manitoba government announced the creation of an independent Capital Region Panel "to provide an avenue for better cooperation and understanding between Winnipeg and its neighbours." According to the announcement, "a more coordinated approach in areas such as land use planning or delivery of services will benefit all concerned."[106] An interim report is expected by June 1999, with the final report scheduled for the fall of 1999. It is clear from this initiative that a decade after the establishment of the Capital Region Committee there are continuing concerns about how to promote better planning and coordination across the Greater Winnipeg area.

TABLE 3
Reform Highlights: Western Canada

BRITISH COLUMBIA
1965   Establishment of regional districts
1978   Regional District Review Committee identified problems
1995   GVRD Livable Region Strategic Plan approved
1999   Province shifted public transit to Greater Vancouver

ALBERTA
1950   First regional planning commission established, in Edmonton
1979   Edmonton's massive annexation initiative
1981   Provision for regional services commissions (15 set up)
1999   Alberta Regional Capital Alliance replaced Capital Forum

MANITOBA
1960   Metropolitan Winnipeg created
1964   Comprehensive study by Michener Commission
1972   Creation of Winnipeg Unicity
1977   Various Unicity amendments, including smaller council
1989   Capital Region Committee established
1991   Bill 68 reduced Unicity council from 29 to 15 members

---

[105]*Ibid.*, pp. 27-28.

[106]Manitoba Government News Release, June 17, 1998.

Overall, the reform experiences of Western Canada provide some interesting variations, especially with respect to British Columbia's regional districts and Manitoba's Unicity. For those troubled by the size and cost of regional governments or amalgamated cities, the regional districts represent a more modest, and flexible, alternative—even if some feel that they have now grown to the point where they need new governing structures. Unicity is intriguing because of its praiseworthy objectives, although they have not been realized.

Concluding Comments

In the almost five decades since Metropolitan Toronto launched the modern era of local government reform in Canada, there have been extensive changes in municipal structures in most provinces. As described in this and the preceding chapter, the reforms have taken the form of:

- the creation or strengthening of upper tier governments, as with Ontario's regional governments, the urban communities and RCMs in Quebec, and British Columbia's regional districts.
- the use of annexations and amalgamations to create large, single tier municipalities, such as with Calgary, Edmonton, Winnipeg Unicity, Toronto, Chatham-Kent, Miramichi, Halifax, and Charlottetown.
- the use of annexations and amalgamations to enlarge small and rural municipalities, notably in Ontario, Quebec, and Newfoundland.
- the use of intermunicipal boards and joint servicing agreements, as in the St. John's Metropolitan Board, the Regional Facilities Commission of Saint John, Edmonton's Capital Region Alliance, the regional services commissions in Alberta, and the recently created Greater Toronto Services Board.

With the notable exception of Winnipeg Unicity, these reforms have been preoccupied with the service delivery role of municipalities and have paid little attention to their representative and political role. This narrow focus is most evident in the various appointed or indirectly elected joint service boards, but concerns about public access and accountability have also been raised with respect to the regional districts and the indirectly elected regional governments. Improving service delivery has also been the rationale underlying most of the amalgamated single tier municipalities created in recent years. The size of some of these new municipalities (notably Toronto) and the large areas encompassing both urban and rural populations (such as Chatham-Kent in Ontario and the Halifax Regional Municipality) raise concerns about their representative role.

The shortcomings of these reforms will be explored more fully in the next chapter, but one must conclude that their limited focus hampered their ability to address the problems which prompted their introduction. Rather than building new foundations for a modern system of municipal government based equally on considerations of effective representation and efficient service delivery, most of the reforms did little more than patch up the cracks in the traditional foundation, leaving the system over-balanced in favour of the service delivery function.

CHAPTER 7
The Limits of Structural Reform and The Potential of Process Reform

The problem is not with amalgamation *per se* but the way in which it has been used or abused. When municipalities are amalgamated to facilitate the downloading of provincial responsibilities, to pursue highly elusive cost reductions, or simply to reduce the number of municipalities and politicians in furtherance of the ideological bent of the provincial governing party, one must question the appropriateness of the reforms.

Introduction

The preceding two chapters have described the extensive structural reforms of municipal government introduced over the past half-century. How effective have these reforms been, and what have been their limits or shortcomings? To answer this question, we begin by considering the main reasons used to justify the reforms and their apparent validity.

The Rationale for the Reforms

The main reasons given for the various structural reforms are:

1. To improve planning and the coordination of services, especially in urban areas.
2. To ensure equity in taxation and in the level of services received, again especially in urban areas.
3. To generate savings through reducing the duplication of multiple municipal jurisdictions.
4. To achieve economies of scale through the creation of larger units of administration.
5. To achieve less government by creating fewer municipalities and fewer municipal politicians.

The first three of these reasons, and to some extent the fourth, all relate to the perceived problems of urban sprawl and will be addressed together under that heading. The third and fourth reasons reflect the belief that "bigger is better" and will be examined under that heading. The fifth reason is essentially a municipal spillover of the neo-conservative agenda currently gripping most governments; it merits and receives separate consideration.

Dealing with Urban Sprawl

This has been the single most prevalent justification for restructuring, underlying the various city expansions through annexation and also the establishment of upper tier governments with jurisdiction over the whole urban area. Proponents of reform, the consolidationists, point to the difficulty in trying to address the needs of an area when jurisdiction is divided among a number of separate municipalities. They cite the dangers faced by a central city which is unable to control adjacent developments which affect its future. They point to the inequities which arise when businesses and wealthier individuals move to the outlying areas, leaving the central city financially weaker even as it often faces a disproportionately heavy burden of costs for programs like social assistance. Unless the city is able to expand its boundaries, or unless an upper tier is created with jurisdiction over the whole area, the central city will continue to decline and inequities in tax burdens and service levels will intensify.

This point of view was well expressed in the (McNally) *Royal Commission on the Metropolitan Development of Calgary and Edmonton,* which reported in 1956 and based its recommendations on the following two principles:

* that it is unjust and inequitable that wide variations in the tax base should exist among the local governing bodies that comprise a metropolitan area where that area is in fact one economic and social unit; and

* that a metropolitan area that is in fact one economic and social unit can ordinarily be more efficiently and effectively governed by one central municipal authority than by a multiplicity of local governing bodies.[1]

---

[1]Royal Commission Report, Chapter 12, p. 5, as quoted in James Lightbody, *The Comparative Costs of Governing Alberta's Metropolitan Areas,* Information Bulletin Number 48, January 1998, Edmonton, University of Alberta, p. 6.

A contrary point of view rejects the notion that unless someone is in charge, problems will not be resolved and production managed in an efficient, coordinated manner.[2] It characterizes this notion as the monopoly model of local government organization and contends that the inevitable result of monopolies is inefficiency and a lack of responsiveness. It asks whether Ontario Hydro or Canada Post can seriously be considered as a desirable model for metropolitan government. This contrary viewpoint, reflecting the public choice theory outlined in Chapter 1, argues that local services are diverse and thus are best provided within a multi-organizational system. Such a system better accommodates and responds to the varying needs and preferences of different parts of the metropolitan area. But the consolidationists reject this view, arguing that this local flexibility, far from being desirable, allows the perpetuation of inequities in the form of wealthy enclaves which evade responsibility for providing financial support to less well-to-do areas.

While the concerns about intermunicipal revenue and servicing inequities are real and valid, Frisken points out that provincial governments can deal with these problems in a number of ways besides restructuring.[3] They can provide unconditional grants to bolster the financial base of assessment-weak municipalities, in much the same way as the federal government has long provided

> Intermunicipal revenue and servicing inequities could be addressed in other ways than municipal restructuring.

equalization payments to "have-not" provinces. Another response is for provinces to take over or fully fund particular local services as a way of ensuring uniformity of service delivery. New Brunswick's Equal Opportunity Program is the best example of this approach, under which that province assumed full responsibility for the administration of justice, welfare, public health, and educational finance.

Paradoxically, the Ontario government has moved in the opposite direction, shifting downward functions which, by their nature, will increase inequities and inconsistencies. As a result of the new service realignment following a *Who Does What* exercise in the second half of 1996, Ontario has given its municipalities increased or total responsibility

---

[2]The explanation of this viewpoint which follows is based on Robert L. Bish, "Amalgamation: Is It the Solution?" a paper prepared for *The Coming Revolution in Local Government* conference, Halifax, March 27-29, 1996.

[3]Frances Frisken, "Jurisdictional and Political Constraints on Progressive Local Initiative," in Timothy L. Thomas (ed.), *The Politics of the City*, Toronto, ITP Nelson, 1997, pp. 163-166.

for such services as social assistance, public health, social housing, land ambulances, and public transit. There is some feeling that the province has been pushing amalgamation so forcefully to ensure that there are larger municipalities to which the downloaded powers can be assigned.

Yet another equalizing strategy that provinces can pursue is to promote a more equitable distribution of public housing throughout an urban area, on the grounds that lower-priced housing is associated with higher levels of demand for publicly funded social services and education.[4] Local resistance to most forms of public housing have limited use of this approach. Ontario set up its own housing agency (the Ontario Housing Corporation) to distribute public housing throughout the Metro Toronto area and, for a time, required municipalities to include "affordable" housing in all new residential developments—a policy withdrawn by the Conservatives shortly after they gained power in 1995.

Provinces can also try to reduce disparities through various regional development strategies. An example would be provincial efforts to limit further growth in already built-up areas coupled with policies and incentives to attract and stimulate growth in less-developed areas. This was the basis of Ontario's regional development initiatives of the 1960s and its Toronto-centred region strategy of the early 1970s—neither of which did much to alter the unfolding development pattern. To the contrary, Stein argues that the provincial government failed to invest in roads, sewers, and water mains in the right places, demonstrating a "failure of nerve" which contributed to the worsening urban sprawl.[5] Stein is even more critical of the Harris government, elected in 1995, which he claims has taken the province out of planning cities (by allowing regions to amend official plans on their own), has cut financial support for cities, and has downloaded provincial costs on them.[6]

While provincial governments have taken the position that varying service standards within a fragmented municipal system must be corrected, they have made very limited use of the many options outlined above. Instead, their preferred solution has been the establishment of new boundaries and/or new upper tier governments with jurisdiction over a metropolitan area. Instead of the provincial government making decisions on major planning and infrastructure issues affecting close to half

---

[4]*Ibid.*, p. 165.

[5]David Lewis Stein, "Special Report: The Regions at 25," *Toronto Star*, January 1, 1999.

[6]*Ibid.*

of the population of Ontario, for example, we get the new Greater Toronto Services Board, which is somehow supposed to fill the gap left by provincial inaction. Thus, we are left with a situation in which the case for municipal restructuring to address urban sprawl seems valid, but mainly because provinces have relied primarily on municipal restructuring, rather than other options, to deal with these problems.

Bigger Is Better

There are several strands to this second argument for restructuring and consolidation. It is held that some municipalities are simply too small and financially weak to discharge responsibilities. A second part of the argument suggests that having several municipalities within one relatively small geographic area (especially an area exhibiting a community of interest) represents duplication of resources and that their reduction will bring savings. It is further alleged that creating larger units of administration will allow economies of scale in the provision of services. Let us look at these points more closely.[7]

Too Small?

When it is said that municipalities are too small, one may properly ask: "too small for what?" It is hard to see how they can be too small for their primary political and representative role. In terms of proximity and ready access, this point seems obvious. McConkey makes an eloquent case for "the humanely scaled political community" which facilitates "the ongoing face-to-face work of acting and discussing together" which epitomizes democracy as "an ongoing interpersonal human endeavour."[8]

But it would be wrong to assume that all small municipalities are inherently democratic. For example, in examining early governance in Western Canadian cities, Careless found that "even in the smallest communities where face-to-face interaction was a daily occurrence, municipal elites emerged with links

> Small municipalities provide proximity and ready access, but they are not inherently democratic.

---

[7]The discussion which follows is largely based on C. Richard Tindal, "Municipal Restructuring: the myth and the reality," *Municipal World*, March 1996, pp. 3-8.

[8]Mike McConkey, "Beyond the Crisis: Proposals for a New Confederation," in Henri Lustiger-Thaler (ed.), *Political Arrangements: Power and the City*, Montreal, Black Rose Books, 1992, p. 161.

to prominent merchants, lawyers and lesser entrepreneurs."[9] Newton goes so far as to suggest that larger units of municipal government are no less democratic than small ones, and cites research which found no major variations among different-sized municipalities with respect to such measures as rates of participation, knowledge of the local government system, awareness of the location of municipal offices, or attitudes toward local services.[10] We will have more to say about the issue of participation in Chapter 10.

If the link between size and democracy is uncertain, so too is the link between size and efficiency, the search for which has been as successful as the search for the philosophers' stone, according to Newton.[11] Proponents of consolidation insist that many municipalities are simply too small to provide the increasingly wide range of services required of them. This argument is persuasive if one assumes that all services must be directly provided by the municipality. But it ignores the growing emphasis on municipalities as service arrangers and not necessarily direct service providers. If a municipality arranges for the delivery of services from a variety of suppliers, public choice proponents claim, it matters less what its own staff resources and delivery capacity may be.

> Even small municipalities can be viable when acting as service arrangers.

This point should not be pushed too far, however. Even with the current emphasis on alternative service delivery strategies, most municipalities will likely continue to provide most of their services "in house." In those instances where many services are contracted out, a municipality still requires a core of qualified staff, including some with new expertise in areas relating to the negotiation and monitoring of contracts. In addition, unless a municipality has some research and analytical capability, it will be hard-pressed to confront the rapidly changing world it faces in a systematic and thoughtful manner. So even if municipalities act more as service arrangers in the future, there will still be individual circumstances in which they may be too small to be viable units.

---

[9]J. M. S. Careless, "Aspects of Urban Life in the West, 1870-1914," in Gilbert Stelter and Alan F. J. Artibise (eds.), *The Canadian City: Essays in Urban History*, Toronto, McClelland and Stewart, 1977.

[10]K. Newton, "Is Small Really So Beautiful? Is Big Really So Ugly? Size, Effectiveness, and Democracy in Local Government," in *Political Studies*, Vol. XXX, No. 2, 1982, pp. 190-206.

[11]*Ibid.*, p. 193.

Wasteful Duplication?

Proponents of consolidation insist that, for example, having four roads departments in four separate municipalities in one urban area represents wasteful duplication and expense. Obviously, money could be saved, they claim, by eliminating this duplication through the creation of one combined roads department. At first glance, this argument seems logical, but where—specifically—will the savings arise? Well, since there will be one department head, not four, three salaries will be saved for a start. Not necessarily. Experience has shown that the new department head may command a larger salary in recognition of a quadrupled workload, and that other costs may arise for additional support staff, upgraded computer equipment, and the like.

What other savings will result from combining the four roads departments? Bear in mind that none of the roads have disappeared as a result of amalgamation. If staff and equipment were deployed at full capacity under the old structure, it is reasonable to assume that the combined staff and equipment will still be needed to look after what are still the same roads. Some rationalization is possible, of course. To use the favourite example of proponents of amalgamation, we can avoid situations where snowplows from two or more levels of government travel over the same roads, some with their plows raised and on their way to a more distant work assignment. But rationalization of service delivery has already been happening in recent years, under the pressure of fiscal restraint. The parochial, "stand-alone" practices of old are no longer affordable; nor are they tolerated by local citizens increasingly determined to see value for their tax dollar.

So the duplication argument leads to a mixed conclusion. Yes, there may be a way to utilize the staff and equipment of four municipal roads departments more efficiently. But must there be consolidation to bring about these savings? Consolidationalists believe so, while others argue that if there are savings to be had through a better deployment of staff and roads equipment, this can be negotiated (and increasingly is being negotiated) through intermunicipal agreement and collaboration.

Public choice proponents dispute the notion that having several municipal departments in one area must be wasteful duplication. They point out that having several separate bodies providing similar products or services is seen as healthy competition in the private sector. They also question why having one large municipal service provider should be desirable when this arrangement is seen as an undesirable monopoly in the private sector. These arguments, of course, reflect the public choice view of a political market place in which informed consumers choose amongst different packages of products and prices (taxes). For public choice proponents, the more separate municipalities there are, the more service choices are available to local citizens.

There is considerable evidence to suggest that it is not the public or private sector that is critical to operating efficiency, but the degree to which competitive forces are at work. "Where there's competition, you get better results, more cost-consciousness, and superior service delivery."[12] Support for this assertion is found in a study of the solid waste collection experiences of two municipalities in the Greater Vancouver area. One had periodic competition because of a contract with a private firm and the other had a permanent public monopoly under which city crews collected all solid waste. During the study period of the 1980s, crew productivity increased sharply for *both* municipalities. According to the study authors,[13] the key factor in explaining this pattern was the regional competitive pressure on solid waste collection producers in the Greater Vancouver area. They explained that public producers are often exposed to unsolicited bids from private firms and to cost comparisons among municipalities in the region.

Having several municipalities in one urban area presents choices for the consumer of municipal services, according to supporters of public choice. Residents or businesses thinking of locating in the area have several combinations of products (municipal services) and prices (tax levels) to choose among—just the sort of consumer choice which is seen as so desirable in the private sector. Those already located within one of the several municipalities can make comparisons and can lobby, pressure, even "vote with their feet" in an attempt to bring about improvements. This public choice argument presumes, of course, that consumers of municipal services are well informed about what is available at what cost in their own and neighbouring municipalities, and that they have the time, resources, and mobility to use this knowledge effectively. Many reject these assumptions.

Opponents of amalgamation argue that the formation of one large municipality embracing a whole urban area not only removes the possi-

---

[12]Jim Flanagan, auditor of the City of Phoenix, as quoted in David Osborne and Ted Gaebler, *Reinventing Government*, New York, Penguin Books, 1993, p. 79.

[13]James McDavid and Gregory Schlick, "Privatization versus union-management cooperation: the effects of competition on service efficiency in municipalities," *Canadian Public Administration*, Fall 1987, pp. 472-488.

bility of consumer choice, but also removes or greatly reduces the opportunity for innovation, creativity, intermunicipal comparisons, and other activities which serve to enhance productivity and to generate cost savings. An examination of five municipalities will typically reveal five different ways of performing a particular function. It is also likely that one way will be superior and more cost-effective. If the five municipalities are amalgamated to form a single municipality, the odds are only 1 in 5 that the superior methodology will be embraced by the new municipality[14] — not a very tempting proposition.

Proponents of consolidation dispute this point, claiming that the new municipality will seek out the best practices of its predecessors. But in the short run at least, most energies seem to be directed to managing the transition to the new municipality. Old and familiar practices and procedures may be continued within the new structure, and not necessarily the most effective ones. Often, one of the former municipalities (usually the largest one) gains a controlling interest in the new municipality and its practices, good, bad, or indifferent, are the ones that prevail.

Reduced Costs?

The contention that amalgamation reduces costs relates back to the previous argument about wasteful duplication. However, since reducing costs has been the primary reason given by provincial governments to explain their amalgamation initiatives in the 1990s, this argument merits careful examination. Those who see cost savings seem to proceed from three main assumptions, whose validity needs to be considered:

1. That the existing range and level of services will continue largely unchanged within the new municipality;
2. That the bulk of the anticipated cost savings will arise from very substantial downsizing of staff; and
3. That economies of scale will result from providing services over larger areas as a result of amalgamations.

Past experience tells us that there are strong upward pressures on costs after an amalgamation. There is pressure to standardize services, by moving to the highest level previously prevailing—that is, by levelling up, not levelling down. There is pressure to standardize salaries and wages, by levelling up to the highest remuneration which previously existed. Additional staff may need to be hired because of a loss of volunteer activity associated with the previous, smaller municipalities. The new

---

[14]This example is provided in an analysis by David Barber, Director of the Cordillera Institute, letter dated July 9, 1998.

municipality may also face demands for additional levels of supervisory personnel, more support staff, or new specialized positions.

Partly because of these pressures, the substantial savings which are claimed by amalgamation proponents have not usually materialized in the past. Sancton makes this point quite forcefully, citing examples from Britain, the United States, and Canada. He notes that numerous studies in the United States have shown that larger municipalities spend more money per capita on most services than do smaller ones, and that the federal government's Advisory Commission on Intergovernmental Relations had reversed its position by 1987 and no longer advocated municipal consolidation.[15] A recent Newfoundland study found no basis for widespread amalgamation as a method of reducing costs and held that a case could be made that greater efficiencies would result from retaining a larger number of smaller municipalities.[16] A study on the determinants of municipal expenditure in Ontario found that within a regional government structure, the larger the municipality, the higher the per capita expenditures.[17]

To be fair, there are contrary points of view. For example, Lowery and Lyons found little support for the contention that a fragmented municipal structure reduces delivery costs.[18] Lightbody claims just the opposite, through an analysis which concludes that costs are higher in the fragmented municipal structure in the Edmonton area than in Calgary's more unified structure.[19]

Vojnovic provides a very interesting preliminary analysis of the effects of five recent amalgamations of Canadian municipalities. His findings demonstrate the futility of generalizing about the link between amalga-

---

[15]Andrew Sancton, "Reducing costs by consolidating municipalities: New Brunswick, Nova Scotia and Ontario," in *Canadian Public Administration*, Fall 1996, p. 272.

[16]Final Report, *Task Force on Municipal Regionalization*, St. John's, September 1997, p. 53.

[17]J. Kushner, I. Masse, T. Peters and L. Soroka, "The determinants of municipal expenditures in Ontario," *Canadian Tax Journal* (1996), vol. 44, no. 2.

[18]David Lowery and William Lyons, "The Impact of Jurisdictional Boundaries: An Individual-Level Test of the Tiebout Model," *Journal of Politics*, February 1989, as quoted in Katherine A. Graham, Susan D. Phillips, and Allan M. Maslove, *Urban Governance in Canada*, Toronto, Harcourt Brace & Company, Canada, 1998, p. 22.

[19]Lightbody, *op. cit.*

mation and costs.[20] In some instances where costs decreased, it was because provincial grants were provided to smooth and sweeten the transition process. In other instances, costs went up significantly, but at least partly because of provincial downloading, increased service standards, or other factors not directly related to the act of amalgamation.

Opinions on this issue are strongly held, and both sides can assemble arguments and studies which support their point of view. It is our conclusion that the bulk of the evidence suggests that amalgamations do not lead to cost reductions. At the very least, one can say that the diverse findings on this issue certainly

> Overall, the diverse findings on this issue do not support the substantial savings claimed by consolidationists.

do not support the substantial savings claimed by proponents of amalgamation. The Golden Report on the Greater Toronto Area cautioned that the cost-saving benefits of amalgamation are "often over-stated," noting that diseconomies of scale can be created, that upward migration of wages and service standards often occurs, and that "with fewer municipalities against which to benchmark, there is less opportunity to measure relative performance and less pressure to keep costs low."[21]

To the extent that savings are achieved as a result of the current crop of amalgamations, it will be because the present era of fiscal restraint prompts governments to treat municipal employees much more harshly. In earlier restructurings, such as the creation of regional governments in Ontario, it was common practice to guarantee all existing employees job security for at least one full year, and then to use attrition as much as possible to achieve the desired downsizing. Today, the amalgamation process is viewed by some as an opportunity to establish an entirely new municipality which has no obligations to past employees—or to past collective agreements, if they can be voided—and which can set up a much leaner, cheaper operation. Indeed, Sancton speculates that proponents of amalgamation find that it provides convenient political cover for further reducing the size of municipal bureaucracies. Years of restraint and cutbacks, accompanied by assertions that all the "fat" had been cut out, left little room or rationale for further downsizing. Amalgamating, however, offers an opportunity for another round of cuts, with any savings

---

[20]Igor Vojnovic, *Municipal Consolidation in the 1990s: An Analysis of Five Canadian Municipalities*, Toronto, ICURR Press, 1997.

[21]Report of the GTA Task Force (Anne Golden, Chair), *Greater Toronto*, January 1996, pp. 212-213.

being attributed to the merger. "Whatever savings are made in these circumstances have more to do with capturing convenient opportunities than with capturing economies of scale."[22]

Even where this strategy is attempted, one result is substantial cost increases in the early going because of the severance packages which must be paid. Another result is often the discovery that there has been excessive downsizing and that too much experience and expertise has been lost. In such cases, new costs arise when additional staff have to be (re)hired. The new city of Kingston, which came into existence on January 1, 1998, experienced these difficulties. A concerted effort had been made to reduce by several hundred the staff complement which had existed amongst the three former municipalities being amalgamated. Within a few months of operation, however, Kingston determined that it was understaffed by close to a hundred and that buyout packages and early retirements had left some types of expertise in short supply and had adversely affected some departments more than others.

Provinces such as Ontario and Nova Scotia attempted to prevent the upward migration of salaries following amalgamation by passing legislation setting out new rules governing the collective bargaining process. Ontario's Bill 136 (the Public Sector Labour Relations Transition Act), introduced in June 1997, initially proposed to remove the right to strike during the negotiation of a first contract following restructuring. The original provisions of the bill were clearly unfavourable to labour and appeared to be a fairly transparent attempt to give municipalities greater bargaining leverage to extract savings from workers under the guise of restructuring. The government backed down, however, in the face of fierce opposition, and the legislation was revised in several respects, including restoration of the right to strike. Nova Scotia passed the Public Sector Compensation Act which prohibited any pay increases for public sector employees between November 1994 and November 1997. While this legislation avoided pay increases in the newly amalgamated city of Halifax, it also left employees of the new municipality with 21 different collective agreements providing widely varying salaries and working conditions, even for personnel with essentially the same job duties[23]— hardly an arrangement conducive to good morale and working relations.

---

[22]Andrew Sancton, "The Politics of Amalgamating Municipalities to Reduce Costs: Some Personal Reflections," *Local Services Research Review*, Newsletter of the Local Government Institute, University of Victoria, Volume 1, Number 2, Winter 1996.

[23]Vojnovic, *op. cit.*, pp. 103-104.

But, what about the savings to be achieved from economies of scale? Economies of scale arise where the per unit cost of delivering a service falls as the quantity of the service provided increases. Such savings are real, but each municipal service is likely to achieve these economies at a different scale of production. The optimum size of government may be different for fire services than for roads or police. For example, studies by Kitchen have shown that the lowest cost per gallon of water supplied existed in municipalities in the range of 25 000 to 35 000 people, whereas the least expensive delivery systems for solid waste collection were found in municipalities under 5000, with per capita costs then rising until municipalities reached about 325 000 residents.[24]

> Economies of scale do arise, but at different population sizes for different services.

If one wants to achieve economies of scale, amalgamation is a problematic choice, because while the larger municipality which results may be more efficient for delivering some municipal services it will also be less efficient for delivering others. Moreover, if municipalities are made too large, diseconomies of scale arise—because of problems delivering services to remote areas within an enlarged jurisdiction and because of bureaucratic congestion. An example of this latter situation is provided by a study of the financial impact of merging the 11 lower tier municipalities and the regional government in Ottawa-Carleton into one large municipality. It concluded[25] that the new single municipality would have increased annual expenditures of between $25 million and $77 million, because the efficient low-cost operational approach of smaller municipalities would be lost and would not be compensated by any significant economies of scale. Most municipalities, and in particular the rural municipalities, have lower service levels and lower administrative costs; both would tend to rise toward Ottawa's levels. The upper end of the range of cost increase (the $77 million) assumes that service levels and administration would move substantially toward Ottawa levels, particularly for fire, police, recreation, and culture. Notwithstanding this study, amalgamation discussions continue in Ottawa-Carleton, with considerable pressure to create one large municipality which is supposed to save money.

---

[24]Harry Kitchen, "Does Amalgamation Really Produce Cost Savings?" paper presented to Municipal Amalgamation Conference, Halifax, April 25, 1995.

[25]The summary which follows is based on Price Waterhouse, *Study of the Financial Impact of One-Tier Government in Ottawa-Carleton*, Final Report, August 27, 1992, p. i.

Providing Less Government

The third and final rationale for amalgamation singled out for discussion is the claim that people are over-governed and desire less government and fewer politicians. This view reflects an anti-government bias which is central to the right-wing revolution which has swept across North America in the past couple of decades. Nowhere has this rationale been more in evidence than in the municipal reform initiatives pursued by the Conservatives in Ontario since their election in June 1995. They premise their restructuring on the notion that local politicians and staff are "the problem," that there are too many of them, they are wasteful in their practices, their operations are inefficient, they tax too readily, and they spend irresponsibly.[26]

The answer, according to the Conservatives, is to provide less government. Every amalgamation in Ontario prompts a press release from the Ministry of Municipal Affairs and Housing which tracks how many fewer municipalities and municipal politicians there are as a result. The statistics are presented as a self-evident gain for society. But it must be understood that what amalgamation brings is not so much less government as bigger governments, farther removed from the local communities they used to serve. People who feel over-governed are often reacting to large and bureaucratic structures that seem engulfed in "red tape." Yet these are the kind of structures which can result when municipalities are enlarged through amalgamation. Proponents of consolidation claim that "customers" will receive improved access through new "one-stop shopping" facilities. Opponents argue that citizens already had such a contact point before amalgamation—in the small, "all-in-one-spot" municipal offices that have disappeared.

If one believes in local democracy, why is it so desirable to have fewer elected local politicians? What are the implications of enlarging municipalities to the point where serving on council ceases to be a part-time activity available to all, and becomes the preserve of the full-time, professional politician? One consequence of this change is that council salaries go up to handle the increased workload, often cancelling virtually all of the savings which were supposed to occur with fewer politicians. Consider the experience in the new city of Halifax where total salary costs for councillors were only reduced by 24% even though the number of

---

[26]T. J. Downey and R. J. Williams, "Provincial agendas, local responses: the 'common sense' restructuring of Ontario's municipal governments," in *Canadian Public Administration*, Summer 1998, p. 234.

councillors was reduced by 60%. What value does one place on the amount of local representation lost, as compared to the savings of 0.07% in the annual operating budget of the new municipality?[27]

Summary: Reviewing the Rationale

What conclusions can be drawn from our analysis of the main reasons advanced for municipal restructuring? The first rationale, dealing with urban sprawl, is the one which most holds up to close examination. A case can clearly be made for municipal consolidation to address the need for area-wide planning, for coordinated economic development, and for promoting greater equity in service levels and tax burdens. As discussed, there are other ways to address these needs, perhaps just as effectively, but since provincial governments have not seen fit to use these other means to any large extent, we are left with structural reform as the option.

It has been argued that "if there is general agreement that regional planning is necessary, it will emerge without a regional government structure,"[28] as the creation of Greater Vancouver's Livable Region Plan would seem to confirm. It is also true that economic growth can occur even with a fragmented structure, as is evident from the dramatic turnaround of Moncton, cited in 1992 and 1993 by the *Globe and Mail Report on Business* as one of the top five cities in which to do business. But in today's global economy, "focus for international competition is difficult when multiple units of government exist within a metropolitan centre." According to Lightbody, businesses today expect a regional environment in which there is some reasonable sense of direction; "where competitive city systems provide this, and where national boundaries and geographic location are increasingly less bothersome, cities that cannot compete will lose out."[29]

There are a number of other circumstances in which restructuring may be appropriate or desirable. If boundaries are keeping apart people with a high degree of interaction who want to be together, amalgamation may be the answer. If municipalities are so small and financially weak that they can't maintain a minimum core of capable staff, amalgamation may be necessary. If a municipality finds that its neighbours remain

---

[27]All figures from Vojnovic, pp. 104 and 118.

[28]Andrew Sancton, *Governing Canada's City Regions: Adapting Form to Function,* Montreal, Institute for Research on Public Policy, 1994, p. 45.

[29]Lightbody, *op. cit.*, p. 13.

parochial and are unwilling to pursue cooperative ventures which would benefit all, it may understandably pursue amalgamation. If two municipalities provide much the same range and level of services, and have much the same salary scales, amalgamation may not produce the upward pressures on services and costs previously cited.

On the other hand, the other arguments discussed above do not make a convincing case for consolidation. Least persuasive, ironically, is the argument most cited by provincial governments and other proponents of restructuring, that it leads to substantial cost-savings. However, it is perhaps understandable that provinces are reluctant to acknowledge that a primary objective, or at least consequence, of amalgamation is instead to redistribute costs to provide greater equity.

> While the case with respect to urban sprawl is strong, the other arguments advanced for amalgamation are much less convincing.

Taking everything into account, it appears that amalgamation has often been pursued for the wrong reasons and to an excessive degree. It has been presented as a positive step because it results in less government, even though this is manifested in larger and more remote local government as well. It has been oversold as a panacea for municipalities facing a financial squeeze because of actions taken by the senior levels of government. In some cases, the provincial level has pushed amalgamation to create larger units of local government which can take on new downloaded responsibilities which, arguably, do not belong at that level. Perhaps worst of all, it has been imposed or strongly promoted by provincial governments as the *only* reform option for municipalities to pursue. Yet it is but one of several structural options and, as discussed later in this chapter, there are also process improvements which are even more beneficial as a reform alternative. The problem is not amalgamation *per se* but the way in which it has been used or abused.

Analyzing the Structural Reforms

Let us now move from an examination of the rationale for the reforms to a closer look at the reforms themselves. While regional governments and urban communities were established in the 1960s and early 1970s, the main form of restructuring has been the expansion of the central city, through annexation or amalgamation, in an attempt to provide a coordinated approach to planning and the provision of services. This "one big municipality" model is found in places such as Calgary, Winnipeg Unicity, Toronto, and Halifax. A second type of reform involves the use of joint servicing boards to address intermunicipal issues and joint servicing possibilities. Examples include the former St. John's Metropolitan Board and the Metropolitan Authority of Halifax, the Regional Facilities Commission of Saint John, and the Greater Toronto Services Board. The regional district of British Columbia is either the most highly developed version of this second model, or a limited version of a regional government—depending on how one chooses to characterize it. As discussed below, neither of these models is free of problems.

The One Big Municipality Model

The strength of this first model is supposed to lie in its ability to address region-wide issues and servicing needs. It is debatable, however, how effective the new structures have been in achieving their objectives. A major problem has been that continuing growth and sprawl quickly over-spill the new boundaries which are created and result again in the lack of unified jurisdiction over the urban whole. There is no better example than the Toronto area which "has probably experienced more formal analysis and diagnostic attention over the post-war years than any well-heeled Hollywood thespian."[30] Yet the resulting network of regional governments (including Metro Toronto) were unable to prevent the continuous urban mass which spread across the "Golden Horseshoe" of Central Ontario. The Montreal Urban Community found itself in a similar position. In response, we now have something approaching a third level of local government in our two largest metropolitan areas. The Greater Toronto Services Board commenced operations January 1, 1999, and a new advisory body known as a commission de développement pour la métropole has been legislated, but not yet set up, for Montreal.

If policy makers continue to take the position that one urban area should be under the jurisdiction of one municipality, it is hard to see how we can avoid the instability and upheaval of periodic rounds of restructuring as new amalgamations are introduced every couple of decades in an attempt to recapture overspilled populations. The end result is the development of municipalities so large that it is difficult to envisage them as units of "local" government.

---

[30]James Lightbody, "A new perspective on clothing the emperor: Canadian metropolitan form, function and frontiers," in *Canadian Public Administration*, Fall 1997, p. 451.

It is not just the growing size of these consolidated municipalities which is a concern. Because their restructuring has been predicated on the need to address servicing matters, it is the service delivery role of municipal government which has received the attention. With the notable exception of Winnipeg Unicity, virtually all the municipal restructuring initiatives paid very little attention to the representative role of municipalities—a role which was often undermined by the reforms. Ontario's experience with regional governments is instructive in this regard, as outlined below.

> Ontario's regional governments illustrate how the reforms can undermine the representative aspect and inhibit public access.

The consolidation of lower tier municipalities reduced the number of councils and, with the enlarged areas, many citizens felt that their municipal government was less accessible and less sensitive to their particular needs. The feeling of alienation was even stronger with respect to the regional councils, which not only appeared remote but also had taken over a number of functions previously exercised at the lower tier. The increase in regional staff made the system seem increasingly bureaucratic and the essentially indirect election of regional councillors did little to generate public involvement in, and support for, the regional system.

One analysis of the Ontario reforms discerns a change in the balance of power at the local level and describes "a major increase in the influence of public servants, especially regional ones, at the expense of local elected officials and residents."[31] Rather than being closely involved in the operations of the municipality, councillors appear relegated to a role of responding to policy proposals put forward by their staff. This analysis further notes that with fewer councils and more formal procedures for handling business, the nature of citizen participation in local government also changed. "The emphasis now was on scheduling an appointment before a council and presenting a brief outlining one's arguments ... instead of a spontaneous appearance and an informal discussion...." The result was a shift of power among citizens since "the new technical rules of citizen participation not surprisingly favour those with formal argumentative skills or those who can afford to hire people with these skills."[32]

---

[31]Henry J. Jacek, "Regional Government and Development: Administrative Efficiency versus Local Democracy," in Donald C. MacDonald (ed.), *The Government and Politics of Ontario,* Toronto, Nelson, 1985, p. 111.

[32]*Ibid.*, p. 112.

Developments since in Ontario have done little to provide reassurance. Granted, direct election of upper tier councils, or at least the heads of these councils, has become more prevalent over the past decade or so. But the latest round of restructuring has again been preoccupied with improving service delivery and with cutting costs. Much less attention has been paid to how well local citizens will be able to participate in a municipal government which has a much larger population and/or covers a much larger geographic area. According to a recent analysis, the representative capacity of the municipal system has been severely hampered by the elimination of significant numbers of elected councillors.[33] Nor is it helped by the current preoccupation with making municipalities more business-like. Instead of concern for enhancing the democratic nature of municipal government, we get promises about improved customer service and one-stop shopping kiosks.

As noted, Winnipeg Unicity stands out among the examples of the one big municipality model because of its innovative efforts to generate citizen participation. Since the community committee of Winnipeg, or some variation of it, continues to be recommended and attempted in municipal restructurings today, let us take a closer look at its possibilities.

What About Community Councils?

When Unicity was created in 1972, 13 community committees were established, each covering a number of wards and consisting of the councillors from those wards. They were originally seen as providing a forum for public involvement and for political decentralization. Each committee was to be responsible for preparing its own budget for services with a local orientation which were assigned to it. In addition, resident advisory groups (RAGs) were to be elected to advise and assist each committee.

Overlooked in the early enthusiasm for these innovative new mechanisms was the fact that the community committees were not lawmaking bodies and had no taxing powers. While there were suggestions that they would in some respects fulfil the role of the former lower tier municipalities, Higgins provides a more accurate description in calling them "sub-committees of the city council."[34]

---

[33]Downey and Williams, *op. cit.*, p. 231.

[34]Donald J. H. Higgins, *Urban Canada: Its Government and Politics*, Toronto, Macmillan, 1977, p. 150.

Even less specific was the mandate of the resident advisory groups— to advise and assist the community councils! As Higgins outlines, the initial response from local citizens was strong, with almost 500 advisors elected at the first meetings of the resident advisory groups.[35] Disillusionment set in, however, with the realization that these groups had little influence and that even if their particular community committee was responsive to their views, the committee only comprised from 3 to 6 of the 51 members (including the mayor) of council.

Other analysts haven't even been as positive as Higgins. Axworthy, for example, feels that the consultative mechanisms made very little impact and notes that in a 1973 survey "less than 5% of citizens recalled ever having contact with the RAGs or community committees."[36] He also describes an increasingly centralized system characterized by bureaucratic "stonewalling." According to Axworthy, "Civic administrators became notorious for not divulging information, for controlling the activity of the junior members of departments in their public dealings, and for refusing public access to information."[37] Another study notes that in 1976 the Unicity council prohibited the community committees from continuing with the allocation of modest sums to various community cultural and recreational groups. This action also blocked the limited financial support which had existed for the RAGs, and in 1981—10 years after the creation of these much-heralded instruments of citizen participation—council was allocating RAGs on average $400 each![38]

In June 1977, the size of the Unicity council was reduced from 50 to 29. The number of community committees (12 since 1974) was reduced to 6 and their vague and limited powers were further reduced. With much larger areas and populations of approximately 100 000, the community councils and RAGs lost the close contact and familiarity with local issues which had been their main strength. When Unicity's council was further reduced to 15 members in the early 1990s, the community committees were reduced in number from 6 to 5, and the RAGs were abolished.

---

[35]*Ibid.*, p. 203.

[36]Lloyd Axworthy, "The Best Laid Plans Oft Go Astray: The Case of Winnipeg," in M.O. Dickerson, S. Drabek and J.T. Woods (eds.), *Problems of Change in Urban Government*, Waterloo, Wilfrid Laurier Press, 1980, p. 117.

[37]*Ibid.*, p. 116.

[38]Mathew J. Kiernan and David C. Walker, "Winnipeg," in Warren Magnusson and Andrew Sancton (eds.), *City Politics in Canada*, Toronto, University of Toronto Press, 1983, pp. 236-237.

Montreal's experience with a similar kind of consultative body has also been discouraging. When the Montreal Citizen's Movement (MCM) was an opposition party, it made much of the importance of neighbourhood councils which would involve the decentralization of city government. In its party platform for the 1986 municipal election, the MCM proposed decentralizing municipal services to 10 neighbourhoods directed by decision-making councils. However, after its election victory, what the MCM set up in 1987 were 9 district (not neighbourhood) *advisory* (not decision-making) councils. All power remained centralized in the city council and its executive committee. With populations of up to 150 000 each, the districts were too large for effective grassroots representation. According to one observer, the district advisory councils (DACs) became little more than a place where local and individual concerns could be raised, and then easily lost in the ensuing paper shuffle.[39]

> Montreal's experience with community councils has, like that of Winnipeg, been disappointing.

Thomas also describes as disappointing the performance of the DACs.[40] He notes that it soon became apparent that the DACs had very limited jurisdiction, lacked decision-making power, and had their agendas set by Montreal's powerful executive committee. Any recommendations from the DACs were sent directly to the executive committee for study, a process which, according to one councillor, "is worrisome in terms of what it says about democracy at city hall."[41]

In 1994, the MCM lost control of council to the Vision Montreal party, led by Pierre Bourque. During the election campaign Bourque had talked about abolishing some of the consultative structures created by the MCM. He made good on his promise, centralizing power even more in the executive committee and turning the district advisory councils into "nothing more than a personal public relations tool."[42] Before the end of his term, Bourque had set up 16 neighbourhood councils and following his reelection in November 1998, he was talking about devolving service delivery to these neighbourhoods. But since he has moved to change the rules of

---

[39]Henry Aubin, "Promises Not To Keep," *Montreal Gazette*, November 8, 1994.

[40]Timothy Lloyd Thomas, *A City With a Difference*, Montreal, Véhicule Press, 1997, pp. 108-109.

[41]Councillor Ingrid Peritz, as quoted in *ibid.*, p. 109.

[42]Editorial, "Democracy, Bourque-style," *Montreal Gazette*, January 12, 1999.

procedure to restrict council debate, limit the length of speeches, and expand the use of closure,[43] it would seem that a centralized regime will continue to operate in Montreal.

A community council was established for the Sackville area of Halifax County in 1988, to head off Sackville's move to incorporate and to separate from the county.[44] Instead, five county councillors from districts in the Sackville area were authorized to meet as a community council, to recommend on matters of local concern and on area rates for services not included in the county's general rate. Following what has been described as "a period of successful operation" in Sackville, a similar community council structure was set up in the Cole Harbour/Westphal area of the county. This concept was incorporated into the legislation establishing regional municipalities in Halifax and Cape Breton, and five community councils were established for Halifax. One of these recently disbanded, citing a lack of issues and low community interest as the reasons.[45]

Notwithstanding the generally disappointing results associated with community committees and other forms of local advisory councils, they continue to be recommended as a form of replacement for lower tier municipalities which are abolished as part of a major amalgamation. Thus, six community councils have been established within the new city of Toronto, to represent (initially at least) the communities of the six municipalities which have disappeared. Similarly, the Constituent Assembly report which called for the amalgamation of all six lower tier municipalities and the Region of Hamilton-Wentworth into a single municipality[46] proposed community councils (their number and areas to be determined) to represent communities of interest. Each committee would be made up of the councillors elected to the amalgamated municipal council from that community, together with other members to be selected by means to be determined. The community committees would provide a mechanism for citizen participation, for monitoring the delivery of services within the particular community, and for making locally specific decisions.

---

[43] *Ibid.*

[44] The discussion which follows is based on Kell Antoft and Jack Novack, *Grassroots Democracy: Local Government in the Maritimes*, Halifax, Dalhousie University, 1998, p. 33.

[45] Communication from Jack Novack, March 22, 1999.

[46] Constituent Assembly on the Municipal Government System in Hamilton-Wentworth, Final Report, *Better Municipal Government*, March 31, 1996.

Community councils or committees created in such circumstances are almost doomed to failure. If they are given any significant powers at all, they will be exploited by those who had opposed amalgamation in the first place and there will be constant pressure to expand the duties of the councils so that they can somehow approximate the municipal councils which were lost. If, on the other hand, as is their more likely fate, they are confined to inconsequential matters without any real budgetary or policy impact, then participation inevitably wanes.

The Joint Services Board Model

This model, by its very name, is also focused on the issue of service delivery, but it can address this issue in a much more flexible manner than the one big municipality model. Since the optimum size for economies of scale varies by municipal service, the best way to achieve such economies would presumably be to arrange for the provision of different services over different combinations of municipalities, usually under the administration of a joint board. These services can be provided by contracting with a municipality or with the private sector—wherever the best deal for the taxpayer can be arranged. The fact that various servicing contracts will come up for renewal periodically also injects a competitive element into municipal operations which, as previously noted, tends to increase productivity among all municipalities in the area. Taking this approach is consistent with the concept of the municipality as a service arranger, not necessarily a service provider.

However, large numbers of boards and intermunicipal agreements result in complex, time-consuming, confusing, and less accountable governing arrangements, claim critics of this approach. Moreover, the existence of such joint arrangements is proof, they argue, that a state of interdependence exists and that amalgamation should therefore follow. When problems arise with the operation of joint boards, pressure for municipal restructuring mounts. For example, the decision to introduce a major amalgamation in the Halifax area was apparently influenced by dissatisfaction with the performance of the Halifax-Dartmouth Metropolitan Authority established in 1962, its internal wrangling, and ineffectiveness in dealing with major challenges.[47] The previous chapter cited a number of

> Intermunicipal boards are criticized for being complex and less accountable and/or are seen as a stepping-stone to full amalgamation.

---

[47]Graham et al., *op. cit.*, p. 83.

other examples of joint boards and their difficulties, including the St. John's Metropolitan Area Board, abolished in 1992 when a number of municipalities were amalgamated in that area of Newfoundland.

Yet various joint service boards continue to exist and to be recommended. The success of joint servicing arrangements in the Moncton area was noted in Chapter 6 as a factor in the recommendation not to impose amalgamation. Nor did the fragmented structure inhibit economic development, as evidenced by the success of the Greater Moncton Economic Commission, with representation from 11 municipalities.[48] There is also no reason why having a variety of servicing agreements should be seen as so complex and confusing, as has been alleged. The experience of bodies such as the regional districts in British Columbia indicates that widely varying functional arrangements can be managed without apparent difficulty. As to the charge of lack of accountability, it can be argued that accountability is enhanced through the use of servicing contracts and performance standards. If the board or the particular servicing arrangement doesn't measure up, municipalities will presumably pursue other avenues.

Moreover, even if joint servicing agreements and joint boards should eventually give way to municipal amalgamation, this should not be seen as a drawback or failure. To the contrary, such initial arrangements allow municipalities to pursue some of the benefits of closer collaboration without necessarily giving up their separate status. At the same time, as various services are merged and harmonized, the municipalities develop relationships which would facilitate amalgamation, should that step be found desirable at some later stage. Moreover, the adjustments and costs of any such amalgamation will be lessened as a result of the groundwork which has been laid.[49]

Whatever its possible strengths, since the joint services board essentially acts as an agent on behalf of the municipalities for whom it provides services, its composition and focus is likely to be weak with respect to addressing region-wide issues. This problem has been evident with respect to a number of joint boards discussed in the preceding chapter. There are also concerns about accountability with joint boards which are made up of appointed or indirectly elected members, especially if they take on a significant number of responsibilities. The best example is provided by the regional districts of British Columbia, which are widely re-

---

[48]Vojnovic, *op. cit.*, p. 19.

[49]This point is also made in *ibid.*, p. 118.

garded as a very successful and flexible instrument for joint service delivery. In the previous chapter, Patrick Smith cites the planning work of the Greater Vancouver Regional District as evidence that effective regional initiatives can be undertaken without municipal restructuring. Yet faced with the prospect of additional responsibilities being given to the districts, Smith and Stewart[50] have recently expressed concern that a municipal accountability crisis is looming. They cite various problems with the makeup of the municipal councils which "provide the predominant basis for indirect election to these large urban/metropolitan regional districts."[51] Among their proposals for reform is a call for direct election of a Greater Vancouver Authority to replace the Greater Vancouver Regional District.

The Two Models Compared

The one big municipality model is better suited to focusing on area-wide issues, but may be suspect in addressing more localized concerns. With a joint services board, it is the area-wide focus which is likely to suffer. There are concerns about a loss of accessibility and a weakening of local democracy because of the elimination of local municipalities through amalgamation under the one big municipality model. Joint services boards also give rise to accountability concerns because of their composition. In somewhat oversimplified terms, then, we face problems with accountability at either the lower tier or the upper tier, depending on which of these two models are used.

choice of model reflects view of what municipal ernment is supposed to be do.

If the choice is one of strong local councils and a regional board that may lack accountability versus a strong regional or megacity council with local community councils to provide token access and representation, the former model better supports our view of what municipal government is supposed to be. We reject the notion that municipalities are mainly vehicles for service delivery, whose boundaries should be made ever-larger to accommodate perceived servicing advantages. We take as our starting point the importance of the local community and the primary role of council as a political mechanism for expressing and responding to the collective concerns of

---

[50]Patrick J. Smith and Kennedy Stewart, *Making Accountability Work in British Columbia*, Report for the Ministry of Municipal Affairs and Housing, June 1998.

[51]*Ibid.*, Report 2, p. 42.

members of the community. It follows that municipalities must be based on communities of interest, not on areas that are convenient for administering services. More emphasis should be given to structures appropriate for governing, not service delivery. If this is done, "municipal boundaries can then be used to delineate real communities, and optimal boundaries for service production can be worked out by other agencies and even by the private sector."[52]

The previous two models are not the only structural choices, however. While two tier regional government systems are no longer in vogue, they may—if properly structured—offer an alternative to the one big municipality and joint board models and provide a middle ground between the positions of the consolidationists and those who favour fragmentation.

The Two Tier Model

It is useful at the outset to recall why upper tier governments were created in the first place. County governments were created by the Baldwin Act of 1849 as a vehicle for the provision of a limited range of services which were best administered over a wider geographic area than individual lower tier municipalities. The regional governments introduced just over 100 years later expanded the role of these county governments (now called regional) by giving them more responsibilities and by extending their jurisdiction over cities (previously separate from the county system).

County councils are made up of members elected initially to serve on the councils of constituent lower tier municipalities. The same system of "indirect election" was retained for most of the original regional governments. It is consistent with the notion that the upper tier exists as an agent of the lower tier, to provide those services which the lower tier may feel can be better handled on an intermunicipal basis. It is this model of municipal government, in which the upper tier exists in a supporting role to the lower tier, that deserves further consideration. The value of a two tier system was well expressed in the report which recommended a system of regional government in Hamilton-Wentworth. In its words:[53]

> The Commission believes that the two tier system for the area offers the best opportunity of reconciling the two main aspects of municipal government—efficiency and access. The larger administrative unit would provide a greater chance for efficiency, but the sheer size, number of

---

[52]Sancton, *Governing Canada's City Regions*, p. 43.

[53]The Hamilton-Burlington-Wentworth Local Government Review (Steele Commission), *Report and Recommendations*, November 1969, p. 72.

people and volume of business would mean that the elected council of the metropolitan community would have difficulty in hearing all persons wishing to express aspects of local concern. There are many functions that are not of overall concern but are of extreme local importance. These functions may be more readily dealt with by the lower tier council who will have the knowledge of local conditions.

The report went on to explain that a two tier system of municipal government allows different decisions to be made and different levels of service to be provided in various areas of the region to best meet the desires and needs of the inhabitants.

Kitchen offers several benefits from the existence of both lower tier and upper tier municipalities.[54] The first is that the larger geographic area of the region can better address and control spillovers (positive or negative externalities) that might arise if some services were provided by lower tier municipalities. As an example of a negative spillover, he cites the problem that could arise if solid waste disposal were a lower tier responsibility and if a solid waste disposal site were opened by one municipality near the boundary of an adjacent municipality, generating negative impacts on the residents of that neighbouring municipality.

A second benefit of a regional level is ensuring consistent standards in the provision of certain services. If, for example, social welfare assistance were administered at the lower tier and if support differed among lower tier municipalities, there would be an incentive for recipients to relocate to those municipalities offering the highest level of support. Until recent changes, this pattern was evident in those few areas of Ontario without a county welfare system, where the separated cities within the county carried a disproportionate share of the welfare burden.

A third benefit of the two tier system, according to Kitchen, is that where spillovers are not prevalent and uniform standards are not required, local preferences can be reflected in the quantity and quality of services provided by lower tier municipalities. In addition, the existence of a number of separate municipalities looking after these services generates a competitive atmosphere which provides a stimulus for improved service delivery.

Bird and Slack also find merit in the two tier system, partly as a way of getting around the fact that each urban service will likely achieve the lowest per unit cost at a different scale of production. In their words:[55]

---

[54]The discussion which follows is based on Kitchen, *op. cit.*

[55]Richard M. Bird and N. Enid Slack, *Urban Public Finance in Canada*, 2nd edition, Toronto, John Wiley & Sons, 1993, p. 35.

... the optimum form of government will likely turn out to be a two tier or multi-tier structure where some services are provided by the upper tier— either a province or a regional government—and some by the lower tier or tiers. Indeed, since most government activities consist of a cluster of functions, what appears to be unnecessary overlap of governmental functions may sometimes represent a rational solution to the spillover problem.

In our view, one of the main problems with the two tier system, at least as it evolved in Ontario, is that the regions became too powerful, assumed too many responsibilities from the lower tier, and gradually came to see themselves as the primary municipal level of government. This led to charges that such an important governing body should not be comprised of indirectly elected members, and to changes which introduced direct election of some or all of the upper tier members, thereby removing any direct voice for the lower tier municipalities. The Ontario government has added to this "top-heavy" arrangement by downloading to the upper tiers a number of additional responsibilities which arguably should have remained provincial.

It is possible to envisage another two tier model in which the upper tier reverts to its traditional role of acting as an agent of the lower tier municipalities. Consistent with the principle of subsidiarity, municipal responsibilities should be vested in lower tier municipalities as much as possible, to the extent that they are capable of handling them. If that division of duties can be better achieved by some modest consolidation of lower tier municipalities, so be it. The limited responsibilities which are better handled across a wider area (such as water supply and sewage treatment and arterial roads) would be the responsibility of the upper tier, on the understanding that it is carrying out these responsibilities on behalf of the lower tier municipalities, who are the primary decision makers. In keeping with this model of a "slimmed-down" upper tier, some of the social service responsibilities recently downloaded to the regional governments in Ontario could be returned to the province where they more logically belong.

> Another possibility is a two tier model in which the upper tier reverts to its traditional role of acting as an agent of the lower tier municipalities.

In this model, the upper tier would not necessarily provide its services directly; it might pursue alternative delivery options which are more cost-effective. In other words, it would act as a service arranger on behalf of its lower tier municipalities, entering into what might be a variety of joint ventures for different servicing needs. The upper tier, as conceived here, would be less like the top-heavy regional governments of Ontario and closer to such governing bodies as the regional districts of British Columbia, the RCMs as they are evolving in Quebec, or the regional county services boards proposed for Newfoundland. It is appreciated that some broader, regional interests may be neglected or poorly managed under such arrangements. But this prospect has to be weighed against the neglect of local community views and concerns that is likely under the one big municipality model.

What About Process Improvements?

After all this discussion about which structures might work best, it is contended that *none* of them are as important as the processes followed by the municipality. Process improvement refers to a wide range of initiatives relating to the way municipalities do the things they do. For our purposes, they include such changes as:

- improving productivity by redesigning work activities;
- stimulating productivity through employee incentive programs;
- achieving cost-savings by pursuing partnership arrangements;
- gaining revenues by being more entrepreneurial; and
- prompting productivity improvement by managed competition.

Ironically, a number of the reports recommending municipal restructuring have acknowledged the potential of process improvements, but that hasn't stopped them from calling for amalgamations. Perhaps the best, and most puzzling, example is provided by the Constituent Assembly report on Hamilton-Wentworth. It estimated that a single amalgamated municipality would reduce costs by 2%, largely by a reduction in middle management personnel and overhead. In contrast, the report found that between 15% and 30% savings could result from improvements in service delivery.[56] Faced with these options, the report inexplicably chose to recommend full amalgamation. The only clue to its rationale may be the suggestion, in an appendix to the report, that restructuring "may help provide the right environment for change."

A rather similar pattern is found in the report prepared for the Ontario government to justify the savings it was predicting from the creation of the new city of Toronto. Sancton's analysis of this report determined that

---

[56]Both of these estimates are cited on p. 35 of the Constituent Assembly Report, *op. cit.*

two-thirds of the savings which were anticipated related to process im-provements which might be introduced by the new municipality.[57] The authors of the initial report tried to link these improvements with the issue of amalgamation by suggesting that creation of the new municipality would produce a "clean slate" which would somehow facilitate imple-mentation of the new processes. The reality is likely to be quite different, according to Sancton. "The persistent day-to-day complications of the amalgamation process itself will constantly intrude on the priorities of even the most dedicated 'new public manager.'"[58]

Whatever circumstances are most conducive to process improve-ments, more attention needs to be given to this aspect of municipal re-form. A number of practical examples follow. Please bear in mind that these examples are necessarily brief in their description, and reflect the situations at a particular point in time (as evidenced from the dates of the published sources on which the examples are based). Some of these examples may have since run into difficulty or even been abandoned— although others may have gone on to even greater success. Either way, these examples are not presented as a definitive statement on the sub-ject; they are intended to be illustrative of the kinds of improvements which can be achieved if municipalities make process reform a priority.

Managing Costs, Not Cutting Expenditures

Too many municipalities react to financial pressures by cutting expen-ditures (often "across the board") until some arbitrary level is reached—usually one which avoids an increase in property taxes. While the motiva-tion may be commendable, this approach results in cuts which are ill considered, usually made in haste, and often without an appreciation of the long-term impact on the municipality. That impact is often one of reduced service standards. The difference with an approach which man-ages costs is far more than semantic. Its objective is to reduce costs while maintaining or even enhancing standards of service.

Cost Management in Pittsburgh Township

A good, and successful, example of a cost management program was introduced in Pittsburgh Township in 1993. The municipality challenged

---

[57]Andrew Sancton, *Toronto's Response to the KPMG Report, Fresh Start: An Estimate of Potential Savings and Costs from the creation of a single tier local government for Toronto*, prepared for the City of Toronto, December 17, 1996.

[58]*Ibid.*, p. 3.

its employees to generate savings of at least 10% of its operating budget, or over $500 000. It also pledged to share 10% of any such savings with the employees. All staff were asked for at least five suggestions. The municipality, wisely, did not emphasize "big savings" items, realizing that many staff could only achieve small savings in their particular area of work. Each municipal department was audited to review the job specifications and operations and to help identify areas for improvement. A monthly newsletter updated employees on progress with the initiative. In addition, bimonthly meetings were held to explain cost components so that employees had a better basis for finding savings. The effort was successful, the savings target was met, and the Pittsburgh Township employees also took home a Christmas bonus of about $700 each. The municipality's efforts placed it among the finalists for the IPAC Award for Innovative Management.[59]

Many factors contributed to the Pittsburgh Township success with cost management. These included:

- a history of good council-staff relations
- effective champions of the new approach
- the involvement of all employees, both in generating ideas and in sharing the savings
- encouraging many small ideas with small savings, rather than looking for a few dramatic breakthroughs [Two-thirds of the cost-saving ideas in Pittsburgh Township involved savings of less than $2000.]

According to Pittsburgh Township's CAO at the time, cost management focuses on the 1001 ways to make 1% improvements, thereby achieving the results.[60] He stresses that the challenge is to ensure that employees feel that they have the authority within their own work areas and, in consultation with supervisors, to make improvements to the process. "Once staff feel a sense of ownership and involvement, quality improves, morale increases and costs go down."

---

[59]Winners and finalists for these annual awards are described in *Public Sector Management*, a quarterly publication of the Institute of Public Administration of Canada, and a good source of examples of innovative practices by Canadian public sector bodies.

[60]Barry Malmsten, "Managing Costs, Not Cutting Expenditures," paper presented to Insight Conference on *Reinventing Municipal Government for the 21st Century*, September 18, 1995.

Seeing Stars in Ajax

Another similar program was launched in the Town of Ajax under the name STARS (Saving Town of Ajax Real Dollars). Its target was to generate 1001 ideas to save money ($500 000 in annual cost savings), including at least two ideas from every employee, and to achieve savings without laying off any permanent employees and without significant cuts in services to Ajax residents. In fact, in the first phase of the program, 2200 ideas were generated, an average of 9 suggestions per person, reflecting participation by 84% of staff, and saving $593 000.[61]

Awarding Oscars in Owen Sound

The city of Owen Sound launched a similar program in August 1995. Its Employees Initiative Program was entitled OSCARS, for Owen Sound Can Achieve Real Savings. Its objective was to generate 400 ideas which would deliver savings or increase revenues by the end of 1995. The program exceeded all expectations and some 640 suggestions were received by the end of the year. By the spring of 1996, 141 of these suggestions had been acted upon, representing potential annual savings for the city of nearly $400 000.[62]

The OSCARS program included a monthly newsletter with features such as:

- a recurring Siskel and Ebert Trivia Contest.
- a number of imaginatively named awards, such as the George Burns "Longevity Award" for those who submitted suggestions in consecutive months and the Archie Bunker "All in the Family Award"—a pizza party given to all employees who have made a suggestion in the competing section group with the highest ratio of entries per employee.
- a "Curtain Calls" section featuring winning OSCAR suggestions.

Besides reinforcing the efforts of employees and building momentum for the project, many of the features in the newsletters exhibited the sense of fun and team spirit so essential to the success of this sort of venture.

Brampton Is Best

To take but one more example, the city of Brampton launched an initiative called BEST (Brampton Employees Save Taxes) in which savings of close to $2 million were achieved in 1996. This was accomplished

---

[61]The preceding summary is based on *ibid.*

[62]Craig Curtis, "Owen Sound: Responding to Change," *Cordillera Institute Journal*, Markham, April 1996, p. 14.

without a reduction in the quality of service—thanks to 2000 cost-cutting suggestions from staff.[63]

How Does It Work?

The evidence is overwhelming. Cost management programs of the sort highlighted above can be a very effective way of reducing costs while still maintaining service standards. How do they do it? Primarily by tapping into the creative abilities of municipal staff—who know their jobs better than anyone else and can find ways to save money if there is some incentive to do so. To those who recoil in shock or horror, and exclaim that staff should always seek out cost savings automatically without extra incentives, we should remember that traditional budgeting practices actively discouraged such efforts. Those who generated savings were "rewarded" by having that money taken away from them and given to areas which were less efficient and which overspent their budgets. They were further "rewarded" by being given less money the following year, since they had obviously had more money than they needed if they didn't use all of it.

The existence of some highly publicized success stories about cost management, however, does not mean that these programs are quickly or easily implemented. It is obviously helpful if a municipality considering such an initiative has a history of good management-staff relations and mutual trust and respect between councillors and staff. If staff suspect that any labour-saving ideas they generate will be used to downsize, they will clearly have little reason to cooperate. Also helpful is any history of staff working in teams, especially teams which cut across functions and levels within the municipality. A third key ingredient is solid cost accounting data, without which it is very difficult to review work processes for possible cost savings.

Joint Ventures and Partnerships

As discussed in earlier chapters, the traditional model of the municipality as a self-sufficient provider of all services needed by its residents is giving way to a new model of the municipality as service arranger, as an enabling authority which draws upon resources from varied sources and stresses collaboration and joint ventures. Here again, examples abound, and several are included to illustrate the benefits of this approach.

---

[63]Report in *Municipal World*, July 1996, p. 27.

Public-Public Partnerships

Cooperative purchasing ventures have been particularly common and have usually extended to other joint ventures.

- An early example from Ontario is the Peterborough Public Buyers Association, which since 1968 has tendered for commonly used goods and services for five municipalities, five educational institutions or school boards, and two hospitals.[64]
- The Elgin Area Administrators Group brings together representatives from St. Thomas, Elgin County, and several of its municipalities, both school boards, the conservation authority, the health unit, the community college, the general hospital, and several other agencies to pool resources, improve communication, and create opportunities for cooperative ventures. In its first year of operation (1995), it saved the taxpayers of Elgin County over $300 000 through such projects as shared busing of students from both school boards and joint banking arrangements for several members. As of mid-1996, new projects were under way involving joint safety training for casual and student employees and busing of students using city transit.[65]
- The York Region Board of Education and York Region Roman Catholic Separate School Board formed a consortium to achieve cost savings in school bus transportation, counselling services, multi-use facilities, and raising revenue in non-traditional ways. This initiative placed them among the winners of the 1997 Ontario Local Government Innovative Public Service Delivery Awards.
- The city of St. Thomas has also entered into a variety of public-public partnerships:
  - ○ It provides complete planning services to five of its neighbouring municipalities in the county, an arrangement which has allowed the city to retain its qualified staff and to coordinate planning and servicing issues with its neighbours.
  - ○ The St. Thomas Economic Development Corporation has a contract with two neighbouring municipalities to provide marketing, promotion, and other economic development services—the cost for which would have been prohibitive had they set up their own separate departments.
  - ○ St. Thomas provides engineering services to the public utilities commission for water main design and construction inspection.

---

[64]Details on this Association are found in the Ministry of Municipal Affairs, *Joint Services in Municipalities: Five Case Studies*, Toronto, April 1983.

[65]This example, and the following ones concerning St. Thomas, are from N. Roy Main, "Wise Men Seldom Wrong," *Cordillera Institute Journal*, June 1996, pp. 12-14.

It similarly provides engineering services to its adjoining municipalities for the design and inspection of underground works.

○ St. Thomas has a contract with the Separate School Board for
sports field maintenance at its newest high school.

Public-Private Partnerships

• The city of Markham took an innovative approach to providing concession services for the new community centre it was developing for
its Milliken Mills community. It negotiated a 20 year lease under which
McDonald's built a restaurant (with compatible architectural design),
a parking lot, and a connection to the community centre. Markham
receives money from the lease, and a share of the gross revenue from
the restaurant, above a certain level.[66]

• Selective use of the private sector has proven to be a cost-effective
approach to meeting transportation needs in a number of Canadian
municipalities. In 1988 Winnipeg began contracting out half of its
rides for the disabled to taxi and van companies. Edmonton does the
same. While rides in Winnipeg increased from 97 000 to 282 000 between 1987 and 1991, costs per trip fell from $21 to $14 over the same
period.[67] Beginning in 1989, Markham has used taxis to cover outlying
bus routes during slow evening hours.[68] Customers contact the transit
office, which dispatches a taxi to the nearest bus stop. The customer
pays the regular bus fare to the cab driver, and the taxi company bills
the municipality for the fare run up by the metre less the amount of
the bus fare. Markham has been saving more than $150 000 a year
since introducing this scheme.

• Public-private collaboration supported an important policy initiative
in Kitchener-Waterloo. Community policing, accompanied by the increased presence of "beat cops," was receiving increasing emphasis
in the early 1990s. But when a downtown Kitchener neighbourhood
wanted a storefront police office, the expense appeared prohibitive.
This problem was overcome when the downtown business association put up the money to rent space for the police operation.[69]

---

[66]This joint venture is described in *Innovative Financing: A Collection of
Stories from Ontario Municipalities*, Toronto, Municipal Finance Officers Association of Ontario and Association of Municipal Clerks and Treasurers of Ontario,
1993, pp. 24-25.

[67]Stevenson, "Canada's Best-Run Cities," in *Financial Times of Canada*,
November 7, 1992, p. 13.

[68]Paul Schliesmann, "Bus-taxi Swap Could Help City Save Dollars," Kingston,
Whig Standard, July 26, 1994.

[69]Stevenson, *op. cit.*, p. 12.

- Qualicum Beach, British Columbia, provides an example of a public-private partnership of great benefit to the municipal partner.[70] It needed a new municipal office building, for which it began to assemble land in the downtown in 1988. By the time funds were set aside for construction in 1994, the town had become aware that the Vancouver Island Regional Library wanted to expand its facilities in Qualicum Beach. Gradually, a multi-purpose complex with both public and private components took shape. The public component, known as the Town Square complex, includes a municipal office and council chamber, a new public library, new policing offices (for the RCMP), an underground parking lot, and a public square to serve as a focal point for the community. The private component includes commercial space within the Town Square complex and new commercial space on the site which had been occupied by the (old) municipal offices. Through this joint venture, the municipality has reduced its capital investment in the project and gained future revenues from such sources as payment for the new downtown parking being provided, taxes from the commercial space to be located within the new complex, and the ongoing lease of the library facilities to the regional library system. The private partner indemnifies the town, through contractual arrangements, for all cost overruns in the design and construction of the new facility. In addition, private sector skills and creativity have been tapped to help in creating the best project possible.

- In 1995 the Region of Hamilton-Wentworth entered into what was described as the largest single public-private partnership of its type in North America. It signed a 10 year $187 million contract with Philip Utilities Management Corporation for the management and operation of its sewage and water treatment facilities, including over 60 pumping stations, reservoirs, and combined sewer overflow tanks. The contract includes a "no layoff" condition and guarantees the Region a minimum savings of $500 000 in its annual operating budget. In addition, any profit that Philip makes beyond $1 million is shared with the Region (which gets 40%).[71]

Public-Private Possibilities and Pitfalls

From the preceding examples, it should be apparent that a variety of arrangements are possible within the framework of a public-private partner-

---

[70]The summary which follows is based on Mark Brown and Jonathon Huggett, "A Public-Public-Private Partnership in Qualicum Beach," *Cordillera Institute Journal*, August 1996, pp. 12-14.

[71]See Hemant Canaran, "Hamilton-Wentworth sets a benchmark in public-private partnership," *Municipal World*, August 1995, p. 6.

ship. Most of these partnerships relate to capital projects and they have been defined as "any situation where the costs, risks and rewards of creating, refurbishing or expanding infrastructure are shared by government and the private sector."[72] There are several models or alternatives with respect to such capital projects, including build-operate-transfer, build-transfer-operate, turnkey operations (design-build), and leasebacks.[73] Of particular interest because of its current topicality is the option of privatization, a very broad term which can cover such arrangements as the sale of an existing facility to a single private owner/operator, an agreement with a private owner/operator to develop a new facility, and employee takeovers.

Privatization

There are a number of potential benefits of partnerships with the private sector, and also some potential drawbacks.[74] Potential benefits include:

- gaining private sector skills and experience which help to minimize project costs and ongoing operating costs;
- reducing the governments' need for up-front capital;
- utilizing the marketing expertise of private sector partners; and
- having access to funding sources, through private sector partners, not otherwise available to the public sector.

Potential drawbacks of private sector partnerships include:

- taking a risk that the private partner's business may fail partway through the project;
- exposing the government financially, if it provides financing guarantees; and
- possible loss of control over the project.

Privatization can be advocated as one way of downsizing government and reducing public expenditures, which is certainly the way it has been presented by the Ontario government. Opponents of this approach fear that by giving municipalities more flexibility to enter into partnerships with the private sector and then downloading responsibility for such capital-intensive services as roads, water and sewer systems, public transit and

---

[72]Ministry of Municipal Affairs, *Study of Innovative Financing Approaches for Ontario Municipalities* (Price Waterhouse), March 31, 1993.

[73]For details on these arrangements, see Chuck Wills, "Structuring and Financing Public-Private Partnerships," a paper presented at the November 22-23, 1993 Insight Conference of the same name, Toronto, Insight Press, 1993, pp. 44-46.

[74]These pros and cons are based on Wills, *op. cit.*, pp. 46-47.

airports, Ontario is creating a situation which will lead to widespread privatization of these formerly public sector operations. This is not automatically a harmful development, but is it in the best interests of the public to have public capital facilities owned or operated by the private sector? To what degree will the relevant government authorities be able to monitor and regulate the quality of the capital facilities and services being provided by the private sector and to enforce the rights of the government authority on behalf of the public?[75]

A further concern is that the shift to privately owned or operated capital facilities is apparently to be accompanied by a marked increase in user fees to finance such ventures. One may ask whether this arrangement is mainly designed to allow governments to avoid the appearance of raising taxes on a tax-weary public, and whether user fees are ultimately the fairest way to pay for the operation of facilities from which a broader segment of the public than those paying the fees will benefit.[76]

What About Privatization of Services?

As noted above, public-private partnerships may be pursued with respect to major capital projects, like water and sewer systems, as a means of funding capital costs that are beyond the scope of the municipality. But what about the movement to contract out the delivery of various services such as garbage collection, road maintenance, or recreation? Unless such initiatives are ideologically driven—out of some notion that reducing the scope of government is, by definition, a positive step—then presumably services would only be contracted out if cost savings and/or improved delivery were to result.

It should not be assumed that privatizing a municipal service will result in lower costs. Even if private companies offer what seems to be an attractive price for providing an existing municipal service, what this offer entails must be examined very carefully. Municipalities need to ask themselves such questions as:

*   What is your basis for judging any such offer? Do you have a sufficient handle on your total cost of providing the service in question and on the level and quality of output you are providing for that cost? Without such measures, you are not in a position to draw comparisons.

---

[75]This issue is raised by Heather Douglas, "New Opportunities for Public and Private Sector Partnerships in Capital Project Financing," paper presented at Insight Conference, *op. cit.*, p. 102.

[76]*Ibid.*, p. 103.

- If everything seems covered, and the private bid is significantly lower, what is the possibility that you are being "low-balled" so that you will make the switch?
- If you privatize, what happens to the affected municipal employees? What policies has the municipality adopted to ensure that they are treated in a fair and humane way?
- If you do privatize and are unhappy with the results, what are your options at the end of the specified contract period? Will you have sufficient expertise left "in house" to resume direct responsibility for the service in question? If not, are there other private suppliers to whom you can easily turn? If there aren't, then are you just going from a situation of a municipal monopoly to one of a private monopoly?

There is no magic in private administration of services. There is no logical reason why private administration should be cheaper, when one considers that a profit margin must be built-in which is not present in public sector administration. To the extent that inefficient public sector operations exist, it is because of such factors as the restraints under which they operate, the lack of positive incentives to reinforce productivity, and the absence of competitive pressures akin to the market place forces which stimulate the private sector. This is evident from the fact that private companies which enjoy a monopoly position are usually prone to higher prices and poorer quality. It is not public versus private which is the deciding factor in whether there will be efficiency. It is monopoly versus competition.

> There is no magic in private administration, and no reason why it should be cheaper than public administration.

Managed Competition, Not Privatization

Instead of pursuing privatization as any kind of end in itself, a number of municipalities have adopted an objective of "managed competition."[77] Under this approach, public sector employees and their managers compete with private firms for the right to provide a given service. If a private firm wins the competition, it signs a contract to provide the service for a specified length of time, during which the government monitors the service provider's performance closely. If public sector employees win, they continue to provide the service, but under a performance agreement with the government. Both the contract and the performance agreement state

---

[77]The discussion of this concept is based on David Seader and Mary K. Lee, "The Formalized Approach to Public-Private Competition (Part I)," *Cordillera Institute Journal*, 1997, Issue I, pp. 5-8.

clearly the method of providing the service, the total cost of providing the service, and the performance standards to be met. If the service is not delivered up to standard and within cost, a new competition is held.

Managed competition can offer a number of benefits.[78]

- It creates a new climate within government which is more dynamic and open to change.
- It gives employees an opportunity to redesign their jobs and to champion changes that, under "normal" circumstances, might not even be considered.
- It forces government to be more focused on efficiency and effectiveness.
- It can reduce costs while maintaining, or even improving, service quality.

The Indianapolis experience with managed competition provides an encouraging example of the kind of relationship which can be developed between unions and management in the pursuit of new approaches in municipal government.[79] When a pro-privatization mayor was elected there a few years ago, over the opposition of a concerned union movement, the first few months of the new administration were quite strained. However, union leadership and the mayor found common ground by agreeing to the "competitive model" already cited. City work units submitted bids in this process and, to the surprise of some, it turned out that union involvement in preparing bids led to an 80% success rate—in contrast to a success rate of only 30% when the union was not involved in the bidding process.

To be competitive in this new operating environment, the union removed narrow, old-style job descriptions that raised costs and priced its members out of work. It replaced them with broader job descriptions that make staff more flexible. According to the leader of the union local in Indianapolis, "the union has cross-trained and upgraded employees to many different tasks. It has meant wages of employees rising to the level paid to the highest skill."[80] Most of the savings realized through managed competition have come from the elimination of management and supervisory personnel, as better-trained and well-motivated workers take greater responsibility for getting the job done. A happy by-product of the

---

[78]*Ibid.*, p. 6.

[79]The description which follows is based on Peter Holle, "Enlightened Unionism," *Cordillera Institute Journal*, 1997, Issue 3, pp. 19-20.

[80]As quoted in *ibid.*, p. 19.

new atmosphere in Indianapolis is a decline in grievances from about 300 a year to about 20 a year.

As the union leader sums up the situation, "we win 4 out of 5 contracts that the union bids. When we do the work, we do it for 25% less than it was done in the past because of competition and because you start asking people to bring their brains to work instead of parking them at the door."[81]

It must be appreciated that Canadian municipalities vary widely in how ready they are to face a system of managed competition. Before it is introduced, there should be in place:

- an awareness of all the specific services and programs provided by the municipality and (ideally) which of these services are core versus ancillary.
- well-developed measures of cost and output in relation to these services.
- a work environment in which productivity improvement has been emphasized as a value and reinforced and rewarded in practice.
- a trusting relationship between employer and employee, so that initiatives to reduce costs are not seen as a threat that will lead to staff layoffs. Involvement of unions is of central importance.

Raising Revenues, Not Just Cutting Costs

Governments traditionally focus on ways of cutting expenditures when faced with a financial crunch. But they are starting to give more attention to the alternative of generating increased revenues. In fact, a number of the preceding examples include at least some emphasis on revenue generation. These include the St. Thomas initiatives in selling services and expertise to neighbouring municipalities and other public bodies, and the Markham joint venture with McDonald's. In addition, some municipalities perform services on private property for a fee, such as cutting trees or unclogging drains. Some sell souvenirs, publications, municipal crests or insignia, and various other items. Some "hire out" specialized equipment for use by other municipalities and organizations or specialized services such as engineering or planning expertise.

American local governments have been very imaginative and aggressive in their revenue generation efforts. For example:[82]

---

[81]*Ibid.*, p. 20.

[82]Osborne and Gaebler, *op. cit.*, p. 197.

- The Milwaukee Metropolitan Sewerage District transforms 60 000 tons of sewage sludge into fertilizer every year and sells it, generating some $7.5 million in revenues.
- Phoenix earns $750 000 a year by siphoning off the methane gas from a large wastewater treatment plant and selling it for home heating.
- It used to cost Chicago $2 million annually to tow away abandoned cars. It now earns that amount of revenue through a contract with a private company which pays Chicago $25 per car for the right to tow them away.
- The St. Louis County Police Department developed new software for use in police reporting and then licensed the software to a private company under an agreement that earns the department $25 000 every time the software is sold to another police department.
- Paulding County, Georgia, built a 244 bed prison, even though it only needed 60 extra beds, so that it could charge other jurisdictions $35 a night to handle their overflow. The new jail earned $1.4 million in its first year of business, $200 000 more than its operating costs.

As these examples illustrate, enterprising local governments are always looking for a possible "deal," they are prepared to take some risks to generate additional revenues, and they are willing to spend money now if such action will earn more money later. Traditional local governments show no such imagination. They tend to be very short term in their focus. They postpone spending on road repairs until the road has to be rebuilt at three times the cost of resurfacing. Osborne and Gaebler illustrate the contrasting mindsets of traditional and enterprising governments with an example from the Los Angeles County Clerk's Department. The average tax auditor in that department generates 140 times his or her salary in increased tax collections. During a 1991 recession, however, Los Angeles didn't hire any additional auditors, on the grounds that "politically, when you're laying off cops and firemen, you can't hire auditors."[83] An enterprising government wouldn't lay off the cops and firemen, claim Osborne and Gaebler. It would train a few as auditors and generate enough additional revenue to keep the rest.

One of the examples of enterprising government in the Canadian context is provided by the city of Waterloo's "Waterloo Inc." initiative. This has involved the formation of business unit teams challenged to deliver products and services using business principles. One of the tasks of these teams is to identify potential new revenue sources. Further details on this Waterloo initiative are provided in Chapter 9, which examines

---

[83]Los Angeles official, quoted in *ibid.*, p. 206.

the kinds of new organizational structure which are being introduced in municipalities.

Two years ago, Peel became the first municipality in Canada to introduce a special composting system which turns garbage into safe, quality garden compost. Expansion plans were recently approved which will convert garbage into an industrial fuel called stabilate, which can be used to generate electricity or to fire cement kilns.[84]

Before he became Prime Minister and forgot to follow his own good advice, Brian Mulroney used to criticize Canada's never-ending efforts at constitutional reform. In his words: "Imagine what might have been accomplished in, say, the field of medical research if the same amount of time, talent and money had been available as in the field of federal-provincial relations."[85] One can't help wondering how much might have been achieved in process improvements and revenue-raising initiatives by applying the resources which have instead been consumed in the process of studying, resisting, and implementing amalgamation.

Concluding Comments

This chapter has been critical of many of the structural reforms which have been introduced. As noted above, the problem is not with amalgamation *per se* but the way in which it has been used or abused. While many of the reforms of the 1960s and 1970s were overly focused on service delivery, they were at least attempting to create boundaries better suited to the perceived needs of the municipalities in question. By contrast, many of the reforms of the past decade have had more dubious rationale. When municipalities are amalgamated to facilitate the downloading of provincial responsibilities, to pursue highly elusive cost reductions, or simply to reduce the number of municipalities and politicians in furtherance of the ideological bent of the provincial governing party, one must question the appropriateness of the reforms.

A further problem is that a number of provinces have been unwilling to allow municipalities to pursue reform options other than amalgamation. It is difficult to understand the provincial rigidity on this point. If

---

[84]Mike Funston, "Peel plans to turn kitchen trash into fuel," *Toronto Star*, October 13, 1997.

[85]Brian Mulroney, *Where I Stand*, Toronto, McClelland and Stewart, 1983, p. 57.

provincial governments must cut grants and download costs to serve their own fiscal purposes, why can't they allow municipalities to decide how best they want to meet these challenges? Some municipalities might choose amalgamation, while others might enter into intermunicipal agreements, contract out service delivery, or introduce special purpose agencies to address municipal needs. There might even be local citizens who prefer to pay $100 or $150 more per year to retain their own separate municipality.[86] Why must there be only one choice for municipalities?

An added concern is that the reform of municipal processes has received limited attention because of the preoccupation with structural reform. The two options are by no means mutually exclusive, although it is felt that the preoccupation with amalgamations has diverted and drained much municipal energy and attention that might have been directed to improving processes. To the extent that the latter involve the adoption of more business-like practices, they bring their own potential problems. No matter how business-like it may become, a municipality is still a government, not a business, and must act accordingly—a theme returned to in Chapters 10 and 11.

---

[86]Vojnovic, *op. cit.*, p. 122.

CHAPTER 8
Intergovernmental Relations

As the federal and provincial levels scrambled to address their deficit and debt concerns in the 1990s, they left municipalities with increased responsibilities but without the authority or the resources to handle them.

Introduction

Discussions of intergovernmental relations usually start with the constitutional subordination of municipalities and the legal framework provided by provincial governments and their constraints on municipal action. Such an approach is valid, as far as it goes, and there is no denying the fundamental significance of the weak and limited legal foundation on which municipal governments rest. But this approach oversimplifies the complex nature of intergovernmental relations. It understates the many ways in which the federal government affects municipalities, both directly and as a result of federal decisions which have an impact on the provinces and then reverberate down to the municipal level. Given the interdependence of governments and government programs, this approach also fails to take into account the fact that municipalities may be affected as a result of various senior level decisions which, on the surface or initially, don't even appear to be related to municipal government.

To illustrate, consider the growing spectre of homelessness, of people begging and sleeping in the streets of Canadian cities. Municipalities respond to this situation in a variety of ways, ranging from increased funding for shelters to regulatory by-laws designed to prevent aggressive panhandling which might annoy shoppers and tourists. But homelessness didn't arise from, nor can it be solved by, municipal actions. It is a reflection of much more serious social problems relating to unemployment, health care, social assistance, and housing and resulting from actions taken by the federal and provincial governments.

In pursuit of its deficit and debt reduction objectives, the federal government has made major cuts in transfers to the provinces for social programs and has made it more difficult for unemployed Canadians to qualify for (un)employment insurance. Provincial governments have responded in kind, with cuts to social programs and to municipal grants. The best (worst?) example is provided by Ontario, which cut welfare payments by 21% and cancelled financial support for the building of affordable housing, putting its faith (misplaced, as it turned out) in the private sector to supply the necessary housing.[1] Meanwhile, the extent of poverty and homelessness worsened. In 1996, 26 000 people in Toronto, many of them suffering from mental illness, used shelters. According to a recent study, there were 37 000 on a waiting list for subsidized housing, and there were over 100 000 at risk of losing their housing because they pay more than 50% of their income on rent.[2]

As often happens, jurisdictional battles claim centre stage. The federal government has been trying for several years to transfer responsibility for some 40 000 social housing units to the provinces. Ontario, in turn, has transferred responsibility for social housing to municipalities as part of a major service swap introduced in 1997 (discussed later in this chapter). Municipalities originally opposed this download as inappropriate and costly, but many are now anxious to take over operating responsibility since they have already become responsible for the costs. It will not be enough, however, simply to stop "passing the buck" on the social housing portfolio. "All three levels of government must take ownership of and responsibility for solving the problem, or it will worsen."[3] It is also clear that their responses, to be effective, must go well beyond the specific issue of social housing, wherever its responsibility rests.

> Wherever this responsibility is "housed," it can only be solved by action on a number of different fronts.

In the discussion which follows, we will look first at the general evolution of municipal relations with the senior levels, and will then examine the way that the functional and financial relationships have been changing. Two areas of concern in these relationships have to do with the impact of disentanglement exercises and the growing provincial invasion of the property tax field.

---

[1] Ian Urquhart, "Homelessness report paints ugly picture," *Toronto Star*, January 16, 1999.

[2] Report of the Mayor's Homelessness Task Force, *Taking Responsibility for Homelessness, An Action Plan for Toronto*, January 1999.

[3] *Ibid.*

Evolution of Provincial-Local Relations

The evolution of provincial-municipal relations in Canada has involved, for the most part, a pattern of increasing provincial supervision, influence, and control. In the early years of their existence, municipalities often had considerable operating freedom, especially where their provincial governments were still in their infancy. Consider Crawford's description of the local autonomy enjoyed by Ontario municipalities following the 1849 Baldwin Act:

> Within the scope allowed, and the scope was extensive, the municipalities had gained the right to local self-government with a minimum of parliamentary or executive control, the elected representatives being answerable in matters of policy to their electors and in matters of law to the courts.[4]

Before long, however, provincial governments began to exercise a growing supervisory role. Departments of municipal affairs were established by the turn of the century in a number of the provinces, "to give leadership and guidance in municipal development and to provide for the continuous study of the problems of the municipalities."[5] This need was first evident in the Western provinces, where a rapid development of local government institutions was made necessary by a sudden expansion of population. Manitoba established a Department of Municipal Commissioner as early as 1886, with Saskatchewan following suit in 1908 and Alberta in 1911. British Columbia appointed an Inspector of Municipalities in 1914, but a full department was not created until 1934. Ontario's experience was somewhat similar, with an office of Provincial-Municipal Auditor as early as 1897 and a Bureau of Municipal Affairs from 1917, but no department until 1935. That same year Nova Scotia created a Department of Municipal Affairs and in 1936 New Brunswick established a Department of Education, Federal, and Municipal Relations.

The common factor here, of course, was the Depression of the 1930s and attendant municipal defaulting on financial obligations. In response, provincial governments established or expanded not only municipal departments but also boards with a variety of administrative and quasi-judicial responsibilities relating to local government. A number of these bodies had originally been formed to regulate public utilities and their

---

[4]K. G. Crawford, *Canadian Municipal Government*, Toronto, University of Toronto Press, 1954, p. 32.

[5]*Ibid.*, p. 345. Chapter 17 of Crawford, on which this section is based, provides a good description of the historical evolution of provincial-local relations.

relations with municipal authorities. As a result of the financial difficulties of the 1930s, many of these bodies were assigned responsibility for controlling municipal financing as well as jurisdiction in other areas such as zoning and assessment. As an example, the Ontario Railway and Municipal Board, created in 1906 primarily to deal with railway matters, was reconstituted as the Ontario Municipal Board in 1932. That same year, the Municipal and Public Utility Board of Manitoba, which had been created in 1926, was given responsibility for approving debenture issues and also the Quebec Municipal Corporation was established.

By the mid-1930s, all but one of the then provinces[6] provided extensive supervision and control over municipalities through a department and, in most cases, a board. In several instances this control was quite sweeping. Nova Scotia provided that every municipal by-law was subject to the Minister of Municipal Affairs, and in Quebec the Lieutenant-Governor-in-Council was empowered to disallow any municipal by-law. All of the provinces except Prince Edward Island required approval of by-laws to incur debt. Other types of by-laws, such as those relating to public health, traffic, and zoning, were also made subject to approval by the appropriate provincial departments and boards. In many cases, municipalities were authorized to exercise specific powers only subject to review or control by some provincial authority. Provincial control was also gradually extended over personnel and the conditions of employment of municipal staff. This included provincial standards of qualification for appointees and the limitation of the right of councils to dismiss employees without provincial approval. In addition, provision was made for the inspection or investigation of the affairs of a municipality both on a regular basis and as a special inquiry at the request of council or citizens or on the initiative of the province.

> Provincial control through departments and boards was widespread by the 1930s.

The post-war period brought a further increase in provincial supervision and control, largely because of the growing service demands on local government arising from the extensive urbanization of the time. As the revenues from the real property tax became less and less adequate to finance the growing expenditures of municipal government, the provinces increased their financial assistance. Most of this increased assistance, however, was in the form of conditional grants, as described below. By attaching conditions, provinces were attempting to ensure that

---

[6]The exception was P.E.I., no doubt because it had few municipalities.

certain services were provided to at least a minimum standard regardless of the varying financial capacities of their individual municipalities. But as municipalities participated in more of these conditional grant and shared cost programs, their local expenditures increasingly reflected provincial priorities.

In some instances, provincial intervention was even more direct, with the provincial government taking over all or partial responsibility for functions traditionally exercised by the local level on the grounds, often quite valid, that the function had outgrown local government—or at least its limited boundaries—and now had much wider implications. This pattern of responsibilities shifting upward to more senior levels occurred with respect to such matters as roads, assessment, the administration of justice, education, public health, and social services. A related development in some of the provinces saw the establishment or enlargement of a number of intermunicipal special purpose bodies which were ostensibly part of the local government structure and yet came under increasing provincial influence and control. Here again there was a valid concern on the part of the province about minimum standards in such areas as health and education, but the end result was a further weakening of municipal government in relation to the provincial level. As one analyst saw it:

> The succession of efforts to enlarge local administrative structures in education, public health, welfare, and toward regional municipalities has simply reduced the number of units confronting the provincial administrator at any one time.... The taxpayer's dollar has been the fulcrum of power for the bureaucrat to use in organizing things, ostensibly for the citizen's benefit but inevitably for the bureaucrat's benefit as well.[7]

By the 1960s, then, local governments had been subjected to three decades of developments which undermined their operating independence and brought them increasingly into the orbit of the senior levels of government.

1. As a result of the Depression of the 1930s, municipalities experienced increased provincial surveillance over their financial activities and they lost their historical place in the social services field to the senior governments, increasingly the federal government.
2. During the 1940s, massive centralization occurred because of the war effort. As part of the tax-rental and then tax-sharing agreements brought on by the wartime emergency, municipal governments were squeezed out of such fields as income tax and sales

---

[7] Vernon Lang, *The Service State Emerges in Ontario*, Toronto, Ontario Economic Council, 1974, p. 61.

tax, and confined to their historical dependence upon the real property tax as their main source of revenues.

3. By the 1950s, the greatly increased demands of the post-war period resulted in further provincial and federal encroachment on the operations of local government.

Even where municipalities retained some jurisdiction over traditional functions, they found themselves increasingly entangled with the senior levels of government. Typical of the pattern which had evolved by the early post-war years is the situation below, describing developments in New Brunswick:

> In many traditional areas of local competence, provincial supervision, regulation or outright control have been deemed the acceptable solutions.... Their overall effect has incorporated municipal affairs more completely in the broader contexts of provincial and federal public administration. Indeed, local autonomy in all but a few ... areas is extinct.[8]

To a considerable extent, this intertwining of activities is inevitable, and reflects the interdependence of the programs and policies of all three levels of government. As O'Brien points out, the various functions of government are interrelated in ways which would require intergovernmental activity even if they were all parcelled out in separate pieces to one level only—which they aren't and can't be.

> The line between health and welfare is not always easy to find. Welfare and social housing are part of one policy. Housing density depends on transit or the automobile. The latter affects the environment and depends on energy policy. Add the need for planning and financing and there is no escaping the fact that governance in our society requires a lot of communication among governments at various levels.[9]

Disentangling or Downloading?

Over the past few decades, there have been a number of provincial initiatives to reallocate and disentangle responsibilities. The approaches taken, the underlying objectives, and the results achieved have varied widely, as will be seen from the descriptions which follow. It will also be ap-

---

[8]H. J. Whalen, *The Development of Local Government in New Brunswick*, Fredericton, 1963, p. 90.

[9]Allan O'Brien, "A Look at the Provincial-Municipal Relationship," in Donald C. MacDonald (ed.), *Government and Politics of Ontario*, Toronto, Van Nostrand Reinhold, 1980, p. 167.

parent that a number of the more recent initiatives seem to be more concerned with downloading than disentangling and result in arrangements which are at least as entangled as before. Let us begin, however, by examining briefly the nature of these initiatives and then considering their potential and their pitfalls.

The New Brunswick Experience

The earliest initiative, and one of the most substantial, began with the Byrne Commission of 1963 (discussed in Chapter 6) and led to the 1967 Program for Equal Opportunity. On the basis of the Commission's identification of services appropriate for the provincial and local levels, the New Brunswick government took over responsibility for the administration of justice, welfare, and public health, and also financial responsibility for the provision of education. Property assessment and property tax collection also became provincial responsibilities. The extent of the provincial takeover, and the fact that the province replaced municipalities in providing services in rural New Brunswick, caused many to worry that the improvement in service allocation and delivery had been achieved at the price of municipal government.

The Quebec Experience

The Quebec government undertook a significant realignment of responsibilities and financing in 1980. School board revenues from property taxes were substantially reduced and their revenues from provincial transfers were increased. To offset its increased costs for education, the province also significantly reduced its transfer payments to municipalities, thereby increasing municipal reliance on the property tax.[10] As a result, the share of school board expenditures financed by provincial transfers increased from 60% to 93% between 1969 and 1989. Even more dramatic, with these changes Quebec municipalities were meeting 96% of the cost of local services through their own fees, charges, and local taxes,[11] a degree of fiscal autonomy not approached in any other province.

---

[10]F. Vaillancourt, "Financing Local Governments in Quebec: New Arrangements for the 1990s," in *Canadian Tax Journal*, 1992, Vol. 40, No. 5, pp. 1123-1139.

[11]Canadian Urban Institute, *Disentangling Local Government Responsibilities —International Comparisons*, Toronto, January 1993, p. 27.

Two further changes were introduced at the beginning of the 1990s, prompted by the provincial government's concern about its growing expenditure burden and its perception that the revenue-raising potential of the property tax had not yet been fully tapped.[12] In 1990 the province transferred to Quebec school boards the expense of maintaining school facilities while authorizing the boards to levy a property tax (which is to be collected by municipalities) covering up to 10% of their expenditures.[13] The result has been to reduce the share of provincial financing of school board operations to about 88%.[14] The following year the Quebec government introduced changes which shift to municipalities greater responsibility and financing obligations for public transit, roads, and policing. Both of these changes can be seen, at least in part, as an attempt by the province to shift back to the property tax the burden for financing some of the expenditures which had been assumed by the 1980 reforms—a move strongly opposed by the Quebec Union of Municipalities.[15]

The Nova Scotia Experience

The disentanglement process in Nova Scotia arose out of a provincial initiative which was originally focused on reducing the number of municipalities in the province. The *Task Force on Local Government* reported in April 1992, and called for a major restructuring of municipal government in the five most urbanized areas of the province, as discussed in Chapter 6. It also cited the position of the Union of Nova Scotia Municipalities that:

> Property services should be supported by property taxes and delivered by municipal government. People services are the responsibility of the provincial government and should be financed by general provincial revenues. Both orders of government should continue efforts to reallocate the delivery and financing of services recognizing this basic principle.[16]

---

[12]This view is frankly expressed by Claude Ryan, Minister of Municipal Affairs, in a December 14, 1990 statement, *The Sharing of Responsibilities Between The Government and Municipalities: Some Needed Adjustments.*

[13]*Ibid.*

[14]Vaillancourt, *op. cit.*, p. 1137.

[15]Katherine A. Graham, Susan D. Phillips, and Allan M. Maslove, *Urban Governance in Canada*, Toronto, Harcourt, Brace & Company, Canada, 1998, p. 72.

[16]Report to the Government of Nova Scotia, *Task Force on Local Government*, April 1992, p. 11.

The report also called for any reallocation of services to be revenue-neutral, again reflecting the position of the municipal association. More specifically, the Task Force proposed that rural municipalities would have to start providing their own policing and roads (as urban municipalities had been doing) and that the province would take over the municipal share of the administration and financing of general welfare assistance.[17] In one of several parallels with the Ontario experience (described below), these disentanglement proposals caused greater concern among rural municipalities than urban. The urban municipalities have larger social assistance obligations (which the province would assume) and they were already paying their own way with regard to policing and roads.

The Liberal government elected in 1993 adopted the principle of service exchange proposed in the 1992 Task Force report. The province would provide a five year period of transition payments and, during this time, municipalities would "be relieved of responsibility for social welfare services and contributions to the cost of correctional services."[18] To offset this shift and to maintain the fiscal neutrality of the swap, rural municipalities would take over the costs of policing and residential streets (services already being paid for by urban municipalities). But as these changes were being implemented, the province became increasingly preoccupied with deficit reduction. As a result, it capped the amount available for equalization payments to financially weak municipalities, causing particular hardship to a number of coastal towns formerly dependent on the ground fishery.[19]

In April 1998, the province and the Union of Nova Scotia Municipalities signed a memorandum of understanding under which the municipal contribution to social service costs is to be phased out between 1998-1999 and 2002-2003. A comprehensive review of roles and responsibilities was initiated, the first phase of which involved the identification of issues affecting the provincial-local relationship. One of the concerns expressed by municipalities was that they should have more say with respect to services for which they have a financial responsibility. For example, rural municipalities complained that service standards, the level of police

---

[17]Allan O'Brien, *Municipal Consolidation in Canada and Its Alternatives*, Toronto, ICURR Press, May 1993, p. 18.

[18]Kell Antoft and Jack Novack, *Grassroots Democracy: Local Government in the Maritimes*, Halifax, Dalhousie University, 1998, p. 11.

[19]*Ibid.*, p. 12.

service, and RCMP budgets are set by the federal and provincial governments, but funded by municipalities. Similarly, it was argued that if
municipalities are required to contribute to the cost of roads, they should
have some say about the roads standards, presently determined by the
province.[20] It remains to be seen whether there will be any further service
exchange in Nova Scotia as a result of this ongoing review.[21]

Ontario's Disentanglement Experience

Social services figured prominently in the reallocation of responsibilities
in New Brunswick and Nova Scotia, and it was also social services which
launched disentanglement in Ontario.[22] The *Report of the Provincial-
Municipal Social Services Review* (PMSSR) recommended in 1990 that
Ontario follow the lead of most other provinces and take complete
responsibility for the cost of social assistance. The province agreed in
principle but was not prepared to absorb the approximately $800 million
in extra costs that this would entail.

The way out of this dilemma was to put more items on the table, and
the *Report of the Advisory Committee to the Minister of Municipal Affairs
on the Provincial-Municipal Financial Relationship* (with a title that long,
it soon became known as the Hopcroft Report after its chair) provided
this broader approach.[23] Set up in April 1989 and reporting in January
1991, the Hopcroft Report proposed that the entire division of powers
between the provincial and municipal governments and the accompanying financial arrangements be reconsidered. It further recommended that:

1. Functions should be assigned clearly and unambiguously to one
    level to the extent possible.
2. The financial relationship should be simplified so that the prov-
    ince would continue to provide conditional grants to municipali-
    ties only in areas where there is a legitimate provincial interest.

---

[20]These examples are from Richard Ramsay, *Report to the Union of Nova
Scotia Municipalities and the Department of Housing and Municipal Affairs*, October 23, 1998, p. 8.

[21]Further information about the review process can be obtained from its web
site, which is www.munisource.org/unsm/review.

[22]The summary which follows is based on David Siegel, "Disentangling
Provincial-Municipal Relations in Ontario," *Management*, Toronto, Institute of
Public Administration, Fall 1992.

[23]*Ibid.*, p. 29.

Once again the province accepted the recommendations in principle, while worrying about the financial implications of some of the shifts in responsibility being advocated—especially since the Hopcroft Report[24] calculated that the changes it was recommending would decrease municipal operating expenditures by about $709 million. The response of the newly elected NDP government was to invite the Association of Municipalities of Ontario (AMO) to appoint municipal representatives to a working group including an equal number of provincial cabinet ministers to look at the possibility of reallocating provincial and municipal responsibilities. The stated objectives were to create better, simpler government; improve the efficiency and effectiveness of service to the public; clarify which level of government is responsible for what services; and improve financial accountability and fiscal management.[25] A key guiding principle was that the exercise had to be "fiscally neutral," leaving neither level of government better or worse off financially as a result of any reallocation of responsibilities. Thus began Ontario's disentanglement process.

> Fiscal neutrality meant that neither level of government was to be better or worse off financially at the end.

From the outset, the province expressed a willingness to take over the municipal share of the cost of general welfare assistance. To maintain the concept of fiscal neutrality, this meant that municipalities would have to assume additional costs in other areas. A draft agreement reached in January 1993 called for the municipal level to assume responsibility for certain provincial highways serving primarily local traffic and for municipalities to pay for the property assessment services provided by the province. There would also be a reduction in provincial unconditional grants, with the effect of all three of these adjustments supposedly offsetting the cost burden associated with shifting welfare to the province.

In the months that followed, a number of concerns were expressed about the draft agreement. Many on the municipal side felt that the province was assuming welfare costs which were inflated because of the prolonged recession and which would gradually decline, whereas the offsetting road costs being shifted to municipalities would remain high or would increase. Small and rural municipalities were especially troubled

---

[24] *Report of the Advisory Committee to the Minister of Municipal Affairs on the Provincial-Municipal Relationship*, Toronto, January 1991, p. 42.

[25] Ian Connerty, "Disentanglement: Changing the Provincial-Municipal Balance," in *Municipal Monitor*, Association of Municipal Clerks and Treasurers of Ontario, Richmond Hill, Kenilworth Publishing, October 1992, p. 182.

by the proposed changes since roads are their primary function. Over-shadowing all of these specific concerns, however, was a growing controversy about the province's "social contract" initiative. A central thrust of this initiative was to help reduce the provincial deficit by imposing very significant cuts in transfer payments to the local level. The arbitrary nature of these cuts, announced as they were after municipalities had already set their budgets and were more than one-third of the way through their 1993 fiscal year, prompted a very negative reaction from the municipal sector and AMO to reject the draft disentanglement agreement and costs.

The *Who Does What* Exercise

Disentanglement returned, albeit with some important changes in approach and emphasis, following the election of the Harris government in June 1995. A *Who Does What* panel, chaired by former Toronto mayor David Crombie, was appointed on May 30, 1996, to begin a complete over-haul of who does what in the delivery and funding of many government services. The stated goal of the panel was "to ensure the very best service delivery by reducing waste, duplication and the overall cost of government at the provincial and local government levels."[26]

The panel's recommendations culminated in a summary report in December 1996, which largely followed the services to property versus services to people distinction cited earlier. It called for increased municipal responsibility with respect to roads, transit, ferries, airports, water and sewer systems, and policing, and increased provincial responsibility for social services (notably social assistance and child care) and education.

The Ontario government's response was a flurry of announcements in one week in mid-January of 1997, in what became known as "mega-week." Its proposed realignment of responsibilities ignored the recommendations of *Who Does What* in several key respects. In particular, the province proposed to download to municipalities increased responsibility for a number of social programs, including public housing, public health, homes for special care, long-term care, and general welfare assistance. In return, the province would assume all of the education costs previously borne by residential property tax payers. The nature and speed of the government's response suggested that it had been pursuing its own internal agenda, while using the *Who Does What* panel almost as a front or a diversion. That agenda, it seemed, was to gain full control of educa-

---

[26]According to Ministry of Municipal Affairs and Housing *News Release*, August 14, 1996.

tion decision making in Ontario.[27] Subsequent events (discussed below) support this interpretation.

In the face of mounting criticism and evidence that fiscal neutrality did not accompany the proposed service swap, the province agreed in late February 1997 to the establishment of two joint provincial-local teams (with the Association of Municipalities of Ontario) to review the mega-week proposals. As a result of these deliberations, a new division of responsibilities was announced on May 1st, 1997.

The government embraced most of the proposals put forth by AMO. Central to the new agreement is the fact that residential property tax payers continue to pay half of the education costs they had been financing (about $2.5 billion). However, the province now sets the education tax rate, which is to remain frozen for several years. With the money saved from not taking over all of the education financing from residential property tax payers, the province found itself able to retain a number of responsibilities relating to social programs that were to be shifted to the local level. It has kept full responsibility for long-term care and for homes for special care, rather than shifting half or all of these costs to municipalities as had been announced. The province also abandoned its plan to split welfare costs 50/50, and has continued with the existing 80/20 formula. However, this cost-sharing formula has been extended to Family Benefits Assistance, which had been 100% provincially funded, so the net result was still to shift some social assistance costs to the local level. In a further concession to municipal concerns, the province indicated that before shifting responsibility for social housing to the local level it would spend some $200 million on capital upgrades.

While these changes represented a number of concessions that the province had earlier indicated it was not prepared to contemplate, statements from the Premier and the Minister of Municipal Affairs suggested that they were quite satisfied with these changes, which still met their objectives. Interestingly, the Minister, in a statement to the Legislature on May 1st when he introduced these changes, explained that the first priority of the whole exercise had been "to reduce taxes by ending the spiralling costs of education in this province."

Since these changes were introduced, the province has dropped use of the "who does what" terminology and now refers to the exercise as a

---

[27]These observations, with which we concur, are made by, among others, Katherine A. Graham and Susan D. Phillips, "Who Does What in Ontario: The Process of Provincial-Municipal Disentanglement," *Canadian Public Administration*, Summer 1998, pp. 186-187.

local services realignment, or LSR. There have been continuing adjustments, especially in relation to the various transition funds which were created to ensure the fiscal neutrality of the exercise. In March 1999, the province announced that effective January 1, 1999, it would share half of the municipal costs for public health and land ambulances, in part to ensure provincial standards in the delivery of these services.[28] Since provincial grant support is being adjusted to reflect this change, there is no net financial gain for municipalities. But the initiative may indicate some provincial sensitivity to the complaint that municipalities should not have to pay for services whose standards are set by the province. This is essentially the same complaint about violation of "pay for say" noted above with respect to Nova Scotia municipalities.

Disentanglement Potential and Pitfalls

A number of advantages have been cited by those who propose the disentanglement of provincial and local responsibilities. These include simplified arrangements, less overlap and regulation from above, and increased local autonomy. It has also been suggested that the local level would be left with clearly assigned services and access to the revenues to carry these out, which would enhance public accountability and lead to more citizen involvement in government. This is an impressive list of advantages, but how were they to be achieved? How would powers be redistributed between the provincial and local levels?

> Disentanglement advantages are supposed to include reduced overlap, increased local autonomy, and greater local accountability.

When municipal institutions were established, their limited role consisted mainly of providing services to property, financed, quite logically, by a tax on property. The property tax came under increasing criticism as the 20th century advanced not only because it was no longer adequate to generate all of the revenues required but also because it was seen as no longer appropriate to finance the services to people which were becoming part of municipal operations. Those looking for a rationale for a new distribution of provincial and municipal responsibilities often seized upon this services to property versus services to people distinction for their purposes. They argued that services to people should be handled by the provincial level. They pointed out that services such as education pro-

---

[28]Ministry of Finance Backgrounder, *Local Services Realignment—1999 Enhancements*, March 23, 1999.

vided benefits well beyond the boundaries of any one municipality and should be financed appropriately. They also noted that social services involve an income redistributive function tied to broad provincial (even national) standards and objectives, should not be open to local variation, and hence were not appropriate for local administration.

These distinctions have been used, at least in part, in several studies related to disentanglement, including New Brunswick's Byrne Commission (1963), the Michener Commission in Manitoba (1964), the Graham Commission in Nova Scotia (1974), and Ontario's *Who Does What* panel (1996). For example, the Graham Commission contended that municipal responsibilities should be divided into two groups: "... local services, which are of primarily local benefit or which might best be provided by municipal government, and general services, which are of more general benefit to the province or which the province might best provide."[29]

Cameron[30] is critical of this approach which suggests that municipal responsibilities don't extend beyond the provision of services, however defined, and therefore ignores the representative and political role of municipal government. Second, he finds the allocation of responsibilities arbitrary and likely to result in a municipal system which is responsible only "for that which is unimportant or inexpensive." Sancton expresses similar concerns and is critical of disentanglement's underlying rationale that municipalities should concentrate on those responsibilities that are inherently local, an approach which he suggests inevitably means a narrower range of municipal functions.[31] He describes the faulty assumption made by municipal advocates of disentanglement as follows:

> To base municipal government's existence on a mission to concern itself with inherently local issues is to insure its quick death. Does anyone really believe that there *any* issues which are still inherently local?[32]

He points out that there are provincial rules and regulations in place for almost any municipal function one can cite, and notes as examples garbage disposal and sewers—which were once thought of as local matters. Indeed, Sancton has demonstrated elsewhere that even metropolitan and

---

[29]Nova Scotia, *Royal Commission on Education, Public Services, and Provincial-Municipal Relations, Report*, Halifax, Queen's Printer, 1974, Vol. II, p. 3: 22.

[30]Cameron, *op. cit.*, pp. 222-235.

[31]Andrew Sancton, "Provincial-Municipal Disentanglement in Ontario: A Dissent," in *Municipal World*, July 1992, p. 23.

[32]*Ibid.*

regional governments have not been able to handle functions such as public transit, water supply, and garbage disposal, which have increasingly come under provincial jurisdiction.[33]

Disentanglement proponents have argued that the exercise will result in a greatly simplified structure and one more easily held accountable, but almost all of the discussions and the changes proposed or introduced relate to which services are to be provided by what level of government. As Sancton has observed, the process has given too much emphasis to "political and administrative tidiness."[34] If, as argued at the beginning of this text, municipalities are to act as a political mechanism through which a local community can express its collective objectives, then it is essential that municipalities be involved in as many activities as possible that are of interest and concern to the local community. This means expanding, not reducing, their sphere of influence. It means becoming (or staying) involved in functional areas in which the municipalities cannot expect to be autonomous. As Sancton wryly observes: "If municipal politicians are not interested in *all* government policies that affect their community, they can hardly complain if many in the community are not interested in municipal government."[35]

Consider the markedly different approaches taken in New Brunswick and Ontario. Under the Program for Equal Opportunity, the New Brunswick government took over responsibility for the administration of justice, welfare, and public health, and also financial responsibility for the provision of education. In so doing, it diminished the role of municipal governments, even to the point of abolishing rural counties and taking over direct provision of some services to rural areas. In contrast, the municipal level in Ontario appears to have been strengthened, not diminished, by assuming a number of additional responsibilities. At this point, however, it is unclear whether Ontario municipalities have really gained responsibilities or just additional costs. So far, the province apparently intends to continue dictating service levels and standards, contrary to the "pay for say" principle. That higher levels of government may have ulterior motives when apparently strengthening the municipal level is evident from the British experience. While senior staff promoted the view that local authorities should be strong and vigorous, one of them indiscreetly revealed that

---

[33]Andrew Sancton, "Canada as a Highly Urbanized Nation," in *Canadian Public Administration*, Fall 1992, pp. 281-316.

[34]Sancton, *Disentanglement Dissent*, p. 24.

[35]*Ibid.*

what the central government really wanted was "local authorities strong enough to do what the centre wanted, to undertake planning and service provision without continued detailed supervision, yet according to centrally determined policies."[36]

Municipal opinions differ on the desirability of the additional responsibilities being shifted downward, especially as between urban and rural municipalities—just as they did in response to the previous disentanglement exercise at the beginning of the 1990s. Small and rural municipalities, which are heavily represented in the Association of Municipalities of Ontario, generally supported the services to property versus services to people distinction, and were opposed to the downloading of social programs. However, the regional governments and a number of the large cities recognized the importance of social programs as a way of "connecting to diverse communities and promoting quality of life" and they also recognized that the quality of life in urban areas is "the key instrument of economic development in a global economy."[37] Accordingly, they were interested in the possibility of greater responsibility for social programs, *if* commensurate financial resources were also provided.

The objective of fiscal neutrality for any service swap has been a primary issue, of course, and has seriously compromised the whole exercise. A true disentanglement exercise would determine what services were best handled by what level of government and would then shift them accordingly, *regardless of* the financial impact. There would be "winners" and "losers" as between levels of government, but since there is only one set of taxpayers in Canada (as governments are fond of repeating), then the overall impact would balance out. If provincial costs went up as a result of a service swap, municipal costs would go down by a corresponding amount and the total provincial and municipal taxes paid should remain about the same.

Whatever superficial logic this theoretical argument has, it totally ignores political reality. It matters greatly to governments which level is perceived as spending more or less—especially in the current climate. As a result, the disentanglement exercises of the 1990s have had as an overriding objective the achievement of fiscal neutrality, a pledge that neither level of government will be better or worse off financially as a result of any service swap. The requirement of this objective is understandable on

---

[36]As quoted in Michael Keating, *Comparative Urban Politics*, Aldershot, Edward Elgar, 1991, p. 105.

[37]Graham and Phillips, *op. cit.*, pp. 194 and 205.

one level, but it effectively destroys the disentanglement exercise. One cannot shift functions to the level where they most logically belong; one must manipulate the final service swap in such a way as to balance the books.

The fiscal neutrality objective turned disentanglement into a mathematical exercise.

The extent to which this financial requirement can distort disentanglement is painfully apparent in Ontario. Logic, and the recommendations of a series of previous studies including those of the *Who Does What* panel, suggested that the province should retain, or assume even greater responsibility for, various social programs. If it wished to take over responsibility for education as well, so be it. The result would be an increase in provincial costs and a corresponding decrease in municipal costs. Instead, the combined forces of the fiscal neutrality pledge and the provincial government's own financial and tax-cutting priorities reduced the disentanglement exercise to "basic arithmetic." Since the province wanted education, it needed to download enough other services to offset that cost. This largely explains why social housing, which wasn't even part of the *Who Does What* panel's deliberations, got tossed into the mix.[38]

The nature and scope of the downloading in Ontario cannot be fully explained or justified by the principle of subsidiarity. That principle proclaims that responsibilities should rest at the lowest level *capable of providing them*. It has been cited in numerous studies, including the Golden Report on the GTA.[39] It is our contention, however, that the Ontario government has downloaded responsibilities which are beyond the capability of the municipal system. Moreover, to overcome this problem, the government also embarked on a very aggressive campaign to force amalgamations, with the intention of creating large enough units to be able to handle this download. In our view, these actions seriously distort what was intended by the concept of subsidiarity.

The Ontario experience is also instructive in another regard. If inappropriate responsibilities are downloaded, the end result is to increase entanglement, not to decrease it. The services which most logically belong under municipal jurisdiction are those which can vary in their provision and their standards from place to place. The great attraction of a separate level of municipal government is that it allows

---

[38]*Ibid.*, p. 187.

[39]Report of the GTA Task Force, *Greater Toronto*, January 1996, p. 163.

citizens in different jurisdictions to choose different servicing priorities through their elected councils. But such variations are not an advantage if they occur with respect to services which need to be provided at a minimum standard across Ontario. If those services fall under municipal jurisdiction, then concerns arise about a lack of common standards, and about problems caused by spillovers and externalities. This is the situation we now face in Ontario. The province has downloaded responsibilities with respect to water and sewage treatment facilities, social housing, public health programs, highways, public transit, and a variety of other matters. Will service standards be maintained, especially by municipal governments facing a serious financial squeeze?

This is essentially the same question which has long been posed in the federal-provincial domain, whenever provinces demand greater freedom to make their own service arrangements. It is epitomized by the public concern over medicare and whether a strong federal presence is the best way of resisting the development of a two tier (private and public) health care system. The questions have been nicely joined in an article by Thomas Walkom,[40] in which he invites those who support the provincial call for a social union in which they would have greater say over social programs to hold their meetings (in winter 1999) in Amberley, Ontario. They would find that they could not get there, which is the point he wants to make.

Amberley is a small community near the Lake Huron shoreline, which used to be accessed from no fewer than four provincial highways. All of these highways have been downloaded to the municipal level. As a result, road standards, snowplowing, even speed limits, change abruptly as one moves from one county jurisdiction to another. According to Walkom, in the winter of 1999 the radio routinely reports that county authorities have pulled their plows off the roads. The police respond by closing the roads, and local residents are advised to "hunker down and wait out the weather." In his view, the lesson from all this is that function follows form. "If you want to destroy a provincial highway network, hand off responsibility for roads to local government. If you want to disable a national medicare system, give more authority over enforcement to the provinces."[41]

One need not go as far as Walkom to have reservations about the impact of downloading responsibilities. The Ontario government appears

---

[40]Thomas Walkom, "Drive slowly: Offloading dangers ahead," *Toronto Star*, January 12, 1999.

[41]*Ibid.*

to recognize the potential dangers by providing that municipal performance must adhere to provincial standards which will be developed or enhanced. These standards may well be desirable or necessary to ensure at
least minimum conditions with respect to such services as water supply,
sewage disposal, or public health programs. But the result is a provincial-
municipal relationship which is arguably more entangled, not less.

Ultimately, it may be that efforts at disentanglement are not only
flawed in ways described above, but pointless or inappropriate. The
needs of citizens may best be addressed by more than one level of government. For example, "acknowledging the legitimate local interest in
human-service delivery, while retaining responsibility for income redistribution at the provincial level, would contribute to recognition of the diversity of circumstances and need across communities and affirm a vital
role for local governments in the social domain."[42]

Federal-Local Relations

The apparent inevitability of overlap and entanglement is also illustrated
by the extent and complexity of the federal-local relationship, a relationship which is not even supposed to exist (at least in any formal sense)
according to the constitution. But exist it does, and, in fact, federal-local
relations have arguably been more prominent both before and after the
brief period in which they were formalized through the federal Ministry of
State for Urban Affairs. As described in Chapter 4, there is no better example than the federal contribution, through financial assistance under
the Dominion Housing Act of 1935 and then the Canada Mortgage and
Housing Corporation of 1946, to low-density sprawl and all of its associated municipal servicing problems. The actions of CMHC also contributed to neighbourhood dislocations and attendant problems because of
what has been described as a bulldozer approach to urban renewal.

To be fair, not all federal urban renewal experiences have been this
negative. Gutstein details the experiences of the Strathcona Property
Owners' and Tenants' Association, established in 1968 to oppose urban
renewal initiatives in Vancouver which were displacing large numbers of
families.[43] The following year the federal government announced that it

---

[42]Graham and Phillips, *op. cit.*, p. 205.

[43]Donald Gutstein, "Vancouver," in Warren Magnusson and Andrew Sancton
(eds.), *City Politics in Canada*, Toronto, University of Toronto Press, 1983, p. 201.

would not provide funds for the urban renewal projects in Strathcona Park unless the residents were involved in the planning process. The result was a working committee comprising government officials and members of the Association, "one of the first instances in Canada of citizens sharing this kind of decision making with government."

Decisions by the Department of Transport concerning rail services have had a critical impact on the economic vitality of communities as have various industrial incentive and other programs offered by such departments as Regional Economic Expansion. One well-documented example shows the federal Minister of Regional Economic Expansion playing a leading role in securing the removal of railway tracks from the centre of Quebec City—an objective that had been voiced for 60 years.[44]

Immigration policy is another federal government responsibility which has affected municipalities, dramatically so in the case of Canada's largest urban centres. But as Frisken notes, "federal immigration policy makes little attempt to ease the strains imposed on cities or city neighbourhoods by large influxes of new immigrants."[45]

These examples should suffice to demonstrate that a kind of federal-local relationship existed long before it was given any formal recognition during the 1970s. Indeed, one study found that by the late 1960s, "more than 117 distinct programs administered by 27 departments in Ottawa influenced metropolitan development plans."[46]

In almost every case, however, the federal programs were introduced without regard to their impact on the local level. Municipalities had no opportunity for advance consultation and little hope of obtaining adjustments after the fact. In many cases, the varied federal initiatives were not even coordinated with each other. During the 1960s, for example, the CMHC financed extensive residential construction in the vicinity of the Malton Airport near Toronto.[47] When the Ministry of Transport sought to expand the airport in 1968, it found that an entire residential community had been constructed on what had been uninhabited farmland. As a

---

[44]See Lionel D. Feldman and Katherine A. Graham, *Bargaining for Cities*, Toronto, Butterworths and Co., 1979, pp. 60-63.

[45]Frances Frisken, "Introduction," in Frances Frisken (ed.), *The Changing Canadian Metropolis*, Volume 1, Toronto, Canadian Urban Institute, p. 19.

[46]Elliot J. Feldman and Jerome Milch, "Coordination or Control? The Life and Death of the Ministry of Urban Affairs," in Lionel D. Feldman (ed.), *Politics and Government of Urban Canada*, Toronto, Methuen, 1981, p. 250.

[47]*Ibid.*, p. 251.

result, its expansion plans were thwarted and it had no choice but to seek a new site for an airport.

By the end of the 1960s, however, developments were under way which appeared to offer the possibility of a much more coordinated approach to the handling of federal activities which affected urban Canada. Two major factors were combining to produce strong pressure for a closer and more formalized federal-local relationship. First, there was a growing municipal interest in the possibility of increased federal funds being made available to deal with major service demands, especially in urban areas. Doubtless this interest was stimulated by the fact that requests to the provincial governments for more financial assistance were constantly rebuffed on the grounds that the provinces were short of funds because of federal dominance of the main revenue fields. As the only national municipal body, the Canadian Federation of Mayors and Municipalities (now the Federation of Canadian Municipalities) took the initiative in promoting the municipal cause, especially after discussions on constitutional reform commenced in 1967. A joint Municipal Committee on Intergovernmental Relations was established and prepared an excellent paper on *The Municipality in the Canadian Federation* for presentation to the annual conference of provincial ministers of municipal affairs in Winnipeg in August 1970.

Municipal interest in federal money and federal concerns about urban Canada prompted closer federal-local relations.

In the meantime, the second factor encouraging a federal-local relationship was developing with the growing federal appreciation that because of the large number of Canadians living in urban areas, the ability of municipal governments to meet their needs was of more than local, or even provincial, interest. In this connection, December 1967 brought a Federal-Provincial Conference on Housing and Urban Development and this was followed by a conference of civil servants in April 1968 at which the federal government outlined a number of specific shared-cost proposals. Within a few months a Federal Task Force on Housing and Urban Development was appointed and its January 1969 report called for a greatly expanded federal role. Headed by the then Minister of Transport, Paul Hellyer, the Task Force did not hesitate to make a number of recommendations involving matters within the jurisdiction of the provincial and municipal governments and appeared to incorporate a number of the proposals which had been made by federal officials at the above-noted April 1968 conference of federal and provincial civil servants.

Thus, for example, the Task Force recommended that the federal government make direct loans to municipalities to assist them in assembling and servicing land for urban growth, acquiring dispersed existing housing for use by low-income groups, and developing urban transit systems. Noting that urban planning must be undertaken on a regional basis to be effective, the report called on the provinces to establish a system of regional governments for each major area. In addition, it recommended that the federal government establish a Department of Housing and Urban Affairs. The Task Force envisaged that the CMHC would retain its role as administrator and implementor of federal housing policy, while the new department would concentrate on advising on policy and coordinating research activities, at least at the federal level and possibly with other governments and agencies as well.

Initially, the federal cabinet appeared not ready to accept such an enlarged role and within a few months Hellyer resigned as Minister of Transport, expressing dissatisfaction with the lack of government action on housing and urban questions generally. He later claimed that he was sabotaged by senior civil servants opposed to his recommendations.[48] While there was undoubtedly some truth to this charge, David Cameron notes that by using "outsiders" on his Task Force, Hellyer was bound to create opposition from the bureaucracy, especially when the tight schedule for preparation of the report left insufficient time for the accommodation of views. Moreover, by making himself chairman, Hellyer "forged an identity between the results of the policy recommendations and his own political future."[49]

The Rise and Fall of MSUA

Ironically, within a year of Hellyer's resignation, his successor, Robert Andras, was designated Minister of State for Urban Affairs and a Ministry of Urban Affairs was established. As recommended by the Hellyer Task Force, the new ministry was not to be a traditional operating department but was to concentrate on policy development and on coordinating the projects of other departments. Also emphasized was the need to increase consultation and coordination among all three levels of government in dealing with the challenges of urbanization.

---

[48]See Hellyer's comments in *City Magazine*, Toronto, December 1977.

[49]David M. Cameron, "Urban Policy," in G. Bruce Doern and V. Seymour Wilson (eds.), *Issues in Canadian Public Policy*, Toronto, Macmillan, 1974, p. 231.

The new ministry began with ambitious objectives considering "the absence of any authority with which to control the legislative or spending proposals of other agencies."[50] One analysis[51] observed that "it was created as a new David without a sling; the new ministry of state could fulfil its mission only with mutual trust and goodwill." These commodities turned out to be in short supply and none of the approaches attempted by the ministry had much success.

Initially, in an attempt to gain credibility, "MSUA offered to represent the interests of municipalities and provincial governments in discussions with other federal agencies."[52] But this role brought it into direct confrontation with other federal agencies and little was accomplished. By 1972 MSUA had adopted a new strategy—it would promote coordination by arranging meetings among representatives of all three levels of government and the various federal ministries whose programs affected urban areas. This approach had already been advocated by the Canadian Federation of Mayors and Municipalities and partly through the efforts of the Federation the first ever national tri-level conference was held in Toronto in November of 1972. The fact that the municipal level was represented in its own right was in itself a breakthrough, but the extent to which the conference might be considered a success depends upon the expectations of those participating in it. A Joint Municipal Committee on Intergovernmental Affairs presented several well-researched papers but little progress was made because of the uncompromising attitude of the provinces, especially Ontario.[53]

A second national tri-level conference was held in Edmonton in October 1973. It was decided to undertake a study of public finance with particular reference to the adequacy of municipal revenue sources, a development seen optimistically as "the first important piece of firm evidence of the success of the tri-level process."[54] But delays in launching the Tri-Level Task Force on Public Finance led to the third national tri-level conference being postponed, forever as it turned out.

---

[50]Cameron in Doern and Wilson, *op. cit.*, p. 245.

[51]Feldman and Milch in Feldman, *op. cit.*, p. 254.

[52]*Ibid.*, p. 255.

[53]For a thoughtful assessment of this first conference, see *Urban Focus*, Vol. 1, No. 2, "The Tri-Level Conference—The Morning After," Queen's University, Institutes of Local Government and Intergovernmental Relations, January-February 1973.

[54]*Urban Focus*, Vol. 2, No. 1, November-December 1973.

With the national tri-level conferences stalled by provincial intransigence, MSUA adopted another strategy. It attempted to move from persuasion to power—which it sought through the Canada Mortgage and Housing Corporation which controlled major expenditures. Here again, however, successes were limited and by 1975 there was "a state of open warfare between MSUA and CMHC."[55] Within 18 months the MSUA personnel were cut by 40%.

It adopted yet another approach at this point. It made no effort to initiate meetings, but let it be known that it would organize them if requested. "MSUA thus evolved from an agency that had flirted with the imposition of policy to an urban consultant active only on invitation."[56] This final phase of MSUA activity was received more favourably, but this was largely because of its much more modest mission, not because of any real support. By the spring of 1979 it had fallen victim to the politics of austerity. "Total savings would be less than $4 million (perhaps closer to $500 000), but the public would be impressed by a government prepared to abolish a whole ministry in the name of fiscal responsibility."[57]

While the reasons for the failure of MSUA are fairly obvious for the most part,[58] viewpoints vary on its original appropriateness or the consequences of its demise. While conceding that "responsibility for urban policy—as policy for cities—must rest with the provinces," Cameron contends that there still could be an important role for a federal body like MSUA "to concentrate on analyzing the impact of federal activities on cities and in turn interpreting provincial and municipal urban policy to federal agencies."[59] What is clear is that because of the failure of MSUA we continue to have federal policies enacted without regard to their urban impact. "Federal initiatives in the cities have been not only incoherent and irrational, often they have been inconsistent and unequal."[60]

In spite of the experience of MSUA, tri-level relations continue in Canada, and are unavoidable given the interdependence of programs and

---

[55]Feldman and Milch, *op. cit.*, pp. 257-258.

[56]*Ibid.*

[57]*Ibid.*, p. 260.

[58]In addition to the frequently cited article by Feldman and Milch, see Cameron in Doern and Wilson, *op. cit.*, and Allan O'Brien, "The Ministry of State for Urban Affairs: A Municipal Perspective," in *The Canadian Journal of Regional Science*, Halifax, Spring 1982.

[59]Cameron in Doern and Wilson, *op. cit.*, p. 249.

[60]Feldman and Milch in Feldman, *op. cit.*, p. 263.

policies at all three levels of government. The need for such a relationship also derives from the very considerable influence which the federal government exerts over Canadian municipalities. To take but one example of the interdependence of the various levels of government, consider the issue of the transportation of hazardous goods. The Canadian Transport Commission held a series of hearings in the mid-1980s on the rail transportation of hazardous materials to the Vancouver port area, only to conclude that broader questions of all forms of movement of dangerous goods were beyond its jurisdiction but needed to be addressed. The result was a tri-level task force to conduct the first such comprehensive study in the Vancouver metropolitan region.[61]

> Notwithstanding the demise of MSUA, the federal government continues to influence how cities develop.

There is ample evidence to demonstrate that the federal government has continued to influence the way Canadian cities develop, even with the death of MSUA. In fact, the federal influence may have been greater during the 1980s, as evidenced by major development projects in almost all of Canada's major metropolitan areas.[62] Some of these projects (such as Harbourfront in Toronto and the Rideau Centre in Ottawa) were the result of election promises, while others reflected the regional influence of a member of the cabinet—such as the Winnipeg Core Area Initiative promoted by Lloyd Axworthy.[63] Whatever their impetus, these projects demonstrated the continuing significance of the federal presence in urban Canada.

The end of the 1980s saw repeated calls by municipalities for a tri-level approach to the funding of infrastructure investment in Canadian cities. Without such support, it was alleged, many basic municipal services which provide the basis for growth and development would begin to crumble. A 1985 study by the Federation of Canadian Municipalities determined that $12 billion in infrastructure investment was needed across Canada. The situation was reminiscent of the late 1960s, when municipal concerns about the high costs of such items as urban transportation

---

[61]Peter Oberlander and Patrick Smith, "Governing Metropolitan Vancouver," in Donald Rothblatt and Andrew Sancton (eds.), *Metropolitan Governance: American/Canadian Intergovernmental Perspectives*, Berkeley, Institute of Governmental Studies Press, 1993, p. 341.

[62]Caroline Andrew, "Federal Urban Activity: Intergovernmental Relations in an Age of Restraint," in Frisken, *op. cit.*, p. 430.

[63]*Ibid.*

systems helped to precipitate the previous period of formal tri-level relations. The difference is that in that earlier period the federal government was actively interested in pursuing a more formal tri-level relationship. No similar interest was evident at the end of the 1980s, as the federal government struggled to reduce its financial commitments wherever possible.

The election of a federal Liberal government in 1993 did lead to one tri-level initiative relating to the infrastructure. As part of a job-creation program promised during the election campaign, the government introduced the *Canada Infrastructure Works* program. Over a two year period ending on March 31, 1996, it pledged to provide $2 billion in federal funding for approved projects, to be matched by the same amount of funding from provinces and municipalities, directed toward upgrading the quality of the physical infrastructure in local communities.[64] Municipalities were generally pleased with the program, which allowed them to address some of their most pressing infrastructure needs. Overall, 60% of the infrastructure funding was spent on water, sewer, and transportation projects, with the remaining 40% going on construction or improvement of various types of community facilities and special projects.[65]

The Changing Financial Relationship

Disentanglement, of a sort, is occurring with respect to intergovernmental financial relations. It has been driven and shaped by the deficit and debt reduction measures which have preoccupied the senior levels over the past decade. In what has been characterized as an era of fend-for-yourself federalism, the federal government has been reducing its transfers to the provinces, while softening the blow by making them less conditional. The provinces have responded in kind, with respect to their financial assistance to municipalities. If this trend continues, municipal governments will find themselves (whether willingly or not) with greater financial independence. They will have to find a growing portion of the funds they need from their own revenue sources, much as they had to do in the early years of their existence.

> As in the beginning, municipalities once again have to rely mainly on their own revenue sources.

---

[64]From Canada Infrastructure Works, *News Release*, February 18, 1994.

[65]According to Federation of Canadian Municipalities, *Year in Review: 1995-96*, p. 21, as quoted in Graham et al., *op. cit.*, p. 188.

The original expectation that municipal expenditures would be financed from the property tax was undermined by the expensive service demands unleashed by the extensive urbanization of the 20th century. The provincial and federal governments have also faced greatly increased expenditures but they have been able to impose a variety of new taxes to finance their needs. While the federal government has unlimited taxing powers under the constitution and the provincial governments can levy any form of direct tax, municipalities are restricted to those tax sources which their provincial governments have seen fit to delegate to them. A number of different taxes have been available to municipalities over the years, but most of these have since disappeared or been reclaimed by the senior levels of government as part of the centralization of finances referred to above. The mainstay of municipal revenues has always been the tax on real property, supplemented in some provinces by an additional tax on business at a rate on a stipulated percentage of the assessed value of the property.

While the property tax was still providing over 80% of municipal revenues in 1930, that proportion had fallen below 50% by the beginning of the 1960s.[66] In its place, grants from the senior levels of government became increasingly prominent, accounting for over 40% of the gross general revenues of Canadian local governments by the beginning of the 1970s. As discussed in Chapter 4, the overwhelmingly conditional nature of these grants threatened to reduce municipal governments to "hollow receptacles into which the values of the federal and provincial government are poured."[67]

Some of the uncertainties surrounding financial assistance were at least partly addressed by revenue-sharing agreements introduced in a number of the provinces. Ontario was the first to take this initiative, in 1973—with its "Edmonton Commitment" to increase its transfers to local governments at the rate of growth of total provincial revenues—but it was also one of the first to abandon revenue sharing, in 1977. In the second half of the 1970s, provinces such as Manitoba, Saskatchewan, and British Columbia introduced plans which guaranteed their municipalities specified levels of transfer payment.

---

[66]Economic Council of Canada, *Fourth Annual Review*, Ottawa, September 1967, p. 219.

[67]Municipal Submission to the first National Tri-Level Conference, *Policies, Programs and Finance*, Ottawa, 1972, p. 20.

While these arrangements were of some benefit while they lasted, the bulk of financial support remained both uncertain and overwhelmingly conditional in most provinces. New Brunswick was the one exception to this pattern in the 1970s, but its proportion of conditional grants had begun to increase by the end of the decade. In 1983 the province announced that it was freezing the 1984 unconditional grant at the 1983 level as part of a series of restraint measures.[68] Growing municipal concerns led to a new unconditional grant formula, but the province introduced a financial freeze again in 1989. According to the municipalities, unconditional grants as a percentage of gross budgets in New Brunswick cities declined from 49.8% in 1974 to 34.9% in 1988.[69]

These transfer freezes (and subsequent reductions) have done nothing to alter Richmond's critical assessment of the provincial-municipal financial relationship and the changes which have been made to it. He compares the approach used quite unfavourably with that of the provincial and federal levels in resolving their problems of fiscal imbalance.[70] Generally, Richmond finds that greater centralization and control by the provinces over local governments has been the result and notes that:

> In contrast to the federal-provincial response, the provincial-municipal mechanism for dealing with financial dilemmas was generally characterized by unilaterally determined transfer mechanisms, a proliferation of conditional grants, an irrational equalization system and a large number of special purpose bodies.[71]

He also points to the harmful effects of the financial restraint experienced by provincial governments and notes that provinces such as Ontario and British Columbia have frozen their contribution to shared cost programs and "left the municipal sector out on a limb when attempting to budget for an ongoing responsibility."[72] The difficulty is illustrated by two examples involving Ontario.[73] In 1971 the province increased its

---

[68]Department of Municipal Affairs and Environment, *Review of New Brunswick's Unconditional Grants to Municipalities*, February 1986, p. 41.

[69]Brief to the Policy and Priorities Committee of the Government of New Brunswick, *Re The Unconditional Grant to Municipalities and Related Matters*, Provincial-Municipal Council, Inc., October 11, 1988, p. 3-3.

[70]Dale Richmond, "Provincial-Municipal Transfer Systems," *Canadian Public Administration*, Summer 1980, pp. 252-255.

[71]*Ibid.*, p. 253.

[72]*Ibid.*, pp. 258-259.

[73]Kitchen, *op. cit.*, pp. 384-385.

support for the capital costs of public transit systems from 25% to 75% and, in addition, agreed to pay 50% of the operating deficit of transit systems—changes which prompted some municipalities to expand their transit facilities. But in 1975 the province imposed a ceiling on the amount it would contribute to operating deficits, and the following year it limited its contribution to a 5% increase from the previous year, at a time when operating costs were increasing much more rapidly.[74] Similarly, municipalities greatly expanded their day care facilities when the province financed 80% of the costs. Here again, 1976 saw the province limit funds for this service to a 5.5% increase, with municipalities locked into more rapidly expanding expenditures over which they had little control.

Siegel explains how this uncertainty surrounding conditional grants can leave municipalities very vulnerable to shifts in provincial policy.[75] Because of initial provincial interest in some program, the municipality is encouraged to develop extensive delivery systems on which local citizens come to rely. Then the provincial government's priorities change, and it shifts its financial support elsewhere. The municipality cannot shift its operations so easily; it has a delivery system in place and a clientele that has come to depend on the service or program in question. The result is that the municipality feels compelled to continue providing the service, but without the provincial funding which first tempted it into this activity.

Cuts in federal transfers have led the provinces to cut transfers to municipalities.

Reference has already been made to declining provincial financial support in recent years in provinces such as British Columbia, Ontario, and New Brunswick. To a large extent, this situation reflects the decline in federal financial support to the provinces. Federal cash transfers to provincial health and social programs were cut by 33% in the first two years of the Canada Health and Social Transfer block grant[76] which replaced two somewhat more conditional programs, the Canada Assistance Plan and Established Program Funding. The 1999 federal budget promises $11.5 billion more for health care over the next five

---

[74]Those steps pale beside the Ontario government's action, arising from the previously discussed *Who Does What* exercise, to phase out all financial support for public transit.

[75]David Siegel, "The Financial Context for Urban Policy," in Richard Loreto and Trevor Price (eds.), *Urban Policy Issues: Canadian Perspectives*, Toronto, McClelland and Stewart Inc., 1990, p. 27.

[76]Matt Sanger, "The Financial Squeeze on Local Government," *The CPPA Monitor*, Canadian Centre for Policy Alternatives, May 1998.

years, beginning with $2 billion more in 1999-2000, but it remains to be seen to what extent the provinces will respond by increasing transfers to municipalities.

Up to now, provinces have been expressing indignation at the cuts in federal transfers even as they have pursued a similar approach with their municipalities. Provincial transfers have been reduced, with the blow sometimes softened by providing the money with fewer strings attached. Alberta and Ontario have been notable in this regard. Alberta terminated its Municipal Assistance Grant and replaced it with a new Unconditional Grants Program. Funds from four other conditional grants programs (relating to urban parks, public transit, policing, and family and community support services) were then transferred into the new unconditional program. But the budget for the unconditional program was then steadily reduced, from $169 million in 1994/95 to $126 million the next year and to only $88 million in 1996/97.[77] In strikingly similar fashion, the newly elected Conservative government in Ontario announced in 1995 that three existing grant programs (the unconditional grant, roads grant, and northern roads assistance) were being converted into a single block grant—the Municipal Support Grant. This new grant was then reduced from what would have been a $1.4 billion transfer to $887 million in 1996 and $666 million in 1997, before disappearing as a separate grant in 1998.

As a result of these and other actions, provincial transfers have gone from being a growing proportion of municipal revenues during the first three-quarters of the 20th century to a sharply declining portion. As noted in Chapter 4, while transfers accounted for close to 50% of municipal revenues in 1971, they represented only 25% of the total in 1993 and just 20% in 1997. The capacity of municipal governments to absorb the transfer cuts, and also to cope with the increase in expenditures from downloaded responsibilities and costs, is constrained by their more limited sources of revenue. The primary local source has always been the real property tax, which was still providing over 80% of municipal revenues as late as 1930.[78] By the mid-1980s, the property tax accounted for barely one-third of municipal revenues.[79] With the growing shortfall in transfer payments, however, the property tax is now back to about 50% as it tries

---

[77]Figures from Alberta Municipal Affairs, *News Release*, February 24, 1994.

[78]Economic Council of Canada, *Fourth Annual Review*, *op. cit.*, p. 219.

[79]Richard M. Bird and Enid Slack, *Urban Public Finance in Canada*, 2nd edition, Toronto, John Wiley and Sons, 1993, p. 64.

to make up the difference.[80] The rest of the shortfall has been offset by an expansion in miscellaneous local revenues, especially in user fees.

Provincial Invasion of Property Tax Field

The ability of municipalities to finance an increasing portion of their expenditures from their own revenue sources is threatened by the fact that the real property tax is less and less their own to use as they wish. Since the beginnings of municipal government in Canada, this tax has been portrayed as the mainstay of municipal finances. Yet municipalities have been gradually losing control over the use of the property tax.

Much of the provincial incursion has occurred with respect to education financing. At one time, education costs were mainly funded from the property tax. Gradually, provincial financial assistance grew, along with increasing provincial control and supervision of educational matters. Provincial governments also amalgamated school boards, in a move paralleling and exceeding in scope the amalgamation of municipalities described in Chapters 5 and 6. Prompted by the desire to reduce costs and to improve access and equity, provinces began—as early as the 1930s in Alberta—to consolidate school boards and school areas.[81]

> The process of school board consolidation has intensified during the 1990s.

This process has continued and intensified in the 1990s. For example, New Brunswick reduced the number of school boards from 42 to 18 in 1992 and then eliminated the remaining boards in 1996, replacing them with provincial superintendents advised by 18 district councils. Alberta reduced the number of school boards from 181 to 57 in a two-stage process which began in 1994. Twenty-two boards were amalgamated into six regional boards in Nova Scotia, along with one province-wide board for Acadian and Francophone education.[82] Effective January

---

[80]Property taxes generated 49% of local government revenues in 1993 and 51% in 1997, according to data in Statistics Canada, CANSIM, Matrix 7093, *Local General Government Revenue and Expenditure, Canada*, as found at its web site, www.statcan.ca, on March 30, 1999.

[81]For a summary of consolidation activities up to the mid-1990s, see Robert Carney and Frank Peters, "Governing Education: The Myth of Local Control," in James Lightbody (ed.), *Canadian Metropolitics: Governing Our Cities*, Toronto, Copp Clark Ltd., pp. 248-251.

[82]The preceding examples are all from Ontario Ministry of Education and Training, Backgrounder, *Education Reform and Finance in Other Provinces,* 1997.

1, 1998, Ontario cut the number of school boards in half, to 66. The Quebec government has recently replaced 159 religious boards with 72 linguistic boards.

There are many issues which could be raised, such as the large size of many of the remaining boards and the extent to which the reforms have involved the centralization of educational decisions within provincial bureaucracies. But our primary concern in this section is with the effect of these education changes on municipal occupancy of the property tax field. Beginning with the Program of Equal Opportunity in New Brunswick in 1967, provinces have been appropriating a portion of the property tax field and directing it to the financing of specified provincial services. As a result, the provincial role in the property tax field is much larger than the role of state governments in the United States. "Not only is the tax now basically provincial in New Brunswick, Prince Edward Island, and, for education, in British Columbia, but the local tax rates are at least partly determined by provincial grant levels...."[83] In New Brunswick and PEI the province acts as the collection agency for both its own property tax levies and those for municipal governments.

The disentanglement exercises of the 1990s have added to this pattern of encroachment. For example, when Nova Scotia took on administrative responsibility for a number of "people services" in the 1995-96 program of service exchange, it still required municipalities to include a provincial education levy in their tax bills, and also to contribute to the social and correctional services programs which are now totally provincial responsibilities.[84] As a result, a substantial portion of the municipal budget and the municipal tax base is devoted to supporting provincial programs.[85] Similarly, under Ontario's realignment of services following the *Who Does What* exercise, the province assumed responsibility for half of the education costs previously paid by residential property tax payers. But the province also took over responsibility for setting the residential property tax rate to finance the other half of those costs, and for setting the property tax rate paid by business properties.

More recently, the Ontario government has demonstrated a willingness to encroach on municipal decision making with respect to property taxes. Throughout 1997 and 1998, the province introduced property tax reform through at least six separate statutes (and an accompanying flood

---

[83]Bird and Slack, *op. cit.*, p. 92.

[84]Antoft and Novack, *op. cit.*, p. 95.

[85]Communication from Jack Novack, March 18, 1999.

of regulations). A central feature of the reforms was to be the greater discretion to set tax policy given to municipalities in the form of various tax tools which they could utilize to mitigate any adverse tax impacts arising from the move to current value assessment. Even though the reform process continued to unfold throughout 1998, making it difficult to finalize budgets, a majority of the authorized municipalities did utilize one or more of the tax tools provided to them. In late October 1998, however, the Minister of Finance announced that the municipal efforts had been inadequate, and that businesses in Ontario were facing unnecessary and unacceptable tax increases. The government passed Bill 79 in December 1998, imposing a cap on tax increases on business properties of 10% in 1998, an additional 5% in 1999, and an additional 5% in the year 2000.

What is striking about Bill 79 is that it implements the view that the province knows best what is appropriate tax policy for local communities. When the Minister of Finance charged that municipalities had failed to use their tax tools properly, what he was really claiming was that they had failed to reduce sufficiently the tax burden on business—a burden which had arisen because of the way the province chose to implement assessment and property tax reform. In our view, if individual municipalities exercise their political judgment and set the tax policies which they deem appropriate, those decisions should be evaluated by their electorates—non-business as well as business—not by Queen's Park.

The main thrust of Bill 79 is to extend provincial control over local financial decision making. The Ontario government has already taken complete control of property taxes with respect to education financing, as part of a series of initiatives which have centralized education decision making in this province. With Bill 79, it is extending its control over that portion of the property tax that was left under municipal control. The 10-5-5 limits may seem large enough for most purposes, and it is true that municipalities can raise taxes beyond these limits as a result of council policy decisions which are not property tax related. But the cap is mandatory for all municipalities and a very dangerous precedent has been established. Bill 79 has moved municipalities on to a very slippery slope from which it would be all too easy for the province to introduce permanent tax controls extending to all types of municipal expenditure.

The gravity of the situation is well expressed by the Executive Director of the Association of Municipal Clerks and Treasurers of Ontario:

> Make no mistake, this is a devastating decision for municipal government in Ontario. For decades, municipal associations have been lobbying for access to more revenue sources to supplement property taxes and reflect

the scope of municipal responsibilities. This decision places the Provincial Government firmly in control of property taxes in Ontario.[86]

Consultation with the Senior Levels

Much of this chapter portrays the municipal level as essentially a passive observer; it is dictated to by the province or adversely affected by thoughtless federal action. This emphasis overlooks the extent to which municipal governments can take the initiative in pressing their viewpoint upon the senior levels and attempting to obtain concessions from them. The consultative mechanisms available to municipalities and their effectiveness will be briefly considered in this concluding section.

The Federation of Canadian Municipalities

The one national association of municipalities is the *Federation of Canadian Municipalities* (FCM). It was founded as the Canadian Federation of Mayors and Municipalities in 1937, during the Great Depression,[87] and one of its main objectives was to pressure the federal government to finance an unemployment relief program. Efforts to improve the financial position of the municipal level have remained a major concern of the Federation over the ensuing years. The Federation has suffered from some internal squabbling about urban versus rural considerations. In 1973, for example, David Crombie organized a meeting at which Toronto, Montreal, Calgary, and Vancouver discussed withdrawing from the Federation.[88] Another problem is that the need to find a middle ground has forced the Federation to espouse generalized positions which reflect the lowest common denominator at times. Its position may also be weakened by the existence of a number of very active provincial associations of municipalities, and there have been recurring suggestions that it become a federation of these bodies.[89]

---

[86]Editorial by Ken Cousineau, in *Municipal Monitor*, December/January 1998/1999, Association of Municipal Clerks and Treasurers of Ontario.

[87]Gregory Brandsgard, "Regina and Saskatoon's Troubled Membership in the Federation of Canadian Municipalities," in Christopher Dunn (ed.), *Saskatoon Local Government and Politics*, University of Saskatchewan, 1987, p. 78.

[88]*Ibid.*, p. 84.

[89]David Siegel, "Provincial-Municipal Relations in Canada: An Overview," in *Canadian Public Administration*, Summer 1980, p. 314.

During the constitutional debate of the late 1970s and early 1980s which led to the patriation of the constitution, the FCM established a Task Force on Constitutional Reform which called for the entrenchment of municipalities into the Constitution of Canada. In a 1980 Task Force report on *Municipal Government in a New Canadian Federal System*, it called for constitutional recognition of autonomy for municipalities in areas relating to law making, finances, and governing structures.[90] When the Canadian constitution was repatriated in 1982, however, there was no recognition of the municipal level of government.

The Federation has rebounded from this setback and has since experienced considerable growth. Its membership more than tripled from 1983 to 1990, going from about 200 members to some 600,[91] and to about 630 at the end of the 1990s. Its staff and budget have also enjoyed a healthy expansion. It gained national profile with its "big fix" campaign to rebuild Canada's infrastructure, described earlier. It has also been active with respect to such matters as federal payments in lieu of taxes to municipalities, urban transportation issues, criminal justice issues, and the impact of reductions in federal social spending on the quality of life in Canadian cities.[92] It also continues to be a strong advocate on behalf of municipalities and their place within confederation, as evidenced by its 1997 policy statement on the future role of municipal government.[93]

Municipal Associations at the Provincial Level

Most provinces have a number of municipal associations representing both staff and councillors, although it is the political associations which are critical to the consultations with the senior levels. Some provinces have several of these associations while others have only one. Obviously, one large association representing all municipalities has the potential to speak with a more powerful voice. But this potential may not be realized, since the attempt to represent a variety of municipal viewpoints may cause internal strife and foster excessive compromising, pleasing no one.

---

[90]The discussion of FCM's efforts to gain constitutional recognition for municipalities is based on Association of Municipalities of Ontario, *Local Governance in the Future: Issues and Trends*, Toronto, 1994, pp. 60-66.

[91]Andrew, *op. cit.*, pp. 440-441.

[92]Graham et al., *op. cit.*, p. 196.

[93] This paper, and much other pertinent information, is available at the web site of the FCM, at www.fcm.ca.

Ontario's experience is interesting in this regard, and it also illustrates the workings of a formalized municipal-provincial consultative process.[94] In 1969 a Municipal Liaison Committee (MLC) was established to provide more coordinated activity on the part of the four political associations then in existence. A series of joint meetings were held between a committee of cabinet ministers and the MLC, and by 1972 these sessions had become regular monthly meetings of what came to be known as the Provincial-Municipal Liaison Committee (PMLC).

During 1973 the PMLC was involved in discussions leading up to the previously cited revenue-sharing arrangement known as the Edmonton Commitment. Other important issues included a proposal to move toward a system of unconditional grants. The consultation mechanism appeared to be working and municipalities were encouraged. However, the provincial government appeared less and less responsive with the financial restraint and minority government position of the second half of the 1970s. Some ministers tended to consult with the MLC only when it was in their interests to do so, and one analysis suggests that the MLC was occasionally used as a scapegoat to cover up for provincial mistakes or to shift the blame for unpopular policies.[95]

The MLC itself was hampered by limited staff and financial resources. It also had difficulty deciding on its proper role. If the MLC was essentially a federation and a policy-presenting body rather than one which made policy, then its members had to reconcile their

> The MLC suffered from limited resources and uncertainty about its role.

desire to reach a consensus with their responsibility to represent the potentially diverse views of their respective associations. Making this reconciliation even more difficult was the fact that the associations tended to compete with one another for profile and recognition.[96] In late 1979 the largest political association withdrew from the PMLC and within a short time the monthly meetings had ceased.

---

[94]The analysis that follows is partly based on Sheila Gordon, *Intergovernmental Relations*, a paper presented to the Ontario Conference on Local Government Seminar, September 26, 1978.

[95]T. J. Plunkett and G. M. Betts, *The Management of Canadian Urban Government*, Kingston, Institute of Local Government, Queen's University, 1978, p. 90.

[96]Gordon, *op. cit.*, p. 14.

By June of 1980, however, a new umbrella municipal organization had been recommended, and the founding convention of the new Association of Municipalities of Ontario (AMO) was held in October 1981. The new structure attempted to combine for strength while still preserving the diversity of viewpoints which often arise on municipal issues. Thus, it contained within it five sections: Large Urban, Small Urban, County and Regional, Rural, and Northern Ontario. Its principle of operation was that all views would be forwarded on any issue which came to it for comment.

The second half of the 1980s was a difficult period for AMO. Without the formal consultative mechanism which had existed in the days of the PMLC, it found it difficult to obtain adequate consultation from provincial administrations preoccupied with reducing their budget deficits and quite prepared to download in fulfillment of that objective. There was also considerable turnover among its limited staff complement.

At the beginning of the 1990s, AMO found itself playing a central role in Ontario's disentanglement exercise, discussed above. The tentative agreement reached on the first phase of this exercise was lost when the province arbitrarily imposed major cuts in transfer payments to the municipal level as part of its social contract initiative, but AMO was an active and effective participant in the negotiations leading to the sectoral agreements under the social contract. It has also made a strong case for provincial recognition of a separate level of municipal government in its calls for a municipal charter.[97] AMO also played an important role on two task forces whose recommendations led to improvements in the distribution of functions and costs arising from the *Who Does What* exercise.

While the increased activities on the part of AMO have been welcome in one respect, they also raise questions about the suitability of the organization to act as *the* spokesperson for all municipalities in Ontario.[98] Partly because of its make-up and internal sections, small municipalities tend to dominate the attendance at AMO general meetings and participation on its executive committee. This imbalance has become more of a concern as AMO's role has shifted from one of lobbying, responding to provincial policy initiatives, acting as a clearing-house for information, providing goods and services to its members and the like, to one of nego-

---

[97]See AMO, *Ontario Charter: A Proposed Bill of Rights for Local Government*, Toronto, 1994.

[98]The discussion which follows is based on Evelyn Ruppert, *A Critique of the Association of Municipalities of Ontario*, 1997, available at York University's web site at www.yorku.ca/faculty/academic. The author worked as a senior policy advisor at AMO from 1990 to 1995.

tiating changes on behalf of its members. Member municipalities have reacted strongly to these initiatives, claiming that the Association could not bind them to any agreement or negotiate on behalf of duly elected councils, and also claiming that agreements reached by the Association favoured one segment of the municipal sector at the expense of others.

Concerns about the Association have led to the formation of alternative municipal forums, such as the Regional Chairs and the GTA Mayors, and also to instances of municipalities acting directly on their own, rather than through AMO.[99] It appears that the make-up of AMO which, in turn, reflects the diversity of Ontario's municipalities, makes it very difficult for it to achieve a consensus or to act as *the* voice for municipalities. The province seems content for AMO to act in that capacity. Whether deliberately or not, this provincial sanction maintains an arrangement in which the Ontario government can claim that it consults with municipalities, while also knowing that the municipal input to this consultation is inherently constrained.

One of the oldest municipal associations in Canada is found in Nova Scotia, where the Union of Nova Scotia Municipalities was established in 1906. It repeatedly endorsed the need for rationalization of municipal political boundaries and for a reallocation of provincial and municipal responsibilities, and with these objectives in mind participated in the 1992 *Task Force on Local Government*, described in Chapter 6. However, it subsequently had misgivings about the recommendations in the report. The Association expressed concern about the lack of clear evidence to demonstrate the savings which were supposed to result from changes to be introduced and the lack of adequate time and opportunity for public consultation in the process.[100] However, it did participate in the service exchange introduced in 1995-96, and is currently participating in a new provincial-municipal review examining service exchanges. Like Ontario, the Nova Scotia association has pursued the development of a municipal charter, and participated in the development of a new Municipal Act (discussed below) which was enacted in December 1998.

The Federation of Prince Edward Island Municipalities was formed in 1967, and currently represents 39 municipalities comprising 80% of the

---

[99]This section is based on the Association of Municipal Clerks and Treasurers of Ontario, *Municipal Administration Program*, 1998, Unit One, Lesson 6, p. 32.

[100]Union of Nova Scotia Municipalities, *UNSM Concerns with the Current Process of Municipal Reform*, 1993.

population living in incorporated areas.[101] Its description of what it does for its members is not untypical of such associations:

a) represent the interests of local government and act as a spokesperson for the membership.
b) protect the rights and privileges of municipal governments.
c) carry out research activities for individual members.
d) act as a clearing-house for information.
e) further municipal interests through municipal cooperation.
f) provide avenues of training and education of municipal officials.

As discussed in Chapter 6, the Prince Edward Island government has undertaken a program of municipal reform, including substantial amalgamations in the Summerside and Charlottetown areas. The Federation's response to the government's *White Paper on Municipal Reform* is revealing in demonstrating the difficulty all municipal associations seem to have in reconciling the diverse views of their membership. In its response, the Federation refers to the difficulty of an association of "diverse units" responding definitively and indicates that it is impossible "to manifest a single compatible response." Instead, it has chosen to act as a "facilitator of communication."[102]

To take one more example, Alberta's most prominent municipal association is the Alberta Urban Municipalities Association (AUMA). But Masson has noted that even though this association's membership consisted of 100% of the province's cities and towns and 94% of its villages, it has been limited in its influence because of internal tensions.[103] He describes a picture very reminiscent of the experience of other associations, explaining that in many policy areas small towns and villages have had much different concerns than large cities, and that these differences have made it very difficult for AUMA to take a firm position. According to Masson, "the government did not see the AUMA as a major political threat since it was aware of the uneasy alliance between its large and small member municipalities and the compromises that had to be made on difficult issues."[104]

---

[101]*History of Federation of Prince Edward Island Municipalities*, 1993, p. 2.

[102]Federation of Prince Edward Island Municipalities, *Response to the White Paper on Municipal Reform*, p. 1.

[103]Jack Masson, *Alberta's Local Governments and Their Politics*, Edmonton, University of Alberta Press, 1985, p. 201.

[104]Jack Masson, with Edward C. Lesage, Jr., *Alberta's Local Governments: Politics and Democracy*, Edmonton, University of Alberta Press, 1994, p. 43.

Notwithstanding the activities of the various municipal associations, Feldman and Graham suggest that since these associations are not accountable to the public and are "somewhat immune to public opinion," their use for the conduct of important intergovernmental affairs may have stifled the emergence of much public concern about important municipal (intergovernmental) issues.[105] They question whether or not an association can represent adequately an individual municipality's specific concerns, arguing that associations generally represent "the lowest common denominator" of opinion among their members, thereby blurring the interests of individual municipalities. They raise a concern that municipal associations partially financed by the provincial level may be unduly influenced accordingly. They also point out that provincial governments can sometimes subvert the focus of a municipal association so that it becomes a vehicle for disseminating information about provincial policy, rather than for expressing municipal views and concerns. In this situation, Feldman and Graham conclude, "municipal representatives tend to be thought of at best as glorified office boys and at worst as whipping boys."

In their view, intergovernmental concerns should be addressed by individual municipalities, particularly in the case of Canada's larger municipalities. Yet it is the actions of very large municipalities like Toronto and some of the regional governments in Ontario in seeking to look after their own interests that are felt to have weakened the bargaining position of the Association of Municipalities of Ontario. Nor should one rule out the possibility that provincial governments might encourage such "one-on-one" negotiations as a means of keeping municipalities off balance through a "divide and conquer" strategy.

> The weaknesses of municipal associations may encourage large municipalities to act on their own, which further undermines the associations.

Legal and Judicial Constraints

This chapter began by noting the subordinate constitutional position of municipal government. That lack of constitutional status did not have to result in the very narrow, limited role for municipalities that evolved in most provinces. That sorry state of affairs reflects the way provinces chose to exercise their powers—by passing acts which imposed detailed

---

[105]Feldman and Graham, *op. cit.*, pp. 21-27.

controls over specific municipal actions, rather than authorizing municipalities to exercise their discretion within broadly defined spheres.

Perhaps even more so, the limited scope of municipal action reflects the way courts have chosen to interpret statutes which grant powers to municipalities. There are innumerable texts documenting how the Judicial Committee of the British Privy Council (as the Supreme Court for Canada at the time) made a series of decisions which interpreted the British North America Act in such as way as to increase the powers of the provinces much more than Sir John A. Macdonald would ever have intended. It appears much less widely recognized how influential the courts also were in shaping the fate of municipal governments—although in the opposite direction.

Traditionally, the courts have interpreted very narrowly statutes which grant powers to municipalities, taking the position that unless a power was specifically provided, it could not be exercised. Two brief examples will illustrate this pattern. Does provincial legislation which enables a municipality to produce, manufacture, use, or supply electricity, also enable it to purchase electricity in order to use and supply it? This seems a foolish question, to which the answer must be yes—except that the courts ruled no.[106] What about the actions of the then Township of Etobicoke, which responded to a provincial requirement to publish notice of a road closing in the "local newspaper" by inserting a notice in *The Globe and Mail* instead of the local Etobicoke paper? *The Globe and Mail* was almost certainly a more effective vehicle for reaching the intended audience, but that didn't matter to the court. The precise law of the province had not been followed, so the action was quashed.

It is argued that such judicial interpretations of specific powers given to municipalities have been overly narrow and confining. Makuch is very critical of the fact that by-laws are not examined in the context of the reason for the legislative provisions purporting to grant the authority to pass them. The problem to be overcome by the legislation granting the power is not considered. He concludes that in a desire to limit the authority of municipalities and thereby protect individuals from abuses of municipal power, the courts have adopted an arbitrary, if not irrational, approach to interpreting municipal powers.[107]

---

[106]*Ottawa Elec. Light Co. v. Ottawa* (1906), 12 O.L.R. 290 (C.A.).

[107]Stanley Makuch, *Canadian Municipal and Planning Law*, Toronto, Carswell, 1983, pp. 118-119.

We concur. Rather than regarding municipalities as analogous to private corporations, as corporate bodies which must be tightly controlled to protect citizens from their excesses, it is suggested that the courts should be more appreciative of municipalities as a level of government with a mandate from the electorate and with a legitimate political role to fulfil. A striking contrast is provided by the situation in many European countries where municipalities are given a power of "general competence."[108] This is the power to take action on behalf of the community beyond the powers given or the duties laid down in specific statutes. The important thing about this power is that it is *not* added on to a long list of specific duties; rather, it is the starting point in defining the municipality. It reflects the concept of municipal government as an extension of the community. In that respect, the importance of the power of general competence lies less in the activities that it makes possible and more in what it symbolizes about the nature of municipal government. Municipalities need not search for specific powers, because the powers derive from the concept of the municipality as the community governing itself. As a result, the municipality is, or can be, concerned with "any needs or problems faced in the community, and not merely the services that it provides directly."[109]

One of the primary objectives of most municipal associations has been the achievement of some form of recognition for municipalities within the constitution of Canada or, at least some provincial recognition of municipal roles and rights by way of a municipal charter or similar declaration. An example of the latter is

> A primary objective is formal recognition of the role and rights of municipalities, whether in the constitution or by provincial declaration.

the *Protocol of Recognition* signed by the Union of British Columbia Municipalities (UBCM) and the British Columbia Minister of Municipal Affairs in 1996.[110] It establishes principles that define all future intergovernmental relations, including a commitment to partnership, information sharing, and early notice of, and consultation on, significant legislative change.

---

[108]Michael Clarke and John Stewart, *The Choices for Local Government*, Harlow, Longman, 1991, pp. 16-17.

[109]John Stewart, "A Future for Local Authorities as Community Government," in John Stewart and Gerry Stoker (eds.), *The Future of Local Government*, London, Macmillan, 1989, p. 239.

[110]The discussion which follows is based on a report in *Municipal World*, May 1997, pp. 24-25.

The protocol also creates a joint council composed of the Minister of Municipal Affairs, three other provincial ministers, and officers of the UBCM, to act as a forum for reviewing legislation, regulations, policies, and programs relating to local government.

In similar fashion, the Association of Municipalities of Ontario (AMO) has called for a charter or bill of rights within which the principles, values, and rights of local government would be enshrined.[111] Under the AMO proposal, the charter would grant greater discretionary authority to local government, as opposed to the "creatures of the province" concept of strict limits on local discretionary authority. It asked for a commitment that municipal government would be guaranteed access to provincial decision making and consultation on all matters affecting municipal government. The AMO paper also proposed new municipal legislation which would be more permissive in nature and would authorize municipalities to act on their own initiative with regard to any matter not exclusively assigned to any other authority nor specifically excluded from the competence of municipal government.

The Potential of New Municipal Acts

Beginning with Alberta, in 1994, a number of provinces have passed or proposed new municipal acts which give municipalities broader authority to operate. Are these the breakthrough which has long been sought and which will give municipalities the discretion and the recognition which they need to take action on behalf of their citizens? Preliminary indications are not entirely encouraging.

The Alberta Municipal Government Act is the most promising of these initiatives. It eliminates over 20 other separate statutes, and defines broad spheres in which municipalities are enabled to take action.[112] It describes three purposes of municipal government and then provides that a council may pass by-laws for "municipal purposes" with respect to eight specified matters. It also authorizes municipalities to exercise natural person powers. However, one analysis [113] points out that if the courts continue to take

---

[111]The discussion which follows is based on Association of Municipalities of Ontario, *Ontario Charter: A Proposed Bill of Rights for Local Government*, Toronto, 1994.

[112]Graham et al., *op. cit.*, pp. 176-177.

[113]Kristen Gagnon and Donald Lidstone, *A Comparison of New and Proposed Municipal Acts of the Provinces*, paper presented at the 1998 annual conference of the Federation of Canadian Municipalities, p. 22.

a narrow and literal approach, rather than giving a liberal and remedial interpretation, municipalities may find that they are only able to take actions pursuant to the eight areas specified in the act and only within the framework of the three purposes of municipal government which were specified. It further notes that nothing in the act requires the province to consult with municipalities and that within six months of the act coming into force, several hundred amendments were enacted.

The same analysis finds that the new Manitoba Municipal Act does not give municipalities natural person powers and while it does provide a wide range of permissive powers, the range is narrower in scope than is the case in Alberta. Nor is there any explicit provision providing for consultation between the province and municipalities in this legislation.[114]

The new Nova Scotia Municipal Act does not give municipalities either natural person powers or broad spheres of jurisdiction. Instead, it continues the traditional approach of giving municipalities a list of specific powers, but it does provide somewhat more autonomy by reducing the number of provincial approvals relating to financing and by-laws. In addition, the Act provides that the provincial government shall give municipalities 12 months' notice of any initiatives that may affect municipal finance.[115]

Ontario's proposed Municipal Act has no broad mechanism for consultation and clearly does not contemplate any kind of joint decision making. It does promise greater municipal discretion through the exercise of both natural person and governmental powers in 13 broad areas or spheres of jurisdiction.[116] While the natural person powers can really only be used to facilitate the exercise of specific authority otherwise granted, they should still be a useful tool. For example, the rather ludicrous court decision cited earlier, in which it was held that a municipality had no authority to purchase electricity in order to use and supply it, would not arise with the provisions of the proposed act, since a natural person can clearly make purchases. The 13 spheres of jurisdiction are outlined in very general terms and are then qualified and potentially constrained by details provided in later sections of the act. The cabinet is also authorized to

---

[114]*Ibid.*, pp. 6 and 17.

[115]Department of Housing and Municipal Affairs, "Municipal Legislation Gets Makeover," October 27, 1998.

[116]The discussion which follows is based on Association of Municipal Clerks and Treasurers of Ontario, *Municipal Administration Program*, 1998, Unit Four, Lesson 1, pp. 37-40.

restrict the powers of municipalities under this or any other act. In addition, the cabinet, by regulation, may establish standards for activities of municipalities and require municipalities to comply with the standards in carrying out the activity. There are at least 99 sections and subsections, dealing with at least 203 subjects, over which provincial regulatory power is provided.[117] While a partial draft of the new Municipal Act was released back in early 1997, it had still not been passed at the time of the provincial election of June 1999.

One analysis characterizes the various municipal act initiatives as "incremental, ad hoc revisions," not the "new blueprints" that are needed to allow municipalities to serve their citizens in the future.[118] Whatever merits the new acts may have, they have certainly done little to change the tendency for provincial governments to act arbitrarily and without consultation when they are preoccupied with their own agendas—especially when it is a financial agenda. The behaviour of the Ontario government in this regard has been noted earlier in this chapter. To take another example, neither British Columbia's *Protocol of Recognition* nor the province's 1997 initiative to review and streamline municipal legislation have protected municipalities from financial cuts introduced by an increasingly cash-strapped provincial government. In early 1999 the Union of British Columbia Municipalities suspended participation in the joint council which had been set up under the Protocol, as a result of a cut of $40 million in provincial grants.[119]

Concluding Comments

Intergovernmental relationships in Canada are complex and often contradictory. While municipalities are legally subordinate to the provinces, they are also greatly influenced by the actions of the federal government—both directly and as a result of the way federal actions impinge on the provinces and ultimately on municipalities. Another contradiction is found in the fact that disentanglement initiatives in several provinces have actually led to greater entanglement, largely because of the inappropriateness

---

[117]Michael Smither, "A Proposed New Municipal Act," *Municipal World*, April 1998, p. 22.

[118]Gagnon and Lidstone, *op. cit.*, p. 23.

[119]John Wawrow, "Mayors revolt over cuts," *Vancouver Province*, January 17, 1999.

of some of the functions shifted to the local level. Also puzzling is the fact that some provinces have accepted that they should be responsible for social programs, including education, and then have continued to finance at least part of the costs of these programs from the property tax. This arrangement seems to defeat the whole purpose of provincial assumption of the functions in question, and it also diverts property tax revenues which are needed to finance municipal responsibilities.

All of the downloading taking place under the guise of disentanglement should also not mask the fact that there has also been a reverse process of greater centralization in some functional areas. Education is the most notable example, but the increased use of provincial performance standards may extend this central control to other areas.

It is difficult for municipalities to advance their concerns effectively, given the limitations inherent in the make-up of their municipal associations. Ultimately, however, a major stumbling block appears to be that provincial governments don't seem especially interested in what their municipalities have to say. The rhetoric about municipal empowerment has led to some improvements in general municipal legislation, mainly in Alberta, but there is still little indication that provinces are committed to genuine advance consultation with municipalities. The governing parties have their own agendas which they have been pursuing with marked determination, especially in provinces such as Alberta and Ontario. Municipalities and other local governments are being reformed to satisfy the fiscal and ideological objectives of these ruling parties, with little regard for the wishes of municipal associations or the feelings of local citizens.

CHAPTER 9
The Governing Machinery

Chapter 7 noted that most of the local government reforms introduced in the second half of the 20th century were preoccupied with improving service delivery and paid too little attention to the political and representative role of municipal government. This same observation applies to the internal reforms described in this chapter.

Introduction

Two earlier chapters examined the extensive changes which have occurred with respect to the external municipal structures, mostly through amalgamation. There have also been changes to the internal governing machinery of municipalities, however, and it is to that important topic that we now turn our attention. The chapter begins by providing a brief description of what it terms the traditional machinery, then examines the coordinating structures which have been introduced at both the council and staff level, and concludes with a preliminary assessment of the new business models which are currently in favour.

The Traditional Machinery

For our purposes, the traditional machinery of municipal government is defined as comprising the municipal council, the municipal staff (usually organized into a number of functionally specialized departments, depending on the size of the municipality), and a number of standing committees providing a link between councillors and staff. It is appreciated that other structures, notably the chief administrative officer or CAO system, are also fairly common, but these are examples of the coordinating machinery which is discussed in the next section.

The Municipal Council

All municipalities in Canada are corporate bodies and as such exercise, and are limited to, the powers granted by their creators, the provincial governments. These powers are exercised on behalf of the inhabitants by an elected council. The provincial legislation usually includes provisions for the form of council and such details as the number of councillors and whether election is by general vote or by ward (a distinction discussed below).

Municipal councils in Canada consist of a head (known as warden or chair in counties and other upper tier governments, as mayor in cities and towns, and as reeve, chairman, or overseer in villages and townships) and a widely varying number of other councillors. While the total membership varies greatly, there has been a tendency to have small councils of from five to 15 members, largely on the grounds that a small group is less unwieldy and more efficient in making decisions. Notable exceptions include the new city of Toronto with a council of 57 (plus the mayor), the city of Montreal with its 51 members, and, initially, Winnipeg Unicity— which also started out with 51 members but has since been reduced twice to a current membership of 15. While some larger councils have appeared in recent years as a result of amalgamations, the general pattern has been to reduce the size of council. The prevailing view seems to be that smaller councils are preferable because they allow for more expeditious decision making.

Perhaps the most distinctive feature of the council as a governing body is that it combines both executive and legislative responsibilities. As an executive body it initiates proposals for municipal action, makes a myriad of specific decisions—such as hiring a particular employee—and supervises the administration of the policies and programs of the municipality. As a legislative body, it makes by-laws which are the laws governing its citizens. At the senior levels of government, these functions are the responsibility of two separate branches: the Cabinet and the Legislative Assembly (House of Commons). The fact that these functions are combined in the council means, among other things, that the line between making policy and administering policy is often quite blurred at the local level. The combination of diverse responsibilities may also help to explain why there has often appeared to be a preoccupation with specific servicing issues to the neglect of the other roles of municipal government.

Methods of Election

One of the distinguishing features of municipal government is the election of members of the municipal councils, a process which supposedly ensures representativeness and accountability. In practice, however, there are three key variables in connection with the municipal election process:

1. Whether election is by general vote, or on the basis of wards.
2. Whether election is for a short term or a long term of office.
3. Whether members are elected directly or indirectly.

All three of these variables have changed over the years, and all are the subject of lively debate and divided opinions. As will become evident from the examination of these three variables, the differing arguments reflect an underlying preoccupation with either the service delivery or the political role of municipal government.

Ward versus General Vote

While directly elected heads of council are chosen by a general vote of the entire municipality, members of council may be elected on the basis of a ward system. If so, the municipality is divided into several geographic areas with a number of members (usually an equal number) to be chosen from each of these areas. Candidates don't run over the whole municipality but only in "their" ward, and the voters are limited to choosing from among the candidates in their particular ward. Whether election is by general vote or ward may be dictated by statute; it may be at the discretion of the local council; or it may be decided by council subject to the approval of the municipal electors.

Both methods of election have their proponents and their alleged advantages and disadvantages. Supporters of the ward system argue that under this approach the voters are much more likely to be familiar with the limited range of candidates from whom they must choose and the candidates will be more aware of the particular needs and interests of their constituents. It is also contended that ward elections ensure that all areas of the municipality will be represented on council, that they mean less expensive campaign costs, and that they bring a higher voting turnout, an assertion which appears to have some validity.

On the other hand, those supporting election by general vote claim that ward elections tend to perpetuate and even accentuate differences and divisions within the municipality. It is argued that a ward council is very parochial in outlook, with councillors worrying about their individual bailiwicks wherein they must seek reelection rather than being concerned about the good of the whole municipality. It is also contended that some representatives get elected on a ward basis who would not have been chosen if they were running over the entire municipality. Election by general vote is therefore felt to result in stronger, better-qualified candidates since they must have support throughout the municipality. It also avoids the apparently unfair situation in which one candidate receives, as an example, 2000 votes in a ward but finishes out of the running while another candidate receives 1600 votes and tops the polls in a different ward. While such situations can arise since the populations of all wards do not stay equal even with periodic attempts at redistribution, they add to the feeling that the "best" person may not be elected under a ward system. Finally, proponents of a general vote assert that it results in a council more capable of taking a broad view of the overall needs of the municipality.

> The larger the municipality, the more election by ward is necessary or helpful.

Whatever the respective merits of the two methods of election, it might be assumed that beyond a certain population size (which is difficult to specify precisely) election by ward becomes almost inevitable to ensure that the citizen will have some prospect of knowing the candidates and that the candidates will not be faced with the financial and time demands of canvassing an excessively large population. While this relationship between the population of a municipality and the method of election generally holds true, there are exceptions, the most notable being election at large in the city of Vancouver. The ward system in this city was abolished before the 1936 municipal election and has not been reinstated in spite of several local initiatives over the years.

Short or Long Term of Office

Another variation in municipal elections concerns the term of office, which has ranged from one to four years. Those favouring the short term argue that it is more democratic because the electorate can retain closer control over the elected representatives. Since an ineffective council can be turned out of office promptly, it is felt that councillors elected for a short term are more sensitive to public views and concerns. On the other hand, it is argued that too much of the time of a short term is used learning the job and gearing up for reelection. The lack of long-term planning exhibited by most councils may be caused, at least in part, by frequent elections. According to Munro, the historical Canadian one year term was influenced by the American practice prevalent in the 19ᵗʰ century but subsequently abandoned as unworkable.¹ Brittain makes the same observation and goes on to argue that:

> This one year term is probably the most effective method ever devised for preventing the adoption of bad measures, but it is equally effective in preventing or delaying good measures.²

In his view the one year term grew out of a lack of faith in representatives and electors and should be abandoned.

In recent decades, the term of office has gradually been extended in most provinces. Three year terms are now in effect for all or some classifications of municipalities in seven of the provinces and in the Northwest Territories and the Yukon. Four year terms are found in the remaining three provinces, Newfoundland, Quebec, and Nova Scotia (which just introduced the four year term in a new Municipal Act passed in December 1998). Most local government reform studies have reflected this trend to a longer term, usually because of their preoccupation with improving the service delivery role of municipal government.

Yet there is little solid evidence to demonstrate that a longer term leads to improved planning and priority setting on the part of councillors. Whether or not that desirable activity takes place seems to be much more a function of how progressive councillors (and senior staff) are and what kinds of processes they use, not such structural features as the term of office. Illingworth reviews the Ontario experience with the standard three year term since 1980 and remains unconvinced of its benefits over the two year term which was previously in place.³

Direct or Indirect Election

A third variation in the method of election, and one which has been the subject of increasing debate in recent years, is whether it is considered to be direct or indirect. In most cases, election is direct in that the voters choose a candidate for a particular position and none other. Examples of indirect election are found with respect to the upper tier county councils in Ontario and Quebec (although the latter were replaced by regional county municipalities in 1979). These councils are considered to be

---

¹W. B. Munro, *American Influences on Canadian Government*, Toronto, Macmillan, 1929.

²H. L. Brittain, in the annual report of the Bureau of Municipal Research, 1945, quoted in K. G. Crawford, *Canadian Municipal Government*, Toronto, University of Toronto Press, 1954, p. 82.

³Dick Illingworth, "Is the Longer Term Better?" *Municipal World*, September 1994, pp. 22-23.

indirectly elected because they are composed of members who were directly elected to the constituent lower tier municipalities and as a result automatically became county councillors.

In Ontario, for example, all townships, villages, and towns are lower tier units in the two tier county system of government. Each of their councils includes a reeve and also, if they are entitled by the number of electors, a deputy reeve. Informed voters know when they are voting for their reeve and deputy reeve that the successful candidates will not only take office locally but will become that municipality's representatives on county council. In that sense they are indirectly elected to county council.

This form of indirect election has often been criticized, particularly on the grounds that it results in a parochial council with each representative feeling loyalty to his own municipality and no one taking a broader view of matters—essentially the same criticism as that which is made against election by ward. However, the traditional defence of the arrangement is that it provides valuable liaison between the two levels of government since the reeve and deputy reeve "wear two hats" and can represent the concerns of each level of municipal government to the other.

This concept of indirect election has been used, in whole or in part, for most of the strengthened upper tier governments created as a result of the local government reform efforts in the various provinces. This is true of Quebec's urban communities, the regional districts in British Columbia, and Ontario's regional governments (at least initially). Where members are being elected in a lower tier municipality to serve on a regional council, however, the ballot specifies both offices—unlike the situation with respect to county council—so the term "double direct" or "joint seat" is sometimes used instead of indirect to describe the method of electing these regional councillors in Ontario. In any event, as noted in Chapter 7, this method of election appears to have contributed to a feeling of alienation toward these upper tier governments and reinforced their image as bureaucratic, unresponsive regimes. In addition, councillors chosen on this basis have little incentive to identify and deal with regional concerns since their reelection depends on satisfying much more specific, localized concerns.

Similar observations are made by Sancton, who notes that most Canadian two tier systems have been structured so that all members of the upper tier council have also been members of the lower tier councils.[4] The advantages of this arrangement are that the upper tier has had to be

---

[4]Andrew Sancton, *Local Government Reorganization in Canada Since 1975*, Toronto, ICURR Press, April 1991, p. 8.

extremely responsive to the expressed desires of the politicians who run the lower tier units and the potential for jurisdictional squabbles between the two tiers is reduced. The big disadvantage is that politicians and voters have focused most of their attention on the lower tier, leaving regional staff and, in some cases, the indirectly elected chair, in charge.[5] Perhaps partly in response to these criticisms, direct election is becoming more prevalent in Ontario's regional governments. Since 1988 (until it became part of the megacity in 1998), all of Metro Toronto's council was directly elected except for the six heads of council from its lower tier municipalities. Ottawa-Carleton moved to direct election of all its regional councillors in 1994. Direct election of the regional chairs was introduced in 1988 for Hamilton-Wentworth and in 1997 for Sudbury and Waterloo.

The method of selection of the head of council is a particularly controversial issue. While most heads of council are elected directly, at large, there are some instances of indirect election. For example, the wardens of the county in Nova Scotia and Ontario and the regional county municipality (RCM) in Quebec are chosen by and from the council membership. This selection process was also adopted for the various regional governments in Ontario except in the first instance when the chair, as the head is called, was appointed by the Ontario cabinet. A similar approach is used for the selection of the head of the Montreal Urban Community.

This practice has been strongly criticized as undemocratic in that it does not give the electorate an opportunity to choose directly the occupant of the most important municipal office. On the other hand, the practice has been persuasively defended in a number of local government studies as being a central feature of a more effective organization of the municipality modelled upon the parliamentary system.[6] It is argued that heads of council chosen by their fellow councillors have, in effect, been given an indication of majority support for their leadership whereas this situation may not apply at all when the heads are directly elected. Moreover, having given their support, council can also take it away again in a vote of non-confidence by not reappointing the particular head of council, thereby adding an important element of accountability.

---

[5]*Ibid.*

[6]Notably the *Report and Recommendations, Committee of Review, City of Winnipeg Act*, Winnipeg, Queen's Printer, 1976, and the *Report of the Royal Commission on Education, Public Services, and Provincial-Municipal Relations in Nova Scotia*, Halifax, Queen's Printer, 1974.

The Underlying Question

As stated at the outset, the differing viewpoints about the three aspects of election just discussed reflect the underlying conflict between the two fundamental roles of local government—the representative, political role and the administrative or service delivery role. Those who emphasize the representative role and who recognize the political nature of local government tend to favour election by ward, while supporters of at large elections show their concern for service delivery when they emphasize the prospect of a stronger calibre of candidate capable of taking a broad overview of the municipality's needs. Similarly, those who argue for a short term of office are emphasizing the representative role, whereas proponents of a longer term are concerned about the increasingly complex demands requiring attention. Finally, direct election of councillors is seen as more democratic, and is therefore favoured by those who emphasize the representative role. However, those concerned with the need for strong leadership and improved priority setting in the face of growing local responsibilities are drawn to the concept of a head of council chosen by, supported by, and responsible to, the council. These distinctions are summarized in the table which follows.

Representative Role	Administrative Role
Election by ward	Election by general vote
Short term of office	Long term of office
Direct election of council head	Indirect election of council head

The Administration

In addition to the council, the government of the municipality includes the appointed staff who are responsible for administering the programs and policies of council and for assisting council in making decisions by providing expert advice. Since councillors serve, in most instances, on only a part-time basis, they come to rely very heavily on the recommendations given by their staff—to the point where there is a widespread concern that staff are too dominant in the policy process. Because they may be in frequent contact with the public, the staff are also potential public relations ambassadors for the municipality. Because of this contact, staff may be even more aware than councillors of the public view on a variety of local issues. Increasingly, staff find themselves acting as brokers or arbiters of conflicting local interests, seeking to find common ground and to build a basis for action. Staff with good negotiating and human relations skills can make a major contribution in this area, but in so doing they are also helping to define the issue and to determine the limits of possible action on the issue, critical elements of the local policy process that most believe are more properly the preserve of council. Some staff have the responsibility for supervising a number of subordinates and demonstrating managerial skill and, as described later in this chapter, some have a special role as a coordinating officer.

There is, of course, a tremendous variation in the number and organization of staff, depending on the population of the municipality and the range of functions. At one extreme, and still found in some Canadian municipalities, is the staff of one, perhaps part-time at that. This individual may act as clerk, treasurer, tax collector, by-law enforcement officer, dog catcher, and building inspector while performing a variety of other duties and all without any formal job description whatsoever.

At the other extreme is the staff of thousands, grouped into twenty-odd functionally specialized departments, with detailed job descriptions and operating manuals and an elaborate hierarchy. In this latter instance, the municipality obviously has much greater staff resources and expertise available. Bigger is not always better, however, and as with all larger organizations, the municipality may have difficulty drawing these resources together into a coordinated operation.

Traditionally, there has been a requirement for municipalities to appoint certain statutory officers, but new legislative initiatives in several provinces have removed or reduced this requirement, ostensibly to provide municipalities with greater flexibility to develop staffing arrangements which best meet their needs. For example, 1998 amendments (Bill 31) to the British Columbia Municipal Government Act eliminated the required titles of municipal clerk, regional district secretary, and treasurer, but did give formal recognition to the position of chief administrative officer. The first draft of the proposed new Municipal Act in Ontario required only the appointment of a clerk. The current draft (not passed as of mid-1999) stipulates that both a clerk and a treasurer must be appointed, but it also provides that neither of them needs to be an employee of the municipality. This provision would seem designed to facilitate the currently popular philosophy of contracting out municipal services.

Probably the most common approach traditionally used to oversee administrative operations has been the establishment of standing committees although, as discussed below, these have often been abandoned or modified in recent years because they were perceived as contributing to the problems of fragmentation and lack of coordination.

Standing Committees: The Council-Administration Link?

Standing committees normally exercise both executive and legislative responsibilities. They provide a general overview of the operations of one or more municipal departments and they also make recommendations and present reports as requested by council. In large municipalities the committees may be policy-advisory only, without any responsibility for supervising the departments. Standing committees are composed of councillors, sometimes with citizen members as well, and the extent of their use depends upon the size of the council, the volume of business and local customs and administrative arrangements.

The use of a standing committee system is held to be advantageous because it speeds up work in council since the committee sifts through the details of an issue and presents a positive recommendation to council. It also allows councillors to specialize in the fields of administration under the jurisdiction of their standing committees rather than to attempt to be knowledgeable in all fields. It is also alleged that the informal atmosphere of a committee meeting encourages more "give and take" in debate, facilitates participation by municipal officials, and also provides a good opportunity for interested groups or individuals to be heard. In this latter connection, it is argued that the delay built in when matters are referred to committee gives public opinion a chance to develop and to be heard and guards against overly precipitous action.

However, there are also a significant number of alleged disadvantages of the standing committee system. While some delay in decision making may be beneficial, referrals from council to one or more committees and back to council can create a very slow process and the opportunity for buck-passing. If committee discussions are duplicated in council, much time is wasted and the value of the committee's specialized scrutiny is lost. There are often too many committees, with the result that a councillor's already limited time is seriously overburdened. An associated problem in many smaller municipalities is the tendency to establish standing committees when they are not necessary given the volume of work. Often

> Disadvantages of a standing committee system include slower decision making, duplicated debate, and reinforced departmentalization.

such committees have no terms of reference, no regular schedule of meetings, and no systematic procedure of reporting to council. As a result, they are not an effective addition for managing the municipality.

Another criticism, and one of particular relevance for the ensuing discussion, is that standing committees tend to reinforce the departmentalization inherent in the municipal organization and thus contribute to a fragmented outlook. This is because members of a committee may put the interests of their particular department or departments first, an attitude which is hardly conducive to a coordinated approach or to a broad view of the municipality's needs. Often difficulties arise in this respect because the committee system has simply expanded with the increase in municipal departments. Yet the departments themselves may have grown without sufficient forethought, and if this structure is poorly organized for coordination, then what can one expect from a committee system similarly designed? Finally, it is argued that committee members tend to become overly preoccupied with matters of administrative detail and internal management of the departments under their jurisdiction. This is a common problem with councils generally but it is felt to be accentuated by the greater contact and familiarity with administration that the specialized scrutiny of committees permits.

Shortcomings in the Traditional Machinery

Just as the pressures of growth and change undermined the traditional boundaries, responsibilities, and revenues of municipal government as discussed in earlier chapters, so these pressures increasingly called into question the traditional internal governing structure and operation of the municipality. In particular, there were growing problems related to leadership, planning and priority setting, accountability and coordination.

Limited Leadership Powers

These weaknesses were focused at the top, in the limited powers given to the head of council. To illustrate, let us consider the Ontario legislation concerning the head of council, which is notable for the fact that its wording is unchanged from the Municipal Act of 1877.[7] As a result, it is hopelessly out-of-date, deals mostly with matters of administration, and does not recognize that the important duties of heads of council are "to

---

[7]According to Paul Hickey, *Decision-Making Processes in Ontario's Local Governments*, Toronto, Ministry of Treasury, Economics and Intergovernmental Affairs, 1973—and there has been no significant change since his report.

lead, to initiate, and to coordinate the efforts of the councillors, the officers, and the many groups in the local communities that work for the betterment and the enrichment of the local citizens."[8] Briefly, the Ontario legislation requires the head of council to preside at council meetings, cause the municipal laws to be executed and obeyed, oversee the conduct of the officers, cause negligence, carelessness, and violation of duty by officers to be prosecuted and punished, and make recommendations to the council to improve the finances, health, security, cleanliness, comfort, and ornament of the municipality. Remarkably, the provisions in the new Municipal Act proposed for Ontario (but not yet passed) are even more limited and brief and don't give any specific powers to the head of council.[9]

While many provinces have provisions comparable to those in Ontario, some of the legislation gives the head of council other duties which strengthen his or her role as leader of the council. For example, the legislation in Manitoba, British Columbia, and Quebec provides a limited form of veto by authorizing the head of council to return any matter to the council for its reconsideration. The latter two provinces and Saskatchewan grant the head of council the power to suspend any officer or employee, subject to subsequent confirmation by council. The fact that the mayor of Unicity appoints the members of that city's executive committee adds to his or her power and influence. In no instances, however, do the heads of council possess significant executive powers. While they are not limited to the largely ceremonial role of their British counterparts, neither are they comparable to the American "strong mayor" who has extensive authority in connection with the preparation of current and capital budgets, planning, hiring, and firing.

While Canadian mayors have little formal power, they have high local political visibility, in large part because of the tendency for the media in a community to contact the mayor for short summaries of municipal business or comments on current controversies.[10] Their ceremonial and symbolic functions are also important and can be the basis for popularity and reelection, but there is no real power to effect change inherent in this

---

[8]*Ibid.*, p. 62.

[9]Ministry of Municipal Affairs (Ont.), *A Proposed New Municipal Act: Consultation Document*, Spring 1998, pp. 146-147.

[10]Andrew Sancton, "Mayors as Political Leaders," in Maureen Mancuso, Richard G. Price, and Ronald Wagenberg (eds.), *Leaders and Leadership in Canada*, Toronto, Oxford University Press, 1994, pp. 179-180.

role. The mayor does not have any real authority over staffing and the administrative structure, but can exercise considerable influence by providing a link between senior managers and council. "With easier access to senior officials than other council members enjoy, and the ability to interpret council's wishes when they have not been clearly stated, the mayor can exert considerable influence within the municipal bureaucratic apparatus."[11] Like the Prime Minister and the Premier at the senior levels of government, a mayor's position can be very strong if backed by a block of votes within the chamber. But as discussed in the next chapter, municipal voters have shown a strong resistance to the introduction of political parties at the local level. As a result, local party support for mayors has mainly been evident in Montreal and Quebec City.

Given these limits on their formal power, heads of council in Canada must rely heavily on their personality and persuasive skills and attempt to enlist council's cooperation. Levine claims that the power exercised by Canadian mayors has historically depended on their personal and popular appeal. The record indicates that mayors, even facing opposition from council members, can accomplish a good deal "if they are competent, shrewd and, most important, popular with the electorate."[12] A number of colourful and long-serving mayors have certainly "put their stamp" on their cities, with names like Elsie Wayne of Saint John, Stephen Juba of Winnipeg, Jean Drapeau of Montreal, and Hazel McCallion of Mississauga coming readily to mind. William Hawrelak of Edmonton was so skilful in courting the voters that he was reelected mayor twice after being ousted from office for various misdemeanours.[13] Observers of rural Canadian political life will have no difficulty identifying examples of reeves and other rural heads of council who have served for 20 years or more, often operating rather like "benevolent despots," but also providing indispensable leadership to their particular communities.

Part of the difficulty for any head of council is that the council itself has serious limitations as a governing body. Except in those few instances where organized political parties operate, the council is made up of a group of individuals with potentially different interests and concerns and no sense of cohesion or collective will. This situation is accentuated when

---

[11]*Ibid.*, p. 180.

[12]Allan Levine (ed.), *Your Worship: The Lives of Eight of Canada's Most Unforgettable Mayors*, Toronto, James Lorimer and Company, 1989, p. 2.

[13]Jack Masson (with Edward C. Lesage, Jr.), *Alberta's Local Governments*, Edmonton, University of Alberta Press, 1994, pp. 183-184.

councillors are elected on a ward basis and parochial views are allowed to predominate over any concept of the good of the municipality. As a result, support for a particular measure is often arranged on the basis of trade-offs. This "log-rolling and back scratching" makes voting patterns even more unpredictable and further complicates the efforts of the head of council to develop a consensus for action.

Because of the lack of cohesion on council, coordination of the activities of the municipality is difficult. This is particularly the case as the range of responsibilities increases and a large number of functionally specialized departments are established. At the provincial and federal levels, each government department is headed by a minister, an elected representative, and all ministers belong to the cabinet where the twin forces of party loyalty and cabinet solidarity serve to facilitate coordination. At the local level, however, there is no comparable arrangement. Perhaps the closest approximation is the establishment of standing committees of councillors to supervise each of the municipal departments, as described above. But it is generally agreed that these committees tend to perpetuate a fragmented outlook on municipal operations by being overly preoccupied with their department(s).

> Among council's limitations as a governing body are a lack of cohesion and of accountability.

There is also a serious lack of accountability within most municipal councils. Granted, all members are normally elected and must regularly seek reelection. But who is responsible for taking the initiative in dealing with the problems facing the municipality? Who is responsible for scrutinizing and criticizing the initiatives taken to ensure that they are in the best interest of the public? Unlike the senior levels, there is no "government" or "official opposition" at the municipal level. Because these matters are the responsibility of everybody on council and yet of nobody, it is almost impossible for citizens to know where to direct criticism or praise. Councillors can claim that they attempted to represent a citizen concern but were outvoted by other councillors, and the possibilities for evading responsibility are all too evident.

Fragmented Administration

The administrative structure of most municipalities has suffered from fragmentation, mainly as a result of the establishment of more and more departments, organized on a functional basis, headed by a specialist in that particular discipline. Not surprisingly, each department tends to be preoccupied with its own area of expertise or specialty, creating what has been increasingly referred to as a "silo" problem. Reinforcing the narrow focus is the existence of provincial departments similarly specialized, each of them maintaining close contact with their municipal counterparts. These provincial departments, at least until recently, have deployed a variety of conditional grant programs to ensure that the municipal departments give high priority to their specialized area. While all of this is understandable, it results in little attention being paid to the overall needs of the municipality.

Where municipalities use a standing committee system, it has already been noted that these committees often tend to reinforce a narrow focus on the activities of "their" departments, to the neglect of a broader consideration of overall municipal needs.

Adding to the fragmentation, of course, is the existence of numerous special purpose bodies which provide a wide range of services that ought to be, but often are not, closely integrated with the services provided by the municipality. It is hoped that the classic example of the street being paved by the council and then being torn up by the utility commission for sewer work is seldom in evidence. But there are many other, more subtle examples of lack of coordination or insufficient liaison between boards and council. School board decisions concerning the location of new schools or the closing of existing ones have an important bearing on the pattern of growth within a municipality. Municipal planning efforts may also be affected by decisions made by such bodies as utility commissions, park boards, conservation authorities, industrial commissions, and planning boards. Similarly, a coordinated approach to social services administration by the municipality may be complicated by the fact that relevant programs are under the jurisdiction of such separate bodies as children's aid societies, health units, housing authorities, and library boards.

Coordinating Machinery

In response to the kinds of weaknesses described above, many municipalities modified their internal governing machinery. At first glance, the resulting organizational forms seemed quite diverse. However, they represented two main types of change:

1. The establishment of some form of chief administrative officer to provide leadership and coordination at the staff level.
2. The introduction of some form of executive committee of council to provide stronger political leadership.

There has been a third type of change more recently, to business models of government, but these are discussed separately in a later section.

Chief Administrative Officer Systems

Chief administrative officers (CAOs) are found in Canadian municipalities under a variety of names and with a variety of powers and responsibilities. Titles used include city administrator, city manager, commissioner, chief commission, and director general. Plunkett uses the term CAO to encompass all types of structure (including manager systems) which have a single appointed officer as the head of the administration. On this basis, he found that by 1989 some 170 urban municipalities in Canada had adopted this structure.[14] Among the larger cities in this category are Vancouver, Edmonton, Calgary, Winnipeg, Saskatoon, Regina, Windsor, Hamilton, Toronto, Quebec City, Ottawa, and the regional municipalities of Ottawa-Carleton, Hamilton-Wentworth, Durham, Halton, Niagara, Peel, Sudbury, Waterloo, Quebec City, Saint John, Halifax, and St. John's.[15]

The earliest and most powerful form of CAO is that of the city manager or council manager system which spread into this country from the United States in the early 1900s. The first Canadian city manager was appointed in Westmount in 1913 and the system is still found particularly in Quebec, where legislation has authorized municipal councils to appoint a manager since 1922. In contrast, not until a 1970 amendment did Ontario's Municipal Act give municipalities the authority to appoint any type of CAO. While the number of CAO positions has increased markedly since, most are not full-fledged managers but rather weaker forms of coordinating officer or expanded clerk-treasurer, as described below.

In the western provinces, the principal form of CAO has been the commissioner, usually found in a group of three or four operating as a board of commissioners. This system, like the council manager system, arose out of the turn of the century reform era and was first established in Edmonton in 1904. Regina, Saskatoon, and Prince Albert followed suit within a decade. In a number of respects, the commissioner system is comparable to a multi-headed council manager system, as can be seen from the ensuing discussion. In fact, it has been replaced by the manager system in cities such as Saskatoon, Regina, and Winnipeg.

---

[14]T. J. Plunkett, *City Management in Canada: The Role of the Chief Administrative Officer*, Toronto, IPAC, 1992, p. 21.

[15]*Ibid.*, p. 25.

The Council Manager System

As it developed in the United States, this system is predicated on a complete separation of the policy and administrative activities of the municipality. It involves the appointment of a professional administrator—the manager—to whom is delegated complete responsibility for administering the programs of the municipality, including the coordination and supervision of all staff. The council is elected at large and on a nonpartisan basis and directs its attention to its representative role and the formulation of overall policies for the municipality. In the "pure" council manager systems found in the United States, there are not usually any standing committees and therefore not any regular council contact with the administration except through the manager.

The duties of the manager may be summarized as follows:[16]

a) To see that all laws and ordinances are enforced.

b) To exercise control over all departments and in accordance with civil service regulations appoint, supervise, and remove department heads and subordinate employees of the city.

c) To make such recommendations to the council concerning the affairs of the city as may seem to him desirable.

d) To keep the council advised of the financial conditions and future needs of the city.

e) To prepare and submit the annual budget to the council.

f) To prepare and submit to the council such reports as it may require.

g) To keep the public informed, through reports to the council, regarding the operations of the city government.

Proponents of the council manager system contend that it provides for greatly improved coordination of administrative activities, frees the councillors from unnecessary detail, and allows them to concentrate on their primary role of policy making. While there is considerable potential for improved coordination in the organization of the manager system, its greatest weakness is the premise on which it is based—that it is possible to separate policy and administration in municipal government. To the contrary, it is very difficult to identify in advance whether a particular issue is a routine administrative matter or has political implications. Even if this distinction could be made, it is not desirable to rigidly separate the two activities. In practice, much policy arises out of ongoing administration and the council's complete separation from the administrative activities of the municipality leaves it "making policy in a vacuum."

---

[16]From the *City Manager Directory*, quoted in T. J. Plunkett, *Urban Canada and its Government*, Toronto, Macmillan, 1968, p. 38.

Moreover, while the system provides for a more effective administrative structure, it does not provide for strong political leadership. Indeed, because of the focus on the manager, he or she is often a more conspicuous public figure than the members of council including the mayor. In addition to producing friction and jealousies which frequently result in the dismissal of managers, this situation also leads to managers becoming publicly identified with particular viewpoints and policies. If, as a result, they become embroiled in political controversies, their role as administrative leaders is impaired and they will likely be replaced. One author dryly observes that a manager's departure from work is often the result of illness or fatigue: "The council was sick and tired of him."[17] Thus the successful operation of the council manager system not only requires a manager who does not dominate his council and usurp its policy making role but also one who does not seem to do so.

The Manager System in Canada

As adapted to Canada, the council manager system has undergone certain modifications which minimize some of the problems noted above and, at the same time, minimize somewhat its strength and coordinating potential. Not surprisingly, these modifications reflect both the different governing principles of Canada and the United States, and the differing conditions which prevailed at the time of the system's introduction.

In most Canadian cities in the early years of the 20th century the need for such an administrative reform seemed less pressing or necessary than in American cities. Corruption and the worst excesses of local party politics were much less evident in Canadian cities, and appointments based on merit were much more prevalent. Moreover, administrative coordination was being achieved informally by utilizing the potential of certain key municipal positions, notably that of clerk and treasurer. Especially where the positions were combined in people with leadership skills, their overall knowledge of the municipality's operations and the influence inherent in their responsibilities for preparing agendas, background reports, minutes, by-laws, budgets, and financial reports, often made them unofficial chief administrative officers. Some municipalities confirmed the coordinating potential of these positions by formally designating the clerk or treasurer as something more—resulting in such positions as clerk-comptroller, clerk-treasurer-administrator, and clerk-coordinator.

---

[17]Wayne Anderson, Chester A. Newland, and Richard J. Stillman, *The Effective Local Government Manager*, Washington, International City Management Association, 1983, p. 68.

Even where the council manager system was adopted, the Canadian version usually incorporated certain features designed to maintain the significance and prestige of the elected council.[18] First, the Canadian council manager system does not attempt to enforce a complete separation between administration and policy. The council usually has a direct relationship with at least its main department heads as well as the manager. This is normally accomplished "by the attendance of the department heads at a meeting of a limited number of standing committees of council when matters affecting their particular areas of jurisdiction are under review."[19] Second, the responsibility for the appointment of staff is exercised by council, not the manager, although often council only exercises this responsibility after receiving recommendations from the manager.

With such modifications, Young feels that the Canadian version managed to avoid the fundamental problem of council's complete separation from administration. He explains that council in a Canadian manager system continues to concern itself with administration but "does so from a much broader viewpoint." The advice and recommendations of staff are coordinated by the manager and "it is this opportunity and ability to place such recommendations within the broader perspective of the city's needs as a whole which represents his greatest value to the council in his capacity as policy advisor."[20]

> The Canadian version of the manager system avoided a complete separation of policy and administration, retaining more of a role for council.

The Commissioner System

This system involves the appointment of a few commissioners, who are charged with supervising and coordinating the various departments under their jurisdiction. They may also meet together as a board of commissioners, under the direction of a chief commissioner, to provide overall coordination of municipal operations. The mayor is sometimes a member of this board.

The commissioner system is similar to a council manager system except in two important respects. The fact that there is more than one

---

[18]See Dennis A. Young, "Canadian Local Government Development: Some Aspects of the Commissioner and City Manager Forms of Administration," in Lionel D. Feldman and Michael D. Goldrick (eds.), *Politics and Government of Urban Canada*, Toronto, Methuen, 1976, pp. 276-278.

[19]*Ibid.*, p. 277.

[20]*Ibid.*, p. 278.

commissioner permits a degree of specialization not possible under the manager system where one person must supervise the entire administrative structure no matter how large and complex. Typically, one commissioner is concerned with hard services (such as water and sewerage facilities and roads), another with soft services (such as health and welfare programs and libraries) and a third (if provided) with finance and planning. Moreover, the commissioners provide a two level approach to administrative coordination, both as individual commissioners in charge of a group of related departments and as a board of commissioners in charge of the entire administrative structure.

The second difference is that policy and administration are not as completely separated under the commissioner system. This is particularly reflected in the mayor's membership on the board of commissioners, although the wisdom and effectiveness of this combination has been a matter of some debate.

As already noted, the commissioner system was found mostly in Western Canada, and has gradually been replaced by manager or CAO positions over the past couple of decades. Some cities, such as Red Deer, Prince Albert, and Estevan, have appointed only a single commissioner, in what amounts to a misnamed manager system.[21] Edmonton's commissioner system was replaced with a CAO system and executive committee in 1984. Winnipeg abolished its commissioner system in 1998 and replaced it with a CAO, a new system of standing committees, and a revamped departmental structure. This change was prompted by an October 1997 report of an organizational review.[22]

Canadian CAOs Today

Plunkett sees the growth of the CAO system in Canada as the result of the growth in municipal departments with the urbanization following World War II and the recognition that the issues confronting municipal governments required more analysis and synthesis than could be provided through such a fragmented departmental structure.[23] He explains that most municipalities can now appoint a CAO under the general municipal legislation of their province. In some cases, the legislation provides for the position only in general terms, but in provinces such as British Columbia and Quebec, duties are specified in the statute. For example, the British

---

[21]Plunkett, *City Management*, p. 53.

[22]This report, by George Cuff, is available at www.mbnet.mb.ca/city/cuff.htm.

[23]Plunkett, *City Management*, pp. 25-26.

Columbia legislation stipulates that the incumbent shall, under the control of the council:

a) supervise and direct municipal affairs and employees;
b) put into effect and carry out council policies;
c) advise the council on matters within its control; inspect and report on municipal works as council requires;
d) be responsible for preparing for council the estimate of revenue and expenditures annually or as council requires;
e) prepare and award all contracts as council prescribes;
f) carry out other duties as prescribed by by-law or resolution.[24]

The success of any particular CAO will depend, in large part, on how well the individual is able to work with the diverse mix of department heads in the municipality. Some of these managers may have strongly opposed the introduction of a "senior coordinating officer," while others may have unsuccessfully sought the position themselves. In either case, they are unlikely to welcome a new CAO or to support the position. If standing committees have been retained, department heads may attempt to use these as a buffer or a means of blocking CAO initiatives.

Plunkett suggests that relationships between CAOs and department heads tend to fall into three categories:

1. *Passive:* CAOs who simply forward, without comment, reports received from department heads.
2. *Active:* CAOs who include with departmental reports an accompanying memo setting out their comments.
3. *Dominant:* CAOs who hold back reports from departments until these conform to their general policy viewpoint.[25]

The second category is probably the most common and certainly the most desirable. It ensures that both the technical knowledge of the specialist department head and the broader perspective of the CAO are sent forward, and it gives council the benefit of the most complete range of information on which to make a decision.

Another problematic relationship which can arise is between the CAO and the head of council, given the way the latter position is defined in provincial legislation. The potential for a clash arises if a mayor has a strong personality and a determination to provide "hands-on" leadership consistent with his or her statutory authority to oversee subordinate officers. While a CAO faced with such a conflict could appeal to the council,

---

[24]From *ibid.*, pp. 28-29.

[25]The descriptions which follow, but not the categorical terms used, are based on *ibid.*, p. 42.

which is ultimately responsible for the management of the municipality, such a course of action is by no means certain of success—especially since councillors are all too inclined to view CAOs with suspicion and to fear that they will become too dominant. Prudent CAOs usually make every effort to avoid an overt power struggle.

No matter how effectively a CAO system may work, it provides administrative, not political, leadership. As we will see, the search for new forms of municipal machinery which can provide the latter has proven to be even more elusive.

Executive Committees

Over the years the most persistent method of attempting to deal with the various problems of political leadership has been the establishment of executive committees of council. As had been the case with the establishment of CAO systems, a major impetus was the turn of the century reform movement, which emphasized a strong executive along with such measures as smaller councils and at large elections in its concern to make municipal government more efficient and less political. This prompted the introduction of boards of control, a form of executive committee which became quite prominent in Ontario during the first half of the 20th century. Other forms of executive committee have also been established in a number of large cities or metropolitan municipalities in an effort to duplicate a cabinet organization and a semblance of the parliamentary system.

Board of Control

As described in Chapter 3, the board of control first appeared in Canada in the city of Toronto in 1896. It was not really a board, but a statutory executive committee of council, assigned important responsibilities relating to such matters as budgets, contracts, and staffing. Its recommendations could only be overturned or altered by a two-thirds vote of council (of which the controllers were voting members). While it didn't last long in other provinces, it became mandatory for cities over 100 000 population in Ontario, although it could be dispensed with by a two-thirds vote of council if affirmed by the Ontario Municipal Board.

It was anticipated that the board of control would provide effective leadership and contribute to a more efficient management of the affairs of the municipality. But the board's similarity to a cabinet was superficial at best; instead of a body unified by the glue of party loyalty and discipline, the board was made up of individuals without necessarily any common purpose. With only four board members, plus the mayor, the board became increasingly overburdened in attempting to oversee the administrative activities of the municipality and usually clashed with standing committees where they were retained. Most serious of all, however, was the friction between the board and the rest of council. The latter were particularly resentful of the two-thirds vote requirement for overturning board decisions.

Gradually, municipalities took steps to abolish their boards of control, until this once so prominent structure remained only in the city of London, but with the two-thirds vote provision removed. Surprisingly, the new city of Kingston, formed through amalgamation of three municipalities at the end of 1997, resurrected the board of control. However, it did so on the apparent assumption that the board would not come with the two-thirds vote provision (which it did) and there has been almost continuous friction between the board and the rest of Kingston city council since its inception. It seems unlikely that the board will survive beyond one term.

Other Forms of Executive Committee

Apart from the board of control, a variety of other forms of executive committee are found in Canadian municipalities. Some of these are similar to the board of control in having a statutory foundation, including those established in a number of the reformed local government structures.

There are also nonstatutory executive committees. By their nature they are much harder to categorize, and often are not even called "executive" committees. However, their purpose is reflected in their make-up, which usually comprises the chairs of the major standing committees in the municipality plus the head of council, and in their mandate, which usually includes responsibility for the budget and for providing leadership and coordination.

Montreal is likely the Canadian city with the longest experience with an executive committee, since there are references to such a body as early as the 1850s. Montreal did, as previously mentioned, establish a board of control in 1910, the result of a new charter prompted by councillors endorsing the views of the reform movement of that time. But charter revisions in 1921 abolished the board of control and provided for an executive committee to be named by council. The mayor was made a voting member of this executive committee but could not be its chair, a deliberate arrangement to attempt to curb the power of the mayor.

Montreal's executive committee was authorized to initiate legislation and to supervise departments, with each member normally assigned a number of specific departments to oversee. Its powers were similar to those of an Ontario board of control, even to the extent of the two-thirds vote provision for council to overturn major decisions of the committee.

By the 1960s, the executive committee had evolved into quite a different, and more powerful, position because of the emergence of dominant political parties within Montreal's council. The Civic Party, under the leadership of Jean Drapeau, controlled a majority of the council seats from 1960 until Drapeau's retirement in 1986. The result was that Drapeau's personal choices for membership on the executive committee were ratified by council and the committee could initiate actions with every expectation that they would be supported by council. A strong executive committee, backed by a majority political party, has continued, first with Jean Doré and the Montreal Citizens' Movement and now with Pierre Bourque and Vision Montreal. However, as discussed in the next chapter, Bourque's first term was plagued by defections from his party and his attempt (later quashed by the courts) to dismiss two members of the executive committee.

The cities of Quebec, Hull, and Laval established executive committees in the mid-1960s, after studies which found that the existing government machinery exhibited weaknesses of excessive council involvement in administrative detail, lack of executive direction, and uncoordinated administration. These executive committees are composed of the mayor (as chair) and four councillors selected by the mayor. According to Hickey, the system was based on the premise that a candidate for mayor runs as the head of a team of like-minded councillor candidates.[26] The existence of what is, in effect, a local political party provides the strong political leadership previously noted with respect to the city of Montreal. For example, the Progrès civique de Québec (PCQ) controlled the council in Quebec City from 1962 to 1989, at which time it was replaced by the Reassemblement populaire de Québec, essentially a Quebec City equivalent of the MCM.[27] The Parti du Railliement Officiel (PRO) has held power in Laval since 1981, winning 16 of 21 seats in the 1997 election.[28]

One of the earliest executive committees in Ontario was established by the new Municipality of Metropolitan Toronto in 1954 under the council's general authority to establish "standing and other committees." This committee was given powers almost identical to Ontario's board of con-

---

[26]Hickey, *op. cit.*, p. 199.

[27]Sancton, "Mayors as Political Leaders," p. 183.

[28]Katherine Wilton, "Some surprises in municipal elections," *Montreal Gazette*, November 3, 1997.

trol, but unlike the board it was not directly elected. Instead, it was composed of the chair of the metropolitan council, the mayors of the six lower tier municipalities in the system, and seven other specified representatives from the lower tier councils. Therefore, each member of the executive committee was there because of a prior position in the municipal government structure.

The way in which the executive committee was chosen and the absence of political parties on council explain, at least in part, the lack of strong political leadership in the Metro Toronto system during much of its existence. Under these past arrangements, the executive committee members were not responsible to the full metro council for their selection nor could they depend on continuing majority support for their proposals. Indeed, there was not even any certainty that the executive committee members themselves would agree on what needed to be done in particular circumstances. They were individuals with different constituencies, different viewpoints, and different, perhaps competing, ambitions.

These constraints continue to affect the executive committee which has been set up in the new Toronto megacity. Known as the Strategic Policies and Priorities Committee, this body is made up of the chairs of Toronto's five standing committees, the chairs of its six community councils, the deputy mayor, the budget chief, and the mayor of Toronto. While it is almost as large as a cabinet, it still lacks cohesiveness and common purpose and depends upon the willingness of the members to cooperate and work together.

Winnipeg Unicity in its philosophical base and its actual experiences provides a striking example of the link between organized political parties and the operation of an executive committee. It will be recalled from Chapter 6 that a major objective of those designing the

> The link between organized political parties and the executive committee was evident in Unicity's design.

government machinery of Unicity was the development of a parliamentary model at the local level. A central feature was the provision for an executive policy committee chaired by the head of council and including the chairs of the three major standing committees established as part of the new structure. From the outset, however, the potential of this arrangement was weakened by the fact that the mayor was directly elected, rather than being chosen from among the councillors as had been proposed in the White Paper which led to the new structure.

A Committee of Review of Unicity reporting in 1976 offered forceful arguments in favour of the development of the parliamentary model at the local level, but acknowledged that the political parties which are an essential component of such a model are not warmly welcomed by the local electorates. The committee felt that it could not legislate the development of a party system but would have to hope for "a full-fledged party system to evolve over the course of time, under the influence of the parliamentary characteristics of our model."[29] These hopes have not been well realized. However, the fact that the mayor appoints the executive committee (since 1989) has strengthened that position.

Edmonton established an executive committee in 1984, replacing the commissioner system which had existed for three-quarters of a century. Described as "the nerve centre of city government," this committee is directed to prepare the annual budget and monitor the administration's financial performance, call for tenders and award contracts, develop long-range policies, act as policy coordinator between the city manager and the council's standing committees, draft by-laws for council's consideration, enter into collective bargaining agreements with city staff, set the council agenda, and direct and coordinate the flow of information and business between council, its committees, and the administration.[30]

Effectiveness of Coordinating Machinery

While generalizations are difficult, it is probably fair to say that reforms at the administrative level have been more successful than those at the political level. In particular, the establishment of a chief administrative officer system has the potential to effect improved coordination and integration of municipal programs and activities. This system may help to develop an expanded research and analytical capability and the provision of more comprehensive advice and recommendations to council, but much depends on whether complementary changes are introduced in the management and decision-making process of the municipality. Designating a CAO also provides a specific focus of accountability and responsibility for the administrative performance of the municipality.

If CAOs are, or appear to be, too dominant, the result is often a mixture of fear and resentment from councillors, which may undermine most of the potential effectiveness of the system. On the other hand, weak CAO systems may be unable to overcome the departmentalization of the municipal organization and the silo mentality which inhibits coordinated action. No matter how well it works, it must also be remembered that a

[29]Committee of Review, *op. cit.*, p. 57.

[30]Masson and Lesage, *op. cit.*, p. 82.

CAO system does nothing to strengthen political leadership and, to the contrary, may even detract from this objective by creating a bureaucratic system and by undermining the power and public status of the council.

The establishment of an executive committee system has been a less effective structural reform, in most instances. Most of these committees have lacked political cohesion and have not had any means, except persuasion, to ensure that their initiatives receive the necessary support of council. The effectiveness of these committees has been dependent upon their method of selection and whether or not they were reinforced in their position and activities by the existence of organized political parties on council. In most instances, they were not, and the committees lacked any power base as a result. On the other hand, bodies such as Ontario's board of control and the executive committees in Quebec backed by a block of party votes were regarded by many as too strong and dominant. Striking a balance in this matter is obviously difficult.

> In most instances, executive committee systems have been a less effective reform than CAO systems.

Are Political Parties the Answer?

Those seeking a strong executive within municipal government often call for the introduction of organized political parties, a topic of great controversy. What is it about parties which would create a strong executive and why are parties opposed so strongly?

Basically, parties perform the same task locally as they do at the senior levels; they organize the council into a governing group and an opposition group. The creation of a governing party is significant because it provides the basis for concerted action. If heads of council are chosen by council, they would presumably be leading members of the majority party or majority group on council, and thus would have a power base to support their leadership. If they in turn choose their executive committee from the ruling group, then the committee has cohesiveness because of the common party affiliation and is somewhat analogous to a federal or provincial cabinet.

Political parties provide the potential for not only strong leadership but also more effective scrutiny of the municipality's activities through an organized opposition or alternative governing group. As a result there is a group within council pledged to scrutinize and criticize municipal activities, an important role which is normally left to everybody—and nobody. The mayor and executive committee members need to retain the confidence of council since they owe their positions to council, not the electorate.

In addition, with political parties the operations of council become more understandable and accountable to the public. Since councillors run as a group on the basis of specific programs, there is a greater likelihood that citizens will vote on the basis of substantive issues and policies instead of on the usual basis of selection among personalities. It is also argued that an election campaign organized around opposing parties and alternative approaches generates greater public interest and a higher voting turnout. In part this is because parties can be expected to play their usual roles of aggregating interests, mobilizing public support, and trying to draw more citizens into the political arena. More importantly, at the end of a term the public can attach responsibility for performance to the governing party since this group had the means to effect change. It is not possible for a ruling party to evade responsibility for action or inaction as individual councillors can and do.

How well things work will depend, of course, on the nature of the political parties involved. Proponents of party politics in local government assume a balanced situation with two or more parties which would alternate in power. If one party dominates council for a lengthy period, there is likely to be insensitivity to public opinion and other abuses, traits exhibited by the provincial and federal governments in the same situation. Another issue is whether there would be local parties, focused on local issues, or just branches of national parties. In the latter case, the concern is that local issues would be neglected and that local election results might reflect the popularity or unpopularity of "parent" parties. On the other hand, purely local parties are often short-lived coalitions of local interests that display little cohesion or concerted action once elected. They may be more properly described as factions that reappear under a variety of names at election time and attempt to ensure the election of certain types of candidates, but do not exercise disciplined party voting within council.[31] Such factions clearly don't provide the basis for a strong governing group or opposition.

Critics of political parties at the local level question the validity of a number of their alleged advantages.[32] For example, evidence from the

---

[31]Harold Kaplan, "Electoral Politics in the Metro Area," in Jack K. Masson and James Anderson (eds.), *Emerging Party Politics in Urban Canada*, Toronto, McClelland and Stewart, 1972.

[32]See, for example, David Siegel, "City Hall Doesn't Need Parties," *Policy Options*, June 1987, pp. 26-27, on which the following points are based.

senior levels of government hardly supports the claim that parties provide clear platforms and alternatives for the voter, or stick to their platforms after elected! Nor is it apparent that parties at the senior levels provide strong leadership—at least according to the complaints often heard from both those within the system and from the public. Accountability at the municipal level arises from the small scale of operations and ready accessibility of the decision makers (in most municipalities) and does not need parties to ensure it. In fact, in can be argued that parties make councillors less accountable to the voters, because they are expected to vote with their party on issues. As for the likelihood of increased voter turnout with parties, how beneficial this would be depends on the reason for the turnout. If municipal electors had gone to the polls in record numbers in municipal elections in the early 1990s to defeat Conservative candidates because of their dislike of Brian Mulroney and the GST, this would hardly be striking a blow for local democracy.[33]

There are, of course, a number of other arguments against the introduction of organized political parties at the local level. Chief among these is the assertion that parties introduce division where none exists or should exist. "There is no political way to build a road," claim proponents of this viewpoint which reflects the lingering notion that local government activities are administrative, not political, in nature. Yet if the actual construction of a road is a matter of engineering, not politics, the decision on where to locate a particular road is certainly political. The decision on whether the traffic problem in question should be solved through building a road or providing an alternative form of public transit is also clearly political. The decision on whether the scarce financial resources of the municipality should be used on transportation or some other pressing need is again political. Indeed, if the municipal council is concerned with establishing priorities in relation to conflicting public needs and demands, its role must be political.

Do parties bring division where none need exist, or do they offer a more systematic and accountable way to resolve existing divisions?

Since political decisions are an essential element of municipal operations then, they are not carried into the local arena by parties. But parties may help to make the unavoidable political decisions more systematic and accountable to the public. At the same time, it must be acknowledged that parties tend to exaggerate differences and also to criticize

---

[33] *Ibid.*, p. 27.

excessively for purely partisan purposes. These traits have often been evident in the actions of the parties operating at the senior levels of government.

Another major objection to parties is the feeling that they bring corruption and unsavoury practices into local government. This feeling was undoubtedly strongly influenced by the excesses of party politics and the spoils system in the United States in the period leading up to the turn of the century reform era. Nor were such practices entirely absent from Canadian local government, as illustrated by discussions in Chapter 3. However, it should be remembered that it is people who are potentially corruptible, not that specialized subgroup known as politicians. If there are opportunities for dishonesty and abuse, some people may succumb to the temptation, but they will presumably do so whether they are individual councillors or members of an organized political party.

Ultimately, it doesn't really matter how soundly based are the arguments for or against political parties in municipal government. In practice, there is a strong public antipathy towards any such move. As the next chapter illustrates, efforts by the national parties to contest local elections have usually been rebuffed. Yet voters have often elected coalitions of like-minded candidates masquerading as non-parties and committed to the defeat of organized parties.

New Business Models

The latest round of internal restructuring has seen the introduction of business models in a number of municipalities. To a considerable extent, these initiatives parallel and reflect developments which have occurred at the senior levels of government, somewhat in Canada, and even more so in other jurisdictions such as Britain, Australia, New Zealand, and the United States. The new approaches have come to be known as the "new public management." Many of these approaches are also associated with the notion of an "entrepreneurial government," as described in the best-selling book *Reinventing Government*.[34] A brief overview of these approaches provides useful background for understanding recent developments in municipal machinery.

---

[34]David Osborne and Ted Gaebler, *Reinventing Government*, New York, Penguin Books, 1993.

The New Public Management

Proponents of the new public management suggest that it involves such features as:

*   providing high quality services that citizens value;
*   increasing the autonomy of public managers, especially from central control agencies;
*   measuring and rewarding organizations and individuals on the basis of whether or not they meet demanding targets; and
*   appreciating the virtues of competition and keeping an open mind on which public purposes should be performed by the private sector rather than the public sector.[35]

Critics of the new public management[36] claim that its philosophy is rooted in the conviction that private sector management is superior to public administration. The solution, therefore, is to transfer government activities to the private sector through privatization and contracting out. Since that obviously can't be done for every government activity, the next best thing is to transfer business practices to government operations. But, claim the critics, private sector management practices are not easily transferred to government. If public management is lethargic, cautious, expensive, unresponsive, or any of the other criticisms levelled against it, these shortcomings have more to do with parliament and politicians than with public servants.

Whatever the merits of these respective arguments, the fact is that the new public management has brought significant change in a number of parliamentary democracies.[37] For example, the British "Next Steps" program called for the establishment of separate agencies to carry out the operational functions of government within a policy and resources framework set by departments. These agencies were given significant financial and managerial freedom, but were held accountable through the limited

---

[35]This summary of NPM features is based on Sandford Borins, "The new public management is here to stay," *Canadian Public Administration*, Spring 1995, pp. 122-132.

[36]The discussion which follows is based on Donald J. Savoie, "What is wrong with the new public management?" in *ibid.*, pp. 112-121.

[37]The following description of the experiences of Britain, Australia, and New Zealand is based on Leslie Seidle, *Rethinking the Delivery of Public Services to Citizens*, Montreal, Institute for Research on Public Policy, 1995. Another useful reference is Peter Aucoin, *The New Public Management in Canada in Comparative Perspective*, Montreal, Institute for Research on Public Policy, 1995.

period contracts given to their chief executives, for performance against specified targets covering financial results, efficiency, throughput, and quality. From its inception in 1988, this program had fostered the creation of 109 separate agencies covering close to two-thirds of the public service by the end of 1995.[38]

A somewhat similar reform occurred in New Zealand in the mid-1980s, stimulated by the severe financial problems facing the country at the time. State-owned enterprises were created to take over "trading functions" formerly carried out by government departments. Legislation passed in 1988 provided that the departments were headed by chief executives employed on a contract basis. They were given full power to hire, dismiss, and reward staff. Annual performance agreements were negotiated between the chief executive and the minister, and ongoing monitoring was instituted, along with performance pay systems. Reform in Australia was also triggered by expenditure restraint in the mid-1980s. Changes were introduced more gradually than in New Zealand, but were similar in providing for more managerial authority and more focus on results. The use of performance standards, performance appraisals, and performance pay resulted in a shift towards a client focus.

By contrast, the pace in Canada has been much slower. The federal government announced in December 1989 that special operating agencies (SOAs) would be established to provide increased management flexibility in return for agreed-on levels of performance and results. But the SOAs were given less autonomy than their British counterparts and by the time of the Liberal election in 1993 (which shifted the emphasis to a new customer service program), these SOAs covered only 3% of the federal public service. At both the federal and provincial level, however, there has been a greatly increased emphasis on results, and it has become commonplace for departments to publish annual business plans on the basis of which their performance is supposedly measured.

NPM at the Municipal Level

Financial constraint has also been a major factor influencing the introduction of new public management features at the municipal level. In response, some municipalities have restructured primarily to bring about downsizing, without necessarily giving much thought to how they might operate differently or more effectively. Others have started from a different premise, by looking at ways of introducing a more results-oriented,

---

[38]Seidle, *op. cit.*, p. 34.

competitive operation. This search, in turn, has led them to undertake internal restructuring.

One impetus, for example, has been the growing emphasis on performance measurement. Assembling data on the total cost of providing services usually involves searching the financial records of several departments and thus highlights the fragmented nature of traditional municipal structures and the silo problem that can arise from having a number of departments each operating in isolation. Using the assembled data to pursue internal improvements and to draw comparisons with best practices elsewhere also draws attention to the departmental structure of the municipality and the extent to which it may inhibit improvements in efficiency. The more competitive atmosphere associated with the use of performance measurement also calls into question traditional municipal structures.

The call for municipalities to become more entrepreneurial has been an additional stimulus to structural reform. The traditional municipal organization was designed around the delivery of various services. As already noted, as new responsibilities were assumed, new departments were established. These

> Performance measurement, a more competitive atmosphere, and entrepreneurial activities have all influenced the move to new business models.

departments were given a budget appropriation, usually reflecting the expenditure pattern of the previous year(s). Their mandate was to deliver their services or programs within budget. Municipal governments today are increasingly concerned with the revenues that can be generated from their activities. They realize that the gap between expenditures and insufficient revenues need not be closed only by cutting expenditures, that it can also be closed by increasing revenues. Municipalities are now directing more attention to the expenditure/revenue ratios of those municipal activities capable of becoming more financially self-sufficient. They are also promoting improvements in the efficiency and effectiveness of service delivery. Both of these developments give municipalities further reason to redesign their organizational structures.

Examples of the New Models

The new governing models which have been introduced vary widely in their scope, sophistication, and underlying rationale. Both Winnipeg and Vancouver reorganized their structures in recent years, largely in an effort to contain or reduce costs. Winnipeg's changes included reducing the number of departments from 24 to 18, reducing the number of senior managers from 32 to 22, and reducing city staff by an average of 23% across all departments, by using early retirements as much as possible— all of this designed to achieve salary savings.[39] Further changes in March 1998 regrouped and reduced the departments to a dozen.[40] In similar fashion, Vancouver reduced its departments from 18 to 10, organized support services into a new corporate services department, and eliminated a number of senior management positions, all the while claiming that its objective was not to downsize but to become more effective.[41]

Winnipeg has also been pursuing the establishment of special operating agencies (SOAs), directly paralleling the separation of service delivery activities which forms part of NPM at the senior levels of government. In Winnipeg's case, these agencies are part of a reshaping of city government that includes such features as:

• a focus on alternative service delivery (ASD) options,
• a planning and reporting cycle that encompasses multi-year business plans, performance measurement, quarterly and annual reports, auditing and evaluation,
• a performance culture built on flexible staffing and structures, training and incentives, and cooperative labour relations, and
• a delegation of authority that is tailored to each SOA's unique business circumstances and lifts fiscal and administrative constraints to smooth the transition.[42]

As a preliminary step, Winnipeg identified more than 30 ASD candidates which might fit under the SOA model. Two areas, animal services and primary materials, volunteered to take the lead in developing the new approaches and presented feasibility studies to council in December 1997.[43] Animal services presented a reshaped business model with a focus on partnering with the private sector, moving towards full registration of animals, and protecting public health and safety. It also projected more than $1 million in reduced tax rate support within three years. Primary services provides the city with sand and gravel and procures con-

---

[39]Katherine A. Graham, Susan D. Phillips, and Allan M. Maslove, *Urban Governance in Canada*, Toronto, Harcourt Brace & Company, Canada, 1998, p. 160.

[40]See web site, www.mbnet.mb.ca/city/html/govern/civicdpt.htm.

[41]Graham et al., *op. cit.*, pp. 159-160.

[42]John Wilkins, "Special Operating Agencies: Reshaping Civic Government in Winnipeg," *Public Sector Management*, Toronto, Institute of Public Administration, 1998, Volume 9, no. 1, p. 14.

[43]The discussion which follows is based on *ibid.*, pp. 14-15.

crete and asphalt for municipal works. Its feasibility study showed that existing profitability and the annual return on assets to the city could be sustained while conserving non-renewable resources.

New business models have been set up in a number of the newly amalgamated municipalities in Ontario, including Toronto, Kingston, and Chatham-Kent. In the case of Toronto, the new city brings together in six new departments the entire organizational structure of the seven former municipalities.[44] The senior management team consists of a CAO and six commissioners. The key administrative groups or clusters are as follows:

- Community and Neighbourhood Services, which includes homes for the aged, children's services, housing, social services, and public health.
- Economic Development, Culture, and Tourism.
- Urban Planning and Development Services.
- Works and Emergency Services, which includes ambulances, fire, transportation, solid waste management, and water and wastewater services.
- Corporate Services, which takes in the office of clerk, corporate communications, real estate, fleet management, human resources, legal services, and information technology.

The new structure features a strong emphasis on public access, including plans to use the Access Toronto electronic network to improve public access and to support one-window service centres where citizens can obtain a building permit, pay a tax bill, or register for a community or recreation program.

Waterloo, Ontario, has been in the forefront of the movement to replace the traditional departmental structure with business units, and because of that pioneering role, its experience is examined in somewhat more detail.

The latest in a series of organizational changes in Waterloo was introduced in February 1996, in the form of five core businesses:

- Development Services
- Public Works Services
- Recreation and Leisure Services
- Protective Services
- Corporate Services

These core businesses are comprised of a number of smaller business units (24 at the beginning of 1999) which have been designed to consolidate most functions and processes that deliver specific products

---

[44]Based on City web site www.city.toronto.on.ca/depts

and/or services to customers.[45] For example, under the Public Works Services unit are six teams covering: roads and storm water management, winter control, recycling and waste management, utilities, parking, and transit. It is expected that business functions and results will be easier to measure and improve with this structure. In addition, the roles people play in the organization have been simplified to reduce layers of hierarchy, to define accountability more clearly, and to broaden responsibility for results to the front lines of the organization.

Business plans and business measurement systems are being developed in Waterloo that link business objectives with the corporate objectives outlined in the city's strategic plan. "Business planning will clearly identify the businesses we should be in, opportunities for cost savings and revenue enhancement and provide a common measurement system to help us make better decisions."[46]

> Waterloo's recent business initiatives built on more than a decade of complementary activities and a supportive corporate culture.

It is important to realize these recent Waterloo initiatives came after more than a decade of complementary activities. In the mid-1980s, the city had embraced the concepts in the book *In Search of Excellence*,[47] with their emphasis on customer, quality, and cross-functional teams. The development of a corporate culture which supported delivering quality to the customer through staff teams was a necessary precondition to the changes which came later.[48] In the early 1990s, Waterloo introduced tools and techniques from total quality management and continuous improvement, which further reinforced the concepts of process improvement, quality, and customer service. It also prepared its first strategic plan. In the early 1990s the city began a pilot project known as *Waterloo Inc.*, in which business teams were formed and challenged to deliver services using business principles. The first pilots were:

---

[45]The description which follows is based on *We're Here For You, Waterloo!*, A Citizen's Guide to City of Waterloo Services, 6th Edition, undated (but presumably 1996).

[46]*Ibid.*

[47]Tom Peters and Robert Waterman, Jr., *In Search of Excellence*, New York, Warner Books, 1982.

[48]Rob Deyman, "Waterloo Inc: Nothing Is Out of the Question," paper presented at the September 18, 1995 Insight Conference on *Reinventing Municipal Government for the 21st Century*, Toronto, Insight Press, 1995.

1. *Fleet Inc.* is a business which owns, manages, and repairs the city's extensive fleet (vehicles).
2. *Utilities Inc.* is comprised of the two operations of water distribution and wastewater collection. Its operations are funded entirely through user rates.
3. *Cemeteries Inc.* operates two cemeteries, a chapel, and a crematorium.
4. *Parking Inc.* operates, maintains, and regulates a variety of surface parking lots and a major parkade in the Uptown area of the city, and it regulates all on-street parking throughout the city.
5. *Development Services Inc.* encompasses the functions of planning, development engineering, parks planning, inspection services, zoning, agreements, and legal administration—that is, the entire process to convert raw land through to the occupancy of buildings and the creation of streets, parks, and other facilities.

Each team was asked to document the total cost or investment, including overhead costs, involved in delivering their products or services, achieve measurement improvement in work processes, and identify potential new revenue sources. Their considerable successes have been documented elsewhere,[49] and paved the way for the creation of business units throughout the organization in 1996.

In contrast to the gradual introduction of change in Waterloo, into a supportive corporate culture, many municipalities are embracing business models and terminology almost as an act of desperation in the face of growing financial pressures. Others have used the occasion of restructuring and amalgamation to introduce what are being touted as the latest and most efficient operating models. In these circumstances, municipal staff are likely to view the new models with suspicion and to fear (sometimes with justification) that the real purpose behind their introduction is not improvement but downsizing and privatizing. Such conditions are hardly conducive to the teamwork and innovation which are critical to the success of these models.

Another potential danger is that municipalities may get caught up in the terminology of the new business models without making the underlying changes in management process which are key to any successes which may be achieved. This problem is a common one when concepts become "fashionable," as was evident when the *In Search of Excellence* writings popularized the notion of MBWA (management by wandering around). Managers were ordered to forsake their offices and were instead to be found loitering around water coolers and coffee pots, giving rise to a variation of MBWA which might more properly be termed management by wandering aimlessly. Currently, it is business jargon which threatens

[49] *Ibid.*

to crowd out real change or improvement. Municipalities are supposed to set up their service delivery business units and their support business units. They are supposed to bring together those activities which constitute their strategic core. All business units must have business plans to justify their existence. One-stop shopping for the customer is the order of the day.

Evaluating the New Business Models

In a number of respects, the new models are not that new at all. We have always had two kinds of government department: line and staff. Line departments are directly involved in providing services to the public, whereas staff departments function as "in house" support to the line departments. The various staff departments of the past are now being drawn together into one unit, called corporate services or the support business unit or something similar. The line departments are also being grouped together into core businesses or core organizational units. The combinations being used for the business units are rather similar to the hard services, soft services, and planning distinctions that many municipalities have used in the past in an attempt to link related departments and activities.

What is new, however, is that not only are the units designed differently—in an attempt to overcome the silo problem inherent in the old departmental structure based on functional specialization—but they are expected to operate differently. There is a very strong emphasis on performance and accountability inherent in these new structures being developed. The line departments or business units are expected to deliver defined service standards within budget limits, in accordance with their business plans. The staff departments/internal service providers are also expected to demonstrate operating efficiency if they wish to be "hired" by the line departments to provide their services. Operations that don't measure up face the possibility of being replaced by an alternative service delivery arrangement. Overall, then, the new structure incorporates (or should) a distinctive new operating philosophy. The rearrangement and repackaging of departments within the structure provides a clearer focus for the application of measurement, comparison, and accountability.

It is suggested that municipalities should concentrate more on these underlying changes in process and operating philosophy and be less preoccupied with couching everything in business terminology, no matter how fashionable that may currently be with their provincial governments.

It is permissible to go on calling departments, departments, even after they are regrouped into more effective combinations. The new public information centre can be called just that; it doesn't have to be known as one-stop shopping or one-window shopping. Employees can be challenged to strive for continuous improvement in performance (and rewarded accordingly), without there being a business plan, just as standards can be set, resources allocated, and results measured and monitored. What is actually being done is far more important than what it is called, especially when so much of the new terminology confuses more than it enlightens.

> It is the underlying changes in operating philosophy and process that are important, not the business terminology.

The concept of a one-window service provider is also not new, and some would argue that the small municipalities which have been disappearing through amalgamation in recent years provided just such a single point of contact for the citizen. While the limited staff of such municipalities may have been found "under one roof," it does not necessarily follow, however, that they were organized in such a way as to provide timely information to citizens and prompt responses to queries. It may well be that some of the new models provide enhanced customer service, but they certainly don't have a monopoly on this feature.

But the whole emphasis on people as customers is (or should be) a major cause for concern. At least some of the proponents of the new public management would like to reduce the role and the rights of local citizens to those of a customer. According to this perspective, the municipality's obligation is to ensure that people get what they pay for and pay for what they get, and receive full value for their expenditures in the process. While this commitment may sound praiseworthy, when carried to an extreme it reduces a municipal government to a service exchange in which user fees are applied to as many services as possible in an effort to operate as close to break-even as possible. There seems to be little appreciation in this approach to the notion that governments quite properly provide services which don't, can't, and shouldn't ever break even. Governments provide such services precisely because they are not revenue generators and hence would never be provided by the private sector. These public goods are paid from the tax dollars which citizens provide collectively. They respond to community needs, needs which cannot be addressed (and won't be) if everything has to measure up financially, and to meet the test of the market place.

This last point is, in our view, the greatest threat of the business orientation which has overtaken municipal government. It is the prospect of the judgment of the market place and of the balance sheet being substituted for the political judgment of elected representatives. However rational and scientific the former approach may appear to be, it represents a diminution of democracy. It parallels the dangers which are present at the senior levels of government, where market forces again—this time the forces of the global market place—are increasingly dictating how governments operate. In effect, we are being told that what we need is "more bang for the buck" rather than "more benefit from the ballot."[50]

Concluding Comments

Chapter 7 noted that most of the local government reforms introduced in the second half of the 20th century were preoccupied with improving service delivery and paid too little attention to the representative and political role of municipal government. This same observation can be applied to the internal reforms described in this chapter. Because of the limited success of efforts to create effective executive committees, the most prevalent reform of coordinating machinery has been the chief administrative officer system. No matter how well this system works, however, it does nothing to strengthen political leadership and, to the contrary, may even detract from this objective by creating a bureaucratic system and by undermining the power and public status of the council. Even more worrying are the new business models which are currently receiving much attention. Their overly narrow focus tends to equate municipal government with efficient and entrepreneurial program delivery, and citizens with customers who need quality service. But citizens have additional rights, and responsibilities, as discussed in the next chapter.

---

[50]B. Guy Peters and Donald J. Savoie (eds.), *Governance in a Changing Environment*, Kingston, McGill-Queen's University Press, 1995, p. 75.

CHAPTER 10
The Municipality and the Public

This is no time to "circle the wagons," with councillors and staff huddled together, clutching their benchmarking reports to their chests for comfort. This is a time to open the circle and invite inside those directly affected by the difficult decisions which have to be made—the local citizens.

Introduction

Since the first chapter, we have emphasized that the most important role of municipal government is representative and political. Yet this role has been undermined almost from the outset, and it arguably faces its greatest threat today, because of the emphasis on making municipalities run more like a business.

We are not opposed to governments operating in a "business-like manner," in the sense of being cost-conscious and concerned with efficiency. It is fine to emphasize productivity and to make comparisons with the private sector where appropriate. It makes sense to be entrepreneurial and alert to opportunities for revenue generation. Indeed, we provided many examples of the benefits of such process reforms in Chapter 7. But municipalities cannot be reduced to a series of business units which are judged solely on their profit and loss statements. Many of the decisions made by municipalities must be judged in relation to the public interest objectives they are meant to serve, not "the bottom line."

Similarly, we have no problem with the notion of municipalities taking better care of their customers. Customer service has often received very little attention in the past and, as discussed below, improvements in this area can be very beneficial. The problem arises when municipalities operate as if they only had customers to deal with and when they neglect their broader and much different responsibilities to their citizens. Good ratings on a customer survey form are welcome, but they don't provide any indication of the health of local democracy. For that we need to look beyond surveys and measures of customer satisfaction to the ways in which citizens participate in municipal government, as electors, as members of local groups, through political parties, and through various tools of direct democracy. All of these aspects are examined in this chapter.

The Citizen as Customer

Municipal governments are facing the combined pressures of growing responsibilities and costs, scarce resources, and a disillusioned public strongly opposed to any tax increase and critical of those services they do get for their money. Many municipalities have responded to this situation in the same way as many private organizations have. They focused on cutting costs and on holding the line on prices (taxes). Whatever short-term gain there may be from such a strategy, it is doomed in the longer term. Indeed, municipalities today face a servicing crisis with respect to their basic infrastructure—partly because of a failure to maintain and upgrade such basic services as roads and water and sewer systems.

Perhaps even more threatening has been the deterioration of the human infrastructure of the municipality. Faced with almost constant criticism, hampered by scarce resources, worn down by years of cutback management, many municipal staff became understandably dispirited and demoralized. As a result, their commitment to productivity, to quality, and to customer service, often suffered. As performance declines, however, public criticism only increases, which in turn prompts a further decline in performance, producing a mutually reinforcing downward spiral.

What Difference Can Customer Service Make?[1]

What happens when, instead of focusing on cutbacks, downsizing, and "doom and gloom," municipalities concentrate on improving the quality of customer service? There is substantial documented evidence, much of it drawn from the experience of private companies, to suggest that the following benefits would arise.

1. The public perception of municipal government would improve. As a result, the disillusionment with government would ease, softening the critical, frequently hostile atmosphere in which municipal personnel have to function.

---

[1]This section is based on Association of Municipal Clerks and Treasurers of Ontario, *Municipal Administration Program*, 1998, Unit Four, Lesson 4, pp. 30-31.

2. The tolerance for current taxation levels would improve, since people are willing to pay for superior products and service. This is evident in the private sector, where people often pay a premium for high quality.
3. Not immediately, but over time, the emphasis on quality would actually result in cost savings. It is true that in some particular circumstances, improving quality through the use of a more expensive raw material will increase costs. Overall, however, improving quality saves money. It does so because almost all quality improvement comes through simplification of design, manufacturing, layout, processes, and procedures—a fact which is evident from the successful cost management exercises pursued in numerous municipalities, as cited in Chapter 7. The result is a striking paradox.

Cost reduction campaigns do not often lead to improved quality; and, except for those that involve large reductions in personnel, they don't usually result in long-term lower costs either. On the other hand, effective quality programs yield not only improved quality but lasting cost reductions as well.[2]

The emphasis on quality also saves all of the costs associated with poor quality, such as those related to recalls and repairs, and those arising from the loss of existing customers and the alienation (through bad "word-of-mouth" publicity) of prospective customers. But municipalities can't lose customers in this way, some will claim. They are in a monopoly position. Those who still think municipalities don't have to compete should ask employees of municipal recreation, garbage, and water and sewer departments, and other staff whose councils have been considering the contracting out of services.

4. The morale of municipal personnel would improve. In part, of course, this improvement would come about because of the less hostile, critical working environment. Even more, however, it would result from staff (and councillors) energized by their pursuit of the positive objectives of top quality and customer service. It is certainly far easier to engender enthusiasm and commitment to such positives than to the largely negative achievement of "holding the line."
5. The improved morale, commitment, and enthusiasm would result in increased productivity and additional cost savings. The end result is an upward spiral of mutually reinforcing positive results, rather than the downward spiral previously discussed.

Citizens Are More than Customers

Having demonstrated the value of customer service, we must also caution that it in no way defines the total relationship between a municipality and

---

[2]Tom Peters, *Thriving on Chaos*, New York, HarperCollins, 1988, p. 98.

its citizens. Customers have rights, such as the right to easy access, to choices, and to quick handling of complaints, but citizens "have both rights and responsibilities to be active in setting the agenda of city government and in debating policy options."[3] Whatever its benefits, the focus on customer service may restrict the public to a largely reactive role.

It bears repeating that municipalities are not businesses. They don't just have occasional and specific contacts with customers; they have ongoing and complex relationships with citizens. "Citizens, unlike customers, have common purposes and rights, and among these are the right to be treated equitably."[4]

> **Municipalities don't just have occasional contacts with customers; they have ongoing relationships with citizens.**

Businesses, by contrast, practise target marketing, differentiate, discriminate, and take whatever actions are appropriate to increase market share or cut costs. If municipalities become more business-like by pursuing business strategies for the customer, this approach opens up the possibility of inequities between individuals, "which runs counter to the equal and universalistic entitlements and obligations associated with citizenship."[5] A narrow focus on how well services are delivered to customers overlooks the fact that "the rationale of public services is not the satisfaction of individual demands, but meeting needs collectively within a framework of public policy."[6]

To take a simplified but valid example, a municipality masquerading as a business may resist providing a service because it is not economic or lacks sufficient customer demand. A municipality mindful of its democratic roots will exercise political judgment in deciding whether a service should be provided, no matter how economically sound or shaky, in response to a perceived need among some portion of the populace.

---

[3]Paul G. Thomas, "Diagnosing the Health of Civic Democracy: 25 Years of Citizen Involvement With City Hall," in Nancy Klos (ed.), *The State of Unicity — 25 Years Later*, Winnipeg, Institute of Urban Studies, 1998, p. 50.

[4]Ole Ingstrup, *Public Service Renewal: From Means to Ends*, Ottawa, Canadian Centre for Management Development, 1995, p. 4.

[5]Jon Pierre, "The Marketization of the State," in Guy Peters and Donald Savoie (eds.), *Governance in a Changing Environment*, Kingston, McGill-Queen's University Press, 1995, p. 57.

[6]Dilys M. Hill, *Citizens and Cities*, Hemel Hempstead, Harvester Wheatsheaf, 1994, p. 228.

As Seidle points out, such terms as customer or client do not capture the nature and complexity of the interaction that occurs when a government official serves someone who is, among other things, "a taxpayer, a recipient of certain monetary benefits from the state, a voter and possibly a member of a political party and/or one or more voluntary organizations with an interest in public policy, and who carries expectations that extend beyond a particular contact with a particular public servant at a particular time."[7] A number of these broader relationships are examined in the remainder of this chapter.

The Citizen as Elector

As noted in earlier chapters, municipal governments began with a very restricted franchise which favoured property owners. The franchise is now quite broad, and essentially gives the right to vote to Canadian citizens, 18 years of age and older, who meet limited residency requirements as specified in provincial legislation. Property owners within a municipality, whether residents or not, also have a vote. However, a disappointingly low proportion of voters take advantage of their democratic opportunities every municipal election year. While the approximately two-thirds voting turnout in federal and provincial elections is not great, it certainly contrasts with the 40% or fewer who cast their vote at the municipal level.

Factors Affecting Voting Turnout

A number of factors are commonly cited as influencing the municipal vote. Studies of voter turnout lend some support to the notion that the turnout is higher in smaller municipalities than in larger ones. This is clearly the finding with respect to recent municipal elections in Ontario, as indicated in the table on the following page.[8] The same type of relationship between population and turnout helps to explain why voting in populous municipalities tends to be higher with a ward system than with elections at large. Socio-economic factors such as the educational level of the electorate and the proportion of home-owners versus tenants also

---

[7]F. Leslie Seidle, *Rethinking the Delivery of Public Services to Citizens*, Montreal, Institute for Research on Public Policy, 1995, p. 9.

[8]Joseph Kushner, David Siegel, and Hannah Stanwick, "Ontario Municipal Elections: Voting Trends and Determinants of Electoral Success in a Canadian Province," *Canadian Journal of Political Science*, September 1997, p. 542.

have an influence.[9] Voting turnout is also affected by the extent of competition for the seats available. Acclamations for the head of council position usually result in a reduced turnout, while a close race for that position can have a very positive impact on turnout. A higher voting turnout is also common when there are "questions" on the ballot in the form of plebiscites or referendums. Indeed, there is an old saying that the most effective way to increase voter interest is to add a liquor licensing question to the ballot.

Municipal Size	1982 Turnout	1988 Turnout	1994 Turnout
Small	57.5%	53.2%	54.0%
Medium	46.7%	45.3%	43.6%
Large	39.9%	36.3%	37.0%

It is widely held that a major negative influence on voting turnout is the complicated nature of the municipal election process. At the provincial and federal levels, voters are accustomed to selecting one name from three or four or so, all of them normally identified by a party label. In contrast, the municipal voter must make choices within several different categories (or from multiple ballots) from among many dozens of individual candidates.

> In the 1984 civic elections in Vancouver, for example, each voter had to choose one of five candidates for mayor, ten of twenty-seven candidates for alderman, nine of twenty-seven candidates for school board seats, and seven of twenty-nine candidates for the parks board.[10]

The rather daunting task facing each Vancouver voter, therefore, was to choose a total of 27 people from a list of 88 names, while also answering "yes" or "no" to a plebiscite on testing the cruise missile in Canada.

Voting turnout may also be low because the act of voting has little meaning for many citizens. Some municipalities have retained historic boundaries that bear little relation to the living patterns of today. Citizens are unlikely to take an active interest in the activities of their municipality if their normal circle of movement for work, shopping, and recreation embraces quite different—and usually larger—areas. Municipal decision

---

[9]R. Vaison and P. Aucoin, "Class and Voting in Recent Halifax Mayoralty Elections," in L. D. Feldman and M. D. Goldrick (eds.), *Politics and Government of Urban Canada: Selected Readings*, Toronto, Methuen, 1976, pp. 200-219.

[10]Donald J. H. Higgins, *Local and Urban Politics in Canada*, Toronto, Gage, 1986, p. 315.

making may not seem relevant because many of the issues of concern aren't handled by municipal councils but by separate boards. This is true in most jurisdictions for such matters as education and public health. Yet, where there are elected school boards, voter turnout is usually even lower than that experienced for the municipal elections. Until changes in 1998, school boards in Ontario spent more than half of the property taxes which were levied by municipal councils. There was supposedly widespread dissatisfaction with the quality of education being provided. Yet only about 25% voted in school board elections.

The limited scope of municipal activities may contribute to the low voting turnout. If municipalities do little more than provide the physical services to support growth and development, as has been the case at least until the recent downloading in some provinces, what is there about this administrative role which will generate citizen interest and involvement? Is the voting turnout so low because the electorate "perceives whether intuitively or through overt knowledge that the social, economic and even environmental problems which beset the city lie beyond the city council's power to solve?"[11] Thomas makes a similar observation about Montreal elections:

> It is possible that Montrealers have come to the same realization as have the citizens in most of Canada's other cities—that the world cannot be changed through municipal politics. City governments are really about managing parks, public safety, potholes and garbage collection.[12]

Peterson goes so far as to claim that low levels of citizen participation in local politics are a rational response to the context in which the public finds itself. He cites, among other factors, the absence of political parties to structure conflict, the lack of issues of burning importance, and limited information about local matters in the newspapers.[13]

Whatever the merits of these points, municipalities often fail to help their own cause. Consider the issues and themes raised by candidates during election campaigns. Are voters given competing "visions" about the future of their municipality? Are they made part of an effort to define local interests and concerns, to identify the priorities that the community

---

[11]Earl A. Levin, "Municipal Democracy and Citizen Participation," in Klos, *op. cit.*, p. 43.

[12]Timothy L. Thomas, *A City With a Difference*, Montreal, Véhicule Press, 1997, p. 145.

[13]Paul Peterson, *City Limits*, Chicago, University of Chicago Press, 1981, p. 128.

wants to address together? Is there even a hint in most municipal election campaigns that a fundamental democratic exercise is under way? The answer to all these questions is no. By far the most common message offered to voters in municipal elections is "vote for me and I won't increase your taxes." While this is a popular thing to say—except to those voters who have stopped believing such promises—it is simplistic and probably also unrealistic. It says nothing about how and where tax dollars should be spent, or about what difficult choices must be made *if* tax increases are to be curtailed. A municipal election campaign provides an excellent opportunity to educate local citizens about the tough choices and exciting opportunities which face the municipality. If some of that excitement could be communicated to the voters, they might gain an understanding of the importance and significance of casting their ballots. Instead, the election campaign is reduced to a parade of candidates attempting to convince us of how frugal they would be if put in charge of our tax dollars.

> Municipal election campaigns do little to demonstrate that a fundamental democratic exercise is under way.

It is acknowledged that promising no tax increases may work as a strategy for the election of individual candidates. But, the issue here is a much broader one—the general lack of voter interest and voting turnout in municipal elections. If the only point is to get individuals elected, then let them promise whatever the voters want to hear. But if the point is to develop an appreciation for the political role of municipal government and the vital issues which a municipal council can help its citizens to face and manage, then the campaign needs to be conducted quite differently.

Potential voters may also be disillusioned by the realization that they are not able to enforce real accountability for actions through the mechanism of periodic elections. How can accountability be allocated, and criticism or praise handed out where warranted? The fact is that there is no clear focus of accountability and responsibility within virtually any of our municipal councils. Without organized political parties, there is no "government" and no "official opposition." Everyone is responsible for everything, which means that no one is really responsible for anything.

For the minority who do exercise their franchise, voting in municipal elections is, at best, an infrequent and rather passive activity. Many citizens want more continuous and direct involvement. They want the opportunity to participate in the process of making decisions, not just to pass judgment "after-the-fact." For such citizens, the normal recourse has been to form or join local groups, as discussed in a later section.

Voting Results: Who Gets Elected?

Until recently, municipal council positions have been considered a part-time responsibility, the preserve of the "gifted amateur"[14] rather than the professional politician. Given the strong influence which business has always wielded over municipal operations, it is not surprising to discover that the most common backgrounds of urban councillors are in business, the public service, education, and community organizations.[15] The percentage of women on municipal council, at least in major Canadian cities, is significantly higher than their representation in provincial and federal governing bodies. Among the reasons which have been given for this situation are that family responsibilities preclude women from taking on the travelling involved in federal and provincial service and that municipal issues are closer to the home and of more interest to women.[16] Trimble challenges both of these explanations, claiming that they are based on incorrect and unflattering assumptions about the nature of city politics and about women's participation in the political process.[17] Moreover, even if women homemakers were interested in social issues, these receive very little attention in small municipalities, where the focus tends to be on roads, snow removal, and other hard service issues.

> Business people are well represented on council, women somewhat, and visible minorities very little.

In contrast to the inroads being made by women on council, visible minorities remain very poorly represented. Even in cities with an ethnically diverse population, such as Vancouver or Montreal, there have been few minority candidates.[18] With the growing cultural diversity of Canada's cities, there will be increased demands that electoral politics be made more attractive and accessible to minority communities.

---

[14]Andrew Sancton and Paul Woolner, "Full-time municipal councillors: a strategic challenge for Canadian urban government," *Canadian Public Administration*, Winter 1990, p. 485.

[15]Katherine A. Graham, Susan D. Phillips, and Allan M. Maslove, *Urban Governance in Canada*, Toronto, Harcourt Brace & Company, Canada, 1998, p. 99.

[16]Chantal Maillé, "Gender Concerns in City Life," in Timothy L. Thomas (ed.), *The Politics of the City*, Toronto, ITP Nelson, 1997, p. 109.

[17]Linda Trimble, "Politics Where We Live: Women and Cities," in James Lightbody (ed.), *Canadian Metropolitics*, Toronto, Copp Clark Ltd., 1995, p. 93.

[18]Graham et al., *op. cit.*, p. 102.

The Role of the Mass Media

Public interest and involvement in municipal government, whether by voting or through other means, can be affected—positively or negatively—by the media coverage given (or not given) to municipal government issues and activities. Local issues usually receive very little coverage in the national electronic media. Yet studies suggest that the general public is particularly interested in local and regional news,[19] and it is coverage of these issues which is most pertinent from the point of view of municipal governments. The adequacy of local news coverage depends on the local radio and television stations (where they exist) and on local newspapers, with the latter being regarded by most citizens as their primary source of information.

It can be argued, however, that the media have contributed to the limited public participation in local government by their generally poor performance in providing information about, and promoting understanding of, local government. News stories tend to concentrate on the supposedly more important and glamorous activities of the senior levels of government. The municipal beat often is assigned to junior reporters and is seen as an unavoidable stepping stone to bigger and better things. Moreover, while local weekly papers may devote considerable space to municipal coverage, even printing the council minutes, the dailies are much more limited and selective in their coverage. As with all news items, there is a tendency to emphasize controversial or sensational matters. The bulk of the council's deliberations is regarded as routine, preoccupied with administrative details, and not especially newsworthy. While there may be some truth in this view, the fact remains that without some media coverage of these ongoing municipal activities, the public is ill informed and lacks the background necessary for an understanding of local issues. Municipal councils and staff often become disillusioned with the media because occasional controversies are highlighted while the vast majority of municipal government activities appear to be largely ignored.

One conspicuous example of media influence relates to the coverage of municipal tax increases. Such increases receive very prominent, and negative, attention in the media. Paradoxically, while the media may

---

[19]See Canada, Royal Commission on Newspapers, *Report* and *Research Studies*, Ottawa, Supply and Services, 1981, and P. Audley, *Canada's Cultural Industries*, Toronto, James Lorimer and the Canadian Institute for Economic Policy, 1983. These studies are briefly discussed in Higgins, *op. cit.*, p. 300.

criticize inadequate municipal services all through the year, at budget time councils are somehow expected to hold the line on taxes. Typical of this kind of media coverage was the response of the *Kingston Whig Standard* when that city's council brought in a 1995 budget which included a small tax increase. The newspaper responded with a large bold headline proclaiming that the "Tax Hike Disappoints Critics and Retailers," and a sidebar quoting one councillor who expressed disappointment that council hadn't been serious about making necessary cuts. The Chamber of Commerce reacted with great indignation, demanding that council reconvene and do the budget again. The controversy simmered for weeks, doubtless in part thanks to the continuing coverage provided by the newspaper and other media outlets. Almost entirely overlooked in all the fuss was the fact that the tax increase for the owner of an average home was $26 over the entire year!

Not only was the budget increase negligible for residential taxpayers, it was made only after prolonged efforts by city council to cut expenditures and to hold the line on taxes. Indeed, the *Whig Standard* subsequently reported on the "heroic struggle" inside city hall to avoid the tax increase and indicated that among the items cut from the 1995 budget were several related to equipment maintenance, equipment replacement, protective clothing, and training and development.[20] It could be argued that councillors had cut too much out of the budget, rather than being too spendthrift.

In early 1999, the *Whig Standard* ran a series of articles documenting the deplorable state of Kingston's aging infrastructure, and suggesting that this situation had arisen because of the failure of past councils to make the necessary expenditures on services and upkeep. Not mentioned was the role that the newspaper may have played in encouraging this unwise frugality in earlier councils.

It should be emphasized that no claim is being made that the budget deliberations of Kingston city council have been above reproach. Nor are we questioning the right of the newspaper to report as it did. This kind of critical coverage is quite common. But it must be recognized that municipal budget deliberations conducted in this atmosphere focus almost entirely on tax rate considerations to the neglect of the basic priority setting exercise which needs to be undertaken. Once again, the result is to reduce what should be a very fundamental political and policy making process into an administrative exercise, preoccupied with juggling and

---

[20] Ann Lukits, "How City Hall employees are spending less money," *Kingston Whig Standard*, February 15, 1995.

cutting expenditure figures until the resulting taxes stay below some pre-determined acceptable level.

To take another example of media influence, it is probably fair to say that the growth mentality which infected most municipalities, at least until recent years, has been encouraged or reinforced by the media. Lightbody, for example, describes the *Edmonton Journal* as "unashamedly a booster press," and notes that it normally endorsed the Citizens' Committee or its Civic Government successors, and the pro-growth interests which they represented. He observes that "While the evidence is insufficient to prove that the Journal was able to structure electoral choice, judging by results we can conclude with some certainty that the environment was scarcely conducive to the emergence of an effective challenge to the Citizens' Committee."[21]

A Bureau of Municipal Research study documented several instances where press coverage appeared to have an influence on the outcome of issues.[22] One analyst suggested that the media influence extended to setting the agenda of public discussion. After studying three small Ontario cities, he concluded that there was a fairly close parallel between the ranking of items in the agendas of the press and of the local political community, and that the daily newspapers had influenced politicians to make particular policy decisions that they might not otherwise have made if left on their own.[23]

Dealing still with newspapers, the degree of concentration of ownership is seen by many as a concern. One worry is that newspapers may be hesitant to provide news coverage and editorial comment which appears critical of any of the varied business interests of their corporate owners. There is also a fear that newspapers will be similarly constrained from critical commentary that might offend major advertisers, notably the property industry. Developments in recent years have done nothing to allay these fears. In particular, Conrad Black, through his Hollinger Corporation, has gained control of Southam and now owns almost 60% of the daily newspapers in Canada.

---

[21]James Lightbody, "Edmonton," in Warren Magnusson and Andrew Sancton (eds.), *City Politics in Canada*, Toronto, University of Toronto Press, 1983, p. 266.

[22]Bureau of Municipal Research, "The News Media and Local Government," in *Civic Affairs*, Toronto, August 1976.

[23]E. R. Black, *Politics and the News: The Political Functions of the Mass Media*, Toronto, Butterworths, 1982.

Whatever their faults, it must be acknowledged that the media often receive very little support from municipalities in attempting to carry out their responsibilities. There are too many examples of municipal governments which at best exhibit no concern for public relations and at worst maintain as much secrecy as possible about their deliberations. While the desire to shield discussions from "sensationalized media coverage" is understandable, attempts to conceal information almost always result in even worse media coverage. Municipal councillors and staff need to take a more positive approach and to use more imagination and sensitivity in developing effective relations with the media.[24]

> Municipalities must accept a fair share of responsibility for what they feel is poor media coverage.

The Citizen and Local Groups

Participation through groups is by no means new, and Chapter 3 described a number of local groups which spearheaded the turn of the century reform movement. Also of long standing are various residents' and ratepayers' associations established to protect the interests of the property owner as principal taxpayer. Over the years, they often broadened their membership and focus. Groups representing the business community and the middle class have also been prominent in a number of cities for more than half a century, often promoting the election of like-minded councillors and attempting to prevent the election of candidates representing labour or socialist viewpoints. More will be said about these "non-party parties" in a later section of this chapter.

According to pluralists, government action is the outcome of a competition among organized groups that seek to protect or promote the interests of their members, although groups supposedly make heightened use of resources only on occasional issues of great concern.[25] But it has been increasingly acknowledged that some groups are better equipped than others with resources and with opportunities to pursue their objectives. Critics contend that the apparently diverse influences implied in the

---

[24]For a good discussion of the media, its influence, and ways of dealing with it, see W. T. Stanbury, *Business-Government Relations in Canada: Influencing Public Policy*, Scarborough, Nelson Canada, 1993, Chapter 10.

[25]Clarence N. Stone and Heywood T. Sanders (eds.), *The Politics of Urban Development*, Lawrence, University Press of Kansas, 1987, p. 13.

pluralist model serve to conceal or distract attention from the fact that one type of group—the business group—is by far the most dominant. This issue has been memorably summarized by Schattsneider in the comment that "the flaw in the pluralist heaven is that the heavenly chorus sings with a strong upper-class accent."[26] Gradually, attention has been shifting to the context in which groups operate, and especially to the economic constraints on political action. The importance of the latter has been advanced, some would say exaggerated, by Peterson, whose views in *City Limits* have been characterized as a kind of pluralism plus. The importance of economic constraints is also evident in public choice theory, and "its extension of the neo-classical model of the market to political life."[27] Numerous examples of both local groups and their economic context will be found in this chapter.

The 1960s and 1970s saw a great increase in local groups, often representing local citizens and neighbourhoods that had not previously been active or influential in public affairs. In addition, a number of these groups attempted to broaden their concerns beyond one specific issue (although it may have caused their initial formation) and sought to change the municipal decision-making process by building in a consultative element. If there was one common feature of most of these groups over the years, it was their attitude towards growth and development. Just as many of the earlier groups, especially those representing the business community, were pro-growth, so many of the later groups, representing neighbourhoods, were concerned with stability and the preservation of existing lifestyles.

According to Magnusson,[28] a new reform politics grew out of this process, one which questioned long-held views about "sacrificing the neighbourhood to the larger community, observing the proprieties of bureaucratic procedure, respecting the judgments of professional planners, and accepting the leadership of elected officials...." Part of this new way of thinking was the belief that municipal politics should be rooted in the ward or neighbourhood, at the level where people would and could be more directly involved in political activity. A similar view was expressed by Fowler in Chapter 4, with his contention that "authentic poli-

---

[26]E. E. Schattsneider, *The Semi-Sovereign People*, New York, Holt, Rinehart and Winston, 1960, p. 35.

[27]Michael Keating, *Comparative Urban Politics*, Aldershot, Edward Elgar, 1991, p. 108.

[28]Magnusson and Sancton, *op. cit.*, pp. 33-34.

tics" is only possible in small scale, diverse spaces where a variety of casual face-to-face interactions occur naturally.[29]

Chapter 4 also noted Sewell's warning about neighbourhood groups becoming taken over by the NIMBY (Not In My Back Yard) syndrome. This pattern has been much in evidence since the 1980s, especially with respect to issues related to the location of waste management sites or "undesirable" residential facilities, such as group homes.

Groups representing the business community merit separate mention. They offer quite a contrast to most citizens' groups, which rely heavily on volunteers, lack funds, have difficulty getting access to information, and often face an unsympathetic city hall. By comparison, business groups usually have a solid financial base, full-time staff to provide continuity, and ready access to information. In addition, "there tends to be an affinity between the interests of the corporate sector and the business or professional background and perspectives of a large proportion of local elected officials."[30] Research by Lorimer and Gutstein in the early 1970s[31] showed that sometimes up to 80% of city councils and land use advisory bodies in Canadian local governments were members of the development industry. That industry is highly organized, with some 80 local associations of the Canadian Home Builders Association and with more than 1000 corporate members in the Urban Development Institute.[32]

Local chambers of commerce, representing local businesses and industry, usually have close ties with, and considerable influence over, municipal councils. There may be joint efforts between these bodies and councils in the promotion of economic development. There has also been an increased link between councils and business as financial pressures prompt municipalities to contract out services and to pursue joint ventures with the private sector.[33]

Groups representing ethnic, racial, and cultural communities have become more prevalent in the past decade or so. In part, this arises from the increased diversity of the populations comprising our cities. We are

---

[29]Edmund P. Fowler, *Building Cities That Work*, Kingston, McGill-Queen's University Press, 1992, pp. 120-133.

[30]*Ibid.*, p. 291.

[31]James Lorimer, *A Citizen's Guide to City Politics*, Toronto, James Lewis and Samuel, 1972, Chapters 7 and 8, and Donald Gutstein, *Vancouver Ltd.*, Toronto, Lorimer, 1975.

[32]Graham et al., *op. cit.*, p. 132.

[33]*Ibid.*

seeing national social movements, such as those relating to women's rights, gay rights, and the environment, pursuing their objectives through action at the municipal level.[34] For example, the gay and lesbian movements have pushed for municipal declarations of gay pride day or week, with distinctly mixed results. In contrast to the receptive regimes in cities like Montreal and Toronto, there have been rejections by municipalities like Hamilton, London, and Fredericton, usually followed by appeals to the Human Rights Commission of the province.

The Citizen and Local Political Parties

Another vehicle for citizen participation in government is through political parties. There has long been, however, strong resistance to overt political party activity at the local level. The word overt is stressed, since many local elected members are widely known to be associated with one of the provincial or national political party organizations. This type of link is apparently quite acceptable to the voters, but a more negative reaction could be expected if the same individuals were to run locally with a more specific party affiliation. Except in Quebec municipalities where organized parties are not unusual, voters in most Canadian cities do not support political parties running for municipal office. This is evident from the experiences of four large Canadian cities, as summarized below. These experiences also illustrate the activities of local citizens' groups.

Political Activity in Winnipeg

Local political activity in Winnipeg received a great stimulus in 1919, when the General Strike of that year polarized the city. A Civic Election Committee was formed by downtown businesses to endorse, and raise funds for, anti-labour candidates. Until the end of the 1980s, this organization, later known as the Metropolitan Election Committee, the Greater Winnipeg Election Committee, and, finally, the Independent Citizen Election Committee (ICEC), continued to elect a majority of the members of council against the efforts of the Independent Labour Party, the CCF, and, most recently, the NDP.

While essentially a pro-business local political party, the ICEC insisted that it was not a party at all and that support for its candidates would prevent parties—especially socialist parties—from bringing their politics and

---

[34]*Ibid.*, pp. 129-130.

policies into the municipal council chamber. As a result, the ICEC was able to avoid accepting the responsibility for leadership in spite of its dominant numerical position within Winnipeg council over the decades.

The year 1972 was a watershed for Winnipeg, ushering in the new Unicity structure of government. A major objective of the new system was the fulfillment of the representative role of municipal government and the encouragement of increased public participation through special consultative machinery. Indeed, Thomas sees Unicity as an attempt to weaken the alliance between public officials and land-based business by promoting citizen involvement and placing "other political actors representing neighbourhoods, broader communities, ethno-cultural groups, non-profits and advocacy groups on a more equal footing with the business interests."[35] The anticipated increase in citizen participation in the decision-making process did not materialize, however, for reasons discussed in Chapter 7. In part, this was because the centre-right candidates of the ICEC dominated the new council and entrenched a pro-development regime in Unicity, one with little sympathy for the community committees or RAGs.[36]

The ICEC continued its domination through the first decade of new Unicity government. By the 1980 municipal election, however, ICEC's veneer of nonpartisanship had worn quite thin, and the NDP scored a breakthrough by capturing 7 seats on the Unicity council, with another 9 going to independent candidates and the remaining 12 to ICEC candidates. Shortly before the 1983 election, the ICEC announced that it was disbanding. One analyst interpreted this step as a clever ploy rather than a sign of collapse. It removed from the scene a name associated with the past council's record, it put off the need for a consensus among the traditional ICEC candidates until after the election, and it avoided the necessity of providing an alternative to the NDP program.[37]

Whatever the motives underlying the dissolution of the ICEC, the election results were quite disappointing for the NDP. They lost one of their seven seats, and nearly lost two others. The local party was undoubtedly hurt by the controversial attempt by the NDP provincial government of Howard Pawley to entrench French as an official language in Manitoba,

---

[35]Paul Thomas, *op. cit.*, p. 47.

[36]Greg Selinger, "Urban Governance for the Twenty-First Century: What the Unicity Experience Tells Us," in Klos, *op. cit.*, p. 89.

[37]Dave Hall, "Twisted Tale of Intentions," *City Magazine*, Winnipeg, April 1984, p. 14.

especially after this became a local referendum issue. In addition, however, the local party was hurt by its own internal divisions between "old guard" members and newer, more progressive members.

The NDP presence on Unicity council was reduced even further, to just two members, in the 1986 municipal election. The other 27 members elected were all independents, although the majority of them represented the now-disbanded ICEC. Indeed, one assessment identified 20 of these 27 "independents" as actively involved with the Progressive Conservative or Liberal parties,[38] continuing the domination of the ICEC type of candidate. According to one observer,[39] the provincial NDP again contributed to the poor showing of the local NDP, this time much more directly. He claimed that the provincial party created confusion for the local party by overruling its decisions, deciding for the local party that it would not run a candidate for mayor, and redirecting key party workers to the elections in Saskatchewan and British Columbia, thereby weakening the local campaign.

In 1989 a reform coalition composed of New Democrats and Liberals was formed under the hopeful name of WIN (Winnipeg into the Nineties).[40] It succeeded in electing members to one-third of the seats on council, establishing for the first time a cohesive reform block on Winnipeg city council. The response to this "threat" by the Conservative provincial government elected in 1990 was to abolish the right of political parties to make contributions to candidates running for city council, while authorizing donations from corporations and unions, actions which have been described as leading to the corporatization of civic government.[41]

In the 1992 election, WIN candidates retained their minority position, holding 5 seats on a council reduced from 21 to 15. But one commentator contends that Winnipeg's long-standing schism disappeared in 1992 when the city council was slashed to 15 and civic politics became a full-time job. "The demands on councillors in the new environment pretty well drove off the last of the bright lights on the right and left, who no longer could pursue civic politics as a hobby."[42] WIN had disappeared by the

---

[38]This is the assessment of Jeff Lowe, "Winnipeg: User-Unfriendly," *City Magazine*, Winnipeg, Spring 1988, p. 9.

[39]Kent Gerecke, "Winnipeg Hits Bottom," *City Magazine*, Winnipeg, Winter 1986/87, p. 35.

[40]Barton Reid, "City Beat," *City Magazine*, Winnipeg, Winter '92/'93, p. 5.

[41]Selinger, *op. cit.*, p. 95.

[42]G. Flood, "Civic Fight Sputters," *Winnipeg Free Press*, September 21, 1997.

time of the most recent (1998) election, but at least five members of the council, including new mayor Glen Murray, are considered "leftish."

Political Activity in Vancouver

As with Winnipeg, it was the threat of political gains by the left which led to the establishment of a pro-business party in Vancouver. The year was 1936, and three CCF candidates were elected in the city's first at large municipal election. In response, business interests founded the Non-Partisan Association (NPA), its very name designed to conceal its real status as a local political party.

The NPA began to run into increasingly strong citizen opposition in the 1960s, concerning both the pace and the location of developments. Vancouver's urban renewal initiatives, for example, were typical of the time in that they involved the displacement of large numbers of families. The Strathcona Property Owners' and Tenants' Association was established in 1968, devoted to halting further such projects in its neighbourhood. The following year the federal government announced that it would not provide funds for the urban renewal project in Strathcona unless the residents were involved in the planning process. The result was a working committee comprising government officials and members of the Association, "one of the first instances in Canada of citizens sharing this kind of decision-making with government."[43] As launched in 1972, the rehabilitation plan became a model for other such programs. Rather than expropriating homes, it emphasized repairs and renovations and provided stability for the Strathcona neighbourhood.

Vancouver's various expressway schemes also prompted strong public opposition which led to their rejection on several occasions. The June 1967 release of the Vancouver Transportation Study triggered a prolonged debate. Leo notes that "citizen protest against the expressway system culminated in November in an acrimonious public meeting attended by five hundred citizens. Some thirty organizations and individuals prepared briefs for submission at the meeting."[44] More significantly, new political parties were formed to challenge the NPA vision of the city.

An important breakthrough appeared to occur in 1972 with the defeat of the NPA and the election of a municipal government controlled by

---

[43]Donald Gutstein, "Vancouver," in Magnusson and Sancton, *op. cit.*, p. 201.

[44]Christopher Leo, *The Politics of Urban Development: Canadian Urban Expressway Disputes*, Monographs on Canadian Urban Government, No. 3, Toronto, Institute of Public Administration, 1977, p. 46.

TEAM (The Electors Action Movement). A coalition of reformers, especially anti-expressway forces, and more conservative business interests,
TEAM did make some noteworthy changes.[45] It restructured the bureaucracy, replacing the commissioner system with a single city manager with
reduced executive powers, and made some moves to open up city hall
to public involvement. Leo concedes that TEAM was a liberal, establishment party, focused on middle-class issues, and with only a limited
concern for matters like "affordable housing, inner-city education, homelessness, racism, and women's issues."[46] But he contends that TEAM
made a valuable contribution by shifting attention from a conservative,
development-oriented approach to city plan-
ning to one which addressed issues of "livability."[47] Whatever its accomplishments, within
four years TEAM was badly divided and in the
1978 election the NPA reemerged as the major
party on council.[48]

> During its limited time in
> office, TEAM did make some
> changes to open up city hall.

But control of council by right-wing interests faced a new challenge
in 1980 when Mike Harcourt, a New Democrat, won the mayoralty and the
Committee of Progressive Electors (COPE) elected three councillors.
COPE was formed in 1968 by the Vancouver and District Labour Council,
with the objective of bringing together labour, ratepayer groups, the NDP,
and other interested groups to establish a base to enter municipal politics.
The left was still in a minority on the 1980 council, however, and discussions were often bitter, with members of the NPA, TEAM, and COPE increasingly polarized. In addition to this constraint on the mayor's activity,
the Social Credit provincial government continued to protect business
interests and obviously had concerns about the election of an NDP mayor.

Harcourt was returned as mayor in 1982, along with four COPE councillors and two independent NDP councillors. Gutstein[49] refers to this elec-

---

[45]Gutstein in Magnusson and Sancton, *op. cit.*, pp. 206-209.

[46]Christopher Leo, "The Urban Economy and the Power of the Local State,"
in Frances Frisken (ed.), *The Changing Canadian Metropolis*, Toronto, Canadian
Urban Institute, p. 690.

[47]*Ibid.*, pp. 690-691.

[48]For an analysis of Vancouver's political parties by a founding member of
TEAM, see Paul Tennant, "Vancouver City Politics," in Feldman, *op. cit.*, pp. 126-
147.

[49]Donald Gutstein, "Vancouver: Progressive Majority Impotent," *City Magazine*, Winnipeg, Spring 1983, p. 12.

tion result as the "first successful challenge to business dominance at the local level in the city's 96 year history." However, there were some difficulties in maintaining a progressive voting bloc on council, and continuing problems with interference from the Social Credit provincial government. Indeed, one book during this period expressed concern that local autonomy was being threatened by the neo-conservative forces in power provincially and their view that local authorities should not be allowed to follow policies contrary to the market-oriented revival being promoted provincially.[50] A similar pattern, even more pronounced, was also evident in British local government during this period, as Margaret Thatcher imposed her view of the appropriate scope of government activity on resistant labour-controlled municipal councils.[51] This same pattern has also been evident in Ontario in the second half of the 1990s, with the provincial Conservative party attempting to rein in what it regarded as excessive spending by school boards and municipalities. As discussed earlier, the province forced major amalgamations on both, took over the setting of the educational tax rate, and imposed ceilings on municipal property tax increases.

On the surface, the 1984 election results were quite similar to those of 1982. Harcourt was reelected mayor, along with five progressive members—four of them from COPE. Opposing them were three members from the NPA and two from TEAM. According to Gutstein,[52] the polarization of the city was completed with this election. As he saw it, Vancouver is really two cities: a working-class east side city and a middle-class west side city—which elect two entirely different councils.

The 1986 election results were quite dramatic, bringing Vancouver's developers back into power at Vancouver's city hall. The NPA captured 9 of the 11 seats on council—including its mayoral candidate, developer Gordon Campbell—and 8 of 9 seats on the school board. According to Gutstein,[53] Campbell was successful in attracting the moderate voters in

---

[50]Warren Magnusson, William K. Carroll, Charles Doyle, Monika Langer, and R. B. J. Walker (eds.), *The New Reality: The Politics of Restraint in British Columbia*, Vancouver, NewStar Books, 1984.

[51]See, for example, Gerry Stoker, *The Politics of Local Government*, London, Macmillan Education Ltd., 1988, chapters 7 and 8.

[52]Donald Gutstein, "Civic Election Wars," *City Magazine*, Summer 1985, p. 12.

[53]Donald Gutstein, "Vancouver Voters Swing Right," *City Magazine*, Winter 1986-87, p. 30. The brief outline which follows is based on the Gutstein article.

spite of his right wing, pro-development record, especially when the alternative was Harry Rankin of COPE, a long-time socialist councillor who was seen by many as quite radical.

Campbell easily won reelection in 1988 and in 1990, but COPE managed to increase its representation on council to three and then to five. The 1993 election was a near sweep for the NPA, with COPE winning only one of the 10 seats on council. The NPA also captured the mayoralty, although with one-third less popular support than Campbell had received in the preceding election.[54] In an ironic twist of fate, the right-wing city council found itself contending with an NDP provincial government led by Mike Harcourt—much as Harcourt, when head of a left-leaning council a decade before, had to contend with interference from the Social Credit provincial government. Domination by the NPA has continued throughout the 1990s and in the most recent (1996) election, it won all the seats on council and on the school board.

Political Activity in Montreal

The modern period of local politics in Montreal can be dated from 1914, according to Guy Bourassa.[55] Since that time, we have witnessed a succession of powerful and popular mayors, often gaining reelection. The regimes over which they presided, however, were often corrupt and financially strapped, and the provincial government had to intervene on a number of occasions, notably in 1918 when the province virtually took over the running of the city by appointing a five member administrative commission.[56] Corruption within the city government finally led to a judicial inquiry, prompted by the urgings of the Civic Action League and its offshoot, the Committee for Public Morality. One of the investigators for this inquiry was Jean Drapeau, then a young lawyer. When the inquiry ended in 1953, the Civic Action League decided to run candidates in the upcoming 1954 election. Drapeau became the League's successful candidate for mayor, and the rest, as they say, is history!

---

[54]Barton Reid, "Civic Elections 1993," *City Magazine*, Fall/Winter '93/'94, p. 8.

[55]Guy Bourassa, "The Political Elite of Montreal: From Aristocracy to Democracy," in Feldman and Goldrick, *op. cit.,* pp. 146-155.

[56]Andrew Sancton, "Montreal," in Magnusson and Sancton, *op. cit.,* p. 67. The following outline of events leading up to Drapeau's long tenure in office is largely based on Sancton's material.

Drapeau's first term of office was a difficult one, because the Civic Action League had not gained control over the council itself. After losing the 1957 election, Drapeau disassociated himself from the Civic Action League but managed to attract most of their city councillors to his new Civic Party. It was as head of this highly disciplined party that he returned to power as mayor in 1960—a position he continued to hold until his retirement prior to the 1986 election.

By the end of the 1960s, however, there were signs of growing citizen activism in Montreal. Potentially strong opposition to Drapeau first surfaced in 1970 in the form of the Front d'action politique (FRAP), which was a grouping of trade unions and left-wing nationalist organizations.[57] Whatever prospects this organization had were dashed by the FLQ kidnapping crisis and Drapeau's success in linking FRAP with the outlawed terrorist group and in capitalizing on the public's desire for stability and security.

Over the next several years opposition to Drapeau grew, not only from radicals who deplored his failure to provide sufficient housing and social and recreational services in the poorer sections of the city but also from middle-class groups concerned with stopping high-rise development, saving the city's older buildings and neighbourhoods, and forcing a more democratic, open system of government.[58] These opposition forces came together in 1974 to form the Montreal Citizens' Movement (MCM), which made a dramatic impact on the November municipal election. Drapeau received only 55.1% of the popular vote for mayor—almost a rebuff in relation to his past results—and his Civic Party won only 36 seats on council, with the MCM winning 18, and a group called Democracy Montreal winning another.

The following year the provincial government took over responsibility for the preparations for the 1976 Olympic Games because of the city administration's poor performance. For the first time there was also clear evidence of corruption within the city administration. One might have expected, therefore, that the opposition forces would consolidate their position and prepare for the overthrow of the Drapeau regime in the 1978 election. Instead, the MCM split apart and was taken over by a group of radical socialists. Its policy orientation alienated the newly elected provincial government of the Parti Québécois which, in any event, was not anxious to tangle with Drapeau and was quite prepared to stay out of city

---

[57]*Ibid.*, p. 73.

[58]*Ibid.*

politics if Drapeau would keep his influential voice out of the sovereignty-association debate. A new party, the Municipal Action Group (essentially a front for federal Liberals) emerged in time for the election, but Drapeau was reelected easily and his Civic Party won 52 of 54 seats on council.[59]

According to Milner, the resurrection of the MCM in the early 1980s was largely due to its new leader, Jean Doré. While Drapeau was returned in 1982 and his Civic Party captured 39 of the 57 council seats, popular support was down—almost 18% less with respect to Drapeau. The 1986 election (which followed Drapeau's retirement) saw a massive victory for the MCM, with only one Civic Party councillor and two independents elected to council. In Milner's view, the Doré-led MCM "appeared reasonable and approachable, especially when contrasted with Drapeau's Gaullist style; its hammering at everyday bread and butter issues corresponded more closely to the emerging public mood than Drapeau's seeming preoccupation with grand projects."[60]

In contrast to the autocratic, secretive style long followed by Drapeau, the new administration was characterized by a cautious and consensual approach. Consultation was the watchword. But the grassroots nature of the MCM soon began to weaken. Developers and business people were not long in courting the new administration and party activists soon found little scope for their activities. Their best leaders had become city councillors or political advisors. Milner's assessment of what happened bears repeating:

> The syndrome is a classic one: the reformist movement takes power and effectively moves toward the centre of the spectrum, attempting to rule in the name of the electorate as a whole, not merely the party activists, who find their activities largely confined to vindicating such limited actions, raising money and recruiting new members. And with no opposition left in City Hall, the external enemy is gone: there's no one, out there, to fight.[61]

Actions taken by the MCM in office increasingly alienated its traditional supporters.[62] During the Overdale controversy, the MCM sided with developers and investors against tenants and community groups of the Overdale housing complex, which was demolished to make way for lux-

---

[59] *Ibid.*, p. 76.

[60] Henry Milner, "The Montreal Citizens' Movement: Then and Now," *Quebec Studies*, No. 6, 1988, p. 5.

[61] *Ibid.*, p. 8.

[62] The summary which follows is based on Timothy Thomas, *op. cit.*, p. 214.

ury condos. It managed to upset both environmentalists and pacifists by allowing the Matrox company to cut down the last stand of black maples on the island of Montreal to expand its parking lot, just after the company had signed a military contract with the United States government. Moreover, when some of the MCM members began to voice their concern over the actions being taken, rules were tightened up to enforce caucus confidentiality—the sort of muzzling action expected of old-line parties, not the MCM.

Four MCM councillors defected before the first term was up. They complained of overwhelming pressure to follow the party line and the silencing of debate within the party. The MCM dissidents set up their own party, the Democratic Coalition of Montreal (DCM), which they claimed was closer to the original ideals of the MCM.[63]

The MCM was easily reelected in 1990, although with only 37 of the 51 seats on council. Critics still found little real change in operating style from the days of Drapeau. The executive committee was still all-powerful, and it was made up exclusively of MCM councillors who were expected to display party solidarity.[64] Rumblings within the party, and some defections, led to some changes in September 1992—including a pledge to increase councillor power through local district advisory committees (discussed in Chapter 7) and to improve civil service efficiency and service delivery.

In addition, the MCM did initiate a number of steps designed to increase citizen access to city hall. One notable feature was the establishment of Access Montreal, a storefront, neighbourhood-based network of public information offices. These offices encompass a broad range of functions, acting as consultation centres, information relay points, and outlets for direct transactions with the city.[65] In spite of some new opportunities for public input, however, critics charged that nothing happened unless it found its way to, and received the approval of, the executive committee. That body was composed of the mayor and six other councillors named by the mayor and approved by council, usually within a week after an election. The executive committee held weekly, closed meetings, which other councillors were not allowed to attend. Nearly

---

[63]Karen Herland, *People, Potholes and City Politics*, Montreal, Black Rose Books, 1992, p. 14.

[64]*Ibid.*, p. 15.

[65]Pierre Niedlispacher, "Access Montreal: Customer-Driven Municipal Services," in James McDavid and Brian Marson (eds.), *The Well-Performing Government Organization*, Toronto, Institute of Public Administration, 1991, pp. 65-67.

every motion presented to council was prepared by the executive committee.[66]

Further evidence of the closed-door, top-down approach to decision making is found in the operation of the city's five council committees. These were established after the 1986 election to allow elected representatives to examine important issues carefully before city hall made decisions. But, one observer points out that Mayor Doré made sure to exclude members of opposition parties from almost all positions on these committees. "By naming MCM councillors to 26 of the 27 committee positions, he got lapdogs instead of watchdogs."[67] It is also charged that Doré steered controversial issues away from these committees, leaving them to spin their wheels discussing secondary matters.[68]

In the November 1994 municipal election, the MCM was reduced to six seats on council. Doré was among the MCM candidates not reelected and he announced his intention to leave municipal politics. However, he did not rule out the possibility of running for mayor again in four years time.[69] Pierre Bourque was elected mayor, and the Vision Montreal party which he headed captured 38 other seats on the 51 member city council. Bourque's first term of office was marked by considerable controversy, however. Numerous charges of violation of municipal party financing rules were laid against the Vision Montreal party, and several convictions resulted.[70] Some 15 councillors defected from the party, and in early 1997 Bourque faced a caucus revolt when he attempted to dismiss two members of the executive committee—an action subsequently ruled beyond his powers by the courts.[71] There was also much criticism of Bourque's efforts to dismantle the public consultation machinery which had been established by Doré and his return to the autocratic governing style that had been associated with Drapeau.[72] In spite of these developments, Bourque and the Vision Party captured the same number of seats in the

---

[66]Herland, *op. cit.*, p. 37.

[67]Henry Aubin, "Promises Not To Keep," *Montreal Gazette*, November 8, 1994.

[68]*Ibid.*

[69]Michelle Lalonde, "Doré Quits City Politics," *Montreal Gazette*, November 8, 1994.

[70]Michelle Lalonde, "Bourque Is Back," *Montreal Gazette*, November 2, 1998.

[71]Graham et al., p. 109.

[72]*Ibid.*

1998 election. Doré did run again for mayor, but finished a humiliating fourth.[73]

Political Activity in Toronto

Citizen activism became prominent in Toronto during the 1960s. A well-documented example concerned an urban renewal scheme for the Treffann Court area of the city, which proposed the usual demolition of buildings.[74] Citizen opposition led, as in Vancouver, to a new approach in which the affected citizens became involved in the development of the urban renewal plans. More generally, the extent of high-rise commercial redevelopment and apartment construction was threatening middle- and upper-class neighbourhoods. Opposition to such projects prompted the establishment or revival of ratepayers' and residents' groups, which became increasingly aggressive in their opposition. "In 1968, a Confederation of Residents' and Ratepayers' Associations (CORRA) was established as a co-ordinating agency; it not only linked the middle-class organizations with one another, but brought them into contact with community groups being formed in poorer neighbourhoods."[75] Equally significant was the creation of the Stop Spadina, Save Our City, Coordinating Committee (SSSOCCC).[76]

Both inner-city poor who felt ignored and middle-class urban conservatives who felt their neighbourhoods threatened agreed that city council had sold out to development interests. In addition to opposing specific development projects, the citizens' movement became influential in the municipal election process. The 1969 election brought a minority of reformers onto city council, and they were quite effective in defining their issues and concerns. The 1972 election results seemed to be a breakthrough (just as they had appeared to be in Vancouver), with the election of a majority of reformers on council and a self-proclaimed member of the reform group—in the person of David Crombie—as mayor.

Once elected, however, Crombie operated as a moderate and, in fact, voted against the reform councillors on many of the major issues facing

---

[73]Lalonde, *op. cit.*, November 2, 1998.

[74]An excellent analysis of this episode is found in Graham Fraser, *Fighting Back*, Toronto, Hakkert, 1972.

[75]Warren Magnusson, "Toronto," in Magnusson and Sancton, *op. cit.*, p. 115.

[76]See Higgins, *op. cit.*, pp. 282-287, and Leo, *The Politics of Urban Development*, *op. cit.*

council.[77] While he was genuinely concerned about the threat to neighbourhoods posed by the excessively pro-growth mentality of previous councils, Crombie was no less committed to private property and private enterprise. Rather, he wanted to find a way of providing continued development without the disruption and dislocation which had accompanied it in the recent past.[78] The Crombie-led council was not radical enough for some and the reform majority soon splintered (as discussed below). But it did establish for the first time a concept that is now taken for granted as common sense—that major development decisions are a legitimate matter of public concern, to be made only after extensive consultation and debate.

> The 1972 election in Toronto seemed to be a breakthrough for reformers, just as it had appeared to be in Vancouver, but not for long.

The reform group which had appeared to capture control of council in 1972 soon split into moderates and more militant reformers, with the latter becoming increasingly critical of Crombie's moderate policies. Ironically, while reform councillors continued to be elected throughout the 1970s, one of them, Michael Goldrick, persuasively argues that the election of 1972 was not the beginning but "the zenith of the reform movement."[79] As he explains, the moderates were satisfied that the reform movement would now ensure that neighbourhoods were protected, the automobile would be treated with common sense, and the style of development would be modified—all objectives of the middle class. The hardline reformers elected from working-class wards, however, believed that the real objective was one of redistributing wealth and power.

> They wanted real, not token, decision-making power shifted to neighbourhoods, not only the style of development controlled but its pace, location and ownership subject to public decision; they challenged private property rights exercised by financial institutions and development corporations and attacked the fortresses of civil service power.[80]

---

[77]See Jon Caulfield, *The Tiny Perfect Mayor*, Toronto, James Lorimer and Company, 1974.

[78]Magnusson in Magnusson and Sancton, *op. cit.*, p. 119.

[79]Michael Goldrick, "The Anatomy of Urban Reform in Toronto," *City Magazine*, May-June 1978, p. 36, an article which provides an excellent analysis of the reform group to that point in time.

[80]*Ibid.*

After the 1974 election, six of the more radical reformers established the reform caucus, a disciplined group which attempted to develop alternative policies to those proposed by the moderates and the "Old Guard." While it was successful in expressing the interests of working-class people, the reform caucus suffered from a negative, obstructionist image in the eyes of the media and from internal differences, partly based on personality conflicts.

A key figure was John Sewell, undoubtedly the most conspicuous and widely identified member of the reform group, and a community activist who had been earlier associated with a number of the citizen confrontations with city hall.[81] Sewell was a very independent-minded politician and while he had made some unsuccessful attempts to build a reform party around himself, when he ran for mayor in 1978 it was as an independent.[82] After one very controversial term, especially in relation to Sewell's defence of various inner-city minorities and his demands for police reform, he was defeated by Arthur Eggleton, a Liberal with strong ties to the business community. Eggleton was elected throughout the 1980s.

In the meantime, however, reform councillors continued to be voted on council, although increasingly identified with the NDP. By 1980 they had 9 of the 23 seats on council, with all but one of the victorious candidates having run with official party endorsement.[83] The differences between reformers and old guard seemed more muted by the early 1980s, partly as a result of the policies which had been adopted by the councils of the time and partly because the economic decline in the country had reduced growth pressures.

It was this economic downturn, Frisken claims, which most influenced the rapid decline in Toronto city council's commitment to restricting the height and density of downtown buildings.[84] Even John Sewell, during his one term as mayor, gave high priority to keeping industrial jobs in the city and attracting new ones. By the mid-1980s, critics were referring to a "let's make a deal" mode of decision making to signify the city's

---

[81]For his personal reflections on these experiences, see John Sewell, *Up Against City Hall*, Toronto, James Lewis and Samuel, 1972.

[82]Magnusson in Magnusson and Sancton, *op. cit.*, p. 123.

[83]*Ibid.*, p. 122.

[84]Frances Frisken, *City Policy-Making in Theory and Practice: The Case of Toronto's Downtown Plan*, Local Government Case Study No. 3, London, University of Western Ontario, 1988, pp. 98-99.

willingness to allow developers building heights and densities that greatly exceeded the limits specified in its Central Area Plan.[85] By this time, as well, a building boom was under way in Toronto, highlighted by such major projects as the new domed stadium and the development of Harbourfront and railway lands at the south end of the city. Indeed, one observer described the air at city hall as full of "echoes of the 1960s," the heyday of the developers and their lobbyists.[86] He claimed that city hall was once again firmly under the control of the development industry which had simply acquired a new level of sophistication in its dealings with the council—a council more pro-development than any since the end of the 1960s.

If the developers were back, so were the citizens' groups—although perhaps not to the same degree. Frisken states that citizen group activity has been both limited and fragmented since the mid-1970s, posing little threat to incumbent aldermen or the conservative make-up of council as a whole.[87] Part of the problem, she notes, is that citizens' groups have become very issue-specific, lacking the tendency towards coalition building that characterized political pressure groups in the early 1970s—such as the previously cited examples of CORRA and SSSOCCC. Nonetheless, such groups as the Federation of North York Resident Associations and resident associations in Markham and Vaughan have been conspicuous.

Given this background, the results of the 1988 municipal elections in Toronto were quite striking. The voters defeated two pro-development aldermen, voted in a majority of designated reform candidates, and chose reform candidates to fill six of the eight city positions on the Metropolitan Toronto council.[88] More specifically, nine of the 17 members of Toronto City Council were considered to be the reform group, of which six were NDP members. One of the nine was acclaimed to office, but all others were endorsed by Reform Toronto, a citizens' coalition which was opposed to the pro-development old guard at city hall.

It is noteworthy that a number of other Ontario municipal election results in 1988 appeared to reflect a victory for citizens' groups over pro-development forces. For example, the heads of council in both Richmond Hill and Markham, very rapidly growing areas just north of Toronto, were

---

[85]*The Globe and Mail*, May 23, 1984, as quoted in Frisken, p. 81.

[86]Geoffrey York, "The Politics of Influence," *Toronto*, November 1986, p. 50.

[87]Frisken, *op. cit.*, p. 93.

[88]Michael Valpy, "Voters Demonstrate Power of Ballot Box," *The Globe and Mail*, November 16, 1988, p. A8.

both defeated after a series of reports about the allegedly excessive influence of the development industry in their municipalities. Cottage owners also used their voting power to elect councillors concerned with the environment and committed to slowing the pace of growth in a number of Ontario's resort areas.[89]

The 1991 municipal election in Toronto featured two candidates for mayor who represented quite contrasting positions on the political spectrum. A former chief commissioner of police and former councillor, June Rowlands, ran against a well-known NDP member and former councillor, Jack Layton. The election victory for Rowlands was strongly influenced by what had been happening to the economy of the Toronto area. The boom which had lasted until the late 1980s had disappeared! Increased unemployment, empty office towers, more homeless roaming the streets, food banks needed for thousands, mounting racial tension and crime—these were now the defining characteristics of the "world-class city" Toronto had sought to become. Such conditions clearly favoured the conservative, pro-development, and "law and order" platform of Rowlands. Moreover, Layton also had to contend with growing voter uncertainty about their wisdom in electing an NDP provincial government the previous year.

There was little real change in the make-up of the council itself. All incumbents who ran were returned and three new councillors were elected. City council remained split with six NDP members, two moderate or swing councillors, and eight right wingers.[90]

Rowlands ran for mayor of Toronto again in November 1994, but this time was defeated by an NDP councillor, Barbara Hall. However, the result was less a victory for the NDP than voter disillusionment with Rowlands, who stumbled in the final couple of weeks of her campaign, and growing respect for the personal qualities of Hall, as she became better known during the campaign.[91] Hall campaigned on a social justice agenda, including more support for environmental projects and more public housing. In addition to Hall's victory, six other NDP councillors were elected—the same number as in the previous council. But they had little room to manoeuvre, since the city had still not recovered from the

---

[89]"Cottagers Pick Slow-Growth Councillors," *The Globe and Mail*, November 16, 1988, p. A24.

[90]This at least was the assessment by Kent Gerecke shortly after the election in "City Beat," *City Magazine*, Winter '91/'92, p. 5.

[91]This summary of the November 1994 election is based on Tom Fennell, "Caught in the Middle," *Maclean's*, November 28, 1994, p. 38.

severe recession which had battered Ontario, and city tax revenues had fallen by $110 million the previous two years.[92]

December 1996 saw the beginning of a very exciting grassroots political movement when Citizens for Local Democracy began to meet, in opposition to the provincial government plans to amalgamate all municipalities in Metro Toronto in the megacity. This group met every Monday evening, with attendance quickly growing from about 200 to more than 1000 at each meeting. C4LD, as it became known, had a steering committee of about 15 people, a "hot line" telephone which provided recorded information about current events and took messages, and a phone tree which called the more than 2000 individuals who had signed in at the Monday meetings.[93] It generated a great deal of interest and debate about the province's plans for the megacity, was addressed by such notables as Jane Jacobs and John Ralston Saul, made presentations at the public hearings on the megacity legislation, and even staged a march from the site of the former Montgomery's Tavern on February 15, 1997, to recall the 1837 rebellion led by William Lyon Mackenzie. Its considerable efforts helped to generate a 76.3% vote against amalgamation in referendums carried out in the six lower tier municipalities in Metro Toronto in February 1997.

> C4LD's activities featured both traditional public meetings and protests and extensive use of the Internet.

Even though legislation creating the megacity was passed in April 1997, C4LD has continued its activities and has broadened them to take in a number of other issues important to local government. For example, some recent newsletters have dealt with such matters as education reform in Ontario, the impact of provincial downloading, and the question of charity casinos. C4LD has no paid staff. It receives no funding from any government source. All of its expenses are met through collections taken at the Monday meetings. It is a noteworthy organization for its ability to generate and sustain such widespread interest in a variety of local government matters and for its extensive use of the Internet to mobilize this interest.

In November 1997, the first election was held for the newly amalgamated "megacity" of Toronto. Barbara Hall ran again for mayor, as did North York's mayor, Mel Lastman, who emerged victorious. Lastman,

---

[92]*Ibid.*, p. 38.

[93]This description is taken from the C4LD Newsletter, March '97 #5, *Whose Ontario?*, available at its web site, www.c4ld.org/C4LD/newsletter5.html.

who is "nominally conservative"[94] and pro-business in orientation, was the preferred choice of the provincial Conservative government, although that hasn't kept him from publicly feuding with Premier Harris and others about issues such as downloading and tax reform. As for the 57 members of the new council, they have as many differences as there are flavours of canned soup. A dozen or so members roughly fit the label of NDPers, and there are another 6 to 10 councillors who will vote with them, depending on the issue. There is also another group of perhaps 20 to 25 councillors who have coalesced around Mayor Lastman.[95] However, Lastman has been careful to spread the jobs of committee and commission chairs across the ideological spectrum.[96] Instead of traditional left-wing and right-wing clashes, the new council has tended to split more along geographic lines, notably with respect to such matters as property tax reform, transportation, and programs for the homeless. While some may welcome the apparent reduction of ideological clashes, the new council lacks a clear identity or any clear sense of purpose. It has been characterized as "a debating society with 56 contesting opinions."[97] Most councillors reject the suggestion that organized political parties may be needed to bring discipline and focus,[98] and Lastman's initial answer is to call for council's size to be cut in half.[99]

Observations About Local Political Activity

Drawing from this admittedly brief overview of experiences in four large Canadian cities, and from the insights of other writings on this topic, what observations can be made about local political activity? Seven separate but related points are discussed below.

---

[94]This apt description was used by Colin Vaughan, "Bright spots on council hard to find," *The Toronto Star*, November 9, 1998.

[95]See Bruce Demara, "New united council a 'soup' of 57 varieties," *The Toronto Star*, May 16, 1998, on which this discussion is based.

[96]*Ibid.*

[97]Colin Vaughan, "Time for council to shape up," *The Toronto Star*, June 8, 1998.

[98]DeMara, *op. cit.*

[99]Philip Mascoll, "Cut council in half, Lastman urges," *The Toronto Star*, April 27, 1998.

No Parties Please, We're Canadian

The first point is that there is continuing resistance to overt political party activity at the local level. This negative response was well illustrated by the results of the 1969 municipal elections for the City of Toronto. The Liberal party, fresh from its 1968 national election victory, was interested in establishing a stronger base in Toronto, partly as a necessary prerequisite to the overthrow of the long-entrenched Progressive Conservative provincial government. The decision to enter a slate of candidates for municipal office was hotly debated, however, and the internal split in the party on this issue resulted in a less than wholehearted effort in the ensuing election.[100] Whatever the reasons, the election results were not encouraging for the national parties. The Liberal party's candidate for mayor, Stephen Clarkson, finished third, with fewer than half as many votes as the victorious William Dennison. Significantly, Dennison had refused to run as an NDP candidate even though he was closely associated with the party. Only three candidates of the NDP and two of the Liberal candidates were elected as aldermen.[101]

Especially No Socialist Parties

The second observation is that where we find political parties at the local level, they are usually purely local creations—often in the guise of a non-partisan group whose primary objective is to keep party politics out of local government, especially if it comes in the form of the NDP. This pattern has already been noted in connection with the rise of the Civic Election Committee in Winnipeg in 1919 and the Non-Partisan Association (NPA) in Vancouver in 1936. In addition, for over two decades after 1934, elections for Edmonton's council "revolved around the slate-making activities of the Citizens' Committee...."[102] The executive of this committee were almost all members of the chamber of commerce. The committee splintered in 1959 when its leader, William Hawrelak, resigned as mayor

---

[100]For an examination of this election campaign by one of the key participants, see Stephen Clarkson, *City Lib*, Toronto, Hakkert, 1972. See also the exchange of views between Clarkson and J. L. Granatstein in Jack K. Masson and James Anderson (eds.), *Emerging Party Politics in Urban Canada*, Toronto, McClelland and Stewart, 1972, pp. 60-67.

[101]Donald J. H. Higgins, *Urban Canada: Its Government and Politics*, Toronto, Macmillan, 1977, p. 239.

[102]James Lightbody, "Edmonton," in Magnusson and Sancton, *op. cit.*, p. 261.

after conflict of interest irregularities, but "aldermen sharing a business orientation retained total domination of council."[103]

One further example is provided by the experience of Brandon, Manitoba, in which the local establishment successfully resisted an effort by the municipal NDP to elect members to city council.[104] The NDP challenge was mounted after the provincial NDP government elected in 1969 implemented recommendations which introduced a ward system in Brandon. In September 1971 a nomination meeting was held which chose a slate of NDP candidates (for mayor and 7 of the 10 council positions) in order to "break the domination of council by Conservatives and Liberals."[105]

The response of the local establishment took a rather familiar form. A Citizens Independent Voters Election Committee (CIVEC) was set up to encourage and support candidates who would be independent of party politics. All of those elected to the executive of CIVEC were active in the Conservative and Liberal parties.[106] By early October CIVEC had endorsed candidates in all 10 wards (of whom 7 were incumbents) as well as the incumbent mayor. The election saw a 55% voter turnout, the largest since World War II—and it is apparent that many of them turned out to support CIVEC. No NDP candidates were elected, and most received far fewer votes than the victorious CIVEC candidates.

In the aftermath of the defeat, a number of explanations were offered for the poor showing of the NDP. These included the rather hurried preparations for entering the municipal election campaign, the overly comprehensive and detailed nature of the election platform, and the lack of credible candidates. Most of all, however, the results were attributed to the effectiveness of CIVEC's campaign against party politics at the local level.

While the NDP, of all the national parties, has shown by far the most commitment to the introduction of party politics at the local level, even it contests municipal elections only sporadically and selectively. Voter resistance to the overt introduction of party politics at the local level remains strong. Moreover, the Liberals and Conservatives have continued to devote their energies to working behind the scenes supporting, and often organizing, local groups of candidates who would oppose the NDP.

---

[103] *Ibid.*, p. 264.

[104] See Errol Black, "Small City Politics: The Brandon Experience," *City Magazine*, Summer 1984, pp. 28-35, on which the following outline is based.

[105] *Ibid.*, p. 29.

[106] *Ibid.*, p. 31.

It is Sancton's view that we are farther away from municipal party politics in Canada than we were in the 1970s.[107] He notes that apart from cities in Quebec, Vancouver is the only major Canadian city whose council is in any way controlled by a political party. The continuing prominence of the Non-Partisan Association (NPA) may be partly attributed to the at large elections in that city, which require extensive campaign finances of the sort more easily obtained by right-wing business candidates.

A Tale of Two Cities

The absence of parties or blocks of candidates does not mean that municipal elections are necessarily devoid of issues, clash, and conflict. This third observation is illustrated by an examination of the contrasting election experiences of Calgary and Edmonton.[108] Calgary's municipal council is described as "a relatively uniform centre-right," in keeping with the private-sector orientation of the city, and its white-collar, entrepreneurial, and politically conservative make-up.[109] Presumably in part because of the general economic prosperity enjoyed by Calgary, incumbents have almost always been returned to office, in elections with very low voting turnouts. Ralph Klein was elected mayor for three consecutive terms, beginning in 1980, and his successor, Al Duerr, won his fourth straight election in 1998. Klein had garnered as much as 90% of the popular vote (for his third and last term), and Duerr won 92% in 1995, although his support fell to a still very impressive 73% in 1998.[110]

In contrast, Edmonton, which is described as public-sector oriented, blue collar, and liberal, has had a "deeply split, often rancorous council."[111] The labour and progressive reform movements have enjoyed considerable electoral success, but have often triggered a pro-business backlash. This was evident at the time of the 1995 election, when there was an organized effort by the business community to defeat Mayor Jan Reimer, who had been elected in 1989, and to promote economic devel-

---

[107]Andrew Sancton, "The Municipal Role in the Governance of Canadian Cities," in Trudi Bunting and Pierre Filion (eds.), *Canadian Cities in Transition*, Toronto, Oxford University Press, 1991, pp. 473-476.

[108]The discussion which follows is partly based on Graham et al., *op. cit.*, pp. 111-112.

[109]*Ibid.*, p. 111.

[110]According to "Calgary Votes 1998," *Calgary Herald*, October 20, 1998.

[111]Graham et al., *op. cit.*, p. 111.

opment. Bill Smith, a tire retailer, ran on a traditional boosterism platform in a campaign that stimulated an unusually high 50% voter turnout. He narrowly defeated Reimer and only five of the incumbent councillors were returned.[112] In the 1998 election, in which voter turnout was back down to a more typical 35%, Smith won a decisive victory, and all 10 incumbents who sought reelection were successful.[113]

Now You See Them, Now You Don't

A fourth observation is that the relative influence of citizens' groups versus development interests seems to wax and wane, acting almost like a self-correcting pendulum swing. In admittedly oversimplified terms, the experience of the past couple of decades suggests that pro-development forces can prevail for some considerable period—until their perceived excesses prompt renewed citizen activism, leading to changes on city council. This activism is difficult to sustain, however, partly for reasons discussed in the fifth observation below, and pro-development forces then assert themselves again.

Thus, for example, the so-called citizens' movement of the 1960s appeared largely to disappear during the 1970s. Much of the progress in reducing the influence of the property industry and of the business community generally over council operations seemed to have dissipated. Whether in Vancouver, Toronto, Winnipeg, or even Montreal, the gains of citizens' groups and the election successes of "reform councillors" were not consolidated. Instead, the traditional pro-business councillors regained some of the ascendancy in the first three of these cities, and soon came to terms with the MCM in Montreal.

The municipal election results in Toronto in 1988 and 1991 serve to illustrate this pattern. The first election occurred towards the end of a boom period in which a "let's make a deal" attitude had returned to city hall. Voters responded by electing a majority of reform candidates, all endorsed by a Reform Toronto coalition opposed to the pro-development stance of the previous council. Just three years later, however, Toronto found itself in a serious economic downturn. Regaining lost jobs and dealing with the perception of increased violence in the streets and neighbourhoods were suddenly more important, and the reform and NDP candidate for mayor, Jack Layton, was soundly defeated.

---

[112]*Ibid.*, p. 112.

[113]Ashley Geddes, "I'm happy inside, Smith says," *Edmonton Journal*, October 20, 1998.

It Goes with the Territory

Reformers tend to take their own election as an indication that the system is working, and to moderate their views.

Part of the explanation for this waxing and waning of citizen influence can be found in a fifth observation, that reformers upon gaining power tend to moderate their positions and objectives. As Lorimer has stated, "the thrust for democratic reforms has been blunted by citizen-oriented politicians once in office. They are inclined to take their own election as an indication that the present political system can work reasonably well...."[114] This pattern was noted with respect to the experience of Toronto's city council after the election of reformers in 1972. It is also apparent in Milner's comments about MCM's move towards the centre in Montreal. In the case of Vancouver, Tennant notes that "because of their success and their exhaustion the various citizens' groups faded away or ... lapsed into routine activities."[115] The economic downturns noted earlier may also blunt the demands of citizen groups. As Thomas notes with respect to Montreal, "In difficult economic times when resources are scarce, groups associated with the MCM chose to focus on their specific needs rather than those of society at large, preferring to deliver at least some benefits to their members."[116]

Citizen influence is also limited by the fact that the various citizens' groups which emerge are far from unanimous in what they hope to accomplish. According to Sancton, some are genuinely committed to various forms of neighbourhood self-government, others want to use local issues mainly as a way of mobilizing the working class for larger battles to be fought in the national political arena, and most are concerned only with the particular issue at hand.[117] Magnusson refers to the fragile political alliances between working-class and middle-class neighbourhoods. As he explains, middle-class neighbourhoods only need to be protected against adverse changes, as they see them. Such changes might well include "halfway" houses and public housing developments, as well as tax

[114]James Lorimer, "Introduction: The Post-developer Era for Canada's Cities Begins," *City Magazine Annual 1981*, Toronto, James Lorimer and Company, 1981, p. 9.

[115]Paul Tennant, "Vancouver Politics and the Civic Party System," in M. O. Dickerson, S. Drabek, and J. T. Woods (eds.), *Problems of Change in Urban Government*, Waterloo, Wilfrid Laurier University Press, 1980, pp. 26-27.

[116]Timothy Thomas, *op. cit.*, p. 143.

[117]Sancton, *The Municipal Role,* p. 473.

increases to support public services. Neighbourhood improvement often took the form of rehabilitation and in-fill construction oriented towards the profitable middle-class market, a process usually referred to as "gentrification." The result, of course, was to displace more of the poor into an inflated housing market.[118]

Sancton is critical of the narrow and limited views and approaches of those who are part of what he terms the so-called "new reform movement." While they lacked a common view of the role of the municipality, he contends that none of them expressed a vision of a stronger, multi-functional municipal government, one endowed with final decision-making power. To the contrary, he claims, most of the reformers are "suspicious of any political institutions, including municipal governments and local political parties, that would have the potential to overrule the expressed preferences of local neighbourhoods and their leaders...."[119]

Frisken points out that citizen activism may be strongly biased against city government initiatives that are sensitive to social needs.[120] It may be aimed at preventing the provision of housing for low-income families, keeping public transit out of residential areas, or otherwise discouraging any municipal initiative that disturbs the status quo. Filion describes efforts by neighbourhood associations to resist affordable housing initiatives in Mississauga, Vaughan, Richmond Hill, Etobicoke, and Pickering, and he concludes that "neighbourhood influence is associated with a tight focus on the immediate interests of residents and a narrow consideration of a decision's consequences, most negative externalities being likely to materialize elsewhere."[121]

We're from the Province; We're Here to Help

A sixth point concerns the influence on local political developments of the provincial party in power and its prevailing attitude and philosophy. This point is obvious in one sense, given the all-pervasive nature of provincial controls over local governments. But, over and above that fundamental

---

[118]Warren Magnusson, "Metropolitan Change and Political Disruption," in Frisken, *op. cit.*, p. 551-552.

[119]Sancton, *The Municipal Role*, p. 473.

[120]Frisken, *op. cit.*, p. 30.

[121]Pierre Filion, "Government Levels, Neighbourhood Influence and Urban Policy," in Henri Lustiger-Thaler (ed.), *Political Arrangements: Power and the City*, Montreal, Black Rose Books, 1992, pp. 176 and 180.

relationship, local political actors may be reinforced or undermined in their efforts depending on the position taken by the provincial governing party. Consider these examples.

Frisken, in discussing the increasingly pro-growth mentality of Toronto's council during the 1970s and 1980s, stated that "in following this course of action the council majority acted consistently with, and sometimes directly in response to, signals or directives from other governments. Ontario Municipal Board and Ontario Cabinet decisions favoured a more rapid pace of downtown development than was provided for in the Plan...."[122]

Mention has also been made of the constraints under which Vancouver operated in relation to the provincial Social Credit government after it elected an NDP mayor. More generally, Magnusson and others warned of the threat to local autonomy in British Columbia in the mid-1980s because of the provincial government's apparent viewpoint that it should curb local initiatives contrary to its governing philosophy.[123] This pattern has also been evident in Ontario since the election of the Conservatives in 1995. Not content to cut off transfer payments to municipalities and to take over education and financial decision making from school boards, the ruling party has been determined to impose its ideological view that the role and size of government—including municipal government—must be reduced. As described earlier, this culminated in an extraordinary intervention at the end of 1998, in which the province, in effect, cancelled the municipal budget and tax decisions already made for that year, and imposed retroactively for 1998 new ceilings on business taxes.

Perhaps no municipality has been more affected by provincial actions than Montreal, however, which has waited in vain for much provincial recognition of, and response to, its prolonged economic difficulties. The Picard Committee appointed by the Mulroney government in 1986 concluded that the governments of Quebec and Ottawa had both favoured development of the rest of the province at the expense of Montreal.[124] To a considerable extent, Montreal suffers from the ongoing wrangling between the federal and provincial governments over the separation question, from its high proportion of anglophones and allophones, and from the fact that it did not support separation in the 1995 Quebec referendum nearly as strongly as the rest of the province.

---

[122]Frisken, *City Policy-Making*, p. 90.

[123]Magnusson et al., *The New Reality*.

[124]Quoted in Timothy Thomas, *op. cit.*, p. 152, on which this section is based.

It's the Economy, Stupid

Bill Clinton's successful campaign slogan when he first ran for President in 1992 underscores the seventh, and final, observation, which relates to the effect of the underlying economic conditions on the local political patterns which unfold. Lorimer, for example, contends that it was the downturn in economic activity towards the end of the 1970s, and the resultant reduction in urban growth pressures, which led to more moderation in city hall—not the citizens' movement or the election of reform councils.[125] According to this school of thought, the prominence of developers and the pro-growth mentality only abated because these features were not compatible with the changed economic conditions.

A decade later, Toronto entered another and even more severe economic downturn, and Fowler describes the impact of the new circumstances on Cityplan 1991.[126] He documents a number of examples of provisions which were dropped from the plan or modified. To cite one instance, a proposal that new development *must conform* to environmental standards became a proposal to *encourage* development to meet environmental objectives.

To a considerable extent, then, one can expect local political activity and council positions on the desirability of growth to increase and decrease in response to underlying economic performance and growth and development pressure. In good economic times, councils feel they can afford the luxury of tighter controls, but such controls tend to be relaxed or abandoned when an economic downturn makes it essential to attract any growth possible. The suggestion that politics is influenced and constrained by economics is hardly a new one, of course, and was highlighted in the introductory chapter.

Consulting with the Public

So far in this chapter, the emphasis has been mostly on public participation through elections, citizens' groups, and political parties. But in addition to these efforts by citizens, there are also many ways in which municipalities can take the initiative and pursue methods of involving their citizens. These initiatives can range from communicating information, to

---

[125]Lorimer, *op. cit.*, p. 9.

[126]Edmund P. Fowler, "Decision Time for Cityplan '91," *City Magazine*, Winter '93, pp. 10-11.

asking for public reaction to some proposed action, to fully involving the public on an ongoing basis in the decisions which have to be made locally. A municipality should think very carefully about what it wants to accomplish and how much it is willing to base its decisions on public input before taking initiatives in this area. Token consultation is worse than no consultation at all. There is little point in inviting public participation, for example, if a decision needs to be made immediately, if the municipality is severely constrained in how it must respond, or if the municipality isn't prepared to commit sufficient resources to make participation meaningful.[127]

Examples of Public Consultation

If municipalities are genuinely interested in consulting with and involving their citizens, the approaches that can be used are limited only by the imagination of municipal personnel. Consider the 10 examples below, all based on actual municipal experiences.[128]

1. Complaints or suggestions forms and drop-off boxes are provided in a few high-traffic areas. The boxes are emptied regularly, with reports back to the public on responses received and actions taken.
2. Stockholm set up a "scribbling wall," a large, prominently located, well-lighted billboard on which citizens are encouraged to express their views about public issues.[129] Sounds crazy, you say? Well, apparently, people responded so enthusiastically that the board had to be cleaned every day, but only after the information on the board was copied and passed on to council.
3. Rather than waiting for citizens to come to city hall, some municipalities take city hall to them, by using a Municipal Information Centre which is staffed by councillors and located at shopping centres or other focal points in the community on a rotating basis.
4. Besides providing a direct report to the local radio station following council meetings, some municipalities include a phone-in segment so that citizens can respond to the actions taken at the meeting.

---

[127]K. A. Graham and Susan D. Phillips, *Citizen Engagement*, Toronto, Institute of Public Administration, 1998, p. 8.

[128]Most of these examples are based on actual experiences described in *Elected Officials Handbook: Practical Aids for Busy Local Officials*, Volume 1, Washington, International City Management Association, 1983, pp. 74-85.

[129]This example is found in Michael Smither, "Encouraging Community Involvement," *Municipal World*, February 1997, p. 5.

5. New residents are welcomed to the municipality with an information package containing such items as the most recent municipal newsletter, street maps, a brief outline of the history of the community, information on municipal personnel, council meeting schedule, telephone numbers and contact persons for various municipal services, and a list of clubs and service organizations. St. Paul, Minnesota entitles its informational booklet, "Owner's Manual," to underscore that it is the local citizens for whom the municipality exists.

6. Some municipalities provide an opportunity during council meetings, immediately after the approval of the minutes of the previous meeting, for public comment on the agenda items.

7. Annual questionnaires are sent to all residents, seeking their views on major priorities and long-term objectives for the municipality. The annual nature of this exercise gives council an opportunity to detect trends and shifts in public opinion.

8. More elaborate and systematic surveys are conducted on how the public values the services being provided by the municipality and how well it perceives that these services are being delivered. Municipalities as diverse as the region of Hamilton-Wentworth, the city of Aylmer, Quebec, and the town of Bedford, Nova Scotia, have undertaken systematic citizen surveys in recent years.[130] The city of North Bay surveyed more than 20 000 households in 1994 to identify customer attitudes towards the levels of service provided.[131] The city of Burlington also carried out an extensive customer survey in 1994, which canvassed the public and identified the areas of greatest satisfaction and dissatisfaction in relation to services provided.[132]

9. Mississauga publishes a *Council Decisions* newsletter, featuring activities and decisions of council and seeking input on future decisions.[133]

10. More and more municipalities are using technology to facilitate public participation. A web site can make information available to those "on line," can be updated with great frequency, and can invite public responses to a variety of current issues.[134]

---

[130]Katherine Graham and Susan Phillips, "Customer engagement: beyond the customer revolution," *Canadian Public Administration*, Toronto, Institute of Public Administration of Canada, Summer 1997, p. 261.

[131]Smither, *op. cit.*, p. 4.

[132]See InterLink Research Consulting, *City of Burlington Service Optimization Study: Final Results*, 1994.

[133]Smither, *op. cit.*, p. 12.

[134]For a discussion of municipal use of the Internet and the implications for municipal governance, see Monica Gattinger, "Local Governments On-Line," in Graham and Phillips, *Citizen Engagement*, pp. 200-222.

The Citizen and Direct Democracy

In several important areas of municipal decision making, municipalities are developing processes which promote public participation in the formulation of decisions. This is a significant shift in emphasis, one which goes well beyond the notion that public participation takes place at election time or should be confined to commenting on specific municipal actions or proposed actions.

Citizens in the Planning Process

One of the most interesting areas of change has been in the field of land use planning. Traditionally, it was regarded as a very specialized area of activity, requiring the application of the expertise of the planners and the political judgment of the elected councils. Except for any minimum legal requirements for public meetings which might exist, public input was not widely encouraged. All that changed with the surge in citizens groups and protest movements, reacting against what was felt to be the adverse public impact of many of the planning decisions being made in the post-war years, especially in urban Canada. Gradually, planning processes were refined to build in much more extensive public consultations at a much earlier stage. In some instances, municipalities developed very elaborate and effective processes.

One of the most notable examples is that of the Greater Vancouver Regional District (GVRD), which launched in 1989 an extensive process of public consultation for updating its 1975 Livable Region Plan. It published a discussion paper and then approved seven broad "livability goals," which formed the basis for a "Choosing Our Future" consultative process lasting 14 months and including regional seminars, a public attitude survey, a children's vision poster program, community meetings, and a television program featuring a public phone-in segment.[135]

As a result of these efforts, the GVRD announced a consensus on "54 steps to a more livable region" that served as a basis for local reviews by each of the then 18 municipalities in the district between autumn 1990 and spring 1991. The goals and steps were gradually refined and reduced in number and these then formed the basis for six "critical choices" forums held simultaneously in May 1993 in different parts of Greater Van-

---

[135]This description is based on Patrick Smith, "More Than One Way Towards Economic Development: Public Participation and Policy Making in the Vancouver Region," in Graham and Phillips, *Citizen Engagement*, pp. 56-57.

couver. Citizens were also encouraged to complete a newspaper insert questionnaire which was delivered to every home in the regional district. Further conferences, consultations, and cable TV broadcasts continued throughout 1993 and 1994.[136] All of these efforts, and many others too numerous to outline here, culminated in the approval of the Livable Region Strategic Plan in October 1995—a formidable achievement for a quasi-upper tier government without any formal responsibility for planning.

Citizens in the Budgeting Process

Another area undergoing change is municipal budgeting. Until the past decade or so, this was normally considered a closed process, with council and staff discussions taking place in private, usually through a series of committee meetings, with compromises and trade-offs sorted out "behind the scenes," and with a final budget presented at an open meeting and adopted with very little discussion. The opportunity for public input was virtually non-existent and there wasn't even much opportunity for the public to become informed about the issues faced and the priorities wrestled with in arriving at the final budget. Without this information, the public had little appreciation of the difficult political decisions underlying the budget process. Gradually, budget meetings were opened to the public, but often citizens were only able to attend as observers. Sometimes, councils invited public comments about specific servicing issues or spending options, but these were sporadic and seldom tied into the actual budget process in any systematic way.

By the 1990s, most municipalities faced growing complaints from citizens, and especially from local business groups, about the level of municipal taxes. There were often criticisms of the budget process itself. It was seen as a long drawn-out affair that began with departmental "wish lists" which were then whittled down by council through numerous lengthy meetings until an acceptable expenditure and tax level were reached. In response to these criticisms, some exciting changes are under way, however, and creative approaches are being developed to involve local citizens in the budgeting process in a serious way.

The response of Burlington, Ontario, was to appoint a citizens' committee to review the city's budget position and budgeting system.[137] The

---

[136]*Ibid.*, pp. 57-59.

[137]The discussion which follows is based on Michael Fenn, "Expanding the Frontiers of Public Participation: Public Involvement in Municipal Budgeting and Finance," in Graham and Phillips, *Citizen Engagement*, pp. 113-136.

committee met throughout the winter and spring of 1992 and it also attended municipal budget meetings that year. It reviewed the proposed current and capital budgets and it examined the budget process as it was understood by the general public. The committee recommended that staff be given firm "end-point" budget directions and then held accountable, that multi-year (three year) current budgeting be adopted, and that more emphasis be given to product and service outputs.[138] One of the by-products of this exercise was that the local media gave positive coverage which helped to reinforce the image of the municipality as open, consultative and well managed.

The Use of Referendums

Proponents of direct democracy often call for the use of tools such as the referendum, initiative, and recall.[139] A referendum involves submitting a policy question or proposed law to the electorate for approval or rejection. The vote can be binding or consultative only. In the latter case the exercise is commonly, but not consistently, called a plebiscite. Canada has had some highly publicized and emotionally charged referendums in recent decades, including the two votes on Quebec separation (in 1980 and 1995) and the vote on the Charlottetown Accord in 1992. The initiative involves citizens proposing new laws which, if supported by enough signatures, are then submitted to voters for approval, a process which essentially allows the public to initiate a referendum exercise on its own. Most direct and dramatic of all is the recall, which allows the public to remove from office an elected representative whose performance is felt to be unsatisfactory.

There are strongly divided opinions on how referendums affect public involvement and democracy. In countries such as Switzerland and the United States, where direct democracy is a common feature, voter turnout is disappointingly low. It has averaged only 35% for referendums and initiatives in Switzerland in recent years.[140] American studies indicate that referendums have little drawing power in getting voters out when held in conjunction with elections and even lower voting turnout when they are

---

[138]*Ibid.*, p. 119.

[139]The discussion which follows is based on C. Richard Tindal, *A Citizen's Guide to Government*, Whitby, McGraw-Hill Ryerson Limited, 1997, pp. 225-226.

[140]Mark Charlton, "The Limits of Direct Democracy," in Mark Charlton and Paul Barker (eds.), *Crosscurrents: Contemporary Political Issues*, 3rd Edition, Toronto, Nelson, 1998, p. 416.

held separately. There are also concerns that the efforts required to get enough signatures to place a question on the ballot leads to domination by large special interest groups with the resources for the task. It is further held that complex issues cannot be reduced to a simple yes or no vote and that shortsighted and ill-considered decisions will result.

The famous or infamous Proposition 13 is often cited in this regard. Passed in California in 1968, it capped property taxes and required a two-thirds local referendum to raise taxes. However welcome these measures seemed initially, they led to severe fiscal and servicing difficulties. This is because the result of Proposition 13 was to give control to one-third of the population plus one, no matter how great the public need.

Most Canadian provinces authorize councils to consult the public directly through plebiscites. In addition, some provinces have provisions for petitions which allow citizens to force a plebiscite.[141] In British Columbia and Alberta, for example, councils must advertise plans for financing long-term capital debt and if a petition against the plans is filed within 15 days, they must go to a general plebiscite. However, 1994 revisions to the Alberta Municipal Government Act raised the minimum number of petitioners required in a municipality from 5% to 10% of the population, with the signatures to be collected within 60 days. The difficulties that this change presents in large urban areas is evident from the fact that in Edmonton or Calgary sponsors of a petition would need to collect 65 000 valid signatures, an average of more than 1000 per day within the two month time limit.[142]

Ontario passed legislation in December 1996 which extended the authority of municipalities to place a question on the ballot of a regular municipal election or at any time. In March 1998 the province released a consultation paper entitled *Municipal Referendum Framework*, which proposed general enabling legislation for referenda. The response of the Association of Municipal Clerks and Treasurers of Ontario was quite negative to what it saw as a threat to the accountability and responsibility of councillors, especially in light of the authorization already provided by the earlier legislation.[143] Notwithstanding its interest in extending the use of public consultation by municipalities, the Ontario government hasn't been very responsive when such mechanisms are used to solicit public views

---

[141]See Graham et al., *op. cit.*, pp. 115-116, on which this discussion is based.

[142]*Ibid.*, p. 116.

[143]For details, see *Municipal Referendum Framework: An AMCTO Response*, available at the Association web site at www.amcto.com/amctoref.htm.

about the appropriateness of provincial initiatives. As noted above, the councils of the six lower tier municipalities in Metro Toronto held plebis- cites on the proposed amalgamation in early 1997, with voters rejecting the megacity by a decisive margin. A citizen-run plebiscite in Hamilton- Wentworth held around the same time produced a 90% rejection of an amalgamation plan which had been brokered by the Ministry of Municipal Affairs.[144] The province refused to acknowledge the validity of either vote.

In the view of André Carrel, "the referendum can play an important and legitimate role in a democracy *if* it is a tool in the hands of citizens, not a toy of the governing elite."[145] He knows whereof he speaks, because Carrel is the administrator of Rossland, a small city in British Columbia which, since 1990, has been pursuing a very exciting exercise of direct democracy.[146] Concerned about the growing rift between citizens and their governments in the aftermath of the collapse of the Meech Lake Accord, the councillors of Rossland and their city administrator searched for new approaches which would allow members of the community to exercise more control over their own affairs. The result was a paper en- titled "A Constitution for Local Government," which gave local citizens three avenues to participate more directly in the city government. First, there would have to be a referendum for any change to be made to the new constitution by-law of Rossland. Second, either council or the citi- zens (providing that 20% of them signed a petition) could subject a coun- cil decision to public confirmation by initiating a referendum within 30 days after the third reading of a by-law. Third, members of the commu- nity (again with 20% backing) could initiate a referendum to force council to take action on an issue.

Interestingly, the initial reaction of the provincial ministry of Municipal Affairs was guarded and resistant. It expressed doubt that council would be able to take actions which, while limited in popularity, were needed to address fiscal, health, safety, or other concerns. In effect, this was really an argument that ordinary citizens don't know what is best for them, and it is up to council to show the way. Rossland's constitutional paper takes the opposite view, making the very sensible claim that "electors are as

---

[144]C4LD, Whose Ontario?, *op. cit.*

[145]André Carrel, "Government: Its Legitimacy, Efficacy and Relationship to Citizens," presentation to Capilano College, January 1998, p. 7.

[146]The discussion which follows is partly based on an article by Susan Dela- court, *The Globe and Mail*, May 21, 1994, and an information package provided by André Carrel.

qualified as members of council to make reasonable and rational decisions. Council members are drawn at random from the electorate; election is not dependent on a test of skills, knowledge or ability."[147]

Another concern expressed by politicians from other municipalities was that the new system was ripe for exploitation by pressure groups. In response to this possibility, the Rossland council proposed a change to the constitution by-law, raising the petition threshold from 20% of registered voters to 33%. When this referendum was defeated overwhelmingly, the mayor of Rossland declared that: "With this vote, the people of Rossland have assumed ownership of their municipal constitution; it is no longer council's experiment to play with."[148]

Perhaps the most important aspect of the Rossland approach is not the number of referendums (there had only been 13 as of the end of 1998, along with one plebiscite) or their outcome, but the changed atmosphere in the community. Instead of just complaining about council action or inaction, more people are discussing policy issues. Because they have been given some say in municipal decisions, they feel a greater responsibility to be informed and to exercise their new power thoughtfully. They are also gaining a sense of ownership of city policy.

Carrel explains that Rossland council has learned that the time to communicate with people about municipal issues is at the definition stage, not when an issue has become a raging controversy, and certainly not after council has made a decision.[149] He emphasizes that the time to start a dialogue with citizens is when there is no pressing issue and no looming disaster. For example, Rossland scheduled four town hall meetings in 1997 to discuss a variety of servicing and financing issues. There were no major problems or controversies; the meetings were essentially "bland and boring" sessions for the exchange of information and ideas. At each meeting, councillors made short presentations, followed by a question and answer period. Yet the first such meeting in 1997, to discuss water, sewer, and solid waste services, attracted over 60 citizens on a snowy February evening. After the meeting, more than 200 citizens (out of 2000 registered voters) completed questionnaires on methodology and

---

[147]City of Rossland, *A Constitution for Local Government*, p. 6.

[148]Quoted in André Carrel, "Direct Democracy," October 22, 1994 presentation, p. 8.

[149]André Carrel, "Municipal Government Leadership," presentation at Capilano College, March 14, 1997, p. 6.

financing options related to garbage collection and recycling.[150] While generalizations are always dangerous, the Rossland experience suggests that given enough support and encouragement, public participation can become as habit-forming as apathy has often been in the past.

> What is important is not the voting but the knowledge that citizens have the right to vote on issues important to them.

But it must be emphasized that holding an occasional referendum will accomplish little in the absence of other changes. In Carrel's words, "a referendum thrown to an angry and frustrated citizenry, like a bone to a hungry dog, is not a democratic act."[151] What is important to the citizens of Rossland is not the actual voting on an issue (which occurs very infrequently), but the knowledge that they have the right to vote on the issues which the community, and not necessarily the council, deems important. The real value of the referendum is when it is provided as part of a series of changes which demonstrate a commitment to openness, consultation, and public participation on the part of the council.

To illustrate, consider the measures introduced by the township of Kenyon in Eastern Ontario, before it disappeared in 1997 in one of the many amalgamations discussed in Chapter 5. These actions included:

- a strategic planning process featuring extensive public consultation, including annual strategy sessions with participants from as many as six local advisory committees of local citizens.
- new approaches to policy making which emphasize public participation and feature public advisory committees to assist council in formulating policy and implementing programs.
- expanded public participation and communication through such means as allowing residents to ask questions during formal council sessions (question periods), encouraging public presentations and participation at monthly Committee of the Whole meetings, and utilizing citizen advisory committees to help in the creation, refinement, and implementation of policies.
- a deliberative and inclusive decision making, through the other initiatives already outlined and also through plans to permit citizen initiatives and referendum petitions, similar to those in Rossland.[152]

---

[150] *Ibid.*, p. 7.

[151] *Ibid.*, p. 6.

[152] This summary is based on Blair Williams, "Reinventing the democratic community: A case study of Kenyon Township in Eastern Ontario," *Municipal World*, November 1996, pp. 13-17.

Concluding Comments

Municipal councillors and staff are overwhelmed with changes and challenges as they enter a new century. Faced with such pressures, there may be a reluctance to encourage public participation because of the fear that it will bring delays, probably opposition to changes, and much time and effort consumed in dealing with this opposition. It may also be that municipal personnel will neglect public consultation more through oversight than deliberate decision, being so preoccupied with the day-to-day challenges that they forget to look outward to their communities.

This is no time to "circle the wagons," with staff and councillors huddled together, clutching their benchmarking reports to their chests for comfort. This is a time to open the circle and invite inside those directly affected by the difficult decisions which have to be made—the local citizens. They have a right to be involved and they can also be a valuable asset and a powerful ally.

CHAPTER 11
Municipalities in the 21st Century

How well municipalities fare in the new century will depend, as always, on how successfully they maintain a balance between their two primary roles: representative/political and administrative/service delivery. The tension between these roles is reflected in two contrasting images of the municipality— as a democratic institution which responds to community concerns and as but one of many players in a competitive market place in which individual interests prevail.

Introduction

It sounds trite to write about the challenge of change, but it is hard to imagine a decade in which municipalities have faced more rapid and wide-ranging changes than those experienced in the 1990s. There is no reason to expect the demands of the global market place to lessen in the new century and little indication that senior levels of government will alter their downsizing and downloading activities. As noted in Chapter 1, municipal governments today find themselves in the midst of another turn of the century reform movement, not yet officially recognized or declared, and are once again facing strong pressures to embrace business principles and to negate the relevance or propriety of politics. This final chapter explores the changes that are needed, the approaches which should be pursued, to help municipalities meet the challenges they face.

The Constitutional and Legal Framework

It has long been suggested that municipalities need, first and foremost, some form of constitutional recognition. Just how vulnerable they are without that recognition became painfully evident when the Ontario government embarked on its very aggressive program of municipal restructuring. There was a court challenge, on both constitutional and statutory grounds, to the legislation (Bill 103) creating the new "megacity" of Toronto. The applicants contended that the legislation violated rights guaranteed by the Charter. His Honour Justice Borins stated that "the evidence supported the conclusion that Bill 103 simply appeared on the government's legislative agenda with little, or no, public notice and without any attempt to enter into any meaningful consultation with those people who would be most affected by it...." In his view, however, "the question for the court is not the government's political posture, but rather its legal and constitutional authority to proceed as it did." On that score, Justice Borins commented that the Charter "does not guarantee an individual the right to live his or her life free from government chutzpah or imperiousness."[1] This strong language was bittersweet for municipal defenders, because it signified that no matter how arbitrarily a provincial government might behave, its constitutional superiority would prevail.

Exactly how the constitutional recognition of municipalities would work, however, is far from clear. L'Heureux argues against any such step, claiming that attempts to protect municipalities by constitution means would achieve the opposite.

> It would favour direct federal intervention and direct dealings between the federal government and the municipalities. The resulting division of powers would be even more complicated and a matter of contention. Given the difficulties the federal government and our ten provinces have now in reaching agreement, it is easy to imagine what would happen if the more than 4600 Canadian municipalities were added![2]

Instead, L'Heureux suggests that it would be more realistic to protect municipal interests by way of provincial constitutions, by including in them such principles as the existence of autonomous municipalities governing local affairs, the election of municipal councils, and the possession by municipalities of independent sources of revenue sufficient to allow them to perform their obligations. The right of a municipality to act by itself in the absence of legislation to the contrary, as well as its right to delegate its powers, might also be included, along with a limitation on the review of municipal by-laws by the courts.[3]

---

[1] All quotes are from the case summary by Michael Smither, "Mega City of Toronto—Challenge Denied," *Municipal World*, October 1997, pp. 20-21.

[2] Jacques L'Heureux, "Municipalities and the Division of Power," in Richard Simeon, Research Coordinator, *Intergovernmental Relations*, Vol. 63, Royal Commission on the Economic Union and Development Prospects for Canada, Toronto, University of Toronto Press, 1985, pp. 200-201.

[3] *Ibid.*, p. 202.

Whatever its advantages or complications, constitutional recognition of municipal governments seems most unlikely. In spite of repeated efforts by municipalities and their associations, no municipal recognition was provided in the 1982 Act which repatriated the constitution and it was also totally ignored in the Meech and Charlottetown Accords. Some very limited progress has been made in provincial recognition of municipalities, as in the *Protocol of Recognition* signed in 1996 by the government of British Columbia and the Union of British Columbia Municipalities, as discussed in Chapter 8. Limited progress has also been noted, again in Chapter 8, with respect to new legislation giving municipalities somewhat broader authority and discretion within which to operate.

But if we judge them by their actions, rather than their words, most provincial governments still don't seem to recognize municipalities as a separate level of government, with their own mandate from their electors and their own obligations to their citizens. Instead, they are still viewed primarily as a vehicle for service delivery which exists to

> In practice, most provinces still don't seem to recognize municipalities as a separate level of government, with a mandate from their citizens.

facilitate provincial objectives, and as an expenditure category which is subject to whatever controls and limits suit provincial fiscal objectives. In fairness, it must be acknowledged that many municipalities have contributed to this unfortunately narrow view of their raison d'être. By downplaying or neglecting their political and representative role, by focusing almost exclusively on how to deliver fewer services as cheaply as possible, they have carried out the limited role assigned to them by the province. In our view, therefore, the first thing municipalities need to do is to redefine their purpose.

Reviving the Political Role

The term "reviving" is used because municipalities were originally established with a political role which was at least as important as the service delivery role. If the settlers in Central Canada in the 1840s had only been interested in receiving services, there would have been no reason for them to push for elected municipal governments. They were already receiving local services from the Courts of Quarter Sessions. What they wanted, clearly, was something more—a say in those servicing decisions, a vehicle through which they could express collective concerns about their communities. No matter how many or what services are provided by municipalities, their primary importance is as an expression of local choice. As Clarke and Stewart explain it, there would be no point, other than administrative convenience, in local governments providing services in which there was no significant local choice.[4]

Chapter 1 described how this political role of municipalities was undermined by a series of developments, including the turn of the century reform movement, the narrowing scope of services and sources of revenue over the first half of the 20th century, the misplaced emphasis of municipal restructuring efforts in the second half of the century, and the reascendancy of the corporate agenda in recent times.

If municipalities are to play an important role in the 21st century, they must reassert themselves as municipal *governments*, featuring elected bodies which make *political* decisions. The municipal council must be recognized as a political mechanism for expressing and responding to the collective concerns of members of the community. Among the important implications of this conception of municipal government are the following points:[5]

- If the municipality is an extension of the community, its identity and its purpose derive from that community, not from the particular services it provides.
- The municipality has a legitimate right to take actions that are needed by that community. The right derives from the nature of the municipality as an extension of the community, and does not depend on what specific powers have been assigned to it.
- The municipality's primary role is concern for the problems and issues faced by its community. The interests and values of the community are expressed and resolved through the municipality. It is "a political institution for the authoritative determination of community values."[6]

If the annual budget exercise in far too many Canadian municipalities is any indication, the only community value which exists is "to hold the line on taxes." That objective frames the whole budget exercise from start

---

[4]Michael Clarke and John Stewart, *The Choices for Local Government*, Harlow, Longman, 1991, p. 2.

[5]The points which are outlined below are largely based on John Stewart, "A Future for Local Authorities as Community Government," in John Stewart and Gerry Stoker (eds.), *The Future of Local Government*, London, Macmillan, 1989, Chapter 12.

[6]*Ibid.*, p. 241.

to finish. Eventually, after much cutting and pruning, and often some staff reductions, the target is met, and the process is pronounced a great success. But how do we know that the decisions made reflect the values of the community? It is true that if you ask local citizens if they would prefer not to have a tax increase, of course they will answer yes. But what if they were asked instead if they would be willing to pay $50 more a year to maintain certain services or certain service standards? The answer to that question might well be yes also. In our view, the typical budget process is totally backwards. It should start by identifying those services that the community wants and needs and is willing to fund. Such an approach could transform the budget process into a real exercise in determining community priorities.

> The annual budget process should start by identifying the services that the community wants and needs and is willing to fund.

Being Strategic and Selective

At one time, governments operated on the basis of "doing more with more." It was assumed that resources were unlimited and that new government initiatives could simply be financed through additional revenues. We then entered an era which supposedly featured more efficient governments "doing more with less." Most recently, the emphasis has been on governments "doing less with less," as they downsize in response to fiscal pressures and global dictates. We don't share the minimalist view of government, believing that a strong public sector is critical to society, and is even essential to support a healthy private sector. But it is clear that governments, including municipal governments, cannot attempt to be all things to all people. It is also clear that municipalities cannot continue with a budget process which amounts to "death by a thousand cuts." The end result is a skeleton operation in which services are provided more poorly and facilities are inadequately maintained. Instead, municipalities need to review their mandates and to define the priorities which will dictate the allocation of their scarce resources. It may be that the community would prefer to see fewer services provided better. Or it may be that the community would accept paying more to avoid losing certain services. It is time to find out the answers to such questions. It can't be assumed that councillors know the answers, just because they have been elected. In that regard, it is interesting to consider the findings of a survey carried out for the city of Burlington in 1994. Overall, the public rating of city services was quite positive. But while staff close to the public had the same perception as local citizens, councillors and senior staff shared a common, but different, view.[7]

Over the past decade or so, many municipalities have used strategic planning exercises as a way of canvassing local citizens (and other stakeholders) with respect to the challenges they face and the priorities they ought to adopt. These can be a very effective means of involving the public, setting priorities, and reallocating scarce municipal resources. In very brief and oversimplified terms, the following steps are involved. [8]

1. *Clarifying the mandate and the mission of the organization.*

For municipalities, this means determining what they must do according to provincial requirements and also what is not ruled out by their mandates—in other words, what things can they do which they are not doing at present. Through this exercise, a municipality can identify its "room to manoeuvre," however limited that may be. A mission statement is a declaration of the organization's purpose. What is this municipality? What basic social and political needs does it exist to fulfil? What makes it distinctive or unique?

2. *Conducting a SWOT analysis.*

This involves an examination of the internal strengths and weaknesses of the organization in relation to the external opportunities and threats it faces. The external examination, normally called an environmental scan, is carried out first. It usually includes a stakeholder analysis, that is, a survey of the customers and clients of the organization, all those who have a stake in the organization's future, those with an interest in the issues facing the organization.

3. *Identifying strategic issues.*

This is the central step in the exercise, and it involves identifying the fundamental policy choices facing the organization. It selects from among the many issues on the horizon those which are of strategic importance and must be addressed by the organization.

4. *Developing strategies and action plans.*

The preceding steps will come to nothing unless the organization develops goals and objectives in relation to each strategic issue, develops

---

[7]Interlink Research Consulting, *Service Optimization Study: Final Results*, 1994, p. 8.

[8]This discussion is based on Association of Municipal Clerks and Treasurers of Ontario, *Municipal Administration Program*, 1998, Unit Four, Lesson 7, which is in turn largely drawn from John Bryson, *Strategic Planning for Public and Non-Profit Organizations*, San Francisco, Jossey-Bass Inc., 1988.

an action plan with clear time lines, and assigns responsibilities for achieving the objectives.

This brief four point summary obviously is far from an adequate description of strategic planning, but it should be sufficient to demonstrate the potential value of this kind of exercise. It gives the municipality a heightened awareness of its external environment and it provides a systematic method of selecting which of the many challenges on the horizon will be addressed with scarce municipal resources. Of particular importance for the discussions in this section of the chapter, it can provide an excellent means of involving the public in municipal decision making. Consider this example from Milton, Ontario, which conducted a strategic planning exercise in the mid-1990s which gave a high priority to public involvement. Actions taken in 1994 included:

- having seniors give their views on what makes Milton a great place to live.
- having elementary school students present their vision on how Milton should grow and develop.
- using posters and public displays to provide information on upcoming *Destiny Milton* events, and also to provide feedback on information obtained through community consultation activities.
- using community representatives to identify community development issues and to provide direction for future action plans.
- carrying out surveys with the assistance of town staff, service organizations, and home and school associations.
- holding "family forums" to discuss community needs and issues.
- holding workshops, focus groups, interviews, surveys, and town meetings to discuss community development issues, and to encourage the development of networks and strategic alliances between Milton residents and their community organizations.[9]

According to a report at the time, "while certain action plans will be implemented by the town, other action plans will be carried out by the residents and community organizations empowered by the strategic planning process."[10]

A strategic planning exercise need not be a technical exercise focused on the completion of a plan. It is (or can be) an ongoing process of debate and dialogue with local citizens, out of which come not only clearer priorities, but also greater public understanding of the issues facing the council and greater council awareness of what is important to the

---

[9]David J. Hipgrave and Gerald A. Grant, "Destiny Milton Strategic Planning Process," *Municipal World*, November 1994, p. 4.

[10]*Ibid.*

citizens. The result is a more solid foundation for fulfilling the political role of municipal government.

Developing More Community Responsibility

Greater involvement of the public through exercises such as strategic planning can help to promote a greater sense of community responsibility for local issues and their resolution. All too often citizens respond to a problem by complaining "why doesn't the government do something about this," even as they decry the size of government and the heavy tax burden they bear. Adding to this paradoxical behaviour is the fact that more responsible actions on the part of citizens might avoid some of the problems which then lead to expensive responses from government. People used to undertake self-help and community-initiated ventures almost as a matter of course. But as the scope of government activity expanded throughout the 20th century, these tendencies disappeared. The notion somehow developed that once the government gets involved with some subject, then it is the government's problem, not ours. Governments have contributed to this unfortunate development by appearing to exclude the public, by acting as if only professionals and experts could have the answers.

Gradually this trend is being reversed. Progressive governments are working with communities to reduce the likelihood of problems arising in the first place. After a century of the medical model of health care, which consumes vast resources to treat people after they become sick, the "healthy cities" movement has revived efforts by municipalities and public health agencies to promote healthy communities and healthy lifestyles as primary methods of avoiding sickness and associated treatment costs. The same emphasis on prevention is evident in the shift to community policing, the opening of "storefront operations," and the provision of youth-related recreational facilities in an effort to reduce crime. Progressive fire departments recognize that their primary task is not to fight fires but to prevent them from happening, and they have devoted increasing resources to public education activities. Members of the community have often led the way with respect to environmental matters, pushing their municipalities to adopt recycling and blue box programs and to promote the three Rs (reduce, reuse, and recycle).

To take one more example, many municipalities have recognized their financial limits and the importance of community involvement by setting up mechanisms which encourage local groups, organizations, or businesses to accept responsibility for providing or maintaining particular facilities or services. A common example is an arrangement under which the municipality provides the site and the boards, but a neighbourhood accepts responsibility for maintaining an outdoor rink in its area. Schemes to "adopt a park" or "adopt a flower bed" are also widespread. A plaque at the site identifies the organization taking on this role.

There is a danger, of course, that these latter arrangements can become little more than a scheme to shift public responsibilities and costs on to private shoulders. If that is the only objective of the exercise, it is unlikely to succeed for long. Equally foolish is the situation in which governments call for greater efforts from volunteers and community associations at the very time that they have been cutting grant support to such associations in the name of fiscal restraint! Adequate government resources and true partnership arrangements are needed "to enable communities in their efforts to rehabilitate housing, create employment, get rid of drug dealers, pimps and slum landlords, foster strong community schools, recover rivers for community use, and improve public health."[11]

Almost lost in all the recent talk about governments pursuing public-private partnerships is the importance of a new partnership between governments and their citizens, one which can generate the volunteer and community efforts which are so needed today. It is scarcely an exaggeration to say that governments spent the first three decades following World War II building a welfare state that largely pushed aside volunteer organizations and the last two decades dismantling these social programs while underfunded charities struggled to pick up the pieces.[12] The response of British Prime Minister Tony Blair to these developments is a new 10 page compact with the voluntary sector in which the government undertakes to respect the independence of voluntary organizations, provide them with stable multi-year funding, and include them in the development of government policies. His government has launched a $120 million program to make it easy and attractive for young people to volunteer, is planning a similar incentive to encourage retired people to get involved in their communities,

> A partnership deserving of more promotion is that between governments and their citizens.

---

[11]Greg Selinger, "Urban Governance for the Twenty-First Century," in Nancy Klos (ed.), *The State of Unicity—25 Years Later*, Winnipeg, Institute of Urban Studies, 1998, p. 99.

[12]This is the perspective of Carol Goar, "Don't mistake price tags for values," *The Toronto Star*, February 13, 1999, on which the following section is based.

and has challenged citizens to "mark the millennium with an explosion of acts of community that touch people's lives."[13]

While a similar initiative from Canada's senior governments would be welcome, municipalities should take the lead in this matter. Gone are the days when volunteers were only associated with the recreation field. With municipal resources so strained and limited, it only makes sense to draw upon community resources and expertise wherever possible. A case in point is Burlington's initiative in appointing a citizens' committee to review its budget process, as described in Chapter 10. In the words of a former community worker and municipal councillor, "civic bureaucratic expertise combined with community initiative can lead to a more dynamic, engaged civic culture and to stronger local democracy."[14]

As this quote suggests, what makes an effective government-community partnership so valuable is not the reduction in government workload but the increased feeling of community responsibility and ownership. The "adopt a park" program cited earlier does help to defray municipal program costs, but its main benefit is enhanced community involvement and a greater sense of ownership. This is reflected in reduced vandalism and general abuse of park facilities which are adopted in this manner. If members of the community have volunteered their time and energy to maintain a park, they view it quite differently; it is "their" park, not just a municipal park. They are not going to damage or neglect "their" park; nor are they likely to tolerate others being similarly inconsiderate. It was always their park, of course, since it was provided through tax dollars, but they didn't see it that way before.

A Vending Machine or a Barn-Raising?[15]

Which view of municipal government is going to prevail in the 21st century? The vending machine view reflects the municipality's role as service provider. This view has always been prominent and has received even greater attention in recent years with the emphasis on municipalities being more business-like and taking care of the customer. People drop

---

[13]*Ibid.*

[14]Selinger, *op. cit.*, p. 99.

[15]These contrasting views of municipal government are described in Frank Benest, "Serving customers or engaging citizens: What is the future of local government?" an article originally published as an insert in the *International City Management Association Journal*, November 1996. Some of the ideas in this article provided the inspiration for the discussion in this section.

money (tax payments) in the municipal vending machine, and the machine dispenses services. Sometimes the machine doesn't work, or is out of the particular product that people want, and they grumble and kick the machine. In response, people may be offered different products and different prices. They may be given a 1-800 number to call; they may even be offered guarantees about product availability or quality. Ultimately, however, there is nothing to encourage a close allegiance between citizens and the municipal vending machine. It is just a service provider. All it wants is for people to deposit their money in exchange for the products. All the people want is the products which satisfy their particular needs. Instead of being citizens of a wider community who have an interest in the needs of others, they are individual consumers. The vending machine view is an extension of public choice theory, focusing on individual choice through markets. It provides a marked contrast to traditional theories of local democracy which focus on the capacity for collective choice through voting.[16]

The barn-raising view incorporates the notion of citizen and community responsibility. People have collective needs and concerns. Instead of saying "why doesn't the government do something," when a problem arises, they are as likely to say "what are we going to do?" The "adopt a park" initiative, properly conducted, is consistent with the barn-raising model of municipal government. So is a strategic planning exercise which draws upon the views and values, hopes and fears, of countless members of the community as a foundation for its planning and priority setting. Technical staff can write a strategic plan, but only the citizens of a community can provide the vision which illuminates such a plan. Storefront operations, efforts to involve and empower local groups and associations, initiatives to promote partnerships amongst groups to tackle community issues—all of these actions reflect the barn-raising model. This model is consistent with the notion, from Chapter 1, of the municipality as an extension of the community, the community governing itself.

Using Resources Wisely

Whatever planning and priority setting exercises may be carried out and however much community responsibility and collective ownership can

---

[16]Michael Keating, *Comparative Urban Politics*, Aldershot, Edward Elgar, 1991, p. 108.

be engendered, municipalities still face the challenge of providing a wide variety of services and programs to their citizens, and doing so with severely constrained resources. As a result, they need to take steps to ensure that they are using their limited resources as wisely as possible. As will be seen, a number of these steps involve the use of efficiency measures, competitive pressures, and other tools and techniques from the business world—even though we have repeatedly rejected the notion that municipal governments should run like a business. There is no inconsistency here. In seeking to use their resources wisely, municipalities should employ any tools which can *assist* them in their decisions. It is not business tools per se, to which we have objected, but situations in which business tools and market forces have dictated decisions instead of simply providing part of the background information on which political decisions are made by councils. These concerns, and how they can be addressed, are outlined in the following sections.

Deciding Who Provides Services

In deciding which services to continue to provide, municipalities need to keep in mind that the provision of a service and the production or supplying of that service are two quite different things. The decision by a council (and its citizens) that a service will be provided does not necessarily mean that municipal staff will be hired or assigned to deliver that service directly. The first decision is a political and policy one—that this municipal servicing need will be addressed. The second decision concerns the best way to address this need and the options include the following:

- a municipality could directly deliver the service itself, using its own staff, in what might be considered the traditional approach.
- a municipality could contract to have the service provided by another municipality.
- a number of municipalities could arrange for the delivery of a service or services on their behalf through the establishment of a joint services board. Both this arrangement and the preceding one allow municipalities to arrange service delivery so as to maximize economies of scale, especially in the case of capital-intensive services.
- a municipality could contract with the private sector for the delivery of the service, through a wide variety of arrangements.

There is no "one best way" with respect to this matter. The point is simply that the municipality should not assume that it will directly provide all services just because that may have been the pattern in the past. It should explore the potential of a different role in which it acts as a service arranger or "enabling authority,"[17] drawing upon a variety of resources (public, private, and voluntary) to address the needs of its citizens. This distinction has also been popularized as steering instead of rowing.[18]

Some use these concepts as a means or rationale for promoting widespread privatization. That is not our objective. We find nothing inherently superior in private administration. In our view municipalities will likely continue to provide directly most of the services required by their citizens. But it makes sense to consider what alternative service delivery options might be available. It also makes sense,

> While alternative service delivery options should be considered, it is likely that municipalities will continue to provide most services needed by their citizens.

by pursuing process improvements, to look at new ways of delivering the services which stay "in house." Neither of these avenues can be explored properly, however, unless the municipality has a clear picture of its existing services and costs.

Knowing and Comparing Costs of Services

This point may seem all too obvious, but one should never assume that municipalities do have this knowledge—even about the exact services they provide, much less about their output quality and their total costs. Remarkably, one expert, discussing municipalities in the United States, claimed that only 4% of them knew the direct cost of each service they provide, only 2% knew the total cost, and only 10% could even tell you what specific services they provide.[19] In recent years, however, there has been growing interest in concepts such as unit costing, activity-based costing, cost management, performance measurement, and the like. All have as their essential focus the identification of the total costs (direct and indirect) associated with providing defined levels of output (a specified quantity and quality of service).

Without this basic information, municipalities do not know, and can not show, what they are getting for their money. They lack a valid basis for comparing staff performance from one year to the next. They lack a basis

---

[17]See, for example, Rodney Brooke, *Managing the Enabling Authority*, Longman in association with the Local Government Training Board, 1989.

[18]David Osborne and Ted Gaebler, *Reinventing Government*, New York, Penguin Books, 1993.

[19]Doug Ayres, quoted in *ibid.*, p. 217.

for comparing their performance with that of other municipalities. Without the information which comes from a good performance measurement system, municipalities are not in a position to evaluate alternative service delivery options. They are not even in a good position to handle the central task of setting priorities, since it is difficult to compare the respective merits of different expenditure claims unless one knows what level of service is being provided by that expenditure and whether this represents an efficient use of resources.

Uses of Performance Measures

Providing information on the total cost of the services is central to any notion of public accountability. It is also a prerequisite to sound decision making. Municipalities are increasingly pursuing user fees and charges in lieu of taxes to raise revenues. How do they know what is a reasonable user fee for garbage pickup, use of ball diamonds, or access to library services? How do they justify fee increases to their citizens? They don't and they can't, unless they know the actual, total costs of providing such services.

Having solid cost data allows the municipality to build budgets on a realistic foundation. Estimates for the coming year are not just based on last year's budget, or on some arbitrary increase (or decrease, in recent years) from last year's budget. Instead, the estimates are constructed by taking the known unit costs for providing a service and multiplying by the number of units to be provided in the coming year. (In other words, if it has been established that it costs "X" dollars per metre to construct sidewalks, then a budget commitment to construct 600 metres of sidewalk will be costed at 600 times "X.")

Budgets built in this manner give the municipality an improved insight into the real causes of any over- or underspending that might occur. A municipal roads department was traditionally considered well managed if it stayed within its budget for the year. More enlightened municipalities might link the budget to the construction and maintenance of "X" kilometres of roads. By so doing, they could at least be alert to situations in which a budget was not overspent but neither were all of the scheduled kilometres of roads built or repaired! With performance measurement, the municipality is in an even better position. It can determine, for the money spent, whether or not the roads were built or maintained at a per unit cost at least equal to the target set *and* it can ensure that any efficiency improvements were not gained at the expense of quality and customer satisfaction. If costs per kilometre of road go down, but the pothole index markedly worsens, then there hasn't been an improvement after all.

Performance measures can be used internally to set improved targets, year by year. These can call for improvements in efficiency and/or effectiveness. Because both kinds of measures are present, there is less risk of the pressure to cut costs leading to service deterioration. For example, municipalities which downsize and/or pursue efficiencies in services like garbage collection may see (at least initially) a reduction in the cost per tonne of garbage collected. But, if they are also measuring things like the percentage of households served at the scheduled time and the extent of customer satisfaction through customer surveys, they will know if the savings are from increased productivity or decreased service.

With solid data on costs and output, the nature of budget discussions between councillors and staff, and the nature of the budget document itself, can change in fundamental ways. In the past, most councillors tried to assert control by digging through hundreds of pages of specific figures in line-item budgets, attempting to find "padding," duplication, or waste. Instead, council can control the budget process by telling staff what results, what service level, it wants to have. Staff then tell council how much that service level will cost. If councils still begin the budget process by calling for expenditure cuts, staff can use cost and output data to show councillors how the level of service will be reduced as a result of such cuts. Whatever service level is agreed upon, that is council's budget control. Staff are free to organize their resources and use whatever approach they feel is appropriate—so long as they provide the service to the defined level and within the cost specified.[20]

Both councillors and staff gain from such an arrangement. Municipal staff gain the freedom to apply their expertise in administration and service delivery. They gain a sense of clear direction from council. They know what is expected of them; they know what they have to do to meet council's objectives. Council gains true policy control over the operations of the municipality; council decides what services will be provided at what level. This is a far cry from the illusory control which councillors have had in the traditional budget process when all they really decide is how much each department can spend.

---

[20]This discussion is largely based on Municipal Administration Program, *op. cit.*, Unit Three, Lesson 5, pp. 32-33, and inspired by the writings of Osborne and Gaebler, *op. cit.*

Performance measures can also be used as the basis for new incentive and reward systems that can unleash creativity and improved productivity in municipal employees. Traditional budgeting systems rewarded those who overspent their budgets (by building a case for additional funds for the coming year) and punished those who actually saved money (by suggesting that they had been given too much and should have less for the coming year). If municipalities use performance measures to get a solid grasp of the real, total costs of providing defined levels of output, they can then offer exciting challenges to their employees. If the employees can meet (or exceed) the defined output level, and do so for less money than budgeted, then at least some portion of the savings can be given to the employees (or to their work area) as a bonus. This kind of "pay for performance" scheme has long been followed in the private sector, and is being introduced in a growing number of Canadian municipalities, as indicated by the examples in Chapter 7.

> Performance measures can be used as the basis for new incentive programs to reinforce staff productivity.

Abuses of Performance Measures

So far, so good. Performance measurement is a business tool which seems to have a number of advantages when applied to municipal operations. But it is also a tool which is open to potential abuses, depending on how it is applied. This is the case when invalid comparisons are drawn or when measures are used by senior levels of government to dictate performance standards that municipalities must follow.

The first problem can easily arise when performance measures are used to make external comparisons with the performance of other municipalities and with private sector performance. Such external comparisons are not without merit. If performance measurement is only used internally, then the municipality doesn't really have any idea of its relative performance. Just how significant is it that productivity improvement of 5% a year has been achieved over the past three years? If the municipality had been operating only half as efficiently as others of comparable size and circumstances, then these improvements are little cause for rejoicing.

For this reason, performance measures are commonly used for external comparisons. This exercise is usually referred to as benchmarking—that is, the continuous process of measuring products and practices against the toughest competition and those organizations regarded as

world-class leaders. These external comparisons introduce a very competitive atmosphere into municipal operations, one which challenges
municipal personnel to improve—not just from year to year, but also in
comparison to their peers elsewhere.

The term benchmarking is usually used in conjunction with the term
best practices. The link between the two concepts is quite direct and
fairly obvious. If external benchmarks are found which suggest that some
municipalities are delivering a service at a comparable standard but more
efficiently, then it makes sense to find out how they are doing this. Great
care must be taken, however, to ensure that such external comparisons
are fair—that we are actually comparing "apples to apples." If so, the
challenge is to identify the management processes, administrative practices, techniques, or "short cuts" that are being used by the other organization to achieve superior productivity. These "best practices" should then
be adopted by organizations seeking to improve their performance.

The problem with this appealing concept is that there are wide variations between organizations in how and where they allocated their costs,
making cost comparisons invalid and misleading. Some indication of the
complexity of external comparisons is evident from a garbage collection
study carried out by the Local Government Institute at the University of
Victoria. It notes that municipal accounting practices vary, as does the
scope of activities included in "operating costs."[21] The handling of such
costs as capital expenditures, debt retirement funds, administrative overhead, equipment replacement funds, and councillor costs differs from
one municipality to the next. Until there is more consistency, the study
cautions that it is impossible to know whether comparisons across local
governments are meaningful. The same is true of efforts to compare municipal performance with those of private companies.

Those pursuing an ideological agenda to downsize the public sector
and to enhance private sector operations can distort performance measures to advance their cause. For virtually every municipal service, it is
probably possible to find a quote from somewhere which promises
cheaper delivery. But there is a danger that the cost comparisons are not
valid and/or that the standards and service quality are not the same. It is
our view that performance measures should not be used as a means of
searching out the cheapest method of service delivery. They should be
used, in combination with other measures such as the incentives and

---

[21]Reported in James McDavid, "Understanding What Makes Local Government Services Efficient: Methods for a National Study of Local Service Production," in *Cordillera Institute Journal*, Markham, April 1996, pp. 10-12.

rewards programs discussed earlier, to stimulate and encourage improvements in the productivity of municipal staff. The question should not be "is anyone doing this cheaper?" Rather the question should be "is staff performance showing desired improvement, year by year?" Steady progress of this sort is more effective than the "quick fix" of what may be an ill-considered privatization venture.

The other problem that can arise is the use of performance measures by provincial governments to force certain standards upon municipalities. For example, the extensive downloading of services in Ontario has been accompanied by a provincial commitment to develop or refine performance standards which municipalities must meet. Without such provincial standards, it could be argued, we could end up with a "hodge-podge" of levels of service, varying with the financial resources and voter tolerance of individual municipalities. But these standards, in the hands of a neo-conservative provincial government, could also be used to force diminished levels of service by insisting that municipalities move to the cheapest operation possible.

Stein outlines an example from "a knowledgeable civil servant" of what might happen with grass cutting in municipal parks.[22] Assume that newer municipalities have in their parks fewer trees which are farther apart. The parks department can string together mowers and cut the grass for, say, $9 an hour. But in an older municipality with many large trees which are close together, this cost-saving measure isn't available, and grass cutting costs $16.50 an hour. What if the province dictates that if some municipalities can cut the grass for $9 an hour, all of them should be able to meet this standard of efficiency? After considering various options, the older municipality decides that the only way it can meet this objective is by cutting down the trees to facilitate the grass cutting.

> Shortsighted decisions arise when efficiency measures take precedence over community values and priorities.

Yes, this is an extreme and far-fetched example. But it not that far off the mark in illustrating the danger inherent in reducing decision making to nothing but a numbers game. It demonstrates the folly of placing efficiency measures above all other considerations. Not evident in this example, of course, is any consideration of the values and priorities of the community.

Performance measures can be a useful tool to assist council; they provide part of the background information. They deserve attention along

---

[22]David Lewis Stein, "Harris' hidden axe," *The Toronto Star*, July 12, 1997.

with the judgment and instincts of the elected councillors and the feelings and values of their citizens and their community. But in the current rush to be seen as more business-like, some municipalities are elevating tools like performance measurement into decision-making models. Benchmarking and best practices reports from consultants replace the considered judgment of councillors. That is the danger which must be avoided, if municipalities are to function as governments and not businesses.

In Praise of Local Democracy

Businesses, if they can help it, only provide services which will generate a profit. They take every step possible to minimize their costs and to maximize "the bottom line." This preoccupation has never been more evident than in the allegedly unavoidable corporate downsizing of recent years in response to global competition. A municipal government which sees itself as a business is apt to take such steps as reducing its involvement in areas which are costly and/or have no potential for raising revenues. But most of the services provided by governments are in the public domain precisely because they can't and shouldn't generate a profit. Governments exist to serve the public interest, not the bottom line.

John Ralston Saul argues that democracy isn't about decisiveness and efficiency; it is about consideration. In his words:

> Efficiency is not the highest example of human intelligence. It is not an important quality in a society; it is a minor, shop-floor necessity. You don't build society on efficiency. You build society on consideration and inefficiency.[23]

Saul is concerned that the anti-democratic forces have reduced society to utility, to function, arguing that functional, interest-based societies are self-destructive "because their view of human intelligence is so narrow and immediate that the society can't actually see where it's going or what the effects of its actions will be."[24] Municipalities steeped in the current business mantra often seem to exhibit that same narrow and short-term focus.

A billionaire financier, now considered a traitor by his erstwhile business colleagues, attacks the notion that measurement and the market

---

[23] John Ralston Saul, "The Good Citizen," *Canadian Forum*, December 1997, p. 15.

[24] *Ibid.*

place should decide the kind of society we have. George Soros contends that every society needs shared values to hold it together and that market values can never serve this purpose.[25] This is because they reflect only what one market participant is willing to pay another in free exchange. In his words: "Markets reduce everything, including human beings (labour) and nature (land) to commodities. We can have a market economy but we cannot have a market society."[26] In addition to markets, Soros claims, society needs institutions to serve such social goals as political freedom and social justice. Are municipalities that kind of institution? How often are concerns about social justice voiced during municipal budget deliberations? Such concerns should frame the budget debate, rather than the perennial concern about zero tax increases. Yet as various writers have pointed out, it is difficult for municipalities to pursue social justice—especially in today's global economy—because policies of redistribution are likely to trigger out-migration by business and the well-to-do.[27]

The municipality of Rossland, British Columbia, seems to have come closer than most to recognizing the importance of local democracy, and it is interesting to hear the views of André Carrel, its administrator. He argues that it is more important for leaders to focus on democracy than efficiency. Echoing the sentiments of Saul, he states that:

> Efficiency is important in the production of nuts and bolts, but inhibits the development of a civil and democratic society. We will not be able to reestablish vital communities by running faster, by using less paper or by creating web pages for our municipalities. Leaders must start by including citizens in the process of governing our municipalities.[28]

He also points out, quite properly, that in a democracy, "the people are neither clients nor customers ... they are the owners."[29]

Municipalities, and indeed governments at all levels, have exhibited a great deal of concern over the past couple of decades about the financial deficit and the performance deficit. Both of these matters are important, but it is the democratic deficit which is especially in need of

---

[25]George Soros, "Toward a Global Open Society," *Atlantic Monthly*, January 1998, p. 24.

[26]*Ibid.*

[27]See, for example, Paul Peterson, *City Limits*, Chicago, University of Chicago Press, 1981.

[28]André Carrel, *Municipal Government Leadership*, presentation at Capilano College, March 14, 1997, p. 4.

[29]*Ibid.*

attention.[30] As Hill cautioned, "the centralization of powers to ministers ... and the decentralization of choice to individuals as parents, tenants and users of services, is in danger of bypassing the elected local council."[31]

Concluding Comments

How municipalities fare in the new century will depend, as always, on how well they maintain a balance between their two primary roles: representative/political and administrative/service delivery. When combined, these roles suggest an appealing and flexible government system which provides varying programs in accordance with the needs and wishes of different communities of local citizens. But as discussed in Chapter 1, various developments over the years have conspired to direct attention to the administrative role of municipal government, to the relative neglect of its political role. This shift in emphasis has been intensified and extended by the new turn of the century reform era in which we now find ourselves and its demands that municipalities become more business-like.

As a result, municipalities are caught between two quite contrasting images of what they are and how they should perform. The first image, admittedly somewhat idealistic, is of the municipality as a vehicle used by the community to identify and to address its collective concerns. It emphasizes the notion of collective action to deal with shared problems and challenges. With this image, the representative and political role is paramount. Municipalities are viewed as local democratic institutions which respond to collective public concerns by providing public services financed from taxes. The ultimate measure of their performance lies in how effectively they respond to the elusive public interest.

> Municipalities are caught between two contrasting images of what they are and how they should perform.

The second image, which seems to be in the ascendancy, portrays the municipality as but one of many players in a competitive market place in which individuals are free to pursue their personal interests by seeking out the services that they find most attractive. The administrative role of

---

[30]Paul Thomas, "Diagnosing the Health of Civic Democracy," in Klos, *op. cit.*, p. 50.

[31]Dilys Hill, *Citizens and Cities*, Hemel Hempstead, Harvester Wheatsheaf, 1994, p. 230.

municipal government is central to this second image. The image is manifestly not one of the collective identification of issues and collective responses. A variety of alternative service providers is seen as offering the range of choice needed for individual consumers of services to pursue their best interests. Charging user fees for these services is favoured over payment through taxes, because the former allows individuals to select only those services they want to use, and to pay accordingly. The ultimate measurement of performance is how efficiently municipalities deliver services as reflected in their bottom line.

The table which follows depicts the key characteristics of these two contrasting views.

Representative/ Political Institution		Administrative/ Servicing Agent
←		→
Collective responsibility	↔	Individual self-interest
Provision of public goods	↔	Varied service providers
Financed by taxes	↔	Financed by user fees
Focused on effectiveness	↔	Focused on efficiency

The second image of municipal government contains within it both positive elements and potential dangers, depending on the extent to which its key features are pushed. The benefits of a competitive atmosphere have long been evident in the public sector, and public choice proponents are persuasive when they contend that the choice for citizens is enhanced when there are multiple local service providers and when there is freedom to access a service or not by paying a user fee or not. As noted elsewhere in this text, there is considerable evidence to suggest that a fragmented municipal structure provides services less expensively than one large, consolidated unit. It is also well documented that "what gets measured, gets done,"[32] and that concerted efforts to promote and reward productivity improvements bear fruit.

On the other hand, we have also noted in this text that whatever efficiency benefits there may be from a fragmented municipal structure are potentially offset by problems caused by the lack of a unified approach to intermunicipal issues and by the perpetuation of servicing and financing inequities. With a number of separate municipalities, individuals are free to choose the one which provides whatever combination of services and

---

[32]Osborne and Gaebler, *op. cit.*, p. 146.

charges best meet their needs—assuming that they have both knowledge of the choices available and the mobility to act upon this knowledge. But this structural arrangement may also allow the creation or preservation of communities of relatively well-to-do individuals who need minimal government services and are taxed accordingly, and who aren't obliged to contribute, thanks to their separate governing jurisdiction, to the costs of the many government services needed by the less fortunate in society, who are located in other jurisdictions. Carried to an extreme, this can result in a kind of social apartheid, in which the elite "feel increasingly justified in paying only what is necessary to insure that everyone in their community is sufficiently well educated and has access to the public services they need to succeed."[33] It is clear that the pursuit of individual self-interest can work better for some individuals than it does for others. Along with what is best for the individual, as measured in strictly financial terms, there has to be some consideration of what is best for the broader community and region in which one moves and interacts.

> Along with what is best for the individual has to be some consideration of what is best for the broader community.

Similarly, an over-preoccupation with the efficiency of service delivery, a tendency to measure municipal operations in the same way as a business, can lead to some harmful distortions. It must be remembered that many of the services provided by government are not provided by the private sector because they do not, and cannot, generate a profit or even come close to operating at break-even. This bad bottom line doesn't make such services a candidate for termination; it is why they belong in the public domain. User charges have their benefits, when applied selectively, but any widespread expansion of their use can be self-defeating. Once again, the self-interested individual will attempt to minimize costs. The wealthier citizens have no need of services such as public transit. They can forego public parks in favour of cottages and private resorts, and may even feel less need for police services thanks to their secure access high-rise or gated community. Indeed, there are now far more private security forces than there are public police. But public programs and services can certainly not be financed solely from user charges paid by the less wealthy in society.

---

[33]Robert Reich, "Secession of the Successful," *New York Times Magazine*, January 6, 1991, as quoted in Murray Dobbin, *The Myth of the Good Corporate Citizen*, Toronto, Stoddart, 1998, pp. 128-129.

Consider the example of municipal bus or transit services. These services never operate at break-even, a fact which seems to cause great controversy—even though the public roads provided for the convenience of the motor car and which are much more heavily subsidized by government also never come close to operating at break-even. Yet the typical response to a transit deficit is to increase the fees and to reduce the service, actions hardly conducive to an improvement in the situation. A totally different way at looking at public transit would be to view it as an essential public good which is also cost-effective when one factors in the costs which would arise without it, in the form of increased air pollution and traffic congestion, greater traffic control costs, time and money lost in commuting, more "fender-benders" and other accidents, and more associated police and court costs. When everything is taken into consideration, it might even be that the much-maligned municipal transit system is a bargain. But when the focus is only on the bottom line, rather than on the broader benefits to society, we are likely to be guilty of shortsighted bookkeeping.

The table above illustrated the key features of the two images we have been discussing along a spectrum rather than in two separate columns, because they represent gradations of behaviour and orientation rather than either/or options for municipalities. It is certainly possible, indeed desirable, to combine the best of both images. Essentially, this approach involves a *moderate* embrace of the features of the second image. Specifically:

- individual self-interest and competitive pressures are powerful forces, but they should not be allowed to prevail to the extent that intermunicipal interests are ignored or harmful intermunicipal inequities perpetuated.
- efficient and economical use of municipal resources is most welcome, provided that such measures are balanced by consideration of effectiveness. The pursuit of the bottom line cannot be allowed to take precedence over pursuit of the public interest.

Under different circumstances, it might not be too difficult to blend the two images we have been discussing, and to add business-like, competitive features to local democratic institutions. Presently, however, we face the added challenge that the very institutions of government (at all levels) seem to be under attack, as a result of the global economy, the dictates of international capitalism, and the neo-conservative ideology which has held sway for the past couple of decades. Not content to have government act in a more business-like manner, there are many who wish to go further and downgrade the role and significance of government in our society, while elevating the importance of the private sector.

One manifestation of this approach is the view that virtually all spending by government is inherently less desirable than spending by and on the private sector. Yet we should know by now that serious problems arise when we fail to maintain an adequate balance between public goods and private goods.[34] In such a society, paradoxes abound. With taxes kept sufficiently low, people can afford increasingly fancy automobiles, even if the streets and highways on which these cars must travel are not well maintained. Children have ready access to television and various forms of entertainment, even as their schools deteriorate and are plagued by increasing violence. People have no shortage of food, alcohol, cigarettes, and other "creature comforts," but lack adequate medical and hospital care when health problems arise from the excesses of consumption. The signs of this dichotomy are increasingly present today, but the book which raised this issue of public-private imbalance is over 40 years old! It is *The Affluent Society*, by Canadian John Kenneth Galbraith, published in 1958.

North Americans now spend more than a *billion* dollars annually on the latest video games and associated high-tech reincarnations of "Pac Man."[35] Yet we continue to debate whether or not we can afford welfare, public housing, public health, environmental programs, and other services which form part of a basic standard of living in a civilized society. The relatively small amount of money spent on local government services is vividly illustrated by Jim Sharpe's comment that:

> ... although the local government bill is not small, it provides education, public health, social services, highways, libraries, fire, police, refuse collection, and a whole range of other public services which most people need and demand, at a total cost that is no larger than the amount we collectively spend on such things as wine and beer, cigarettes, eye shadow, tennis rackets and a flutter on the horses.[36]

To update and localize the point, half a million dollars a day is spent by visitors to the casino in Ottawa-Hull. Yet municipalities throughout Eastern Ontario (and elsewhere) began their budget deliberations this spring, as

---

[34]The discussion which follows is based on C. Richard Tindal, *A Citizen's Guide to Government*, Whitby, McGraw-Hill Ryerson Limited, 1997, pp. 315-316.

[35]This discussion is based on *ibid.*, p. 316.

[36]L. J. Sharpe (ed.), *The Local Fiscal Crisis in Western Europe, Myths and Realities*, London, Sage Publications, 1981, p. 224.

usual, by proclaiming that services would be cut as much as necessary because over-burdened taxpayers simply could not afford any increase in property taxes.

It is highly unlikely that paying taxes will ever become a popular pastime in Canada. But it is through such taxes that a society provides the goods and services which serve and enhance the public good. This community need and collective responsibility provide a marked contrast to the emphasis on individual preferences and choices which has been receiving growing attention. Unless and until citizens show more commitment to governments and their roles within the governmental system, municipalities will remain vulnerable to the pressures to convert them into quasi-businesses. To resist these pressures, therefore, municipalities need to do as much as possible to demonstrate their value and relevance to their communities.

There is an additional, and compelling, reason for municipalities to reassert their political role and to reforge links with their citizens. It is that this relationship represents the best hope for municipalities in the future. Experience has shown that there is little to be gained by relying on the senior levels and waiting to see what may trickle down from above. Far better to build strength upward from the community, from the citizens municipalities exist to serve. That means taking into account the views and concerns of all citizens, not just propertied or business interests. It means being efficient where possible, but also being prepared to provide services or programs which aren't necessarily cost-effective, if they are needed to address a public need. It means being mindful of the bottom line but also dedicated to the public interest.

Select Bibliography

Advisory Commission on Intergovernmental Relations, *A Look to the North: Canadian Regional Experience*, Washington, 1974.

Allen, Edwin G., *Municipal Organization in New Brunswick*, Ministry of Municipal Affairs, Fredericton, 1968.

Anderson, Wayne, Chester Newland, and Richard J. Stillman, *The Effective Local Government Manager*, Washington, International City Management Association, 1983.

Andrew, Caroline, "Federal Urban Activity: Intergovernmental Relations in an Age of Restraint," in Frances Frisken (ed.), *The Changing Canadian Metropolis: A Public Policy Perspective*, Vol. 2, Toronto, Canadian Urban Institute, 1994.

_____, "Recasting Political Analysis for Canadian Cities," in Vered Amit-Talia and Henri Lustiger-Thaler (eds.), *Urban Lives*, Toronto, McClelland and Stewart Limited, 1994.

Antoft, Kell, *A Guide to Local Government in Nova Scotia*, Halifax, Centre for Public Management, Dalhousie University, 1992.

_____ and Jack Novack, *Grassroots Democracy: Local Government in the Maritimes*, Halifax, Centre for Public Management, Dalhousie University, 1998.

Association of Municipalities of Ontario, *Local Governance in the Future: Issues and Trends*, Toronto, 1994.

_____, *Ontario Charter: A Proposed Bill of Rights for Local Government*, Toronto, 1994.

Aucoin, Peter, *The New Public Management in Canada in Comparative Perspective*, Montreal, Institute for Research on Public Policy, 1995.

Axworthy, T., "Winnipeg Unicity," in Advisory Committee on Intergovernmental Relations, *A Look to the North: Canadian Regional Experience*, Washington, 1974.

Baker, M., "William Gilbert Gosling and the Establishment of Commission Government in St. John's, Newfoundland, 1914," *Urban History Review*, Vol. IX, No. 3, February 1981.

Banfield, Edward C., *The Unheavenly City*, Boston, Little, Brown and Company, 1968.

_____ and James Q. Wilson, *City Politics*, New York, Random House, 1963.

Barbour, George et al., *Excellence in Local Government Management*, Washington, International City Management Association, 1985.

Beck, J. M., *The Government of Nova Scotia*, Toronto, University of Toronto Press, 1957.

Bettison, David G., J. Kenward, and L. Taylor, *Urban Affairs in Alberta*, Edmonton, University of Alberta Press, 1975.

Bird, R. M. and N. E. Slack, *Urban Public Finance in Canada*, Toronto, Butterworths, 1983 and Toronto, John Wiley & Sons, 1993.

Bish, Robert L., *Local Government in British Columbia*, Richmond, Union of British Columbia Municipalities in cooperation with the University of Victoria, 1987.

_____, *The Public Economy of Metropolitan Areas*, Chicago, Markham Publishing Company, 1971.

_____ and Vincent Ostrom, *Understanding Urban Government: Metropolitan Reform Reconsidered*, Washington, American Enterprise Institute for Public Policy Research, 1973.

Black, E. R., *Politics and the News: The Political Functions of the Mass Media*, Toronto, Butterworths, 1982.

Borins, Sandford, "The new public management is here to stay," *Canadian Public Administration*, Spring 1995.

Bourne, Larry S. (ed.), *Internal Structure of the City*, Toronto, Oxford University Press, 1971.

Boyer, J. Patrick, *Lawmaking by the People: Referendums and Plebiscites in Canada*, Toronto, Butterworths, 1982.

Brittain, Horace L., *Local Government in Canada*, Toronto, Ryerson Press, 1951.

Brooke, Rodney, *Managing the Enabling Authority*, London, Longman in association with the Local Government Training Board, 1989.

Brooks, Stephen, *Public Policy in Canada: An Introduction*, Toronto, McClelland and Stewart, 2nd Edition, 1993.

Bryson, John, *Strategic Planning for Public and Non-Profit Organizations*, San Francisco, Jossey-Bass Inc., 1988.

Bunting, Trudi and Pierre Filion (eds.), *Canadian Cities in Transition*, Toronto, Oxford University Press, 1991.

Cameron, David M., "Provincial responsibilities for municipal government," *Canadian Public Administration*, Summer 1980.

_____, "Urban Policy," in G. Bruce Doern and V. Seymour Wilson (eds.), *Issues in Canadian Public Policy*, Toronto, Macmillan, 1974.

Cameron, John R., *Provincial-Municipal Relations in the Maritime Provinces*, Fredericton, Maritime Union Study, 1970.

Canadian Federation of Mayors and Municipalities, *Puppets on a Shoestring*, Ottawa, April 28, 1976.

Canadian Urban Institute, *The Future of Greater Montreal: Lessons for the Greater Toronto Area?*, Conference Proceedings, Toronto, 1994.

_____, *Disentangling Local Government Responsibilities—International Comparisons*, Toronto, 1993.

Caulfield, Jon, "Reform as a Chaotic Concept: The Case of Toronto," *Urban History Review*, October 1988.

_____, *The Tiny Perfect Mayor*, Toronto, James Lorimer and Co., 1974.

Charlton, Mark and Paul Barker (eds.), *Crosscurrents: Contemporary Political Issues*, 3rd Edition, Toronto, Nelson, 1998.

Clarke, Michael and John Stewart, *The Choices for Local Government*, Harlow, Longman, 1991.

Clarkson, Stephen, *City Lib*, Toronto, Hakkert, 1972.

Cochrane, Allan, *Whatever Happened to Local Government?*, Buckingham, Open University Press, 1993.

Colton, Timothy J., *Big Daddy*, Toronto, University of Toronto Press, 1980.

Constituent Assembly on the Municipal Government System in Hamilton-Wentworth, Final Report, *Better Municipal Government*, March 1996.

Craig, Gerald M. (ed.), *Lord Durham's Report*, Toronto, McClelland and Stewart Limited, 1963.

Crawford, K. G., *Canadian Municipal Government*, Toronto, University of Toronto Press, 1954.

Dickerson, M. O., S. Drabek, and J. T. Woods (eds.), *Problems of Change in Urban Government*, Waterloo, Wilfrid Laurier University Press, 1980.

Dobbin, Murray, *The Myth of the Good Corporate Citizen*, Toronto, Stoddart, 1998.

Downey, T. J. and R. J. Williams, "Provincial agendas, local responses: the 'common sense' restructuring of Ontario's municipal governments," *Canadian Public Administration*, Summer 1998.

Dunn, Christopher (ed.), *Saskatoon Local Government and Politics*, Saskatoon, University of Saskatchewan, 1987.

Dupre, J. Stefan, *Intergovernmental Finance in Ontario: A Provincial-Local Perspective*, Toronto, Queen's Printer, 1968.

Economic Council of Canada, *Fourth Annual Review*, Ottawa, Queen's Printer, 1967.

Eden, Lorraine, "Provincial-Municipal Equalization in the Maritime Provinces," *Canadian Public Administration*, Winter 1987.

d'Entremont, Harley and Patrick Robardet, "More Reform in New Brunswick: Rural Municipalities," *Canadian Public Administration*, Fall 1997.

Federation of Canadian Municipalities, *Municipal Government in a New Canadian Federal System, Report of the Task Force on Constitutional Reform*, Ottawa, F.C.M., 1980.

_____, *Management and Planning Capabilities in Small Communities*, Ottawa, 1982.

_____, *Brief to the Royal Commission on the Economic Union and Development Prospects for Canada*, October 1983.

Feldman, Lionel D., *Ontario 1945-1973: The Municipal Dynamic*, Toronto, Ontario Economic Council, 1974.

_____, "Tribunals, Politics and the Public Interest: The Edmonton Annexation Case—A Response," *Canadian Public Policy*, Spring 1982.

_____ (ed.), *Politics and Government of Urban Canada*, Toronto, Methuen, 1981.

_____ and Katherine Graham, *Bargaining for Cities*, Toronto, Butterworths, 1979.

Final Report, *Task Force on Municipal Regionalization*, St. John's, September 1997.

Finnis, Frederick, *Property Assessment in Canada*, Toronto, Canadian Tax Foundation, 1979.

Foot, David K., *Boom, Bust & Echo*, Toronto, Macfarlane Walter & Ross, 1996.

Fowler, Edmund P., *Building Cities That Work*, Kingston, McGill-Queen's University Press, 1992.

Fraser, Graham, *Fighting Back*, Toronto, Hakkert, 1972.

Frisken, Frances (ed.), *The Changing Canadian Metropolis: A Public Policy Perspective*, 2 vol., Toronto, Canadian Urban Institute, 1994.

_____, *City Policy-Making in Theory and Practice: The Case of Toronto's Downtown Plan*, Local Government Case Study No. 3, London, University of Western Ontario, 1988.

_____, "Canadian Cities and the American Example: A Prologue to Urban Policy Analysis," *Canadian Public Administration*, Fall 1986.

Garreau, Joel, *Edge City: Life on the New Frontier*, New York, Doubleday, 1991.

Gerecke, Kent, "Winnipeg Hits Bottom," *City Magazine*, Winter 1986/87.

_____, "City Beat," *City Magazine*, Winter 1991/92.

Gertler, L. O. and R. W. Crowley, *Changing Canadian Cities: The Next 25 Years*, Toronto, McClelland and Stewart Limited, 1977.

Goetz, Edward G. and Susan E. Clarke (eds.), *The New Localism*, Newbury Park, Sage Publications, 1993.

Goldrick, Michael, "The Anatomy of Urban Reform in Toronto," in Dimitrios Roussopoulos (ed.), *The City and Radical Social Change*, Montreal, Black Rose Books, 1982.

Goldsmith, Michael, *Politics, Planning and the City*, London, Hutchinson, 1980.

Goodman, J. S., *The Dynamics of Urban Government and Politics*, New York, Macmillan, 1980.

Gottdiener, M., *The Decline of Urban Politics: Political Theory and the Crisis of the Local State*, Newbury Park, Sage Publications, 1987.

Graham, Katherine A., Susan D. Phillips, and Allan M. Maslove, *Urban Governance in Canada*, Toronto, Harcourt Brace & Company, 1998.

Graham, Katherine A. and Susan D. Phillips, *Citizen Engagement: Lessons in Participation from Local Government*, Toronto, Institute of Public Administration of Canada, 1998.

_____, "Who Does What in Ontario: The Process of Provincial-Municipal Disentanglement," *Canadian Public Administration*, Summer 1998.

_____, "Customer engagement: beyond the customer revolution," *Canadian Public Administration*, Summer 1997.

Granatstein, J. L., *Marlborough Marathon*, Toronto, Hakkert and James Lewis and Samuel, 1971.

Gutstein, Donald, *Vancouver Ltd.*, Toronto, James Lorimer and Co., 1975.

Gyford, John, *Local Politics in Britain*, London, Croom Helm Ltd., 1976.

_____, Steve Leach, and Chris Game, *The Changing Politics of Local Government*, London, Unwin Hyman, 1989.

Hanson, Eric, *Local Government in Alberta*, Toronto, McClelland and Stewart Limited, 1956.

Herland, Karen, *People, Potholes and City Politics*, Montreal, Black Rose Books, 1992.

Hickey, Paul, *Decision-Making Processes in Ontario's Local Governments*, Toronto, Ministry of Treasury, Economics and Intergovernmental Affairs, 1973.

Higgins, Donald J. H., *Urban Canada: Its Government and Politics*, Toronto, Macmillan, 1977.

_____, *Local and Urban Politics in Canada*, Toronto, Gage, 1986.

Hill, Dilys, *Citizens and Cities*, Hemel Hempstead, Harvester Wheatsheaf, 1994.

Hobson, Paul A. R., *The Economic Effects of the Property Tax: A Survey*, Ottawa, Economic Council of Canada, 1987.

Hodge, Gerald, *Planning Canadian Communities*, Toronto, Methuen, 1986 and Scarborough, Nelson Canada, 1991.

Isin, Engin F., *Cities Without Citizens*, Montreal, Black Rose Books, 1992.

Jacobs, Jane, *The Death and Life of Great American Cities*, New York, Random House, 1961.

Jones, George and John Stewart, *The Case for Local Government*, London, Allen & Unwin Inc., 1985.

Joyce, J. G. and H. A. Hosse, *Civic Parties in Canada*, Ottawa, Canadian Federation of Mayors and Municipalities, 1970.

Judge, David, Gerry Stoker, and Harold Wolman (eds.), *Theories of Urban Politics*, London, Sage Publications, 1995.

Kaplan, Harold, *Urban Political Systems: A Functional Analysis of Metro Toronto*, New York, Columbia University Press, 1967.

_____, *Reform, Planning and City Politics: Montreal, Winnipeg, Toronto*, Toronto, University of Toronto Press, 1982.

Keating, Michael, *Comparative Urban Politics*, Aldershot, Edward Elgar, 1991.

Kellar, Elizabeth K. (ed.), *Managing with Less: A Book of Readings*, Washington, International City Management Association, 1979.

Kitchen, Harry M., *Local Government Finance in Canada*, Toronto, Canadian Tax Foundation, 1985.

Klos, Nancy (ed.), *The State of Unicity—25 Years Later*, Winnipeg, Institute of Urban Studies, 1998.

Kushner, Joseph, David Siegel, and Hannah Stanwick, "Ontario Municipal Elections: Voting Trends and Determinants of Electoral Success in a Canadian Province," *Canadian Journal of Political Science*, September 1997.

L'Heureux, Jacques, "Municipalities and the Division of Power," in Richard Simeon, Research Coordinator, *Intergovernmental Relations, Vol. 63*, Royal Commission on the Economic Union and Development Prospects for Canada, Toronto, University of Toronto Press, 1985.

Landon, Fred, *Western Ontario and the American Frontier*, Toronto, Mc-Clelland and Stewart Limited, 1967.

Lang, Vernon, *The Service State Emerges in Ontario*, Toronto, Ontario Economic Council, 1974.

Leo, Christopher, "The Urban Economy and the Power of the Local State," in Frances Frisken (ed.), *The Changing Canadian Metropolis: A Public Policy Perspective*, Vol. 2, Toronto, Canadian Urban Institute, 1994.

_____, *The Politics of Urban Development: Canadian Urban Expressway Disputes*, Monographs on Canadian Urban Government, No. 3, Toronto, Institute of Public Administration, 1977.

Levine, Allan (ed.), *Your Worship: The Lives of Eight of Canada's Most Unforgettable Mayors*, Toronto, James Lorimer, 1989.

Lightbody, James, *The Comparative Costs of Governing Alberta's Metropolitan Areas*, Edmonton, Western Centre for Economic Research, Information Bulletin No. 48, January 1998.

_____, "A new perspective on clothing the emperor: Canadian metropolitan form, function and frontiers," in *Canadian Public Administration*, Fall 1997.

_____ (ed.), *Canadian Metropolitics: Governing Our Cities*, Toronto, Copp Clark Ltd., 1995.

Lindblom, Charles E., *The Policy Making Process*, Englewood Cliffs, Prentice-Hall Inc., 1980.

Lithwick, N. H., *Urban Canada: Problems and Prospects*, Ottawa, Central Mortgage and Housing Corporation, 1970.

Loreto, Richard and Trevor Price (eds.), *Urban Policy Issues: Canadian Perspectives*, Toronto, McClelland and Stewart, 1990.

Lorimer, James, "Introduction: The Post-developer Era for Canada's Cities Begins," *City Magazine Annual 1981*, Toronto, James Lorimer and Company, 1981.

_____, *The Developers*, Toronto, James Lorimer, 1978.

_____, *A Citizen's Guide to City Politics*, Toronto, James Lewis and Samuel, 1972.

_____, *The Real World of City Politics*, Toronto, James Lewis and Samuel, 1970.

_____ and Carolyn MacGregor (eds.), *After the Developers*, Toronto, James Lorimer, 1981.

Lorimer, James and E. Ross (eds.), *The City Book: The Planning and Politics of Canada's Cities*, Toronto, James Lorimer and Company, 1976.

Lowi, Theodore, *The End of Liberalism*, 2nd Edition, New York, W. W. Norton, 1979.

Lustiger-Thaler, Henri (ed.), *Political Arrangements: Power and the City*, Montreal, Black Rose Books, 1992.

Magnusson, Warren, "The Local State in Canada: Theoretical Perspectives," *Canadian Public Administration*, Winter 1985.

_____, "Urban Politics and the Local State," *Studies in Political Economy*, 16, 1985.

_____, "Community Organization and Local Self-Government" in Lionel D. Feldman (ed.), *Politics and Government of Urban Canada: Selected Readings*, Toronto, Methuen, 1981.

_____ and Andrew Sancton (eds.), *City Politics in Canada*, Toronto, University of Toronto Press, 1983.

Makuch, Stanley M., *Canadian Municipal and Planning Law*, Toronto, Carswell, 1983.

Mancuso, Maureen, Richard Price, and Ronald Wagenberg (eds.), *Leaders and Leadership in Canada*, Toronto, Oxford University Press, 1994.

Manitoba, Government of, *Proposals for Urban Reorganization in the Greater Winnipeg Area (White Paper)*, Winnipeg, Queen's Printer, 1970.

Manitoba Royal Commission on Local Government Organization and Finance, Winnipeg, Queen's Printer, 1964.

Masson, Jack, *Alberta's Local Governments and Their Politics*, Edmonton, University of Alberta Press, 1985.

_____, with Edward C. Lesage, Jr., *Alberta's Local Governments: Politics and Democracy*, Edmonton, University of Alberta Press, 1994.

Masson, Jack and James D. Anderson (eds.), *Emerging Party Politics in Urban Canada*, Toronto, McClelland and Stewart Limited, 1972.

McDavid, James and Brian Marson (eds.), *The Well-Performing Government Organization*, Toronto, Institute of Public Administration, 1991.

McDavid, James and Gregory K. Schlick, "Privatization versus Union-Management Cooperation: The Effects of Competition on Service Efficiency in Municipalities," *Canadian Public Administration*, Fall 1987.

McEvoy, John M., *The Ontario Township*, University of Toronto, Political Studies, 1st Series No. 1, 1889.

McIver, J. M., "Survey of the City Manager Plan in Canada," *Canadian Public Administration*, Fall 1960.

McQuaig, Linda, *The Cult of Impotence: Selling the Myth of Powerlessness in the Global Economy*, Toronto, Penguin Books Canada Ltd., 1998.

Mellon, Hugh, "Reforming the Electoral System of Metropolitan Toronto," *Canadian Public Administration*, Toronto, Spring 1993.

Milner, Henry, "The Montreal Citizens' Movement: Then and Now," Hanover, *Quebec Studies*, No. 6, 1988.

Minister of Urban Affairs, *Strengthening Local Government in Winnipeg: Proposals for Changes to the City of Winnipeg Act, Discussion Paper*, Winnipeg, February 27, 1987.

Ministry of Municipal Affairs (Ont.), *A Proposed New Municipal Act: Consultation Document*, Spring 1998.

_____, *Study of Innovative Financing Approaches for Ontario Municipalities* (Price Waterhouse), March 31, 1993.

_____, *Toward an Ideal County*, January 1990.

_____, *Report of the Consultative Committee to the Minister of Municipal Affairs, County Government in Ontario*, Toronto, January 1989.

_____, *Joint Services in Municipalities: Five Case Studies*, Toronto, April 1983.

_____, *Performance Measurement for Municipalities*, Toronto, 1981.

Municipal Finance Officers Association of Ontario and Association of Municipal Clerks and Treasurers of Ontario, *Innovative Financing: A Collection of Stories from Ontario Municipalities*, Toronto, 1993.

Municipal Submission to the first National Tri-Level Conference, *Policies, Programs, and Finance*, Ottawa, 1972.

Munro, W. B., *American Influences on Canadian Government*, Toronto, Macmillan, 1929.

New Brunswick, Government of, *Local Government Review Panel, Miramichi City: Our Future—Strength Through Unicity*, and *Greater Moncton Urban Community: Strength Through Cooperation*, April 1994.

_____, *The Commission on Land Use and the Rural Environment: Summary Report*, Fredericton, April 1993.

_____, *Strengthening Municipal Government in New Brunswick's Urban Centres*, Ministry of Municipalities, Culture and Housing, December 1992.

Newton, K., "Is Small Really So Beautiful? Is Big Really So Ugly? Size, Effectiveness, and Democracy in Local Government," *Political Studies*, Vol. XXX, No. 2, 1982.

Nova Scotia, Government of, *Interim Report of the Municipal Reform Commissioner, Cape Breton County*, Department of Municipal Affairs, July 8, 1993.

_____, *Task Force on Local Government*, April 1992.

O'Brien, Allan, *Municipal Consolidation in Canada and Its Alternatives*, Toronto, Intergovernmental Committee on Urban and Regional Research, May 1993.

_____, "Holding Pattern: A Look at the Provincial-Municipal Relationship," in Donald C. MacDonald (ed.), *Government and Politics of Ontario*, Toronto, Nelson, 1985.

_____, "The Ministry of State for Urban Affairs: A Municipal Perspective," *The Canadian Journal of Regional Science*, Halifax, Spring 1982.

_____, "Local Government Priorities for the Eighties," *Canadian Public Administration*, Spring 1976.

Ontario Economic Council, *Government Reform in Ontario*, Toronto, 1969.

_____, *Municipal Reform: A Proposal for the Future*, Toronto, 1971.

_____, *Municipal Fiscal Reform in Ontario: Property Taxes and Provincial Grants* (by John Bossons et al.), Toronto, 1981.

Osborne, David and Ted Gaebler, *Reinventing Government*, New York, Penguin Books, 1993.

Peters, B. Guy and Donald Savoie (eds.), *Governance in a Changing Environment*, Kingston, McGill-Queen's University Press, 1995.

Peters, Thomas J., *Thriving on Chaos*, New York, HarperCollins Publishers, 1988.

_____ and Robert H. Waterman, Jr., *In Search of Excellence*, New York, Warner Books, 1982.

Peters, Thomas J. and Nancy Austin, *A Passion for Excellence*, New York, Random House, 1985.

Peterson, Paul E., *City Limits*, Chicago, University of Chicago Press, 1981.

Plunkett, T. J., *City Management in Canada: The Role of the Chief Administrative Officer*, Toronto, Institute of Public Administration, 1992.

_____, *The Financial Structure and the Decision Making Process of Canadian Municipal Government*, Ottawa, CMHC, 1972.

_____, *Urban Canada and Its Government*, Toronto, Macmillan, 1968.

_____ and Meyer Brownstone, *Metropolitan Winnipeg: Politics and Reform of Local Government*, Berkeley, University of California Press, 1983.

Plunkett, T. J. and Katherine Graham, "Whither Municipal Government," *Canadian Public Administration*, Winter 1982.

Plunkett, T. J. and James Lightbody, "Tribunals, Politics and the Public Interest: The Edmonton Annexation Case," in *Canadian Public Policy*, Spring 1982.

Plunkett, T. J. and G. M. Betts, *The Management of Canadian Urban Government*, Kingston, Queen's University, 1978.

Price, Trevor (ed.), *Regional Government in Ontario*, Windsor, University of Windsor Press, 1971.

Price Waterhouse, *Study of the Financial Impact of One-Tier Government in Ottawa-Carleton*, Final Report, August 1992.

Regional District Survey Committee, *Summary Report of the Regional District Survey Committee*, Victoria, Queen's Printer, 1986.

Report of the Advisory Committee to the Minister of Municipal Affairs, on the Provincial-Municipal Relationship (Hopcroft Report), Toronto, January 1991.

Report and Recommendations, Committee of Review, City of Winnipeg Act, Winnipeg, Queen's Printer, October 1976.

Report by the Task Force on Representation and Accountability in Metropolitan Toronto, *Analysis and Options for the Government of Metropolitan Toronto*, November 1986.

Report of the GTA Task Force, *Greater Toronto*, Queen's Printer, January 1996.

Report of the Municipal Study Commission (Parizeau Report), Montreal, Union of Quebec Municipalities, December 1986.

Report of the Special Representative (Drury Report), *Constitutional Development in the Northwest Territories*, Ottawa, 1980.

Report of the Task Force on Nonincorporated Areas in New Brunswick, Fredericton, Queen's Printer, 1976.

Report to the Government of Nova Scotia, *Task Force on Local Government*, April 1992.

Richardson, Boyce, *The Future of Canadian Cities*, Toronto, New Press, 1972.

Richmond, Dale, "Provincial-Municipal Transfer Systems," *Canadian Public Administration*, Summer 1980.

_____ and David Siegel (eds.), *Agencies, Boards and Commissions in Canadian Local Government*, Toronto, Institute of Public Administration of Canada, 1994.

Rothblatt, Donald N. and Andrew Sancton (eds.), *Metropolitan Governance: American/Canadian Intergovernmental Perspectives*, Berkeley, Institute of Governmental Studies Press, 1993.

Roussopoulos, Dimitri (ed.), *The City and Radical Social Change*, Montreal, Black Rose Books Ltd., 1982.

Rowat, Donald, *International Handbook on Local Government Reorganization*, Westport, Greenwood Press, 1980.

_____, *Your Local Government*, Toronto, Macmillan, 1975.

Royal Commission on Education, Public Services, and Provincial-Municipal Relations in Nova Scotia. Report (John Graham, Commissioner), Halifax, Queen's Printer, 1974.

Royal Commission on Metropolitan Toronto. Report (H. Carl Goldenberg, Commissioner), Toronto, Queen's Printer, 1965.

Royal Commission on Metropolitan Toronto. Report (John Robarts, Commissioner), Toronto, Queen's Printer, June 1977.

Royal Commission on Municipal Government in Newfoundland and Labrador. Report (H. Whalen, Commissioner), St. John's, Queen's Printer, 1974.

Rutherford, Paul (ed.), *Saving the Canadian City: The First Phase 1880-1920*, Toronto, University of Toronto Press, 1974.

Sancton, Andrew, "Reducing costs by consolidating municipalities: New Brunswick, Nova Scotia and Ontario," *Canadian Public Administration*, Fall 1996.

_____, *Governing Canada's City Regions: Adapting Form to Function*, Montreal, Institute for Research on Public Policy, 1994.

_____, "Canada as a Highly Urbanized Nation," *Canadian Public Administration*, Fall 1992.

_____, *Local Government Reorganization in Canada Since 1975*, Toronto, ICURR Press, April 1991.

_____, "Montreal's Metropolitan Government," Hanover, *Quebec Studies*, No. 6, 1988.

_____ and Paul Woolner, "Full-time municipal councillors: a strategic challenge for Canadian urban government," *Canadian Public Administration*, Winter 1990.

Savoie, Donald J., "What is wrong with the new public management?" *Canadian Public Administration*, Spring 1995.

Schneider, Mark, *The Competitive City*, Pittsburgh, University of Pittsburgh Press, 1989.

Seidle, Leslie (ed.), *Rethinking Government: Reform or Revolution?*, Montreal, Institute for Research on Public Policy, 1993.

_____, *Rethinking the Delivery of Public Services to Citizens*, Montreal, Institute for Research on Public Policy, 1995.

Sewell, John, *The Shape of the City*, Toronto, University of Toronto Press, 1993.

_____, *Up Against City Hall*, Toronto, James Lewis and Samuel, 1972.

Sharpe, L. J., "Failure of Local Government Modernization in Britain," *Canadian Public Administration*, Spring 1981.

_____ (ed.), *The Local Fiscal Crisis in Western Europe, Myths and Realities*, London, Sage Publications, 1981.

Sharpe, L. J. and K. Newton, *Does Politics Matter?*, Oxford, Clarendon Press, 1984.

Shields, John and B. Mitchell Evans, *Shrinking the State: Globalization and Public Administration "Reform,"* Halifax, Fernwood Publishing, 1998.

Shortt, Adam, *Municipal Government in Ontario, An Historical Sketch*, Toronto, University of Toronto Studies, History and Economics, Vol. II, No. 2, undated.

_____ and Arthur G. Doughty (eds.), *Canada and Its Provinces: A History of the Canadian People and Their Institutions*, Toronto, Glasgow, Brook and Company, 1914, Vol. XVIII.

Siegel, David, "Reinventing Local Government: The Promise and the Problems," in Leslie Seidle (ed.), *Rethinking Government: Reform or Revolution?*, Montreal, Institute for Research on Public Policy, 1993.

_____, "City Hall Doesn't Need Parties," *Policy Options*, June 1987.

_____, "Provincial-Municipal Relations in Canada: An Overview," *Canadian Public Administration*, Summer 1980.

Smith, Patrick J., "Regional Governance in British Columbia," in *Planning and Administration*, 13, 1986.

_____ and Kennedy Stewart, *Making Accountability Work in British Columbia*, Report for the Ministry of Municipal Affairs and Housing, June 1998.

Stanbury, W. T., *Business-Government Relations in Canada: Influencing Public Policy*, Scarborough, Nelson Canada, 1993.

Stein, David Lewis, *Toronto for Sale: The Destruction of a City*, Toronto, New Press, 1972.

Stelter, Gilbert A. and Alan F. Artibise (eds.), *Power and Place: Canadian Urban Development in the North American City*, Vancouver, University of British Columbia Press, 1986.

_____, *Shaping the Urban Landscape: Aspects of the Canadian City-Building Process*, Ottawa, Carleton University Press, 1982.

_____, *The Canadian City: Essays in Urban History*, Toronto, McClelland and Stewart Limited, 1977.

Stewart, John, *The Responsive Local Authority*, London, Charles Knight and Co. Ltd., 1974.

_____ and Gerry Stoker (eds.), *The Future of Local Government*, London, Macmillan, 1989.

Stoker, Gerry, *The Politics of Local Government*, London, Macmillan Education Ltd., 1988.

_____ and Stephen Young, *Cities in the 1990s*, Harlow, Longman, 1993.

Stone, Clarence N. and Heywood T. Sanders (eds.), *The Politics of Urban Development*, Lawrence, University Press of Kansas, 1987.

Task Force on Housing and Urban Development. Report, Ottawa, Queen's Printer, 1969.

Task Force on Nonincorporated Areas in New Brunswick. Report, Fredericton, Queen's Printer, 1976.

Tennant, Paul and David Zirnhelt, "Metropolitan Government in Vancouver: the strategy of gentle imposition," *Canadian Public Administration*, Spring 1973.

Thomas, Timothy L. (ed.), *The Politics of the City*, Toronto, ITP Nelson, 1997.

_____, *A City With a Difference*, Montreal, Véhicule Press, 1997.

Tiebout, Charles, "A Pure Theory of Local Expenditures," *Journal of Political Economy*, Vol. 64.

Tindal, C. R., *A Citizen's Guide to Government*, Whitby, McGraw-Hill Ryerson Limited, 1997.

_____, *Municipal Councillor's Course*, 2ⁿᵈ Edition, Kingston, St. Lawrence College, 1997.

_____, *Structural Changes in Local Government: Government for Urban Regions*, Monographs on Canadian Urban Government, No. 2, Toronto, Institute of Public Administration of Canada, 1977.

Tomalty, Ray, *The Compact Metropolis: Growth Management and Intensification in Vancouver, Toronto and Montreal*, Toronto, ICURR Press, 1997.

Vaillancourt, F., "Financing Local Governments in Quebec: New Arrangements for the 1990s," *Canadian Tax Journal*, Vol. 40, No. 5, 1992.

Vojnovic, Igor, *Municipal Consolidation in the 1990s: An Analysis of Five Canadian Municipalities*, Toronto, ICURR Press, 1997.

Walisser, Brian, *Understanding Regional District Planning: A Primer*, Victoria, Ministry of Municipal Affairs, June 1987.

Weaver, John C., *Shaping the Canadian City: Essays on Urban Politics and Policy, 1890-1920*, Monographs on Canadian Urban Government, No. 1, Toronto, Institute of Public Administration of Canada, 1977.

Weller, G. R., "Local Government in the Canadian Provincial North," *Canadian Public Administration*, Spring 1981.

Whalen, H. J., *The Development of Local Government in New Brunswick*, Fredericton, 1963.

Whittington, Michael S. and Glen Williams (eds.), *Canadian Politics in the 1990s*, 3ʳᵈ and 4ᵗʰ Editions, Scarborough, Nelson Canada, 1990 and 1995.

Wichern, Phil H., Jr., *Evaluating Winnipeg's Unicity: Citizen Participation and Resident Advisory Groups*, Research and Working Paper No. 11, Winnipeg, Institute of Urban Studies, University of Winnipeg, 1984.

_____, Evaluating Winnipeg's Unicity: *The City of Winnipeg Act Review Committee, 1984-1986*, Research and Working Paper No. 26, Winnipeg, Institute of Urban Studies, University of Winnipeg, 1986.

Yates, Douglas, *The Ungovernable City*, Cambridge, M.I.T. Press, 1977.

Using the Internet

Listing all of the web sites pertinent to local government would require as many entries as the preceding "hard copy" items. The brief annotated list which follows features general sites dealing with broad categories or containing numerous links to other sites.

www.intergov.gc.ca is an excellent site with links to all three levels of government. The federal and provincial sites provide information by department and agency, including media releases, recent announcements, and new legislation or regulations. Within the municipal section are found individual municipalities, alphabetically, by province and territory. Municipal addresses follow a standard format consisting of the type of municipality followed by its name, the provincial short form, and ca. For example, the address for Edmonton, Alberta, is cited as www.city.edmonton.ab.ca. and that of Oakville, Ontario, is cited as www.town.oakville.on.ca.

www.acjnet.org is a site providing access to both federal and provincial legislation and also case law.

www.munisource.org is a site maintained by the Maritime Municipal Training and Development Board. It has direct links to over 2700 municipal sites in 26 countries and a "municipal forum bulletin board."

www.municipalworld.com is the address for *Municipal World* magazine and includes a discussion forum and a series of links to other sites.

Most of the municipal associations in the various provinces have their own web sites. These are usually cited in the links in the entries noted above. But they include www.fcm.ca for the Federation of Canadian Municipalities, www.ubcm.ca for the Union of British Columbia Municipalities, www.amo.com for the Association of Municipalities of Ontario, and www.unsm.com for the Union of Nova Scotia Municipalities.

Most Canadian newspapers are also available on-line. Many of these can be found at www.canada.com. Addresses include www.thestar.com, www.theglobeandmail.com, and www.montrealgazette.com.

www.localgov.org provides information on city, county, and state governments from several organizations, including the International City Management Association.

Index